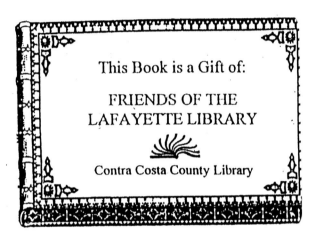

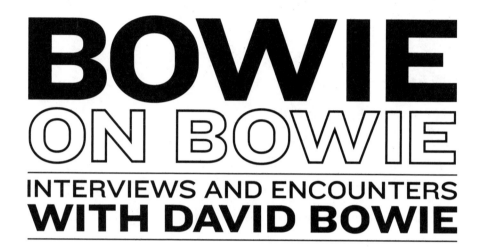

BOWIE ON BOWIE

INTERVIEWS AND ENCOUNTERS WITH DAVID BOWIE

EDITED BY SEAN EGAN

CHICAGO
REVIEW
PRESS

An A Cappella Book

Published by Chicago Review Press, Incorporated
814 North Franklin Street
Chicago, Illinois 60610

ISBN 978-1-56976-977-5

Cover and interior design: Jonathan Hahn
Cover photograph: Photofest

Library of Congress Cataloging-in-Publication Data
Bowie on Bowie : interviews and encounters with David Bowie / edited by Sean Egan.
 pages cm. — (Musicians in their own words)
 Summary: "Bowie on Bowie presents some of the best interviews David Bowie has granted in his near five-decade career. Each featured interview traces a new step in his unique journey, successively freezing him in time in all of his various incarnations, from a young novelty hit-maker and Ziggy Stardust to plastic soul player, 1980s sell-out, and the artistically reborn and beloved elder statesman of challenging popular music. In all of these iterations he is remarkably articulate and also preternaturally polite as almost every interviewer remarks upon his charm. The features in this book come from outlets both prestigious—Melody Maker, MOJO, New Musical Express, Q, Rolling Stone—and less well-known—the Drummer, Guitar, Ikon, Mr. Showbiz—but no matter the renown of the magazine, newspaper, or website, Bowie lets us approach the nerve center of his notoriously creative output"— Provided by publisher.
 Includes bibliographical references and index.
 ISBN 978-1-56976-977-5 (hardback)
 1. Bowie, David—Interviews. 2. Rock musicians—England—Interviews. I. Egan, Sean, editor. II. Bowie, David, interviewee.

 ML420.B754B693 2012
 782.42166092—dc23

                                                                2014042080
Printed in the United States of America
5 4 3 2 1

CONTENTS

INTRODUCTION

In 2013, David Bowie thrilled a world that had assumed he had long retreated into unannounced retirement by releasing *The Next Day*, his first album in ten years. Its refusal to pander to audience expectation in the manner of autopilot latter-day albums by peers like The Rolling Stones and The Who was a mark of the individualism for which he has always been renowned. A UK No. 1, it made a career-high US No. 2.

The only disappointment was that he decided not to speak to the press.

At the turn of the seventies, the man born David Robert Jones on January 8, 1947, was exploiting the moon landings to get into what was then called the Hit Parade with his space-dream-gone-wrong anthem "Space Oddity." In 1971, he was half-heartedly promoting *Hunky Dory*, an album so good as to now be considered an all-time classic, but which he was barely interested in at a juncture where his creative energies were focused on *The Rise and Fall of Ziggy Stardust and the Spiders from Mars*. The strangeness of the mouthful of a title of that 1972 work was representative of a unique record which, though a naked tilt for stardom, played with notions of sexuality and artifice never essayed by any previous musician. With *Aladdin Sane* (1973), he seemed intent on proving he was too profane and knowing to be a pop star, yet too cynical and vain to be a rock star. He stepped out of that (very listenable) contradiction with the "plastic soul" of *Young Americans* (1975) and the chilly epics of *Station to Station* (1976). Miraculously, he sidestepped the scorn of the UK's punk rock movement of '76/'77 by both being absent from the country and producing *Low*, *Heroes*, and *Lodger* (1977–1979), the "Berlin trilogy" whose nigh-suicidal experimentalism could in no way be bracketed with the complacency and careerism of the rock aristocracy that had so aroused New Wave fury.

Admittedly, there was a subsequent album trio informed by somewhat less integrity in the shape of 1983–1987 stinkers *Let's Dance, Tonight,* and *Never Let Me Down,* but Bowie ultimately took hold of himself sufficiently to ensure that that period was not what it seemed at the time: the preamble to the sort of long, slow decline seen with so many "heritage" acts. The Tin Machine experiment was an artistic failure, but nobody could accuse someone who was subsuming his stardom into an intellectual heavy metal band of resting on his laurels. Bowie started to haul himself back to artistic credibility with *Black Tie White Noise* (1993), and if the consensus that his last great album is 1980's *Scary Monsters (and Super Creeps)* has not subsequently been dented, his post-'93 work has always been interesting and, crucially, adventurous.

Bowie's career was brought to a rude halt in mid-2004 when he suffered a heart attack. It was a shocking occurrence for such a preternaturally youthful-looking man, although the fact that several of the features in this book make reference to his chain-smoking of Marlboro cigarettes diminishes that shock. It caused the cancellation of the final fourteen dates of the *A Reality* tour, which itself had already been marred by an audience member throwing a lollipop in his eye. The ten-year silence that followed was ominous. Pulling out of the hat *The Next Day* was in Bowie's long tradition of surprising the world.

Bowie has been one of popular music's greatest interviewees since January 1972, when he famously told the *Melody Maker* he was gay. Although he wasn't yet a big star, it was a groundbreaking moment. Far from coming back to haunt him when he shortly made his stab at teen idoldom, it assisted him. Record-buying youth initially responded with the same revulsion as their parents, then performed a somersault when they gleefully realized that being a fan of Bowie was something with which they could shock their elders, ever the wont of the young.

Over the years, Bowie has pretty much failed to give an uninteresting interview. It might be said that he has habitually used the media for his own ends, whether it be the disputable gay quote, the mischievously headlines-generating call for a new dose of fascism in 1976 or the name-dropping of writers and painters in any number of interviews in an anxious attempt to prove he's not an archetypal rock thicko. Yet he has paradoxically also been honest, declining to be coy about his ambition, his private life, and even his developing ennui. (Who can forget his comment, also in 1976, "I really, honestly and truly, don't know how much longer my albums will sell . . . And I really don't give a shit"?)

This was all assisted by the fact that Bowie became famous at a point in history when rock journalism was coming into its own: the back pages of this quintessential seventies star do not suffer from the opening passages of sixties banality that afflicts coverage of so many musicians of older vintage.

Bowie on Bowie presents some of the best interviews Bowie has granted in his nearly five-decade career. Each interview traces a new step in his unique journey, successively freezing him in time as young novelty hit-maker, hairy hippie, Ziggy Stardust, Aladdin Sane, The Thin White Duke, Plastic Soul Man, fragile Germanic exile, Godfather of the New Romantics, Eighties sell-out, Tin Machinist, and, finally, permanently artistically reborn beloved elder statesman of challenging popular music. In all of them, he is remarkably articulate. He is also extraordinarily polite. No clichéd rock mutha, he is a man whose charm almost every interviewer remarks upon. He is also disinclined to the hard-sell: it's remarkable in how many of these interviews Bowie's latest product is barely discussed, Bowie preferring instead to analyze his own past or expound on his latest, often arcane, theories.

These print exchanges are actually of greater interest than Bowie's audio and film interviews. It may be unfair, but it is inescapably the case that it's difficult to concentrate on (for which read: take seriously) his intel-lectualizing when distracted by the cockney inflections that have remained miraculously intact throughout his globe-trotting and longtime nonres-idency of the UK. Bowie on film has the added distraction of his eerily un-matching eyes.

The material in this book ranges across all of Bowie's career—except the last ten years. Bowie's retreat from music-making meant there was nothing to promote. That lack of promotional duty created a Bowie-quote desert from 2004 onward. That he elected album producer Tony Visconti to be his interface with the media upon his comeback suggests that, during his absent decade, Bowie discovered something which previously had not occurred to him: although he enjoyed talking about himself and his art, he didn't need to.

The features herein come from outlets both prestigious (*Melody Maker, Mojo, New Musical Express, Q, Rolling Stone*) and less well-known (*The Drummer, Guitar, Ikon, Mr. Showbiz*). It barely matters either way. Whatever the renown of the magazine, newspaper, or website, Bowie—the first artist to consistently employ the act of the interview as a means of artistic expression in itself—provides great copy in all.

—SEAN EGAN

DON'T DIG TOO DEEP, PLEADS ODDITY DAVID BOWIE

Gordon Coxhill | **November 15, 1969,** *New Musical Express* **(UK)**

David Bowie's first two albums (1967 and 1969, both eponymously titled in his native UK) were over-quota with feyness. They were also the work of a man audibly not quite sure what to do with his talent.

However, the second album spun off the single "Space Oddity" (and was re-titled after it in some territories). The tale of an unstable astronaut sentencing himself to a lonely death in the desolate depths of space hardly seemed the sort of thing to reap dividends from the euphoria surrounding Neil Armstrong's giant leap for mankind, but it established Bowie as a chart artist—as well as a distinctive voice.

It's interesting to note the ambivalence Bowie expresses about fame in this half-page *New Musical Express* feature. Although his next album, *The Man Who Sold the World*, was released a year later, he kept such a low profile in the two years after this early success that some considered it a form of retirement. —Ed.

It looked like a piece of master planning, but it wasn't. It looked like a monster hit, and it was. David Bowie's "Space Oddity," inspired by a visit to the film "2001," was released just as the world was staying up all night to watch the moon landing.

Like the modest, self-effacing young man he is, David passed the credit on to his record company, but as it was written last November, he can hardly disown his amazing foresight!

"Put it down to luck," he said over the phone from Perth where he was about to begin a short tour of the Haggisland. "I really am amazed at the success of the record, even though I had confidence in it.

"I've been the male equivalent of the dumb blonde for a few years, and I was beginning to despair of people accepting me for my music.

"It may be fine for a male model to be told he's a great looking guy, but that doesn't help a singer much, especially now that the pretty boy personality cult seems to be on the way out."

Much as David takes his songwriting seriously, he is amused by pundits who examine his material looking for hidden meanings even he is totally unaware of. "My songs are all from the heart, and they are wholly personal to me, and I would like people to accept them as such.

"I dearly want to be recognised as a writer, but I would ask them not to go too deeply into my songs. As likely as not, there's nothing there but the words and music you hear at one listening.

"I see you've noticed that my songs are seldom about boy and girl relationships. That's because I've never had any traumas with girls.

"I like to think myself a pretty stable person, and I've never had a bad relationship with an intelligent girl. And if a girl isn't intelligent, I don't want to know."

Although David made a very good impression on the recent Humble Pie tour, he maintains he is a songwriter first, and even denies he is a good performer.

"It was my first tour," he told me, "and I never stopped being surprised the concerts even went on. It appeared so badly organised to me, but I suppose everybody knew what they were doing.

"For me, it was nothing near an artistic success, mainly because I was limited to a twenty minute spot, and I ended up accompanying myself after a mix-up.

"I was very pleased to see that 'Space Oddity' went down well, I thought the audiences would miss the orchestral backing which was on the record.

"I throw myself on the mercy of an audience, and I really need them to respond to me. If they don't, I'm lost. But all the same, I'm determined to be an entertainer, clubs, cabaret concerts, the lot.

"There is too much false pride within the pop scene, groups and singers decrying cabaret without ever having seen the inside of a northern nightclub.

"I just want to sing to as many people as want to hear me, and I don't care where I do it. Mind you, I refuse to have my hair cut or change my appearance for anybody. I'm quite happy with the way I look, and people will have to accept me the way I am, or not bother at all."

A former commercial artist, David played tenor sax with a modern jazz group, "went through the blues thing," during which time he switched to vocalist, and then joined a traditional French mime company, where he met and worked with Marc Bolan.

"Marc has been a great influence on me, not so much with his music, but with his attitude to the pop scene. He shuts himself off from the destructive elements, and prefers to get on with his work.

"That's how I intend to be, in fact I ran away from London a while back when people started talking about me, and didn't come back unless it was really vital."

Inevitably, the underground cropped up, and David had some interesting comments on the movement, "I thought when the whole thing started," he said, "that a whole lot of new, musically-minded groups were going to appear with some meaningful music and try and spread it around. Well, we've got the music, and most of it is very good too, but I can't figure out the attitude of so many of the underground groups.

"It seems to me that they have expanded their own personal little scenes to a certain extent, and then they stop, content to play to the converted. That doesn't get them anywhere, and in the end both the audiences and the groups will get fed up with the same faces and places.

"A lot is said and written about the musical snobbery with the fans, but I think the groups are just as bad. For some reason, even the words entertainer and cabaret make them shudder."

Obviously, having a hit record and being able to command the money that goes with it, is going to make a few changes to David's life, not least of all in his bank balance.

He seems to have made a good start already. "I've bought a big car and a nice little house which needs a lot more time and some money spent on it before it will be as I want it.

"I suppose other little things will crop up as time goes on. At the moment, I'm more concerned with remaining a 22 year old, or even going back a year to 21.

"This business might keep you young mentally but I feel almost middle-aged physically. I often regret not leading a more normal teenage life. From the time I was about 16, I never kicked a football over a common with my mates, I haven't had to chat up a girl like an ordinary teenager for ages, and believe it or not I miss it.

"I have to try and figure out if a girl knows who I am and whether she wants me for what I am or my name. It's a more difficult problem than it sounds, but as I was saying, I haven't had much trouble with girls, touch wood."

The immediate future for David looks bright, with as much live work as he wants, an LP on release this week (14), and even the prospect of his own TV show.

But the usual pressing worry about follow-ups hasn't caught up with David yet. "Follow-up?" he queried, "but the first one's still alive at the moment. Actually I haven't even thought about it.

"I'm not sure if I've got a suitable song for another single, but even if I have, I don't want to be one of those singers whose career depends on hit singles and they are virtually dead for six months of the year.

"I hope to get some free time to do some writing when I return from Scotland, but even then I can't write just because I've got the time. But it's a bit early in life for all my ideas to have dried up, isn't it, so I suppose I'll come up with something."

At the moment, David seems to be the sort of person much needed in pop: full of original thought, a willingness to work, a hatred of the hard drug scene and class distinction in music, and common sense enough not to let the fame and adulation surely coming his way turn his head.

I'm sure he has been around long enough to withstand the pressures, and if he can't, he'll be wise enough to run.

OH YOU PRETTY THING

Michael Watts | January 22, 1972, *Melody Maker* (UK)

This is almost certainly the most famous David Bowie interview ever published.

When UK music weekly *Melody Maker* despatched Michael Watts to interview him at the start of 1972, Bowie was a man on the comeback trail. The three years since "Space Oddity" had been in the charts was an age in an era where visibility was all-important for musical artists. That part of this was voluntary—Bowie's immersion in the Beckenham Arts Lab seems to have genuinely been a greater passion for him than music and stardom at the start of the decade—would have been of little import to those kids scared that their affections might be moored to a has-been.

His comeback was one of the most spectacular of all time. *Hunky Dory*—his December 1971 offering—was hailed as an instant classic, chock-full of great melody and instrumentation while cleaving to the alternative zeitgeist. Yet, astoundingly, it transpired to have been an album knocked off in a hurry to appease a record company disgruntled by the length of time Bowie's magnum opus was taking to reach fruition. Said opus—*The Rise and Fall of Ziggy Stardust and the Spiders from Mars*—was playing on the turntable as Bowie held court to Watts. It too was a classic, and it too cleaved to the zeitgeist—a new one, exulting in trash and flash rather than stoned profundity. This was truly a man on fire creatively, if one hardly interested in philosophical consistency. He was also a man clearly tilting for stardom on his own terms.

Note how blasé and skeptical Watts remains in the face of Bowie's posturing. As subsequent interviews in this book will attest, he was right to do so. However, although Bowie's "I'm gay" assertion was not quite truthful, it was a huge risk: even most hippies and rock consumers were repulsed by homosexuality at the time. Yet his gambit paid off as perfectly as he predicted to Watts. On a related note, the feature gave rise to one of Bowie's other famous quotes: the one about becoming huge before crashing down to earth. The first part of that prediction came true. —Ed.

Even though he wasn't wearing silken gowns right out of Liberty's, and his long blond hair no longer fell wavily past his shoulders David Bowie was looking yummy.

He'd slipped into an elegant-patterned type of combat suit, very tight around the legs, with the shirt unbuttoned to reveal a full expanse of white torso. The trousers were turned up at the calves to allow a better glimpse of a huge pair of red plastic boots with at least three-inch rubber soles; and the hair was Vidal Sassooned into such impeccable shape that one held one's breath in case the slight breeze from the open window dared to ruffle it. I wish you could have been there to varda him; he was so super.

David uses words like "verda" and "super" quite a lot. He's gay, he says. Mmmmmm. A few months back, when he played Hampstead's Country Club, a small greasy club in North London which has seen all sorts of exciting occasions, about half the gay population of the city turned up to see him in his massive floppy velvet hat, which he twirled around at the end of each number.

According to Stuart Lyon, the club's manager, a little gay brother sat right up close to the stage throughout the whole evening, absolutely spellbound with admiration.

As it happens, David doesn't have much time for Gay Liberation, however. That's a particular movement he doesn't want to lead. He despises all these tribal qualifications. Flower power he enjoyed, but it's individuality that he's really trying to preserve. The paradox is that he still has what he describes as "a good relationship" with his wife. And his baby son, Zowie. He supposes he's what people call bisexual.

They call David a lot of things. In the States he's been referred to as the English Bob Dylan and an avant-garde outrage, all rolled up together. The New York Times talks of his "coherent and brilliant vision." They like him a lot there. Back home in the very stiff upper lip UK, where people are outraged by Alice Cooper even, there ain't too many who have picked up on him. His last but one album "The Man Who Sold The World," cleared 50,000 copies in the States; here it sold about five copies, and Bowie bought them.

Yes, but before this year is out all those of you who puked up on Alice are going to be focusing your passions on Mr. Bowie, and those who know where it's at will be thrilling to a voice that seemingly undergoes brilliant metamorphosis from song to song, a songwriting ability that will enslave the heart, and a sense of theatrics that will make the ablest thespians gnaw on their sticks of eyeliner in envy. All this, and an amazingly accomplished band, featuring super-lead guitarist Mick Ronson, that can smack you round the skull with their heaviness and soothe the savage breast with their delicacy. Oh, to be young again.

The reason is Bowie's new album "Hunky Dory," which combines a gift for irresistible melody lines with lyrics that work on several levels—as straightforward narrative, philosophy or allegory, depending how deep you wish to plumb the depths. He has a knack of suffusing strong, simple pop melodies with words and arrangements full of mystery and darkling hints.

Thus "Oh! You Pretty Things," the Peter Noone hit, is, on one stratum, particularly the chorus, about the feelings of a father-to-be; on a deeper level it concerns Bowie's belief in a superhuman race—homo superior—to which he refers obliquely: "I think about a world to come/where the books were found by The Golden Ones/Written In pain, written in awe/by a puzzled man who questioned what we were here for/Oh, The Strangers Came Today, and It looks as though they're here to stay." The idea of Peter Noone singing such a heavy number fills me with considerable amusement. That's truly outrageous, as David says himself.

But then Bowie has an instinct for incongruities. On "The Man" album there's a bit at the end of "Black Country Rock" where he superbly parodies his friend Marc Bolan's vibrato warblings. On "Hunky Dory" he devotes a track called "Queen Bitch" to the Velvets, wherein he takes off to a tee the Lou Reed vocal and arrangement, as well as parodying, with a storyline about the singer's boyfriend being seduced by another queen, the whole Velvet Underground genre.

Then again, at various times on his albums he resorts to a very broad Cockney accent, as on "Saviour Machine" ("The Man") and here with "The Bewlay Brothers." He says he copped it off Tony Newley, because he was mad about "Stop the World" and "Gurney Slade": "He used to make his points with this broad Cockney accent and I decided that I'd use that now and again to drive a point home."

The fact that Bowie has an acute ear for parody doubtless stems from an innate sense of theatre. He says he's more an actor and entertainer than a musician; that he may, in fact, only be an actor and nothing else: "Inside this invincible frame there might be an invisible man." You kidding? "Not at all. I'm not particularly taken with life. I'd probably be very good as just an astral spirit."

Bowie is talking in an office at Gem Music, from where his management operates. A tape machine is playing his next album, "The Rise And Fall of Ziggy Stardust And The Spiders From Mars," which is about this fictitious pop group. The music has got a very hard-edged sound, like "The Man Who Sold The World." They're releasing it shortly, even though "Hunky Dory" has only just come out.

Everyone just knows that David is going to be a lollapalooza of a superstar throughout the entire world this year, David more than most. His songs are always ten years ahead of their time, he says, but this year he has anticipated the trends. "I'm going to be huge, and it's quite frightening in a way," he says, his big red boots stabbing the air in time to the music. "Because I know that when I reach my peak and it's time for me to be brought down, it will be with a bump."

The man who's sold the world this prediction has had a winner before, of course. Remember "Space Oddity," which chronicled Major Tom's dilemma, aside from boosting the sales of the stylophone? That was a top ten hit in '68, but since then Bowie has hardly performed at all in public. He appeared for a while at an arts lab he co-founded in Beckenham, Kent, where he lives, but when he realised that people were going there on a Friday night to see Bowie the hit singer working out, rather than for any idea of experimental art, he seems to have become disillusioned. That project foundered, and he wasn't up to going out on one-nighters throughout the country at that particular time.

So in the past three years he has devoted his time to the production of three albums, "David Bowie" (which contains "Space Oddity") and "The Man" for Philips, and "Hunky Dory" for RCA. His first album, "Love You Til Tuesday," was released in 1968 on the new Deram label but it didn't sell outstandingly, and Decca, it seems, lost interest in him.

It all began for him, though, when he was 15 and his brother gave him a copy to play an instrument; he took up sax because that was the main instrument featured in the book (Gerry Mulligan, right?). So in '63 he was playing tenor in a London R and B band before going on to found a semi-pro progressive blues group, called David Jones and The Lower

Third (later changing his name in '66 when Davy Jones of The Monkees became famous). He left this band in 1967 and became a performer in the folk clubs.

Since he was 14, however, he had been interested in Buddhism and Tibet, and after the failure of his first LP he dropped out of music completely and devoted his time to the Tibet Society, whose aim was to help the lamas driven out of that country in the Tibetan/Chinese war. He was instrumental in setting up the Scottish monastery in Dumfries in this period. He says, in fact, that he would have liked to have been a Tibetan monk, and would have done if he hadn't met Lindsay Kemp, who ran a mime company in London: "It was as magical as Buddhism, and I completely sold out and became a city creature. I suppose that's when my interest in image really blossomed."

David's present image is to come on like a swishy queen, a gorgeously effeminate boy. He's as camp as a row of tents, with his limp hand and trolling vocabulary. "I'm gay," he says, "and always have been, even when I was David Jones." But there's a sly jollity about how he says it, a secret smile at the corners of his mouth. He knows that in these times it's permissible to act like a male tart, and that to shock and outrage, which pop has always striven to do throughout its history, is a balls-breaking process.

And if he's not an outrage, he is, at the least, an amusement. The expression of his sexual ambivalence establishes a fascinating game: is he, or isn't he? In a period of conflicting sexual identity he shrewdly exploits the confusion surrounding the male and female roles. "Why aren't you wearing your girl's dress today?" I said to him (he has no monopoly on tongue-in-cheek humour). "Oh dear," he replied, "You must understand that it's not a woman's. It's a man's dress."

He began wearing dresses, of whatever gender, two years ago, but he says he had done outrageous things before that were just not accepted by society. It's just so happened, he remarks, that in the past two years people have loosened up to the fact that there are bisexuals in the world—"and— horrible fact—homosexuals." He smiles, enjoying his piece of addenda.

"The important fact is that I don't have to drag up. I want to go on like this for long after the fashion has finished. I'm just a cosmic yob, I suppose. I've always worn my own style of clothes. I design them. I designed this."

He broke off to indicate with his arm what he was wearing. "I just don't like the clothes that you buy in shops. I don't wear dresses all the time, either. I change every day. I'm not outrageous. I'm David Bowie."

How does dear Alice go down with him, I asked, and he shook his head disdainfully: "Not at all. I bought his first album, but it didn't excite me or shock me. I think he's trying to be outrageous. You can see him, poor dear, with his red eyes sticking out and his temples straining. He tries so hard. That bit he does with the boa constrictor, a friend of mine, Rudy Valentino, was doing ages before. The next thing I see is Miss C. with her boa. I find him very demeaning. It's very premeditated, but quite fitting with our era. He's probably more successful than I am at present, but I've invented a new category of artist, with my chiffon and taff. They call it pantomime rock in the States."

Despite his flouncing, however, it would be sadly amiss to think of David merely as a kind of glorious drag act. An image, once strained and stretched unnaturally, will ultimately diminish an artist. And Bowie is just that. He foresees this potential dilemma, too, when he says he doesn't want to emphasise his external self much more. He has enough image. This year he is devoting most of his time to stage work and records. As he says, that's what counts at the death. He will stand or fall on his music.

As a songwriter he doesn't strike me as an intellectual, as he does some. Rather, his ability to express a theme from all aspects seems intuitive. His songs are less carefully structured thoughts than the outpourings of the unconscious. He says he rarely tries to communicate to himself, to think an idea out.

"If I see a star and it's red I wouldn't try to say why it's red. I would think how shall I best describe to X that that star is such a colour. I don't question much; I just relate. I see my answers in other people's writings. My own work can be compared to talking to a psychoanalyst. My act is my couch."

It's because his music is rooted in this lack of consciousness that he admires Syd Barrett so much. He believes that Syd's freewheeling approach to lyrics opened the gates for him; both of them, he thinks, are the creation of their own songs. And if Barrett made that initial breakthrough, it's Lou Reed and Iggy Pop who have since kept him going and helped him to expand his unconsciousness. He and Lou and Iggy, he says, are going to take over the whole world. They're the songwriters he admires.

His other great inspiration is mythology. He has a great need to believe in the legends of the past, particularly those of Atlantis; and for the same need he has crafted a myth of the future, a belief in an imminent race of supermen called homo superior. It's his only glimpse of hope, he says—"all the things that we can't do they will."

It's a belief created out of resignation with the way society in general has moved. He's not very hopeful about the future of the world. A year ago he was saying that he gave mankind another 40 years. A track on his next album, outlining his conviction, is called "Five Years." He's a fatalist, a confirmed pessimist, as you can see.

"Pretty Things," that breezy Herman song, links this fatalistic attitude with the glimmer of hope that he sees in the birth of his son, a sort of poetic equation of homo superior. "I think," he says, "that we have created a new kind of person in a way. We have created a child who will be so exposed to the media that he will be lost to his parents by the time he is 12."

That's exactly the sort of technological vision that Stanley Kubrick foresees for the near future in "A Clockwork Orange." Strong stuff. And a long, long way away from camp carry-ons.

Don't dismiss David Bowie as a serious musician just because he likes to put us all on a little.

DAVID AT THE DORCHESTER

Charles Shaar Murray | July 22 and 29, 1972, *New Musical Express* (UK)

As can be gleaned from the opening sentences of this two-part *New Musical Express* feature, by the summer of 1972, Bowie was a star. Having clearly got over the ambivalence about fame expressed in the 1969 interview with Gordon Coxhill in the same paper, Bowie had nakedly lunged for commercial success with the June 6 release of *The Rise and Fall of Ziggy Stardust and the Spiders from Mars* and had been successful.

The mixture of androgyny, science fiction, identity meshing, novel ideas, and great art involved in that work and its promotional campaign was so intoxicating that not many bothered to point out—or even think about it deeply enough to apprehend—that it wasn't the concept album about an interplanetary gender-bender it was touted as. (Note how Bowie avoids the interviewer's question when asked about a song cycle involved in *Ziggy*.) That it went largely unnoticed that only a handful of its songs revolved around the title character was partly due to the fact that his persona was becoming indistinguishable from Bowie's: Ziggy seemed omnipresent.

Although Bowie might at this point still have been playing crummy venues like Friars in Aylesbury, his standing was already patently the precursor to the "huge" status predicted herein for Bowie by Charles Shaar Murray (and, of course, predicted by Bowie himself to Michael Watts at the start of the year). In some respects Murray is solicitous as only a journo who has decided he is in the presence of the World's Most Important Musical Artist can be—but, having said that, Murray was right.

Incredibly, however, Bowie was at this juncture even more than World's Most Important Musical Artist. The second part of this feature appeared opposite a rave review of Mott The Hoople's new single "All the Young Dudes," written and produced by Bowie. As touched on in the article, he was at this point lending his composing and producing talents—as well as the pixie dust that is fame-by-association—to artists he admired such as Mott, Lou Reed, and Iggy Pop. In all cases, he revitalized their careers.

The incident at the turn of the seventies to which Bowie refers wherein he unsuccessfully tried to persuade an audience of the merits of "things that are visually exciting" denotes him being ahead of his time in attempting to purvey what became known as glam rock—of which Ziggy Stardust (the character) was the primary titan.

Note: for "Anji" read "Angie" [Bowie]. —Ed.

PART ONE

Jill and Lyn are seventeen and they're into Bowie. They've both seen David work three times in as many weeks.

They've both got "Ziggy Stardust" and neither of them like Marc Bolan.

Jill says she likes the way David looks. She doesn't necessarily think he's good-looking, she just likes the way he looks.

They and me and a sweaty hallful of other people saw David Bowie and the Spiders From Mars work Friars in Aylesbury at the weekend. The phantom waver of the Ziggy banner put in an appearance as well, and it was alright, the band were all together and Ziggy played guitar.

The Spiders are a surrealistic vision of rock band. Trevor Bolder's silvered sideboards hang several inches off his face, and Woody Woodmansey's hair is an orange Vidal-Sassoon duck's ass similar to David's. Through the show at top speed until the final encore of "Suffragette City" where David pulls off his most outrageous stunt and goes down on Mick Ronson's guitar.

David Bowie is Gonna Be Huge.

The day after the gig he's holding an extended press conference at the Dorchester Hotel, held especially for the planeload of American writers flown in for the weekend. In the foyer everything is frosty, air-conditioned elegance, in slow-motion after the sweltering dusty street.

Down the mirrored corridors of the second floor, through the door into a suitably chic room where assorted media people are eating cakes and sandwiches and drinking tea and/or Scotch.

Lou Reed and his band are there, all the Spiders, and curled up in a corner in a Bolan T-shirt, eye-shadow and silvered hair is Iggy Pop.

When I got there David was wearing an entirely different outfit. Before I left he'd changed into a third.

David's wife, lithe and crewcut, is smoothing things down, getting together drinks and being assaulted by Lou's roadie. When I arrived, he'd just bitten her in the stomach and as she's very slim the bite had gone direct to her abdominal muscles and everybody was falling about.

Woody pours me sumptuous Johnny Walker Black Label and peach juice. Lou Reed is talking quietly to David. He's wearing shades and maroon fingernails. Periodically, horrified waiters enter to deliver yet more Scotch and wine and sandwiches.

MURRAY: **At the moment, the most popular rock journalist words appear to be funk, camp and punk. To what extent do you think you've brought these words into essential usage?**

BOWIE: I think it's most probably due to the general inarticulacy of the Press. They're very small minded. They do indeed revolve around those three words.

Not revolve around. They just crop up . . .

Yes they do. Funk, I don't think I have anything to do with funk. I've never been considered funky. Would you say that? I wouldn't . . .

Would you want to be?

Yes. It's a muddy kind of thing. Camp, yes, I understand the camp thing. Once upon a time it was, I think, put down in the category of entertainer, but since the departure of old fashioned entertainers the re-emergence of somebody who wants to be an entertainer has unfortunately become a synonym for camp.

I don't think I'm camper than any other person who felt at home on stage, and felt more at home on stage than he did off stage.

Nobody ever called Jerry Garcia camp.

No, right, but he's a musician and I'm not a musician. I'm not into music, you see, on that level. I don't profess to have music as my big wheel and there are a number of other things as important to me apart from music. Theatre and mime, for instance.

You say you don't consider yourself a musician, but for somebody who's producing music of a very high grade, I would reckon that you're entitled to be called a musician.

Okay then, I'll shift my emphasis. I wouldn't think I would ever be considered a technocrat on any instrument. I have a creative force which finds its way through into a musical form.

You were saying you didn't consider yourself to be a musician.

In that terminology, in that definition: that a musician is a virtuoso on his instrument? By no stretch of the imagination. I play a good alto, I played a bit actually on the Mott album, which is quite pleasing for me, having not touched a sax for a long time.

You used it on "Hunky Dory."

Yes, but for just a few phrases. I've used it quite heavily on the Mott thing. (Mick Graham: You used it on stage) What? Yeah, I did a James Brown thing for a couple of gigs. We did "Hot Pants" and we blew a bit. We did it at some of the gigs where there seemed to be a lot of Mods, so we thought we'd throw it in. I ad-libbed most of it.

I remember five years ago trying to run a blues band and failing completely because people were standing at the front shouting "Geno Geno! Play some Tamla!"

Oh yeah, but I was a great soul merchant, a James Brown merchant, I've always dug his very funky things, but I'd never considered that I was capable . . . I'm never gonna try and play black music 'cause I'm white. Singularly white!

There is a distinct kind of white funk. Velvet Underground for instance. Going by that as a yardstick of funk and not Albert King. Wouldn't you say that what you are doing is into a certain kind of funk?

Yes, I couldn't put my finger on what it is. Of the rock 'n' roll things that we write, they would definitely be in the Velvets bag, because that's my biggest influence in rock 'n' roll, more so than Chuck Berry, the archetype.

I'd say that Lou Reed was to you as Chuck Berry was to the Stones.

Yes, very much so, that's a very good analogy and I agree with it entirely. In fact I've said the same myself on numerous occasions.

The second pre-conceived question I came with was that rock and roll is increasingly becoming a ritual. Instead of the very down to earth stance of, say the Dead. It's becoming very much of a spectacle, very formulised.

I've not seen many bands where I've noticed that.

Alice is a very extreme example. I think you come into it to a certain extent. I think Bolan does. Sha Na Na in their own particular way also . . .

Well, you must firstly tell me your feelings on this before I know quite what your question is . . .

I have mixed feelings about it, in some cases it works. I think it works when you do it, but sometimes I get the feeling that the audience is being excluded.

Yes, I do feel that a great deal more theatres does not necessarily mean props. As you saw with us, we were using no props. We're not into props.

If we have a theatricality it comes through from us as people, not as a set environment or stage. Like playing an instrument, theatre craftsmanship is something that one learns.

There are going to be a lot of tragedies and a lot of clangers dropped over the next few years when a lot of bands try to become theatrical without knowing their craft. I'm a very professional person, and I feel that I contribute all my energies into my stage performance, that when I'm on stage I give more to an audience than to anybody else when I'm off stage. I've worked hard at it. I was with a mime company and I've had other theatre experience.

What I'm trying to say is that it's important to know about the things you do and to have learnt it, as it is to learn your instrument. As the theatrical expression evolves a lot of it is going to be on a secondary modern school amateur dramatics level.

There will only be the odd few bands who have the knowledge to master their theatre. Iggy has natural theatre. It's very interesting because it doesn't conform to any standards or rules or structures of theatre. It's his own and it's just a Detroit theatre that he's brought with him. It's straight from the street.

Remember we have only been on the road for three months, so it's still coming together, but I wish myself to be a prop, if anything, for my own songs. I want to be the vehicle for my songs. I would like to colour the material with as much visual expression as is necessary for that song.

One thing I've noticed is the way you use words, like in "Andy Warhol"

where you transform the word "Wall" into the word "Warhol." I mean, the way you listen to speech and incorporate it into sound.

One can say a sentence to three people and it'll take on an entirely different meaning for each of those three people. I think if any of my stuff becomes at all surrealistic it's because that's the purpose of it.

It's to give people their own definitions. I certainly don't understand half the stuff I write. I can look back on a song that I have just written and it means something when I first wrote it and it means something entirely different now because of my new circumstances new this or that. I get told by so many people—especially Americans—what my songs are about.

You'd better watch out or you'll have your very own A. J. Weberman rooting through your garbage.

I have one already! He's not quite at garbage level yet, but he's certainly very adamant about what I mean. It's disconcerting to say the least, Alarming.

But America is made up of academics. They're very [G]ermanic in that respect. Because they're so subconciously aware of being a new nation that has no accepted roots in the old world, they strive for their own culture as fast and as quickly as they can. Whatever isn't needed is soaked up by the media and becomes part of the American way of life.

They're terribly self conscious about everything. The level to which rock music has become an academic subject is just incredible. I could walk into a shop and see row upon row of books about any aspect of rock. I mean writings about writers. There are even books on Meltzer. Layer upon layer. It's a build up. They're making their own culture.

Another line of yours I wanted to ask you about is in "Five Years." You said "I never knew I'd need so many people."

Basically what it means is realising the inevitability of the apocalypse, in whatever forms it takes. I was being careful not to say what form it would take because that to me would be incredibly sad and I just tried to get that feeling over in one line.

It's like the things that you flash on supposedly when you're dying running down the street and . . .

His whole life passed before him.

Yeah really it's like that, the grasping for life.

Do you feel worried by people who regard you as the guru?

I'm not that convinced, at the moment, that I am anybody's guru. I know there's a lot of interest in what I'm doing, and we seem to be getting our goodly fair share of exposure, but I'm not convinced that we are leading any particular cult.

But it's happening almost in spite of you, people examining your albums almost line by line.

Okay, well if this is going to be an inevitable situation with the chronicles of rock, and one must presume that it will be, then I would strive to use that position to promote some feeling of optimism in the future, which might seem very hypocritical related to "Five Years." There the whole thing was to try and get a mocking angle at the future.

If I can mock something and deride it, one isn't so scared of it. People are so incredibly serious and scared of the future that I would wish to turn the feeling the other way, into a wave of optimism. If one can take the micky out of the future, and what it is going to be like . . .

It's going to be unbelievably technological. There isn't going to be a triangle system, we aren't going to revert back to the real way of life. That's not going to happen.

It's certainly not a new thing. My God I haven't got any new concept. I juggle with them, but what I'm saying, I think, has been said a million times before. I'm just saying again that we've gotta have optimism in the future.

"Five Years" struck me as an optimistic song.

It is, it is. The album in fact should be taken that way. "Starman" can be taken at the immediate level of "There's a starman in the sky saying boogie children," but the theme of that is that the idea of things in the sky is really quite human and real, and we should be a bit happier about the prospect of meeting people.

On the second side of "Ziggy Stardust" the songs seem to go in a cycle. But when you play live you don't necessarily play them in that order.

I must admit I speculate on the prospect of a show which would be "Ziggy Stardust," but the way I want to do it requires a lot of planning and we haven't had time for that.

I'd rather leave it alone until it's gonna be done properly. I don't want to do anything unless it's gonna be done well.

In the other room I saw a tape box of the Mott album. The only title I recongnised was "Sweet Jane."

That's right, Lou came down. I've got Lou singing it at the moment. I've got to put Ian on, but he doesn't know the lyrics yet.

So you recorded it with Lou Reed singing on Mott's backing?

Lou phrased it so Ian can pick up how it was.

How does it sound when Mott play it?

Fabulous, it's really good. I'll play it for you. The album is fabulous. They've never written better stuff. They were so down when I first met them.

They were having troubles with Island, weren't they?

Oh, everything was wrong. Everything was terrible, and because they were so down I thought I was gonna have to contribute a lot of material. Now, they're in a wave of optimism and they've written everything on the album bar one Lou Reed number and the "Dudes" single I did for them.

They were being led into so many different directions, because of general apathy with their management and recording company. Everybody was very excited about them when they first came out and then, because they didn't click immediately, it fell away. When I first saw them, and that wasn't very long ago, I couldn't believe that a band so full of integrity and a really very naive exuberance could command such enormous following and not be talked about.

The reactions at their concerts were superb, and it's sad that nothing was done about them. They were breaking up, I mean, they broke up for three days and I caught them just in time and put them together again, cause in fact all the kids love them.

(At this point, Bowie put on the rough tape of the Mott album. First

cut was Lou and Mott's "Sweet Jane." It sounded great, the best Mott I've heard. While it was playing, Reed entered the room. I hoped to get him to join the conversation, but he just came over and kissed David).

Reed: That's it. (exit).

I was hoping to get a two-way interview.

Bowie: That was a two-way interview.

PART TWO: BACK AT THE DORCHESTER

The story so far; Lord Ziggy And His Pals are holding court at the Dorchester, drinking, looning, doing interviews and generally having a day of good jolly superstar fun.

In addition to getting her midriff bitten by Lou Reed's manager Ernie, Lady Ziggy (alias Anji Bowie) had fun by sinking her teeth into the generously proportioned left breast of American rock historian Lillian Roxon.

Among a welter of other happenings which even Lou Reed doesn't wish to discuss, this reporter (a shy, young small-town kid bewildered by such extravagant debauchery) continued his epoch-making interview with David Bowie.

We enter the conversation after David and Lou Reed had conducted what Ziggy described as "the shortest interview on record."

MURRAY: You retired after "Space Oddity." Would you ever do it again?

BOWIE: I can't envisage stopping gigging for the next year at least, because I'm having such a good time doing it.

I've never enjoyed it more. I feel I'm one with the band I'm working with and that hasn't happened before for me. I've always felt I was dragging people into doing things. I had a band once before which had the same lead guitarist.

Yeah, I saw you work at the Roundhouse once with Country Joe about two years ago.

That Roundhouse gig was the kind of thing I cite, in that I was into something there that the band wasn't into. They were very much still only wanting to be musicians at that time, and it came off as no more than everybody dressing up.

Was that the one you came to where I was wearing a silver superman suit?

You weren't. You did "Cypress Avenue."

We did one at the Roundhouse about the same period when we appeared very much the same as we are appearing now, and that was with Mick Ronson. I was in a cartoon strip and we all dressed up as a different super hero.

Who were you?

No one in particular, but superhero type figures. We had silver suits, the thing that I used to wear for "Space Oddity," that silver cat suit, which is exactly the same as this.

It hasn't changed at all in three years, if you think about it, but it's different material. I was in silver lame and blue and silver cloak, and silvered hair and blue hair and the whole thing, glitter everywhere. The whole thing was on that scale.

Were they ready to cope with it at the time?

No, they weren't. We died a death. And, of course, the boys said look, I told you so, let's get back to just being a band again.

That's the period that broke me up. I just about stopped after that performance, because I knew it was right, I knew it was what I wanted to do and I knew it was what people would want, eventually.

I didn't know when, though, so I held on. I knew it would happen, because I've always been excited about seeing things that are visually exciting and it's always knocked me out. I like seeing people pretending.

I have a great imagination. I'm not a vegetable. I like to let my imagination run wild and I thought, well if that does that to me, it has to do it to other people as well 'cause I'm just a person. I'm not quite that much of a superman. And, anyway, I'm glad I stuck it out really.

Could you name four or five specific records that influenced you early on?

Yes, "Alley Oop" by the Hollywood Argyles—just a feeling that came from it. I'm afraid I'm not very technical on things like that and all I can say, at best, is that it was a feel that I had an empathy with.

I don't know what it was, whether it was the zaniness of the record or what.

Is that the one about the caveman?

Yeah, and that was Kim Fowley as a matter of fact. He was the Hollywood Argyle that did it, and I loved parody because . . .

Zappa?

Yes, I admire Zappa but there again I prefer Charlie Mingus. I like my parody to be a little softer because I'm a pacifist person by nature and hostility in any form, even on a mental level, I find not endearing.

I think Zappa may have a problem with feeling that he was not accepted on a Mingus level and he had to find himself an audience. I don't think he's ever forgotten that.

But . . . "Pithecanthropus Erectus" is not quite the same as "Brown Shoes Don't Make It"?

Well, that's the strength of my view on parody. I'm a softer person by nature. I'm not hostile. I don't believe I'm an aggressive performer either. I like the situation that I seem to develop with the audience which is generally on a very human level and they're quite friendly.

It's neither screamy nor rebellious: it just has a good feeling to it. I love my audiences. I think I've not been to too many gigs, where the feeling is that nice. It's a very warm feeling I get from audiences.

Correct me if I'm wrong, but isn't there one cut on "Man Who Sold The World" that is a parody of Marc Bolan?

Oh yes, yes. That was "Black Country Rock." I Bolanized it. I do that to a lot of people.

Apart from the obvious one, "Queen Bitch," which of the others are notably parodic?

I did a lot of Newley things on the very first album I made, "Love You 'Til Tuesday." That's a very strange album.

Has it been reissued?

It will be. It's been out once. They brought it out when I had "Space Oddity," but it didn't do so very well. I expect they'll bring it out in a few weeks time. I guarantee they'll bring it out.

Other songs: D'you want some more songs?

Of course, "Waiting For The Man," I'll have to say that one. In fact a lot of Lou's material. Especially that one because it sums up a lot of his early writing, and his writing has changed considerably since those days. I think his new material on the album that we're gonna do will surprise a lot of people as well.

It's miles different from anything he's ever done before. On "Waiting For The Man" I think Lou captured, for me better than anybody else, the feeling of New York, that particular area of New York, that he was living in and in those times.

The other great New York record of our times is "Summer In The City."

Yeah, I agree with that. I was a devoted fan of the Spoonful. I loved them.

Another record was the Mingus "Oh Yeah" album, particularly "Ecclusiastics," which I drew an enormous amount of pleasure from. I felt it very 1990s—very 2001—that whole album. I was into that kind of jazz.

Before Santana came, I was into the English scene and I was never able to relate to that stuff because of my earlier interest in Coltrane and Mingus as well. A lot of Zappa's things flatten me actually.

Any of Zappa's stuff make it with you?

"We're Only In It For The Money," because I mean I saw huge potential in that area for Zappa, but I don't understand Zappa, and I'm not that intrigued by him to try to unwrap his problems or try to find out why.

Were you ever tempted to get into the James Taylor thing of autobiographical songs?

Yeah, I had a spasm of that, but thank God I got out of it.

Out of all your material, with which songs do you feel most comfortable? D'you ever listen to any of your stuff and think it could have been better if you'd done it later?

Oh yes, lots of times. A lot of "Man Who Sold The World," although that was one of the best albums I made. It was a whole traumatic period.

What's gonna be the next post-Ziggy development? Have you started to think about a new album?

No, not at all. I'm still totally involved with Ziggy. I probably will be for a few months getting it entirely out of my system, and then we'll don another mask.

Thanks a lot, and I hope you and Ziggy will be very happy together.

Oh, no. I hope YOU and Ziggy will be very happy. Ziggy's my gift to you.

It had been the last interview of a long day of raps, zaps and varied craziness, and I was keeping David from an immediate departure to enjoy a fortnight's holiday. So we shook hands and said our farewells. David's alright you know. He may even be the "shining genius" his ads say he is. Whatever, he's a gas. Long live Ziggy Stardust! We needed him.

GOODBYE ZIGGY AND A BIG HELLO TO ALADDIN SANE

Charles Shaar Murray | January 27, 1973, *New Musical Express* (UK)

The start of 1973 found David Bowie reinventing himself.

Ziggy Stardust—the character with whom he was so synonymous that some of the public seemed confused that it wasn't his actual name—was departing the stage. He was about to be replaced—the *New Musical Express*'s Charles Shaar Murray revealed—by a construct called Aladdin Sane.

Bowie and Murray's solemn discussion of the characteristics of this non-existent individual (who, it would transpire, was essentially a lightning flash painted across Bowie's face and a drop of liquid placed on his left clavicle) would have struck many weaned on the less theatrical idols of the sixties as preposterous. However, the kids buying records in the seventies—especially in the UK, where glam rock had made outlandish image as important as music—lapped up such make-believe stuff.

In Bowie's case, it was eminently forgivable. Murray found him putting the finishing touches to an album—also called *Aladdin Sane*—which, with *Hunky Dory* and *Ziggy*, would make it three classics in a row.

Note: for "Anji" read "Angie" [Bowie]. —Ed.

JANUARY 17, LONDON WEEKEND SOUTH BANK STUDIOS

As the cab pulls up outside London Weekend's South Bank studios, it's possible to see the David Bowie Travelling Cosmic Circus elegantly disembarking from a limo about 50 yards up the road.

That fluffy scarlet head of hair lights up the grey South Bank as the fluorescent crocodile of exotic humanity ducks into a side entrance, not to be seen for some little while.

In Studio 3, an organ and electric piano are set up, apparently unconnected to anything vaguely resembling an amplifier. Floor managers, camera operators, and directors are milling about excitedly, and a token audience is lolling unconcernedly in their display racks.

After what is apparently considered a decent interval, Georgie Fame appears behind the organ, Alan Price behind the piano.

Evidently it's rockanroll day on London Weekend's "Russell Harty Plus" show. In rapid succession Fame and Price, David Bowie and Elton John are being wheeled in, put behind microphones and wheeled out.

So anyway, Fame's looking very smooth and Talk-Of-The-Townish, grinning hugely, and Price looks morose in his black suit. They crank up the backing track, and Fame begins to sing this abysmal little song presumably their new single, and every so often Price leans into his microphone to mime the backing vocals. They run it through a couple of more times and then tape it.

No one applauds. They leave. Why are musicians that good playing music that bad?

Instant bustle. The piano and organ are muscled off, and the floor manager starts worrying about where Russell Harty's chair is going to be placed during Bowie's segment.

"These boys move around a lot, they tell me," he says to another headphoned soul as a silver drum kit and a brace of Marshall amps make an appearance.

Now there's a stir over at the corner of the studio as Bowie and his entourage enter at the side. David is looking more than somewhat bizarre in a green quilted tuxedo and yellow trousers, waistcoat and boots.

His eyebrows have vanished, replaced by finely sketched red lines. He's wearing red eye shadow, which makes him look faintly insect-like. He is thinner than ever. With him, Trevor Bolder, with sideboards yet unsilvered, looking faintly bemused; Mick Ronson with his second best Les Paul and striped satin jacket; and Woody Woodmansey in a city-gent outfit that contrasts oddly with his extravagantly deranged blond coiffure.

While David gets acquainted with the directors, rejecters, inspectors, dejectors, neglecters, collectors and lesser flora and fauna, a snatch of the backing track to which the man and his arachnid companions are to mime, is played back by the technicians.

Strange electronic whooshings and burblings, very weird.

Then David is securely behind his microphone, the Spiders are in position and the backing track comes up again. Well, who'da thought it—it's "Drive-In Saturday," premiered a few months back in Fort Lauderdale, Florida—all arranged and produced and tied up and coming straight atcha for the new single.

Almost immediately Bowie stops the proceedings and requests that the backing track be played louder. It's pumped up to maximum volume, and he goes through it again.

It's a slow, intense song, more like "Five Years" or "Rock And Roll Suicide" than "Jean Genie" or "Suffragette City," and you're gonna be humming it for the next six months.

The second song is a solo number, for which amps and drums vanish. Sandwiched between the two numbers is an interview, and Bowie's descent from the stage to the tandem armchairs in which Russell Harty will interview him is meticulously rehearsed.

Then the stool and dual mike are set up on the stage, and Bowie's up there sitting behind his curiously unwieldy Harptone guitar, performing Jacques Brel's "My Death."

The exceptional nature of David Bowie's gifts as a composer occasionally tend to blind one to his excellence as an interpreter of the work of others. His performance of "My Death" is riveting, dramatic without ever intruding into the treacherous realms of hamminess, showing a devastating empathy with the lyrics.

Even the technicians have stopped futzing around with the lights, carrying ladders and muttering into their headsets. They're listening to this bizarre creature singing a song by a French composer of whom maybe only half of them have heard.

As Bowie approaches the last section, one of his guitar strings gives under the strain and hangs away from the neck, one razor-thin silver streak under the lights. He cracks up the entire studio by announcing the calamity in the song, and then finishing, just perfectly.

"Cat Stevens would have given up," mutters a member of the audience in the opposite tier.

Break. Bowie and Co. vanish to their dressing room.

After allowing a discreet interval, I wend my way up to find David in the process of . . . getting made up and getting into his stage suit. The dazzling outfit that freaked out the entire studio was, it appears, merely his street garb.

As ever, Sue Fussey is ministering to his hair, now longer on top and at the back, pushed behind his ears at the side.

A gentleman named Pierre LaRoche is tending to his make-up, and the man behind his clothes, Fred of the East End, is there as well. Fred resembles a young lady who had taken it into her head to impersonate Leslie Howard.

His clothing firm, he informs me, is known to the world and points east as "Play It Cool And Play It Loud." David's clothes are mostly from the "Cool" section.

Greetings and small-talk are swapped and it's agreed that after the taping Bowie will have a microphone pushed into his face so that we can discuss the state of the world (and points east).

He vanishes to reappear moments later in full splendour in a more than somewhat mind-snapping outfit which he is to describe as "a parody of a suit and tie." A solitary ornate earring dangles from one ear.

The interview with Harty is moderately amusing, as Mr. H concentrates mainly on Bowie's appearance and outrage quotient. It is, it appears, too much of a technicality to actually discuss music.

But David despite being uncharacteristically nervous, holds his end up brilliantly, making his points and still managing to play it for laughs, like asking "Where's the camera?" in the middle of a long and serious rap, or reproving Harty for his obsessive interest in Bowie's stockings with a limp-wristed, "Silly!"

Then it's time to tape "My Death." During the recording, many of the audience are watching the monitor screens rather than the glittering figure on stage. Maybe the televised image seems more real.

Strange, because in the soft focus, Bowie's face bears an unnerving resemblance to that of Marlene Dietrich in her prime. When the false ending comes up, the floor manager whips the audience into applauding. The clapping fades into an embarrassing silence when Bowie sings the penultimate line. And after the last line there's still a little hesitation before everybody assures themselves the song has finally ended.

A few minutes later, in the midst of a cluttering cafeteria, amid eating and conversational noises and a welter of P.A. announcements requesting various people to report to various places—at once, thenk-yo!—a David Bowie interview takes place.

It begins with a somewhat impertinent comparison of the new expanded Spiders-plus line-up with the Elvis Presley Roadshow—as if they'd let a freaky pinko faggot like my main man David plays God's own city, gawddam.

"It's a nine-piece, not quite as large as Elvis', I would imagine. I think Elvis travels with a heavy string section and everything.

"I would like to get one thing straight: it's not an additional Spiders. The Spiders are still Trevor, Woody and Mick. We've just got in some back-up men on tenor saxes and piano and voices.

"I read in some of the papers that the Spiders were expanding—no way. It's three Spiders, me and back-up musicians."

Does this increased instrumentation imply an equivalent visual enhancement?

"Again I'm concentrating mainly on the music and I shall work on the theatrics of the thing if I have enough time, because I never believe that time can be eaten away as quickly as it is when we're working as we are at the moment.

"Our next gig is on the 14th of February at Radio City in New York. Before then we have to finish the present album on the 24th of this month, which is next week. Then I sail, and as soon as I get to New York I've just got ten days to rehearse the whole thing.

"We were kept very much to ourselves in America, and we were very wary of America the first time. Next time we may be able to get out and about a bit more. We were very paranoid about it."

Was the paranoia justified?

"I never can tell, because I'd quite got to like it by the time I was leaving. I quite adore the feeling of being in New York."

Mentally if not physically, David Bowie enjoys living dangerously.

"I enjoy being on a tight-rope. It gives me an excitement that I need in life."

But could he live on that tight-rope if he wasn't an artist?

"Probably not, but there was never a point in my life when I wasn't living on a tight-rope, and I was always playing music in some way or another. I don't know—I suppose that if I wasn't working in music, I'd still be travelling. I'm very fond of travelling—moving from one society to another."

One of the most unnerving aspects of sitting and talking to David Bowie is that you don't really know at what point in time the conversation is taking place. In an article of two or three moons ago, I described Bowie as "a man in the '70s looking back on the '80s from a position somewhere in the next century."

"That's exactly how I feel a lot of the time. I think it's probably a forced position, but it's a position that I wish to adopt to keep my writing intact and to progress in the direction I'd like."

When Ziggy Stardust is quietly cast aside to that particular mental attic where old alter egos are put out to pasture, who, I asked will emerge in his place?

"A person called Aladdin Sane. Aladdin is really just a track. The album was written in America. The numbers were not supposed to form a concept album, but looking back on them, there seems to be a definite linkage from number to number.

"There's no order; they were written in different cities, and there's a general feeling on the album which at the moment I can't put my finger on.

"It's a feeling I've never yet produced on an album; I think it's the most interesting album that I've written, musically as interesting as any of the things I've written. 'Drive-In Saturday' is one of the more commercial numbers.

"I think everybody wants another 'Jean Genie', but we're bringing out 'Drive-In Saturday' as a single."

Some of the letters concerning David that go through the NME's extraordinarily complex filing system seem to regard David Bowie and Ziggy Stardust as being virtually interchangeable and some of them refer to Ziggy without even mentioning David himself. A lot of them, therefore, regard Ziggy Stardust as being more important than his creator.

"Yes, they're probably right as well. I don't necessarily think David Bowie's at all important. I think the concept and the atmosphere which is created by the music that I write is more important than I am.

"I've always felt like a vehicle for something else, but then I've never really sorted out what that was. I think everybody, at one time or another, gets that kind of feeling: that they aren't just here for themselves, and more often than not they turn to the Bible and agree that it's probably Jesus and God and all of that section of religion. There's a feeling that we are here for another purpose. And in me it's very strong.

"It's a question of probabilities. I just work out probabilities. I see things that are happening at the moment and try and draw them to some focal point where they meet in the future.

"I usually pick different eras and go back and pick incidents that happen in the thirties and forties and push them through to the eighties and see what conclusions could come from what happened then."

Psychic co-ordinates?

"Psychic co-ordinates, yes, that's very good. There's another word and I can't think of it, but I saw on television the other night someone who'd written a book on the subject and it's done with computers now, apparently. But I'm just a writer. I couldn't get involved with writing on a computer. I would feel I was absolutely null and void, and I enjoy writing and putting my own theory of probability into it. It wouldn't necessarily be very accurate. And I'm sure that a computer would come up with a different answer to me."

The question of the black holes (negative anti-matter areas in space) is another concept that Bowie finds intriguing.

"Yes, absolutely fabulous. There's one just outside New York."

Elizabeth, New Jersey, no doubt. I inform Bowie I became anti-matter myself, after passing through this fearsome town in the late summer of 1970.

"Yes, really? You went through it? There have been quite a few losses."

David's smooth acceptance of this particular bizarre flight of fantasy threw me so completely that I forgot my next question, a fact which he noted with ill-concealed amusement.

"You get nervous doing chat shows," I told him—"I get nervous doing interviews." I was more than somewhat on the defensive.

"I get nervous doing interviews,"—he replied—"because I get scared of incessantly repeating myself, like a broken record."

Another mention of Aladdin Sane causes him to warm once again to his theme. "I don't think Aladdin is as clearly cut and defined a character as Ziggy was. Ziggy was meant to be clearly cut and well-defined with areas for interplay, whereas Aladdin is pretty ephemeral. He's also a situation as opposed to just being an individual. I think he encompasses situations as well as just being a personality."

Was whoever sang "Space Oddity" less of an assumed character than whoever it is who sings "Jean Genie"?

"I can't really relate to that man at all, because he was undergoing adventures back then which I've not come across for a number of years. His way of life is very different to mine, very very different.

"I can't connect with him or relate to him at all. I can't think how he was thinking. The only link is 'Space Oddity.' That's the only number to come out of that period that I still have a feeling for. 'The Cygnet Committee' is the only other one."

"Space Oddity" was, of course the first of Bowie's songs to use a particularly neat device, that of changing the change of narrator around the pun of "Here (am I sitting in my tin can)" and "(Can you) hear me, Major Tom?".

He admits: "I must own up to the Beatles for creating that kind of feeling. The one thing that I really adored about Lennon's writing was his use of the pun, which was exceedingly good. I don't think anyone has ever bettered Lennon's use of the pun. I played on it more; Lennon would throw it away in one line. I tend to build a song upon it. I treat my puns a lot more seriously."

Bowie's other major cop, from Lennon, was pinching the backing vocal line from "Lovely Rita" (from "Sgt. Pepper") and incorporating it into "Star" (on the "Ziggy" album).

"I have to interplay with other writers, because I've always been a fan. If I wasn't a fan, I'd probably be far more individual—the other kind of individuality where it's very, very ingrained in the self. Because I'm very involved with society on my level, I have to use the tools that the present society has been created with, musically. That's why, I lift from—and use—and am intrigued by—other writers and their music."

But this recycling of past devices, I ventured, makes it all too easy for certain uncharitable souls in the Press to brand Bowie a mere pasticheur.

"I think I know the one you mean. That was the heaviest piece I've ever seen, and I noted that he's changed his attitude since that piece of writing. I was more incensed because he was talking about the Lou Reed album, and he was complaining basically about the mix of the album, which I had very little to do with myself. I was very brought down by it. I'd just tried to do what I could for Lou.

"I must explain that I don't necessarily know what I'm talking about in my writing. All I try to do in my writing is assemble points that interest me and puzzle through it, and that becomes a song and other people who listen to that song must take what they can get from it and see if information that they've assembled fits in with anything I've assembled and what do we do now?

"All I can do is say: have you noticed *that* and have you noticed *that* and—what does it mean? That's all I can do with a song. I cannot say, 'this is where it's at.' I cannot do that because I don't know! I don't know!

"All I can do is assemble information that I've received. I've written a song on the new album which is just called 'Time,' and I thought it was about time, and I wrote very heavily about time, and the way I felt about time—at times—and I played it back after we'd recorded it and my God, it was a gay song! And I'd no intention of writing anything at all gay. When I listened to it back I just could not believe it. I thought well, that's the strangest . . ."

At this point a massive steak arrived (Bowie D., for the consumption of).

"Charles, let's switch off. While I eat."

JANUARY 20. TRIDENT STUDIOS. LONDON

Saturday night at Trident Studios. The door swings open and the entrant is nearly knocked off his teenage feet by a blast furnace rendition of "John I'm Only Dancing" clawing its way out of the jumbo-sized speakers. Mick Ronson sits in the corner in a bejewelled Marilyn Monroe T-shirt and the ubiquitous Miss Fussey's there as well. David, resplendent in an outside velvet po' boy cap, waves an exuberant hello from behind the control panel where he's sitting with Ken Scott, engineer and/or producer to all the nicest and niftiest names.

The new cut of "John" has a murderously high energy level, which by comparison makes the single version sound like one man with a three-stringed acoustic. It virtually blisters the ears to make it even more obvious that the Spiders are one of our best bands.

All but two cuts from the new album were finished by Saturday—and that particular brace of tunes lacked only vocals. The excellent reason was that Bowie had not yet written the lyrics.

The title cut comes up, and he passes over his notebook containing the lyrics. At the top of the page it says "Aladdin Sane: 1913-1948-197? Copyright David Bowie 1972. So there."

Imagine, if you will, the music that would have been played in a '30s cabaret if the atom bomb had been used during the First World War. "Who'll love Aladdin Sane?" asks the voice, while Mike Garson plays an ornate night-club piano that gradually disintegrates into gleaming ice-shards of notes. Incredibly sinister stuff, and Garson's work on this album is going to make a lot of people own up about rock keyboards—about who can play, and who can't.

Then there's "Cracked Actor," about an ageing Hollywood star who picks up a young teenybopper for sexual reasons, but the poor fool doesn't realise that's she's only with him because she's a smackhead . . . and thinks that he's her connection. A very Hollywood song, and slightly influenced by Iggy Pop and the Stooges—though there's some Lou Reed and some Randy Newman in there as well. And then there's the aforementioned "Time": "Time, he flexes like a whore" and the incessantly repeated line: "We should be on by now."

Apart from the two singles (there's a re-mixed "Jean Genie" too), there's

"Watch That Man," which is loud and heavy and you can dance to it, and the lovely "Prettiest Star," a new version of a song written for his wife Anji, and originally issued as a single as the follow-up to "Space Oddity."

It died, sadly, a horrible death. Plus as an extra bonus—a fine version of the Stones' "Let's Spend the Night Together," which sounds, well, strange coming from David. It figures, though. As the thunderous sound screams out only inches away, Ronson is sound asleep on the couch.

It is decided that some extra bass parts are needed, so Trevor Bolder is hastily summoned, and Ronson stays on to supervise. As he's tired, the Mercedes is summoned to take Bowie back to Beckenham. And, by the same token, a tube takes me back to Islington. As he leaves I notice that the ashtray matches his boots.

"Who'll love Aladdin Sane?" Easy one, chillun. You will.

Aladdin Sane is coming to getcha. And you're gonna love every moment of it.

BOWIE FINDS HIS VOICE

Robert Hilburn | September 14, 1974, *Melody Maker* (UK)

Among other things, this *Melody Maker* feature takes in Bowie's 1973 covers LP *Pin Ups*, *Diamond Dogs* (1974), his in-concert album *David Live* (also '74), and the recording of the start of a new phase of his career, *Young Americans*.

    Diamond Dogs—the semi-concept album that marked Bowie's farewell to glam rock, red hair, Ziggy Stardust, and relatively orthodox rock—had (galvanizing taster single "Rebel Rebel" excepted) been greeted with mixed reviews. Bowie, though, was clearly over it, effusive about his next studio project. As he himself says herein, "Everything I do I get bored with eventually." —Ed.

"I really shouldn't do this," teased David Bowie as he walked across the room of his Beverly Hills hotel suite toward a mound of tape equipment. I had come to talk to him and hear his new live album (a two-record set from his current United States tour), but there was something else he wanted to play first.

"This isn't the new album, but the one after it, and the record company doesn't like me to do that. They want me to talk about the new one, the live one that'll be out soon. But I'm so excited about this one. We cut it in a week in Philadelphia and it can tell you more about where I am now than anything I could say."

This was Bowie's first interview since he began his massive US tour last June, a tour that included such ambitious staging that many reviewers have hailed it as the most spectacular rock show ever.

Bowie doesn't like interviews and rarely does them anymore. They are, he feels, unnecessary links between him and his audience.

Like so many, he feels his music conveys everything he wants to say.

Besides, he hates to read quotes months later when his views on a subject may have changed drastically.

And David's views—he's the first to admit—do change often and drastically.

He was a bit nervous when he entered the room. He simply walked over to the tape equipment and rummaged through some boxes until he found the right one, and began threading the machine and adjusting the controls.

For those who still take note of his fashion, he now parts his hair down the side—a bit like the 1930s look.

The popular Ziggy hairstyle is gone. He was wearing black tux trousers, a blue and white check shirt and bold white suspenders. His shoes were black, rather like a conservative banker might wear. No platforms.

Satisfied the tape equipment was working properly, he moved to a chair and listened as the music came from the speakers.

From the opening track (a new version of "John, I'm Only Dancing") it was clear some changes had been made in Bowie's style.

The musical backing featured a strong touch of rhythm and blues, but mainly it was the confidence, increased shading and range of his voice. It was far less one-dimensional than in the past. More human and "authentic."

The next track—"Somebody Up There Likes Me"—was even more telling. It was a socio-political commentary, very direct in its lyrics.

The other tracks—including a ballad about love having slipped through one's grasp, and a lament about the loss of emotion in this era that contains the line, "Ain't there one damn song that can make me break down and cry?"—were also more direct and accessible than much of Bowie's previous work. There's no resort to science fiction or indirect statement.

When the tape ended, there was less nervousness in Bowie's manner. He was obviously delighted with the new album. It was as if the music gave him greater confidence.

Later, the nervousness would reappear from time to time and when it did he would usually end his comment with a nervous laugh as if to underscore his uncertainty about the particular answer.

"I think it is the closest thing I've ever done on record to being very, very me," he said. "I always said that on most albums I was acting. It was a role, generally.

"And this one is the nearest to actually meeting me since that very first 'Space Oddity' album, which was quite personal. I'm really excited about it."

There seemed to be much less tension and more focus in the new album—tentatively titled "One Damn Song"—than in the recent "Aladdin Sane" and "Diamond Dogs" albums.

I asked him about that. He said he had been through a strain on both of those albums.

"'Aladdin Sane' was a result of my paranoia with America at the time," he said. "I hadn't come to terms with it, then. I have now, I know the areas I like best in America.

"I know the kind of people I like. I've been here a long time—since April. I've had a chance to clarify my feelings. And I'm quite happy over here. I found different people.

"But I ran into a very strange type of paranoid person when I was doing 'Aladdin.' Very mixed up people, and I got very upset. It resulted in 'Aladdin' . . . And I knew I didn't have very much more to say about rock 'n' roll.

"I mean 'Ziggy' really said as much as I meant to say all along. 'Aladdin' was really 'Ziggy' in America. Again, it was just looking around, seeing what's in my head.

"The 'Pin Ups' album was a pleasure. And I knew the band (the Spiders) was over. It was a last farewell to them in a way. 'Diamond Dogs' was the start of this new album, actually.

"Things like 'Rock and Roll With Me' and '1984' were embryonic of what I wanted to do. I tried all kinds of things. It was not a concept album. It was a collection of things.

"And I didn't have a band. So, that's where the tension came in. I couldn't believe I had finished it when I did. I had done so much of it myself. I never want to be in that position again.

"It was frightening trying to make an album with no support behind you. I was very much on my own. It was my most difficult album. It was a relief that it did so well."

Was he worried during "Diamond Dogs" about where he was going next musically?

"No, I knew it was toward this album. Even then. The songs on 'Diamond Dogs' that I got the biggest kick out of—like 'Rock and Roll With Me' and '1984'—gave me the knowledge there was another album at least inside of me that I was going to be happy with.

"I mean, if I can't make albums that I'm happy with, I'll not make them. I won't just go in and knock off dozens of albums. They must mean something to me.

"It just happens that I write very fast. I write a lot. That's why I seem to have so many bloody albums out."

Though the new album, then, is a departure for Bowie, he gave clues to it all along. Even during the peak success of "Ziggy Stardust," he had said he was not interested in just being a rock 'n' roller.

He wanted a broader, more multi-directional career. While the new album is the boldest step in that direction, songs like "Time" on "Aladdin Sane" gave hints of his future.

"Exactly," he said. "It has always been there. It was just a question of when I was going to come out of my particular closet. The answer, obviously, was when I had the confidence to.

"Presumably, the next album will be a further graduation. But, maybe, it'll be a retrostep. We'll see." The nervous laughter popped up briefly.

I asked him about the rhythm and blues influence. Was it something new?

"No. But it's only now that I've got the necessary confidence to sing like that. That's the kind of music I've always wanted to sing. I mean those are my favourite artists . . . the Jackie Wilsons . . . that type.

"That was one of the great things about this trip. I could go to any black place in America and not be recognised. And that was really fantastic.

"The only time, really, we got any kind of recognition on a large scale was at the Jackson 5 concert because there was a younger audience.

"But at most of the R&B shows, they're married couples, not kids, so it was marvellous for me to be able to go out and rave and yell. I went to the Apollo a lot, saw dozens of people."

When did the vocal confidence come to him?

"When I started rehearsing with the band for this tour, I suddenly realised I was enjoying singing again. I hadn't enjoyed it in a long time.

"It was just a way to get my songs across. But when I started rehearsing, I began enjoying it and I found I actually had a voice.

"That's really exciting for me. My voice has improved in leaps and bounds. I've been flattered by some of the things the musicians have said about my singing.

"I'd really like to be recognised as a singer. I'd love that."

Was singing always a goal?

"I don't know," he smiled. "Once upon a time . . . when I was very young . . . like 22 or something . . . I had my eye on that, but I never really took it seriously.

"I didn't have any sort of faith in my voice. I knew that I had an individual voice, but now I'm beginning to believe it's good as well.

"Maybe, I just want to be a crooner . . ." That laughter popped up again.

One of the most interesting songs on the new album is "Somebody Up There Likes Me," a warning about the danger of hero worship.

"There are several things on this album that lead from other things I've done," he said.

"Really, I'm a very one-track person. What I've said for years under various guises is that 'watch out, the West is going to have a Hitler!' I've said it in a thousand different ways. That song is yet another way.

"I just feel we are very open to . . ." he continued, then paused and broke off his thought by saying he hates to pontificate in that way. He just feels, he said, we all have a temptation to let others make our decisions for us—to lead us.

"That's what Ziggy was. That's what they all are . . . all the little characters I come up with."

Wasn't it ironic, then, I suggested, that so many of Bowie's own fans look to him as a leader—someone to give them answers.

"That's just it," he said. "That's what I said in 'Rock and Roll With Me.' I mean, the verse of that talks about that . . . you're doing it to me. Stop it." Again, the nervous laugh.

"That's why I'm happy my music is going in the new direction. It's responsible music. I mean, one could play an enormous game with people, but I am not prepared to do it. I could see how easy it was to get a whole rally thing going.

"There were times, frankly, when I could have told the audience to do anything, and that's frightening. Well, I've got that responsibility so I've got to be very careful about what I do with it. It needs a bit of forethought."

How does he feel his audience will respond to this new album?

"When we were recording, a bunch of kids stayed outside the studio all night until 10 o'clock in the morning, so we let them in and played some things from the album and they loved it, which was amazing. Fabulous, because I really didn't know what they'd think about the change in direction."

What about the absence of science fiction in the new album? Was that part of his increased confidence?

"Yes it is in a way. I used a lot of science fiction patterns because I was trying to put forward concepts, ideas and theories, but this album hasn't anything to do with that.

"It's just emotional drive. It's one of the first albums I've done that bounds along on emotional impact. There's not a concept in sight."

He'd felt a concept was important?

"Yes, very much so. That's what I felt my area as a writer was, but I've obviously changed. When I finished this album, I felt. 'My God, I'm a different writer than I used to be.' Before you put it all together, you don't know what you've really got—just bits and pieces.

"But then when we listened to it all together, it was obvious that I had really, really changed. Far more than I had thought. Every time I play a finished album I get a shock. I think—wow, is that where I am now?"

It seemed like a good time for Bowie to put on another tape. This one was the live album, which is due to be released this month (September).

Titled "David Live," it contains 17 songs, most of them vastly redesigned instrumentally from the original album versions, and sung with the greater character and texture of Bowie's improved style.

The first track—"1984"—burst into the room, and again he settled back in a chair to listen. While the album was playing, several of the musicians travelling with him and some of the MainMan staff came into the room to hear it.

Bowie was very much a musician, not a "personality" in the manner of so many rock stars when they listen to their own music.

He was like a fan pointing out special touches—some crisp guitar lick or a particularly hot saxophone solo—that delighted him. There were, quite justifiably, many reasons for his delight.

Though it is a bit dangerous making such judgements on the basis of a single listening, "David Live" is quite possibly the best live rock album I've ever heard—an urgent, highly accessible, brilliantly performed collection.

One of its special features is the absence of the long delays (for crowd applause) between songs. Just as one song dies down another begins. The result is a lively continuing pulse.

As with Dylan and "Before the Flood," "David Live" updates Bowie's material—even though some of it is only a few months old—in a way that almost makes the original version irrelevant.

Bowie's vocals give all sort of new insights and interpretations to the lyrics, particularly on songs like "Changes" and "All The Young Dudes." The album's only non-Bowie song is "Knock On Wood," the old R&B hit.

Here is the order of songs on the album:

- SIDE ONE: "1984," "Rebel Rebel," "Moonage Daydream," "Sweet Thing."

- SIDE TWO: "Changes," "Suffragette City," "Aladdin Sane," "All The Young Dudes," "Cracked Actor."

- SIDE THREE: "Rock and Roll With Me," "Watch That Man," "Knock on Wood," "Diamond Dogs."

- SIDE FOUR: "Big Brother," "Width of a Circle," "Jean Genie," "Rock 'n' Roll Suicide."

The album, clearly, is a testament to a phase in Bowie's career that is as satisfying as the "Rock of Ages" album is to the first phase of the Band's career. And Bowie does, quite definitely, feel it is the end of a phase of his career.

When someone suggested the live album could be subtitled "David Bowie Vol. 1," he smiled in agreement.

The first step in the new phase— even before the arrival of the next studio album—is the termination of his elaborate stage show.

When his Los Angeles concerts are finished, he'll recross the U.S. with another tour, but this one, without the huge staging, will be a fairly straight concert.

"I think I always know when to stop doing something," he said. "It's when the enjoyment is gone. That's why I've changed so much. I've never been of the opinion that it's necessarily a wise thing to keep on a successful streak if you're just duplicating all the time.

"That's why I tend to be erratic. It's not a matter of being indulgent, I don't think. It's just a case of making sure I'm not bored, because if I'm bored then people can see it. I don't hide it very well.

"Everything I do I get bored with eventually. It's knowing where to stop.

"I have now done what I wanted to do three or four years ago. Stage an elaborate, colourful show . . . a fantasy . . . and I don't think I want to go any further with it because I know it can be done.

"I know I could do an even bigger, grander kind of production. But when I know it can be done, I don't have to do it any more.

"Doing a straight show is very exciting to me now, suddenly jumping into a new kind of tour after this one. I couldn't imagine just doing the same show over and over again. It would be terribly boring. That's why I gave up the last time. That's why I 'retired' last time."

Besides the new musical direction, Bowie's current enthusiasm is boosted by some new musicians who'll be joining him later in the year.

He feels he finally has a band again. Andy Newmark, a drummer with Sly & The Family Stone, and Willie Weeks, a bassist who has worked with Aretha Franklin among many, will join him as soon as their present obligations are finished,

Both men worked with Bowie on the new studio album and, like many who have read so much about the controversial Bowie Image, they approached the project with a bit of uncertainty.

"When Andy and Willie came to see me in the studio, they were very wary," Bowie admits with a smile. "They didn't know what to expect. They came in looking for silver capes and all, I imagine.

"But once we started playing the songs, it worked itself out. It ended in a very, very solid friendship and a group that is going to work with me."

Thus Bowie, as he prepares to recross the U.S., seemed more confident and enthusiastic than on his first two visits here.

He agreed things were going well. It might be just the kind of quote that'll make him shudder in some future moment of depression, but now it fits.

"Yes, I really am more confident. I'm not sure it is supreme confidence or anything, but I am happier."

BOWIE MEETS SPRINGSTEEN

Mike McGrath | November 26, 1974, *The Drummer* (US)

It's difficult to imagine two artists as apparently dissimilar as David Bowie and Bruce Spring-steen. Springsteen is perceived to be suffused with authenticity: a man of the people making conventional-and-proud-of-it rock 'n' roll oriented around the concerns and pleasures of the proletariat. Bowie—although from not much less of a working-class background than "Brooce"—is viewed as someone who spurns grit for the "arty-farty," his lyrics playing with reality and his music mocking the very idea of conventionality.

Mike McGrath's piece appeared in *The Drummer*, an alternative newspaper published in Philadelphia, where Bowie had relocated to record the "plastic soul" album *Young Americans*. Although one could never imagine Springsteen holding forth on flying saucers, as Bowie did once Bruce had taken his leave, the article displays that Bowie and Bruce possessed more in common than might be assumed.

When it was written, incidentally, Bowie was more of a star than Springsteen: the latter's commercial breakthrough would come the following year with the *Born to Run* album. It was the same year that Bowie achieved his own milestone in Springsteen's home country when "Fame" reached No. 1 there. *Young Americans*, said single's parent album, failed to include the version of Springsteen's "It's Hard to Be a Saint in the City" that caused Bowie and Bruce to coalesce in the first instance. (It would not be released until the 1989 box set *Sound + Vision*.)

McGrath observes, "When people learn that you spent a decade interviewing rock stars, they always ask, 'What are they like in person?' The honest answer is that they're never like they are onstage. It was like a couple of working guys hanging out; Bruce a little uncomfortable (as he always was offstage) and Bowie an alien trying hard to pass for one of us, which he could never do. To an outsider they would have seemed almost too relaxed, too soft-spoken. Couldn't they feel the insane energy coursing through the room as these titans met?"

For added layering, the article's sidebar gives a glimpse into the mind of the Bowie obsessive. —Ed.

When Bruce Springsteen played The Tower Theatre recently, announcements were made of upcoming concerts—when David Bowie's scheduled Civic Center appearance was announced it was greeted by a large negative roar from the crowd. It caught off-guard a number of startled onlookers, including the announcer, who voiced concurrence with the crowd.

Some weeks later, during the recent Beach Boys concert at The Spectrum, the upcoming pair of Bowie shows were announced and greeted by a contest of boos and cheers from the crowd. It was obviously as fashionable to support Bowie as dismiss him. Also, judging by the crowds attracted, a lot of the booers came to see him anyway.

And at one a.m. Monday morning the 25th of November, David Bowie met and welcomed Bruce Springsteen while recording his latest album at Sigma Sound. In an open and candid evening he touched on his recent concert performances and spoke of audiences and flying saucers.

At seven o'clock Sunday night a group of about a dozen and a half Bowie freaks stood watch outside the main entrance of The Barclay on Rittenhouse Square. Some had orange, Bowie-cut hair; others just stood with their hands in their pockets waiting for a glimpse of someone that would make their vigil worthwhile.

Mike Garson plays keyboards for Bowie, as well as being his musical director. As we left the Barclay for Sigma Sound Studios on North 12th Street, the kids outside called him by name. We stopped and talked to them for a few minutes. One displayed a gorgeous, large matte color close-up of Bowie, possibly from Monday night's concert.

Mike: That's nice; you gonna give it to Bowie?

Girl: No, I want him to sign it for me!

Mike is a 28 year old keyboard player who's been with Bowie for two years, has never been with one act that long before, and has no plans to move on. He comes, very noticeably, from Brooklyn, where his wife is awaiting his return at the end of this concert tour (about a week) so she can drop their second child in his lap. "We planned it so the kid'll be born the day after I get back."

He began playing classical piano at the ripe old age of seven (his three year old daughter already plays), went from there to jazz, and then to rock.

Along the way he worked for people like Martha and the Vandellas and Nancy Wilson. A lot of influences: Bach, Beethoven, Art Tatum, Chick Corea, Stravinsky.

And, like Chick, Mike is a Scientologist. Not pushing hard for the cause—just mentioning that he was skeptical of it for about six months, took the plunge, and that it's helped him cope both as a musician and a person.

How did he become Bowie's musical director? "I was playing a gig, working with an avant garde jazz group, and one night I got a series of phone calls . . . the third was from Bowie. I didn't know who he was. I was heavy into jazz and had never come across him. I played four chords for him and Mick Ronson. . . . I was hired for eight weeks. . . . That was a hundred and twenty weeks ago."

The Mike Garson Band opened up the show Monday night. For them, the Spectrum ShowCo sound was perfect. A tight professional rhythm and blues-jazz-rock set of opening numbers was greeted first with mild indifference and later with boos, catcalls, and conspiratorial clapping designed to drive the group from stage. Never faltering once, they did their eight warm-up numbers and left the stage to return for one more after the intermission. Finally, after being subjected to an incredible verbal barrage, the group faded into the background and Bowie took the stage.

Bad sound, a weak voice, and shortened muddled versions of older songs interspersed with poor renditions of his new R&B numbers, combined to make this show his weakest yet in the city. Audience reaction was kind, bringing him back for one of his infrequent encores.

The next day consisted of bad reviews, bad feelings, and angry phone calls to WMMR-FM from concert goers who felt that the man had not delivered their money's worth (or as one leatherneck offered during the Garson's band's warm-up, "Get those niggers off the stage!")

Garson: He liked the show— he didn't know the sound was bad either. You know we can only hear the monitors blasting away on stage and they sounded fine. The audience reaction seemed very very good. . . . In actual fact, the reviews on this tour have been better overall than the *Diamond Dogs* tour.

On Bowie: "He wanted to do something without the theatrics; he may go back to them, he may not. For this time he wanted to just get out there and sing. He's not afraid of change, he's always changing. . . . He's full of surprises."

"On a good night his voice is better now than it ever was."

We arrived at Sigma Sound a little after eight. Producer Tony Visconti was arched over a mammoth sound board, pressing buttons, being generally pleasant to the half-dozen engineers and musicians in the control room, and peering into the large windowed studio directly in front.

The album was practically finished. The first rough mix had been accomplished since Bowie recorded the basic tracks some weeks ago, and this week had been devoted to clean-ups and overdubs. This was the final night in the studio for the album—the final touches would now be made.

I'm Only Dancing (She turns me on) was being played back. Pablo was in the studio, overdubbing a cowbell and some chimes onto an already lushly produced cut. Visconti easily shows his pleasure with the final product as Pablo finishes up. The cut is full and rich, almost a Phil Spector R&B wall of sound—Bowie's voice mixed way into the background.

10:30 and the jokes disintegrate into bad puns and poor taste; Tony explains palmistry to a member of the band—says that the late Bruce Lee's lifeline (gleaned from a gigantic close-up of his open fist) showed that he should've lived till 90.

11:30: Out of the corner of the studio comes an old, small brown guitar amp. Tony proudly announces that it belonged to Chubby Checker and was used to record the original version of "The Twist." He sings, "Got a new dance and it goes like this . . ." The amp's specialty is a fine dirty sound that you can't get from an amp unless it was made well about twenty years ago. After hearing a few licks played through, every guitar player in the room plots its theft.

Seven minutes to midnight: The door opens and in saunter Ed and Judy Sciaky, escorting the night's special guest star, a road weary Bruce Springsteen, fresh off the bus from Asbury Park, New Jersey. Bruce is stylishly attired in a stained brown leather jacket with about seventeen zippers and a pair of hoodlum jeans. He looks like he just fell out of a bus station, which he had.

It seems that one of the tracks Bowie laid down was Bruce's "It's Hard to be a Saint in the City." Tony Visconti called Ed at WMMR and asked him if he could get Bruce into the studio. Contacted finally on noon Sunday, Bruce hitched into Asbury Park, then via the nine o'clock Trailways to Philly, where Ed met him "hanging with the bums in the station."

Said Bruce of his Odyssey: "That ride had a real cast of characters . . . every bus has a serviceman, an old lady in a brown coat with one of these little black things on her head, and the drunk who falls out next to you."

An hour later, the time passing with some more overdubs and a few improvised vocals by Luther of the Garson band (who sings a fine lead and whose vocal power adds a lot of strength to an already powerful album), enter David Bowie and Ava Cherry, white haired soul singer for the band.

David breezes in, takes account of the night's progress, lets his piercing eyes cast across the room a few times, listens to a tape and then leaves Tony to his work so as to chat with Bruce.

Five people hunched up in a far corner of the lobby, looking more like the fans (half a dozen of whom were still standing outside, savoring the vibrations) than the stars themselves.

David reminisces on the first time he saw Bruce—two years ago at Max's Kansas City—and that he was knocked out by the show and wanted to do one of his songs ever since. When pressed for another American artist whose songs he would like to record (as he did for British artists on the *Pin-Ups* album), David thinks a while and replies that there are none. A tired but interested Bruce lets a grin escape.

The conversation turns to a common problem: Stage jumpers.

Bowie: It doesn't bother me so much that they do it; I just wonder: What are they gonna do when they get there?

Bruce: Once I was onstage sweating so hard I was soaked with it. Really soaking wet. And this guy jumps up on stage and throws his arms around me; and I get this tremendous electric shock from the guitar. This guy doesn't even feel it! I'm in agony and he doesn't feel a thing; he wasn't feeling anything anyway, but I'm getting this shock and the guy won't let go. Finally my drummer, Mad Dog, comes over and beats the guy off.

Bowie: And the guy went back to his friends saying, "Hey man, Bruce was really wired." . . . The worst was when a guy jumped up on stage and I saw the look in his eyes—all luded out—he was gone. Real scarey look in his eyes, and all I could think was, 'I been waitin' for you. Four years and I been waitin' for one like you to jump on stage.' And I just smiled at him, and his eyes got okay again; then I looked closer and saw he was holding a brick in his hand . . .

Bowie is a tall skeletal leprechaun. Red beret tipped extremely to one side, the other revealing a loose patch of orange hair, leaning away from ears that uncannily resemble a Vulcan's up close. Intense hawk eyes; if they fix on you friendly it warms the room; unfriendly or even questioningly you're forced to turn away from them. Red velvet suspenders over high waisted black pants and a white pullover sweater complete the bizarre outfit, which, like any other, grows on you as the hours pass.

In fact, Bowie grows and fleshes out as the hours pass. From the secluded, mysterious figure portrayed by the press into a man of odd habits, but more personable as some time passes between you.

After an hour, I couldn't understand how Mike Garson could say he was easy and friendly to work with; very short and direct in his instructions to the band as he stands with Visconti at the board, overseeing some back-up vocals. After a few hours, a break, and some chatter about flying saucers, the person seeps through. A real person.

The studio is a warm, fur covered cavern at three a.m. Heads and bodies sway in time to a slow one. Yellows, blues, reds, and greens dimmed as low as possible light the control room and studio. The control room is a starship with endless banks of futuristic controls; punch panel, mixing decks, tape decks, blinking lights. A starship manned by a motley bunch of pirates. Obviously hijacked.

The talk turns toward the sound last Monday at the Spectrum. (**Bowie:** "It's the pits. The absolute pits.") Visconti is assigned to work on its improvement. A five o'clock sound check will be of little use since it's brought up that the acoustics change tremendously when the place fills with fourteen thousand sound absorbing bodies.

If anyone can look tired and energetic at the same time, it's David. Part the curtains in the studio and the silent sentinels below come to life and wave frantically; their big moment—contact with the event.

Bowie tries to record a vocal solo. It sounds terrible, the voice is hoarse and tired. "It's much too early yet—I'm not quite awake . . . I won't be able to record anything till about half past five."

He re-enters the studio and wraps a set of incredibly long, slender lingers around a cold steak sandwich (never having encountered one before, he was taught the correct hold and given seven different explanations as to what a hoagie was).

More on the Spectrum: "I was dreading it really. Everybody whoever played there warned me how terrible it was. I don't think you can get good sound there, but we'll try."

After a promise to meet again and talk further in New York. Bruce heads off with Ed and Judy for a five a.m. visit to the Broad Street diner. Max's Kansas City had been his first professional gig. Bowie was in from the start. Bruce leaves without having heard his version of Saint. The feeling is that it's not ready yet.

Bowie: "There's one that you people probably haven't even heard of here, 'cause the U.S. government threw a blanket over it. It's all over Canada though . . . happened about three, four weeks ago in Akron, Ohio. Same sort of thing that Prof Carr is saying happened at Patterson Air Force Base. There was a decompression accident and they have a ship and four bodies: three feet tall, caucasian, although weathered all over to make up for it, same organic stuff: cocks and lungs and such, but different, bigger brains.

"You know Barry Goldwater is resigning from politics to become President of a UFO organization. . . he's not really resigning from politics, he just realizes they can't keep it all secret much longer and he wants to be at the top when it breaks. It will break soon."

Next on the Bowie agenda is a long voyage down the Amazon; David will not fly and his next concert tour is in Brazil in January. Maybe the long boat ride will ease that throat. On some tracks of the new album (a single record which may include the Springsteen tune) his voice is clear and firm. On others it's mixed way back, so that Garson's group and the full production overpower a weak, hoarse attempt.

There is however, not a bad cut on the album. Hell, you can even dance to it.

As the sun came up and David talked on a bit of the Russians and their 3,000 flying objects sending communicative signals into space (Klattu Barrada Nikto?), the room took on the warm perspective of the remnants of an all night talk-rap-fantasize session. The kind where you come away fulfilled, for no other reason than you felt you got to know a handful of people a bit better.

A warm room, hard to leave. But work was about to resume, the sun was getting higher, and the deadline for this copy becoming tighter and tighter. A firm handshake, as firm and strong as Bruce's; they are much alike.

Outside, a dozen sentinels are huddled in cars, standing on the sidewalk, sitting on the steps, waiting for a little of the magic to pour out. This is Bowie's final night in the studio. When he leaves, they'll get into their cars and beat him to the Barclay. One last look at the man who makes his albums in Philadelphia.

BEHIND BOWIEMANIA

This issue's cover features a collage of pictures that used to cover Marla "Bowie" Feldstein's wall in her room in her parents Lower Merion home. "Used to" only because her room is in the process of being repainted (a scant minimum of a dozen Bowie posters adorn dry walls), and a "better job of hanging them" will be accomplished when the painting is done.

Marla, along with her friends Pat, Leslie, and Debbie, slept and waited outside the Electric Factory ticket office on Lombard Street from Thursday until Saturday so they could buy seats in the first rows for Bowie's Spectrum appearance. They got them.

They are also the backbone of the crew that waits for a glimpse of David as he travels between The Barclay and Sigma Sound. Marla has seen David in concert thirteen times: Twice in February of '73 (with the Spiders), all six shows recently at the Tower Theatre (including holding tickets for the cancelled matinee), three times in New York (Nov. 1, 2, 3), and the two Monday shows at The Spectrum.

Their opinion of the critically received Spectrum performance? "It was definitely better than the three shows in New York . . . We liked it because we know everything about Bowie—A lot of people don't like it because they were into the image, clothes, hair . . . But he does work too hard I think. His voice needs a rest."

Besides seeing their idol on stage, Marla credits herself in a joking way with helping to get Bowie on the Dick Cavett show. She saw Cavett get out of a car in downtown Philly and screamed at him, "Do a show on Bowie!" Cavett allegedly turned and mumbled "OK."

It also so happened that Marla and her crew were in New York for the taping of the show (to be aired December 5). "He was so nervous, we kept clapping at everything to make him feel better. He does about an hour and sings Young American, 1984, Can You Hear Me, and Foot Stomping.

"He sings to us at concerts; if he walked out of the hotel and there were 20 people there, he would know us."

Probably because Marla and her friends were among the privileged few to hear the first sounds on the new album when David invited them into the studio for a small celebration as a token of thanks for their devotion. They also know everyone in the band by name, call them at home, and are well known by doormen and engineers.

"I don't know how much I've spent on him . . . my mother would know. I don't know where I get the money . . . I'm 16. I save my lunch money—75 cents a day makes $3.50 a week."

Much of the weekend was spent in vigil by Marla and her friends. Unfortunately, now that school's in session, she has to be home early; too early to catch late riser Bowie as he leaves the hotel at one in the morning.

The final critical word? "There's nothing he ever did that I don't like."

BOWIE: NOW I'M A BUSINESSMAN

Robert Hilburn | February 28, 1976, *Melody Maker* (UK)

In 1976, David Bowie—even despite his drug problems in this period, details of which would only emerge later—appeared to be a happier soul, something that would seem to be a direct result of having dismissed his notoriously "heavy" manager Tony Defries in 1974.

Perhaps it was this new mood that enabled Bowie to be relaxed enough to have acquired a sense of perspective on himself as an artist. *Melody Maker*'s Robert Hilburn got him to review his work and found him almost injudiciously frank. Bowie dismisses *Young Americans* as unlistenable, albeit not undanceable, and can't even be bothered bigging up his latest album, *Station to Station*.

Bowie also talks about his acting debut in *The Man Who Fell to Earth*, for which he would be critically praised. He never did take up some other roles mentioned herein, though: in *The Eagle Has Landed*, a Ziggy Stardust film—and as prime minister of Great Britain.

Reveals Hilburn, "I interviewed David several times between 1972, when he was on the Ziggy Stardust tour, and this time in Los Angeles. I always found him challenging and provocative: moving so fast in ever-changing directions that it was hard at times to know what was real and what was simply theatrical embellishment—in other words when his comments were part of the role he was playing at the time. There was always a germ of truth in what David said, we came to learn, but he was especially open and vulnerable in this interview. It was the closest I ever got to feeling he was speaking from the heart. In retrospect, I feel he was always speaking more from the heart than we had imagined." —Ed.

For David Bowie, the second encore at the Cow Palace arena in San Francisco was an especially satisfying moment. When Bowie played the same city in 1972 on the Ziggy Stardust tour, only 1,100 people showed up to see him at the 5,000-seat Winterland Auditorium. The turnout was so disappointing that Bowie skipped San Francisco entirely on his next U.S. tour.

But this time—boosted by the success of his "Fame" single and all the attention he has received in the past four years—Bowie played the 14,000-seat Cow Palace (the city's largest rock hall) and the response was phenomenal.

Though his 90-minute set started slowly as Bowie concentrated on new material, he worked up such an enthusiasm in the arena with his versions of such early, well-known works as "Changes," "Rebel Rebel" and "Jean Genie" that a rare thing happened after the first, rather obligatory encore.

The audience continued yelling for Bowie long after the house lights—normally the sign that a concert is irrevocably over—were turned on. An excited, but apparently unprepared, Bowie finally came back on stage to do a hastily assembled version of "Diamond Dogs."

Though he messed up some of the song's lyrics, the audience continued to roar its approval and kept doing so for a full five minutes after the house lights were again turned on. One Cow Palace official said it was the strongest response he had seen a rock act receive there in years. Bowie, clearly, has arrived as a rock superstar in America.

"Incredible," Bowie said after the show as he attended a brief backstage reception at the Cow Palace, where he accepted a silver cape from promoter and ex-Fillmore boss Bill Graham and a plaque from a radio station noting that "Fame" had gone to No. 1 on its chart.

"It was a lovely night," Bowie said. "And it should be even better in Los Angeles. The numbers were a bit tough for us tonight. We were a four and the audience was a four. That can sometimes mean resistance. In L.A. we'll be a five—in the realm of the magician—and the audience will be a six—meaning comfortable, agreeable. That should really be something."

By all accounts, Bowie is a happier, more confident and relaxed person on this tour than on past ones. He looks it onstage and confirms it in conversations off-stage. Gone is the rock 'n' roll superstar pose of the Ziggy Stardust tour, and the elaborate staging and icy, detached manner of the "Diamond Dogs" tour in 1974.

The setting and mood this time finds Bowie in more of a continental, cabaret role as he comes on stage wearing a stylish white dress shirt (complete with French cuffs), a black waistcoat (with a box of European cigarettes visible in one pocket), and black slacks.

The stage, except for sound and lighting equipment, is free of extra devices. Bowie's manner is warm and inviting.

An even greater contrast between this tour and earlier ones is that Bowie is not as isolated and detached as he was.

After the first of three concerts at the 18,000-seat Forum in Los Angeles, for instance, Bowie—accompanied by his wife Angela and five-year-old son Zowie—stopped by the Forum's fancy lounge for a reception that was attended by approximately 200 persons, including Ringo Starr, Rod Stewart, Alice Cooper, Neil Sedaka, Lou Adler and the US President's son, Steven Ford. He rarely made such appearances in the past.

Though the commercial success of "Fame" and "Young Americans" in America would be the most obvious reason for Bowie's new attitude, he says the fact that he now feels comfortable with his business/management affairs is an even more important factor.

His periodic announcements that he was going to stop touring were due, he says, to frustrations that built up on those tours.

"Record sales can only do so much for your confidence," Bowie had said, sitting in his San Francisco hotel room a couple of hours before his concert.

"Real confidence comes from things much closer. It comes from being able to put together a tour like this one almost single-handedly and see it come off so well; see people around me enjoying themselves.

"Over the last year I've become a businessman. I used to think an artist had to separate himself from business matters, but now I realise you have more artistic freedom if you also keep an eye on business.

"Things were handled so badly (on past tours) that it was painful to go out to receptions and be with everybody and have false gaiety, because there wasn't any gaiety. There was often bitterness and terrible arguments happening.

"So, I preferred to stay on my own, get the tour over and end up saying, 'I'll never tour again.' I wasn't trying to be particularly mysterious or clever about it. I just couldn't imagine ever touring again by the time I'd get through with a tour.

"There's a song—"Word on a Wing"—in the show and on the new album that I wrote when I felt very much at peace with the world. I had established my own environment with my own people for the first time.

"I wrote the whole thing as a hymn. What better way can a man give thanks for achieving something that he had dreamed of achieving, than doing it with a hymn?"

A hymn? From David Bowie?

Bowie acknowledges he is in a certain transition period these days.

"Yes, I do feel like I'm starting over again in a way," he said, commenting on the sense of rediscovery that seems to fill much of the "Station To Station" album.

"Word On A Wing," for example, the album's title track, carries a sense of optimism and celebration ("Raise your glasses high . . . it's too late to be hateful . . .").

"I think there's a certain maturity now. You can hear it in the album. I've always said I'm terribly vulnerable as a writer. You can just look at the records and see what I'm feeling.

"It sometimes takes me a while to get away from the album and actually see what it all means to me. But I can go back over the earlier albums and see exactly what was happening."

What about "Hunky Dory?"

"There was a feeling of optimism and enthusiasm in the album that reflected my thinking at the time," Bowie responded.

"There's even a song—'Song To Bob Dylan'—that laid out what I wanted to do in rock. It was at that period that I said, 'okay (Dylan) if you don't want to do it, I will.'

"I saw that leadership void. Even though the song isn't one of the most important on the album, it represented for me what the album was all about. If there wasn't someone who was going to use rock 'n' roll, then I'd do it.

"Ziggy Stardust was saying, 'If I'm going to do it, what attitude will I adopt to do it with? The track 'Ziggy Stardust' summed the attitude up in one song. The 'Aladdin Sane' album was Ziggy's viewpoint about 'Oh, God, I actually have made it and it's really crazy and I'm not sure what to make of this . . .'

"The album was full of self-doubt. It was half still posing (as Ziggy Stardust), but at the back of it saying I don't know If I wouldn't be happier back at home."

On "Diamond Dogs," Bowie said, it was as if he were seeing his plans and earlier optimism shattered. Though the album dealt outwardly with society, it reflected his own turmoil.

"It's all microcosm, macrocosm," he said. "I mean, I think songwriters—if they are pontificators with theories—are usually talking about themselves."

By the time Bowie recorded "Young Americans" he was always making plans to break away from the tensions which he felt had put a strain on his relations with his old management company.

"'Young Americans' was the celebration of getting over it," he said. "'Fame' was a happy song. The melodic feel, everything about it, is happy. I don't play 'Young Americans' much. It's one of the most unlistenable albums I ever made. But I dance to it. It's good to dance to.

"'Station to Station'? I'm still too close to it, But it's like 'Let's start over.' This time I'm going to take a little more time about it and make sure everything stays in bounds. But you never know what is going to happen.

"It's a bit like walking a tightrope. You slip once and regain your balance and make it to the other side. But it doesn't mean that you've learned enough never to slip again. Circumstances change. There's always a bit of danger."

Despite the emotional and artistic ups and downs of the past four years, Bowie feels he has kept close to his own goal of building a multi-directional career that escapes the limitations of being stereotyped in any given field (eg rock 'n' roll).

"I think I've kept fairly well on the track despite it all," Bowie said. "I think I'm doing about what I thought at the time. I am making films. I still haven't become overground, really. I have just become the largest-selling of the underground."

In his first film, The Man Who Fell To Earth, Bowie plays Thomas Newton, an industrialist who succumbs to the pressures that build around him.

"It rang so true," Bowie said, speaking of the role. "The film, I suppose, for me, is sort of allegorical on a very private scale, but it won't be to the public. They'll see more a sort of Howard Hughes figure because it's certainly an exaggeration.

"But it's very much the thing of someone with a purist idea in the beginning and the whole concept becoming corrupt as it is carried out. It's a very, very sad film."

Besides having another film role suggested (to play alongside such as Michael Caine and Donald Sutherland in The Eagle Has Landed, the story of a World War II plot by the Germans to kidnap Winston Churchill), Bowie eventually wants to make a movie of "Ziggy Stardust."

But there is another area of involvement—admittedly long-range—that also intrigues him. It's the idea of Candidate Bowie.

When asked about his eventual goal he replied, in the teasing way he has that makes the remarks seem at once both entirely possible and totally designed for effect: "The only thing I know is I want to be Prime Minister of England one day"—he broke into sudden laughter and resumed the thought—"that's the only thing I know.

"Otherwise, I'm sort of a happy, carefree sort of guy . . . I just want to have a revolution in England." Again, he laughed.

But later, Bowie returned to the idea of politics; this time a bit more seriously. "The one thing I want to do when I get back to England is see what is happening there politically," he said.

"When I'm a lot older and know what I'm talking about politically, I would like to get into our politics back home. I still have my Grand King complex. I'll never lose that. I'm ultra Capricorn.

"Politics is one reason I think it is good to avoid being classified as a (particular kind of) artist. It's good to retain one's individuality. The only reason one uses the Sinatra figure to explain what I mean about maintaining a persona is that he is about the only person who has done it.

"He's someone who is not just an actor or a singer. He transcends all those areas. He's even something of a public figure. That's what I want to be felt about me.

"It's the idea of seeing what you can do with the human persona, how far you can extend the ego out of the body. I think my music is never looked at as just music.

"You have to have one's attitude toward David Bowie in there as well. It's all very McLuhanish, isn't it. I'm trying to make myself the message, which is the 20th century form of communication."

But surely, someone asked, there must be some area of artistic involvement that is close to Bowie's heart? What, for instance, would he like to see written (singer, performer, songwriter, actor?) under his name on his tombstone.

"Tombstone!" Bowie replied, somewhat startled, but his eyebrows were raised. "I'd like a memorial. I'd never be content with a tombstone."

GOODBYE TO ZIGGY AND ALL THAT . . .

Allan Jones | October 29, 1977, *Melody Maker* (UK)

The cover of the issue of *Melody Maker* in which Allan Jones's interview appeared featured not just Bowie's photo but one of The Clash, who had that week unsuccessfully tried to bring their brand of snarling, street-wise rock to war-torn Belfast. Times had changed since the last time Bowie had agreed to do interviews (he hadn't promoted his January 1977 album, *Low*). Decadent, self-indulgent gestures like his 1976 call for a new dose of fascism were not the flavor of the day in the era of punk, which is possibly why he felt compelled to spend a chunk of the interview denying he meant the comment seriously, or had ever given a Nazi salute.

In fact, Bowie was one of those established acts who managed to escape the wrath of the new wave: his ceaseless experimentation and lack of interest in pursuing easy bucks meant that he had never acquired the patina of the "sell-out." Even so, many must have been the rock lover who raised an eyebrow at his admission herein that Recording Artist had not been for him a vocation but a flag of convenience for a painter in search of a new medium. —Ed.

Thursday afternoon waltzes with the grace of Astaire on styro-foam heels through the swinging doors of the Dorchester, to be met by a venerable welcome. Brash, playboy confidence is at once surrendered to the air of mellow retreat that haunts the atmosphere like the foretaste of old age.

A cosmopolitan chorus of accents embracing several continents provides a fractured soundtrack to the inconspicuous efficiency of the darting platoons of bellboys and porters, who look, in their smart green uniforms, like the well-scrubbed buglers of some private army.

Their genteel buoyancy is a subtle contrast to the grim and laboured services of the older butlers, who carry silver tea-trays to impatient customers with a one-toe shuffle across the verdant wall-to-wall that recalls the hesitant walk of arthritic tightrope walkers out for a stroll along Niagara's furious currents.

Thursday afternoon wonders where it will find the European Man.

David Bowie's hands flutter before him as if he was attempting to describe some indefinable abstract design to a blind man, or attempting, even, to conjure from the space before him a tap-dancing showbusiness dove.

He smiles quickly and nervously. Thin lips spread narrowly over tiny rodent teeth. His laugh is like the crackling bark of static. Infectious, nevertheless. He chatters briskly, but without impatience. His accent will veer from the clipped Cockney inflections of Michael Caine's Harry Palmer to the smooth, theatrical modulations and husky definitions of an actor in a provincial company impersonating some elder statesman of the stage with impertinent skill.

He is so entertainingly polite that you feel sure he could charm the wings off an angel.

David Bowie is in London for the solitary purpose of selling his new album. And he makes no elaborate excuse for the frustrating brevity of his individual engagement with the media.

"The only reason I've decided to do these interviews," he later admits, "is to prove my belief in the album. Both 'Heroes' and 'Low' have been met with confused reactions. That was to be expected, of course. But I didn't promote 'Low' at all, and some people thought my heart wasn't in it.

"This time I wanted to put everything into pushing the new album. I believe in the last two albums, you see, more than anything I've done before. I mean, I look back on a lot of my earlier work and, although there's much that I *appreciate* about it, there's not a great deal that I actually like. I don't think they're very *likeable* albums at all.

"There's a lot more heart and emotion in 'Low' and, especially, the new album. And, if I can convince people of that, I'm prepared to be stuck in this room on the end of a conveyor belt of questions that I'll do my best to answer."

This is an opinion. David Bowie's two most recent albums, recorded in Berlin in collaboration with Brian Eno, are among the most adventurous and notably challenging records yet thrust upon the rock audience. Inevitably controversial, these albums have combined the theories and techniques of modern electronic music with lyrics that have found Bowie dispensing with traditional forms of narrative in pursuit of a new musical vocabulary adequate to the pervasive mood of despair and pessimism that he has divined in contemporary society.

"Towards the end of my stay in America," he reflects, "I realised that what I had to do was to experiment. To discover new forms of writing. To evolve, in fact, a new musical language. That's what I set out to do. That's why I returned to Europe."

David Bowie, as you reach this sentence, is explaining the circumstances and sequence of events that provoked his retreat from his exile in America and his eventual decision to return to Europe.

"The conditions were thus," he begins, his hands busily searching for pack of Gitanes. "I was at a point where I wanted to leave America. I had been, as I like to put it, 'staying' there for more than two years. I'm wary of saying that I 'lived' there. 'Living' in America is a real commitment, and it was a commitment I wasn't prepared to make.

"So, as I say, I'd been 'staying' there for some time, and I realised that I'd become tired of the country. And I was also getting quite tired with my methods of writing. I wanted to move out of the area of narrative and character. I wanted, generally, to re-evaluate what I was doing.

"I realised that I'd exhausted that particular environment and the effect of that environment upon my writing. I was afraid that if I continued to work in that environment I would begin repeating myself. I felt that that was the way I was heading.

"There was no enjoyment in the working process—I'd exclude from that 'Station To Station.' That was fairly exciting because it was like a plea to come back to Europe for me. It was one of those self-chat things that one has with oneself from time to time."

He suddenly throws down his pack of cigarettes as if annoyed with himself. "Christ, no . . . what am I talking about? A lot of that and 'Young Americans' was damn depressing. It was a terribly traumatic time. I was in a terrible state. I was absolutely infuriated that I was still in rock and roll.

"And not only *in it*, but had been sucked right into the centre of it. I had to move out. I'd never intended to be become so *involved* in rock and roll . . . and there I was in Los Angeles, right in the middle of it.

"Whether it's fortunate or not I don't know, but I'm absolutely and totally vulnerable to suggestion by environment, and environment and circumstances affect my writing tremendously. To the point of absurdity sometimes.

"I look back on some things in total horror. . . . And, anyway, I began to realise that the environment of Los Angeles, of America, was by this time detrimental to my writing and my work. It was no longer an inspiration to be caught in that environment.

"I realised that that was why I was feeling so claustrophobic and cut off. I was adopting such a hypocritical stance. There was this incredible fight between materialism and aestheticism. My commitment has certainly never been to rock and roll. I've made no secret of that. I was just a hack painter who wanted to find a new medium to work in, frankly.

"And rock looked like a very good vehicle. But one was always fluctuating between the temptation to become a rock star and the sentimental ties with wanting to be an artist—and there I was living right in the middle of this crazy and filthy rock and roll circus. It really was no more than a circus.

"And I should not have been in it. I should not have become such a major part of it. It was frustrating for me. Now I'm fit and happy and well again. I'm enjoying the process of work for the first time in years. It's more than work. That's why I say that I'm not interested in posterity.

"I'm now more concerned with my work being appreciated on a more personal level. Once I had all those big dreams. Oh, I had all those dreams, man. Great ambitions. I had them until I learned about simply enjoying the process of working and the process of living.

"I'm happy now. Content. I feel more than a product on an assembly line and no more a means of support for 10,000 people who seem to revolve around every fart that I made."

David Bowie crushes out a Gitane and immediately another is between his lips. His finger flicks at his lighter.

"My role as an artist in rock," he says, "is rather different to most. I encapsulate things very quickly, in a very short space of time. Over two or three months usually. And generally my policy has been that as soon as a system or process works, it's out of date. I move on to another area. Another piece of time.

"I have to answer these questions in naive analogies, I find, because I've always fought against considering my role, my position in this *thing*, this rock and roll game.

"I've never wanted to consider myself a *part of it*. It tends to hinder me. That's when I start pulling on my hat of solitude. That's when I usually clear off to Japan or somewhere. I never intended to become a part of it. Yet, at the same time, yes, I've challenged it and enjoyed—occasionally—the controversy.

"But you wouldn't believe how much of it was entirely unwitting. I think I did play *outside* the boundaries of what is considered the general area of rock and roll. Some of it, just pure petulance, some of it was arrogance, some of it was unwitting, but, inevitably, I kept moving ahead.

"Ziggy, particularly, was created out of certain arrogance. But, remember, at that time I was young and I was full of life, and that seemed like a very positive artistic statement. I thought that was a beautiful piece of art, I really did. I thought that was a grand kitsch painting. The whole guy.

"Then that f----r wouldn't leave me alone for years. That was when it all started to sour. And it soured so quickly you wouldn't believe it. And it took me an awfully long time to level out. My whole personality was affected. Again I brought that upon myself.

"I can't say I'm sorry when I look back, because it provoked such an extraordinary set of circumstances in my life. I thought I might as well take Ziggy out to interviews as well. Why leave him on the stage? Looking back, it was completely absurd.

"It became very dangerous. I really did have doubts about my sanity. I can't deny that the experience affected me in a very exaggerated and marked manner. I think I put myself very dangerously near the line. Not in physical sense, but definitely in a mental sense. I played mental games with myself to such an extent that I'm now very relieved and happy to be back in Europe and feeling very well. . . . But, then, you see I was *always* the lucky one.

"'David Live,'" says David Bowie, "was the final death of Ziggy. God, that album. I've never played it. The tension it must contain must be like vampire's teeth coming down on you. And that photo on the cover. My God, it looks as if I've just stepped out of that grave.

"That's actually how I felt. That record should have been called 'David Bowie Is Alive And Well And Living Only In Theory.'"

"Berlin," Bowie observes, reflecting upon the environment in which he has recorded his last two albums, "is a city made up of bars for sad, disillusioned people to get drunk in. I've taken full advantage of working there to examine the place quite intensively. One never knows how long it's going to remain there. One fancies that it's going very fast.

"That's one of the reasons, sure, that I was attracted to the city. It's a feeling that I really tried to capture in the paintings I did. I made a series of paintings while I was there of the Turks that live in the city. There's a track on the new album called 'Neukoln,' and that's the area of Berlin where the Turks are shackled in very bad conditions.

"They're very much an isolated community. It's very sad. It's very, very sad. And that kind of reality obviously contributed to the mood of both 'Low' and 'Heroes.'

"I mean, having encountered an experience like that it's hard to sing 'Let's all think of peace and love. . . . ' No, . . . David, why did you say that? That was a stupid remark. Because that's exactly where you should arrive after seeing something like that. You should arrive at a sense of compassion. The title track of 'Heroes' is about facing that kind of reality and standing up to it.

"The only heroic act one can f--- well pull out of the bag in a situation like that is to get on with life and derive some joy from the very simple pleasure of remaining alive, despite every attempt being made to kill you."

It will be remembered that Bowie's performances in London last year were prefaced by his controversial pronouncements on Britain and the possibility of fascist rule here. His comments were interpreted by some as advocacy of extreme right-wing politics; others saw in his remark a prophetic nature, a warning rather than a gesture of support for fascist policies.

"I can't clarify those statements," Bowie says wearily when the subject arises. "All I can say is that I've made my two or three glib, theatrical observations on English society, and the only thing I can now counter with is to state that I'm NOT a fascist. I'm *apolitical*.

"The more I travel the less sure I am about exactly which political philosophies are commendable. The more government systems I see, the less enticed I am to give my allegiance to any set of people, so it would be disastrous for me to adopt a definitive point of view, or to adopt a party of people and say '*these* are my people.'

"I guess it was all pretty glib. But then again, I'm not one for delicate social niceties. If I take a jump into the pool, I generally swallow all the water."

He is reminded of his fascist salute to the country when he arrived at Victoria Station, and is asked to define its significance.

He virtually explodes from his chair.

"That *didn't* happen. THAT DID NOT HAPPEN. I was so *livid* with that cameraman. I *waved*. I just WAVED. Believe me. On the life of my child, I *waved*. And the bastard caught me. In MID-WAVE, man. And, God, did that photo got some coverage . . . as if I'd be foolish enough to pull a stunt like that. I died when I saw that photo. And even the people who were with me said, 'David! How could you?' The bastards. I didn't . . .

"GOD, I just *don't* believe in all that."

David Bowie was 30 this year. It's significant, he feels, that he feels no resentment now of the passing of time: in his early 20s, he reflects, the very thought of growing older appalled him—"it was an *horrendous* thought." Now he accepts with equanimity the responsibilities of maturity, and even the eventuality of death.

"I think having a son made an enormous difference to me," he remarks. "At first it frightened me, and I tried not to consider the implications. Now it's *his* future that concerns me. My own future slips by. I'm prepared for it, and I'm prepared for the end.

"There are still so many people on an immortality kick, though, and it amuses me now. We'll do *anything* in our power to stay alive. There's a feeling that the average lifespan should be longer than it is. I disagree. I mean, we've never lived so long. Not in any century that man's been on this planet.

"Not so very long ago no one lived pass the age of 40. And we're still not happy with 70. What are we after exactly? There's just too much ego involved. And who wants to drag their old, decaying frame around until they're 90, just to assert their ego? I don't, certainly."

In this context of age and the process of change, I inevitably mention the minions of the new wave presently battering at the doors of success and achieving now the kind of publicity that Bowie enjoyed five years ago.

"The sad thing about it all," he says, "is that it's being called a *movement*. I wish the people involved were being treated as individuals. I'm so worried for them. I'm dissatisfied with them because I can't tolerate people who want to form, or be part of, movements.

"It should always come back to individuals. I think there are now some individuals who have some very exciting ideas. Some of them, at least. I only hope they survive. Because I totally sympathise with their indignation."

It is suggested (as the hounds bark at the door in an attempt to bring to a conclusion this brief interview), that both "Low" and "Heroes" betray an extraordinary pessimism, and there is, in the jagged atmosphere of the music they contain, an anticipation of violence and imminent disaster.

"I'm afraid I *am* pessimistic," Bowie offers. "I'm not at all optimistic about the future. But I'm not totally resigned to the situation. There is, I hope, some relief in compassion—and I know that's not a word usually flung at my work—and 'Heroes' is, I hope, compassionate.

"Compassionate for people and the silly desperate situation they've got themselves into. That we've *all* got ourselves into, generally by ignorance and rash decisions. Decisions to join or remain within sets of people.

"We haven't moved on at all from that tribal thing—you know, if you don't understand it, have a swing at it with an axe.

"You know, people simply can't cope with the rate of change in this world. It's all far too fast. Since the Industrial Revolution there's been this upward spiral with people desperately trying to hang on, and now everybody's started to fall off. And it'll get worse.

"There isn't really much cause for hope," says David Bowie finally. "But I haven't given in yet. I think there's some fight left in me still. Somewhere.

I'm not a brave man and I do see it all as a vast enormous joke. A very bad joke at that. But there is one area of optimism.

"Even bothering to write about it all and think about it is some kind of fight against it. But even so, I can't help thinking that it's all nearly over."

He turns his eyes towards heaven.

"Just give us a date, will you?" he asks.

12 MINUTES WITH DAVID BOWIE

John Tobler | January 1978, *ZigZag* (UK)

This piece from British magazine *ZigZag* is interesting for the fact that, unlike much of this book's contents, it was not conducted by an avid fan, but by someone who could so take or leave Bowie that he muddles up *Diamond Dogs* and *Young Americans*. Recalls Tobler, "The interview was done for RCA to use as a promo tool for *Heroes*. Bowie was not one of my heroes, and many would correctly say that I was the wrong man for the job. But it was work, and I respected Bowie for his success."

ZigZag was born out of a semi-fanzine ethos. As such, at this point it was still a relatively rough-and-ready publication, as can be seen from the article's peculiar syntax and grammar, as well as the decision to run the interview verbatim.

The nature of a verbatim transcript always makes for a slightly stilted feel, but over and above that, the mood seems to become somewhat awkward when Tobler, perhaps insensitively, refers to Bowie's old friend and rival Marc Bolan as having recently "snuffed it."

The fact that Tobler was only granted an audience of under a quarter of an hour ("Maybe I was given a bit longer, but whoever edited it for use in *ZigZag* thought that was a good headline") didn't stop *ZigZag* making Bowie the issue's cover star.

Note: for "Bryan" read "Brian [Eno]." —Ed.

Zig Zag: The last couple of albums, which is really what you're here to talk about, have been, to some people, somewhat inaccessible. I think you said at some point that you were determined not to be predictable. Is that what it's about?

David Bowie: Well no. There's a predictable answer. What it really is is that I'd got tired of writing in the traditional manner that I was writing in in America, and coming back to Europe I took a look at what I was writing and the environments that I was writing about and decided I had to start writing in terms of trying to find a new musical language for myself to write in. I needed somebody to help with that 'cos I was a bit lost and too subjective about it all, so I asked Bryan Eno if he would help me and that's really how the whole thing started. It was really a process of trying out new methods and new processes of writing rather than for the more obvious line of being unpredictable, and 'cos I've brought out two now of the same nature, and that's not predictable with me. I've gone against myself you see, can't even predict myself!

ZZ: I hear that um Eno was really very impressed when he first met you and Iggy, and you seemed able to hum "no pussyfooting . . ."

DB: (Laughs) Yeah, I know his work quite well.

ZZ: Do you in fact have a tendency to try and investigate the more 'off the wall' happenings in music?

DB: They're the ones I tend to gravitate towards. I've got a particular code of working, which is if it works its out of date so I generally apply that to every given situation, in music or on tour or whatever and especially music. I hardly ever listen to anything that's currently in vogue or popular. I tend to buy rather obscure kind of things.

ZZ: Such as?

DB: Well, let's see, the last things really that I bought were Steve Reich and Philip Glass things which I've been listening to for quite some time, but, again when it comes to music my influences tend to come more from observation of the environment that I'm in, which is fairly obvious when you look at the albums and where they were made, they tend to very much mirror where I was, you can tell more or less which street in the city I was in. 'Young Americans' you know is Philadelphia and 'Diamond Dogs' is definitely L.A. and New York.

ZZ: It's funny you should talk about 'Diamond Dogs' cos you also said you made that as a plastic soul album which you . . .

DB: No 'Young Americans.'

ZZ: Yeah, sorry "Young Americans," that it was just a joke record.

DB: No it was not a joke record. It was seriously a plastic soul album. It was definitely me, portraying as a white Englishman, my view of American Black Music, somebody who watches more from outside than actually getting involved with it inside.

ZZ: Do you in fact prefer the current disco type of sound to the soul music of the 60s which I'm sure you are more familiar with.

DB: Er no, I'm not a big fan of disco at all. I loathe it. I really get so embarrassed that my records do so well in discos, I've had two enormous disco hits now, can't hold my head up when I go into arty clubs, yes of course I was a big fan of the soul sound of the 60s. That was part of a somewhat sketchy musical education that I had, a quite diversified one as well to boot.

ZZ: Indeed. I gather you're embarking on a tour very soon.

DB: Next year I'm planning to do a world tour, yes.

ZZ: Who are you gonna use backing you?

DB: That's very difficult to say at the moment. One would like to work with Eno and Fripp on stage but of course to get Bryan out of his apartment takes about a week so to get him on the road is an impossibility, but I think he'll do selected cities with me. If he's never been there before he'll probably come and play. He tends to work in that fashion.

Fripp is a bit more easy to accommodate I mean, he can go on the road and its no great pain, but I don't know whether he'd want to do a very long tour. He seems to be about a 4-week man. (laughs) Neither of them are crazy about touring, so I'm gonna have to look for other guys as well.

ZZ: Mmmmmm. Were you a great fan of either King Crimson or Roxy Music?

DB: Roxy I liked their first album very much indeed. I thought that was very exciting. The whole concept was very new and lovely juxtapositions that I hadn't heard before. King Crimson. I was always, funnily enough Fripp was one of the only virtuosos that I liked, I'm not a big fan of virtuosity, but Fripp always appealed to me, his playing.

ZZ: It was said when you were doing "Low" that your poetic muse at one time had deserted you momentarily, and that was why many of the songs were short lyrically, as opposed to the somewhat lengthier stuff you had done before. Is that still . . .

DB: I guess there was some truth in that, I mean it can be applied to what I said earlier that it was strictly a question of experimentation and discovery. I had no statement to make on "Low." It was low in profile in its own way and it was a very indulgent album for me to find out what I wanted to do musically. The strange thing that came out of "Low" is that in my meanderings in new processes and new methods of writing, when Eno and I listened back to it we realised we had created new information without even realising it and that by not trying to write about anything we had written more about something or other that one couldn't quite put one's finger on than we could have had we actually gone out and said, 'let's do a concept album.' It was quite remarkable so we thought, great fine, let's do that again, it's quite exciting, so we did that with "Heroes." We used an immense amount of imagery and juxtaposed one against the other and used incredibly startling methods of writing, anything from random selection out of books, musically as well, I mean, chord changes. We were quite arbitrary sometimes and the total effect astonished both of us when we sat back and listened to the finished thing.

ZZ: Do you intend to pursue this direction rather than getting back to the more lyrical . . .

DB: No, er yes! (laughs) We've always said, because we are both arty, we've both said we'd do a trilogy so our triptych will be completed. We will do one more at least. We do have a very solid relationship with each other. I think it also is very strong outside of the musical area, because when we're together the last thing generally we talk about is music um, as you probably well know, Eno's a wonderful conversationalist and one can sit there and laugh all night and also I'm working on Fripp's next album. He's asked me to do some work with him in America when I go over there. I don't know what yet. I'm very excited about it. I don't know what he wants me to do.

ZZ: Are you sort of using the lyrical side of your ability to do Iggy's albums, I mean, not that you write the words . . .

DB: Well, one must look at it this way. Jim hadn't worked for um at least 2 years, had been thru some very bad times, and needed more than a little bit of support emotionally and mentally as well as materially and I think he resolved most of his problems on the first album, and if it shows at all my influence or attributes won't be quite as recognisable in any future stuff that we're doing and we're doing another album after this. Jim is very much in charge of his own situation and he realises what he wants to write and what he wants to write about. He's becoming an excellent song writer. I think he always was an excellent song writer but he had that lapse and that peaking thing.

ZZ: Really. He was most impressive on stage.

DB: Oh he's fantastic. I've always thought he was for me, rock 'n' roll, absolute rock 'n' roll, uncompromising rock 'n' roll.

ZZ: Did you in fact go out with him on the first tour because you were somewhat sceptical about whether he could cut it alone.

DB: No not at all. He encouraged me to play piano with him and I thought the idea was thoroughly enticing and very tempting and I did it for the nerve of it really. I never enjoyed a tour so much, because I had no responsibilities on my shoulders at all, I mean I just had to sit there, drink a bit, have a cigarette, wink at the band, I mean ya know, and watch him.

ZZ: Right, which is something to watch.

DB: Oh yeah.

ZZ: You said a couple of years ago that you didn't really care if your LPs continued to sell or not.

DB: Yeah.

ZZ: Does that apply to Iggy as well in any way because you're very much involved.

DB: No that was personalised to my albums, of course I really want Jimmy to regain his old audience and find an even bigger, newer one because I've always considered him very important. No that applies strictly to my albums.

ZZ: Does it still apply?

DB: I still feel very much that way although now I have to go against myself because I'm so excited about the new stuff I want people to hear it so I'm rather in a quandary . . . "Well I don't care," but then on the other hand I do care 'cos I think they're really good. I think they're really good albums.

ZZ: Do you look back on the stuff you've done and say, "Well that one wasn't really . . . ya know."

DB: Oh yes, yes I look at them all and there's not one I like, I . . . the only one I *like* is "Young Americans" because its the only likeable album, but the others, one could hardly apply the adjective *likeable* to any of them. Some of them I think were sketchy ideas that I didn't work on hard enough. That didn't quite cut it. Its like painting really I mean, not every painting that you do is gonna be good but you've done them and there you are. I tend to look at albums rather like that. I admit some of the ideas didn't come off, but there's some good work in there somewhere though. There's a logical sequence. I mean if it just seemed to meander on and didn't seem to make any sense to me. I can just about see the year that I wrote that album, or I can say, "Yes, that describes that environment and that year very well" I think. Which is very good, sort of what I set out to do.

ZZ: There's been a number of people involved with you all through this time and you're unlike many, many other rock stars in that you never seem to go backwards to these people with the odd exception. Mick Ronson for example. Do you ever see Mick Ronson?

DB: I haven't seen Mick Ronson for years. But to flatten your other point my rhythm section has been with me for 4 albums and 2½–3 years I think (laughs).

ZZ: But you basically discovered them. No I was thinking of people like . . . I mean it was rather bizarre that both Marc Bolan and Bing Crosby both of whom you worked with snuffed it recently.

DB: You really want me to . . . what do I say?

ZZ: I mean do you see anything sinister in that?

DB: No I don't.

ZZ: I'm glad to hear that. You did do a Bing Crosby T.V. show didn't you?

DB: Yes I did.

ZZ: Which could be very interesting to see. . . . Do you have any plans to work with anybody else, like the Astronettes or anybody?

DB: No, there's one band that I can mention. I like them very much indeed. They're an unrecorded band in America called Devo. I've been listening to them for a long time since they sent me their tapes and I hope if I have the time at the end of this year to record them. Its sort of like three Enos and a couple of Edgar Froeses in one band. Most peculiar. That's very nut-shelling of what they're like.

ZZ: Right. We should ask about this new film that you are doing.

DB: Its a partial life story/biography of Egon Schieler, an expressionist painter of early 19th Century and its sort of a fairly quiet, intimate study of his relationship with his model and its a nonsensationalist film. Again its a reaction against the last film I made. Most of the things I do are reactions to the last things I did, rather than just for the sake.

ZZ: You turned down a young Goebbels film didn't you?

DB: Yes (laughs) that's fairly predictable.

ZZ: Great OK. Thanks very much. Its good to see you, come back soon.

DB: Thanks.

CONFESSIONS OF AN ELITIST

Michael Watts | February 18, 1978, *Melody Maker* (UK)

In this reunion with Michael Watts from *Melody Maker*, Bowie talks about the "I'm gay" quote that had, in the same paper six years previously, made Bowie (and Watts to some extent) famous.

The interview is also interesting in that it reveals that Bowie—often thought to be of the opinion that all publicity is good publicity—feels that there are, in fact, limits to how he should present himself.

As well as turning thirty, he talks about working with directors David Hemmings and Nicolas Roeg, and his "cut-ups" writing technique, which has so often given his lyrics a uniquely fractured air.

The Egon Schiele biopic, mentioned not for the first time in this book, did go ahead as *Excess and Punishment*, but without Bowie's involvement.

Notes: for "Nick" read "Nic" (Roeg).

for "Neue" read "Neu!"—Ed.

This interview with David Bowie was conducted at brief intervals during four days' filming of Just A Gigolo. The interviewer had to put up with the film crew playing trumpets and old gramophone records of German marches, as well as a film extra belting out songs at the piano. "I hate these blues sessions," says Bowie. Once, a long time ago, however, he used to play sax behind Sonny Boy Williamson . . .

I haven't talked to you since February 1973, when you were performing at Radio City Music Hall in New York. You've since left, amid a lot of publicity, MainMan Management and Tony DeFries. How do you feel now about DeFries?

(Long pause) Yes, that's an interesting question. My anger was spent a good couple of years ago, and all the feelings of being used, done-out-of and whatever, I think they've more or less melted into the mist.

I suppose now it was all rather important in a way. I certainly would not have achieved the degree of notoriety, I think, without all that nonsense going on. If I was an egoist I guess I could say that I would've done because my performance was good enough, but one doesn't know.

Without some of those initial ridiculous fusses, some the best things never come to light. It did come to light through the efforts of him and the crazies who were running around at that time, and so I guess I'm thankful for that period in one way.

But I'll never condone completely what went on. I don't know whether I was absolutely manipulated but I believe all my business was manipulated. I believe that a lot of what were initially very good ideas were cheapened for the sake of getting something out economically rather than going the whole hog and doing things properly.

Stage shows were never what they were supposed to be because suddenly the money was not there to pay for what I wanted initially. Things would always be done on a shoestring and I could never understand why, because apparently we were very, very popular and . . . "where's the money?"

All that was involved. We have settled now. I don't think any of it was amicable, but it's mellowed out now. We have an understanding with each other. We have to deal with each other from time to time—but not on a personal level.

You would never go back to him?

Oh, Lord *no*! That's absolutely . . . it couldn't be further from my mind. I have literally no idea of what he does, where he is and what kinds of things he does anymore. It was an astonishing, chaotic period. Very tumultuous.

What are your feelings now about the sex angle? (In January 1972, at the outset of his career with MainMan, Bowie confessed to the MM that he was bisexual, the first rock star to make such a declaration. The remark had huge reverberations.)

It seems easier for people to assimilate that now than it ever was before. I've got two views about it. Initially, I thought it was a good polemicist's basis; it was something to throw in people's faces. But on the other hand it had a disastrous effect on my credibility as a composer and writer for a long, long time.

Why did you tell me?

Do you know, I've never really understood why. It certainly wasn't a premeditated thing. I was starting to build Ziggy, he was starting to come together, and I was naturally falling into the role; and it was using one's own resources, and you sort of pick up on bits of your own life when you're putting a role together. Bang! it was suddenly there on the table. It was as simple as that.

I read that article again for the first time the other day. It's very coy and embarrassing.

Yes, but imagine in a few years' time, that will become an archetype interview of that period. You mustn't feel embarrassed. No, no! I know exactly what you mean, but you wait and see. Mark my words, mark my words. It's the old McLuhan thing about cliche, archetype.

I'm sure only a few years after he'd made them Chaplin was very, very embarrassed by his first movies—but all these years later! There was nothing like that before then, and a whole school of something or other has come from them.

And I was sort of half serious then when I said that I'd developed a school of pretension within rock and roll. I can see why I said that. I don't necessarily agree with it now. I only said it as, again, a throwaway. But there is some strength in it, I think. Quite definitely.

I remember an interview about 18 months ago in the Village Voice with Cherry Vanilla (once Bowie's American publicist at MainMan). It was a piece about marketing gays…

Oh God. Marketing gays.

And she said, "we peddled David's ass like Nathan's sells hotdogs."

Good Lord. Chronic, isn't it? I hope she meant it tongue-in-cheek. I know what she meant, yeah. She worked very hard at pushing that side of me, because it gave her very easy access into headlines. And all the time that

that was going on, of course, I was in another country, so it was hard for me to keep any sort of control.

My compromise at the time was to live with it when I got to America and found out how I'd been set up to be over there, and I thought, "my God, I can't fight this enormous snowball. I'll have to work with it and gradually push it back down to something more manageable."

But I'd just started with Ziggy, and I couldn't suddenly drop it then. He was Ziggy, he'd been created, and that was my piece at the time, my theatre piece. I thought, "well, I'll have to use what Ziggy's got and be what God's given him" (short laugh).

And so I had to work with him for a little while in those first few months in America.

You put yourself on the line, too, by involving yourself in other artists' careers. I've always wondered why, considering that you've had such personal success, you should want to build, or re-build, others' successes: Lou Reed, Iggy Pop and now Devo.

I guess it's because there is still a lot of fan in me. I do get impressed with new things. I can't help but be. I like to feel that if I can't do that myself then I'd like to be part of it and try and . . . Especially people who are not being noticed.

I would love to be responsible for helping somebody. I think that's great for my ego.

They've not been acts of unadulterated kindness?

Oh, no, no. Good Lord, no.

But you did receive some rather horrible criticism, particularly in relationship to Lou, that you were coming up on his back.

I did read a lot of that, of course, and I never denied it because it seemed such a shallow observation of what I was doing. There are very, very few parallels between me and Lou Reed.

I think I've only ever written one song like his, and that was "Queen Bitch," and it was only recognised as a Lou Reed song—and I know this for a fact—because I wrote next to it "For Lou."

"Andy Warhol" was next to it.

Oh yes, yes. Those two together. But I don't think my career was based on those two songs, and there is very little else that I have done that is anything near approaching what Lou Reed does or has done. I find it very hard to find a comparison between me and Lou.

I've never written about street people or such, or the gossip of the day, walked like him, dressed like him, looked like him or even performed like him. I think that's really shallow. We got on very well. I found him very witty, in a very New York way. And the same again, I might add, applies to young Iggy as well, 'cause I've also read that a coupla times.

But, you know—and I did it partly for the amusement factor—I've always noticed that if I put out certain names as my influences to see if people would pick up on them and then say I was definitely influenced by them, then every time I've done it it has always come back. Always, always, always!

I could say that my greatest influence, in fact, was Tiny Tim, and they'll say, "ah, of course! Quite obviously David Bowie has lifted an enormous amount from Tiny Tim." Always it works in that fashion.

I don't blame anybody because I do it purposely—I certainly used to do those red herrings just to see how it affected people—but it amused me that they would take something like that and convolute it and make it into a statement of their own.

Let's move from the past to the present. How do you feel about this film as compared with The Man Who Fell To Earth?

A totally different kettle of poissons. This has so far been a far more enjoyable experience. For one reason or another I'm a lot closer to David than I was with Nick (Roeg). Nick is less approachable. David is a far more generous personality.

Roeg's an intellectual.

David not so much; though, of course, he is of a sophisticated nature. Creatively, quite as extraordinary as Roeg in his way.

Do you feel that movie was a success?

I think that's debated by everybody that's seen it. I think there's a lot of pro, a lot of the reverse. I still have only seen it the once—the one time that I saw it in the cinema—and I still feel that I learned more by the actual process of making it than seeing the film in a finished state.

I didn't enjoy it as a movie to watch. It's very tight. Like a spring that's going to uncoil, it's full of terrific tensions. Of course, that's part of the so-called magic of the film; that it's got these very inhibited feelings in it.

There's a repressed feeling of something or other boiling under the surface all the time. It's never allowed to come out, so it leaves you with that terrible feeling that you've had a restricted viewing of something.

Would you agree that it's a film about a man who originally is pure but ends up being corrupted and disgusted with himself?

The way Nick interpreted that purity, looking at the way it's cut, he seemed to have interpreted that purity in a perverse way. There's something awkward about it, gawky; there's something not right about that person's purity. I suppose on surface value that's the film Nick was making, yeah.

Nick had a lot of other intentions that he never confided—well, not to me, anyway. He's a secretive man. And, indeed, at that time I was also pretty closed about talking, with anybody, really.

Yes, I want to ask you whether you saw parallels between yourself and Thomas Newton, the strange character that you played, which is why you took the role.

Oh, that's a dangerous trap to fall into! Sort of, it was quite easy for me. When I did it was hook, line and sinker, I would've thought (Laughter). I mean, Nick exerts such a tremendous influence over one psychologically that one does carry the weight of the image around for a bit afterwards.

He was a cold, inexpressive character. This is what your image was at that point.

I think I was very frightened of expressing any kind of emotion then, which of course, followed with the most dramatic and traumatic experiences on the "Station To Station" tour when I became over-emotive. I went through great waves of despondency and ecstasy . . . and I'd kept a lot of things pretty well repressed for a few years.

So that was a very cathartic point in your life?

Oh, Christ, yeah. I feel much more on an even keel now.

But you're a volatile man, to say the least. It could happen again?

Yes, I get scared stiff of the idea of touring again because of all kinds of experiences that one has. Once bitten, *maybe* twice shy. I hope that I don't get back into that situation again.

Do you mean drugs, and other things as well?

All the things. The testing of one's personality to the fullest: can you cope on a tour? When you're shouldering the responsibility of the whole thing, it's quite easy to break up. Either way, you close up or you let loose. My tendency goes either way. God knows how it's gonna affect me. But I'm a lot healthier and fitter beforehand this time.

You appear to be enjoying acting, anyway.

I'm finding it enthralling to be really getting into a person's flesh this time around. I really feel very much at home with this character, being led and shown how to do it.

But you've always been interested in creating personae!

Oh yeah, yes, but I've never approached it this way. It's impossible to explain, really, but it's a question of following through thoughts rather than just like a parrot reciting the words . . . This is wonderful! (Breaks off).

It sounds like (assumes brittle, actorish voice), "well, of course, there's only 3,584 words in Othello. As Peter Brooks used to tell me, now you know all the words, all you have to do is get them in the right order." (Laughter) I hate talking about acting. I don't know enough about it.

I think you ought to tell me how you got involved in the movie about Egon Schiele.

It was originally suggested to me that I should play the part by Clive Donner, the guy who did The Caretaker and Mulberry Bush. He sent me the original script and I jumped at the idea of it, 'cause Schiele was somebody I was aware of.

Wally was one of his girlfriends—pronounced "Valley." Wally is just a working title. I think it will be changed. It will go through the time from as he was leaving Klimt as a pupil and setting himself up as a painter, through his prison sentence and to the end of his relationship with his girlfriend, Wally.

Charlotte Rampling is on the boards to play her at the moment. I don't have much say in the actual casting. Donner I don't know that well, but he's very, very intelligent. It seems that all the time I pick on the English and European directors.

The next person that I'm meeting in a couple of weeks' time is Fassbinder, with the possibility of doing The Threepenny Opera with him, a re-make. He's now getting into doing English language films.

I've seen him in Berlin a couple of times, but I've never been introduced to him or had a chance to chat to him. Supposedly a strange sort of guy, very weird. This is such a strange sort of movie for him.

I think it's everybody's efforts to pull the strange quantities together and see what comes out—an idea that I go along with completely. Planned accidents.

Whatever happened to The Eagle Has Landed and Stranger In A Strange Land?

Eagle Has Landed I was turned down for the part, and Stranger In A Strange Land I didn't want to be involved with because I thought it would be a bit typecast (short laugh). It was also during the MainMan period. But I was violently against doing Stranger In A Strange Land, having realised it would be, you know, "get out of that one."

I'd be alien for life. I'd just be stuck out there. All I'd be offered would be people with green skins and varying colour hair—that would be the only character change I could make, hair colour.

People do associate you with futuristic things, don't they?

I don't know now whether it's so futuristic. I never thought of myself as a futurist. I always thought I was a very contemporary sort of figure, very Nowish. Rock is always ten years behind the rest of art; it picks up bits and pieces.

I mean, I only picked up Burroughs years after it all happened in literature, and actually applied it to my work. The application wasn't made until years after it was a dead and gone style; it'd been finished in literature a long time.

And that happens with rock. It's only just reached Dada now. So, as far as putting me as a futurist, I think the fact is I'm as contemporary as I feel I need to be, and a lot of the rest of what's going on pays a retrospective look to what's gone down before.

It's work generally in an atmosphere that's about five years behind. There's so much of it that it seems to represent today, but it isn't, in fact: it's using references and feelings and emotions from a few years back.

I've always thought there was a lot of England 1890s about you as well. Beardsley and Wilde, etc.

Oh, yes! That was a very strong influence, the idea of the Aesthete, the elitist (laughs)—a point which Brian (Eno) and I share. I think there's a large snob factor in what I do.

You once said to me, "I'm an actor, not an intellectual," and yet critics see in your records ideas rather than emotions.

I've decided I'm a Generalist now!

A Generalist?

Yes. I thought that just about covered all grounds. It encompasses anything I wish to do, really. I find, for instance, I really want to paint seriously now, and not toy with it, and I am painting very seriously now, every available moment.

And I'd like to be known as a painter one day when I get up the nerve to show them. But I want at the moment to be known as a Generalist rather than as a singer or a composer or an actor. I think a Generalist is a very good occupation to have.

How about this contrast of ideas and emotions? Critics do tend to find more ideas in your work than other musicians'.

Again, I think the sum total of the parts is greater than the input, very much so, and especially on the latter stuff that I've done. There were a considerable amount of very diverse ideas that went into the album, but the sum total of all those ideas is something extraordinarily different to that which I expected to come from the album when I made it.

For me, listening to "Heroes" is quite as new an experience as any other listener listening to it. They're never what I expected them to be.

There was, apparently, a quite casual, happy atmosphere in the studio with Eno. But the music didn't turn out that way.

No, no. I thought it was a nice, exercising process, but it turned out to be a substantial piece of work, which was very satisfying.

"Low" is, in fact, more bleak than "Heroes," I think.

Yes, it is. But that was a come-down period, a withdrawal time.

Tony Visconti, who helped produce it, told me that you made "Low" because you felt you were becoming predictable.

Yes, yes—I felt I was very predictable, and that was starting to bore me. I was entering an area of middle-of-the-road popularity which l didn't like, with that disco soul phase, and it was all getting too successful in the wrong way. I want and need creative, artistic success.

I don't want, need or strive for numbers. I want quality, not a rock 'n' roll career. My ego is such that I do wish to be recognised as offering something fairly worthwhile, and when I feel it is getting a bit ploddy it embarrasses me and I wish to move on.

Do you think there is a general theme to your records?

(Pauses, then mischievously adopts a Dr. Bronowski voice) "Is there an element of the irrational in the human spirit?" (Laughter) Yes, I think the irrational is very much part of it all, and the combination of the wrong elements in the wrong place at the right time.

That's very vague.

Yes, I don't think I would like to subject myself to complete analysis of my work, really.

With the exception of "Hunky Dory" and "Pin Ups," there's a very chilly, technological feel about much of it.

A bit chilly, you think? I think it's not expressed in general, emotive terms: love or anger, or whatever the emotional scale is somewhere above top C (grins). The emotions on it are those rarely touched by writers, I think. That's what gives it the chilly feeling.

But I don't think they are chilly emotions—I think they are just rather surprising emotions that are lurking in one's head somewhere that are very rarely expressed, possibly because one doesn't feel there's an occasion to express that kind of emotion.

I still don't know whether there is an occasion to express that emotion, but I'm expressing it on those records if anybody needs it!

Well, they obviously do because they're buying the records. Although, without knowing their sales, I would have said that the last two albums didn't do as well as the others.

Oh, no, of course not, no.

And that doesn't bother you at all?

Not at all. It's rather pleasing in a perverse kind of way.

That does smack of snobbery.

Yes, I know it does. Brian says he's most embarrassed that "Before And After Science" is doing so well in New York—of course he's lying through his teeth, he's very pleased. But he said, "I did everything to put people off buying it. I went over there and did my utmost to dissuade people from purchasing the aforesaid article." In fact, "Before And After Science" is receiving a very good reaction in the States.

But as far as you're concerned, isn't there a chance of you losing your audience?

Oh quite.

But it doesn't bother you?

No. No. There comes a time when you go through the most ridiculous posture of saying, "I'd be really pleased if everybody stopped buying my records so I could go away and do something else." There's an ounce of lunacy at the back of one's mind when the album comes out. "Let's see if this one can really crash, really bomb." There's a little bit of oneself that actually thinks it.

Because that would mean there's now no constraint to make a record for that particular audience?

Absolutely. And then you can take the whole bull by the horns and just record something underneath a table with a cassette recorder, or whatever, and all those things one says one's gonna do one day.

But Lou Reed tried that with "Metal Machine Music," didn't he, and it didn't work for him?

I haven't talked with Lou for a long time, so it's hard to know exactly what was at the back of his mind. 'Course, he promptly started producing very commercially-orientated albums after that, so I don't quite know whether that was a ploy to lever himself off RCA.

And he went back to his basic theme, writing about that kind of netherworld.

Yes, yes. I don't think he's too interested in writing about anything else, though. I don't know—I think Lou stays in New York too much. Having said that, of course, I now hear that he's staying in Japan, so it's not entirely true.

Let's talk a bit about the collaboration with Eno. What do you think you've taken from him?

That's a nasty question, a nasty question.

What has he injected to my music? is probably the more accurate, and what he's injected is a totally new way of looking at it, or another reason for writing. He got me off narration, which I was so intolerably bored with.

Narrating stories, or doing little vignettes of what at the time I thought was happening in America and putting it on my albums in convoluted fashion: Philadelphia, or New York or Los Angeles, "Panic In Detroit" and "Young Americans." Singer-songwriter askew.

And Brian really opened my eyes to the idea of processing, to the abstract of communication. I don't think we agree with each other on everything. We're certainly not that simpatico where we embrace what each other says with open arms.

It's possible also that my word-manipulation in songs has slightly changed his ideas. He enjoys the way that I work with words and melodies.

How do you?

I still incorporate a lot of Burroughs ideas, and I still purposely fracture everything. Even if it's making too much sense. I now fracture more than I would've done in the past. But it's still a matter of taking my three or four statements and interrelating them.

Not as literally as I used—I don't use the scissor method very much—but I'll write a sentence and then think of a nice juxtaposition to that sentence and then do it in a methodical, longhand fashion. A lot of me goes into it now, whereas at one point it was getting very random.

It was far more random on "Low." On "Heroes" it was a bit more thought about. I wanted a phrase to give a particular feeling. But never a song as a whole—I never had an overall idea of the feeling.

Each individual line I wanted to have a different atmosphere, so I would construct it in a Burroughs fashion. There are two or three themes in each song, but they are interlinked in such a way as to produce a different atmosphere per line, and sometimes a whole batch of lines.

But I didn't want to restrict myself with one process, so I would use straightforward narrative for maybe two lines and then go back to disorientation. "Heroes" was the most narrative, about the Wall, on that album.

On "Low" a "New Career In A New Town" . . .

That didn't have any words, though. (Intrigued). But did it give you the impression afterwards that it had? Yes, it does, doesn't it? That's exactly what I mean, that the sum of all the parts produces an astonishing feeling, and that you really feel that you understood something from it.

"Be My Wife" was quite specific. Was it genuinely anguished, or were you being tongue-in-cheek?

It was genuinely anguished, I think. It could've been anybody, though. But

I think as a generalisation what you find on both albums is a potpourri ranging from narrative song to, I suppose, in its own way, surrealism. In fact, some of the songs are very like those I used to write a long time ago, not so very different from something like "Quicksand" which was on "Hunky Dory."

What's "Sound And Vision" about?

That was an ultimate retreat song; actually, the first thing that I wrote with Brian in mind when we were working at the Chateau. It was just the idea of getting out of America, that depressing era I was going through. I was going through dreadful times. It was wanting to be put in a little cold room with omnipotent blue on the walls and blinds on the windows.

But I do think Brian and I are very good collaborators. I've never been happy collaborating with anyone before to the extent that I do with Brian. We do have such varied interests that it makes for some very interesting speculations in the studio. It's nice to have a friend like that and to work in that relationship. I never thought I would work like that. I always felt very singular.

How did you get on with Bob?

(Long pause)

Bob Fripp.

Oh, I thought you meant Bob Dylan! Didn't get on with him at all. I had a dreadful time with Bob Dylan. Absolutely ghastly. I talked at him for hours. I was fairly flipped out of my head, if I remember, and I just talked and talked.

The funniest part about it was that I'd been talking about his music and what he should do and what he shouldn't and what his music did and what it didn't, and at the end of the conversation he turned to me and—I hope it was in jest, but I have a feeling it wasn't—he said (falling into a banal American accent), "you wait till you hear my next album."

I thought, "oh no, not from you, please! Not that, anything but that!" I don't know whether I was in the correct state to appreciate him, but it was the first and last time I ever met him.

He never made any other contact with me (laughs uproariously). That was in New York. I didn't find him odd, that was the problem—there again, when people meet me they generally don't find me as odd as they would have me be, so I guess it's one of those things where you build up a particular picture.

I lost all that fascination for him, I must admit, quite a number of years ago, though. Once I had quite a thing about him.

Does any rock person now hold any interest for you?

I really don't think so, I really don't think so. At this particular stage I do feel incredibly divorced from rock, and it's a genuine striving to be that way. I refuse to listen to records, refuse to listen to music in general.

Not even Kraftwerk?

No . . . I don't think they have found their niche—I could turn that into a pun but I don't think I'd better! I've found a lot of their earlier work more invigorating than their later stuff, actually. I liked a lot of the stuff that seemed to be free-form.

That was when Neue were with them, of course, and you had two very frictional elements working against each other—Neue who were into complete volume against Florian's very methodical planning.

I can't get the same satisfaction out of them now, though I like them as people very much, Florian in particular. Very dry. When I got to Dusseldorf they take me to cake shops and we have huge pastries. They wear their suits. A bit like Gilbert and George, actually . . . God, whatever happened to those two? I used to really like them. . . . When I came over to Europe—'cause it was the first tour I ever did of Europe, the last time—I got myself a Mercedes to drive myself around in, 'cause I still wasn't flying at that time, and Florian saw it.

He said, "what a wonderful car," and I said "yes, it used to belong to some Iranian prince, and he was assassinated and the car went on the market, and I got it for the tour."

And Florian said, "ja, car always lasts longer." With him it all has that edge. His whole cold emotion/warm emotion, I responded to that. Folk music of the factories.

Were you influenced by Kraftwerk when you made "Low"?

I dunno if I was in a musical way. Some of their premises for wanting to make music I found interesting.

You say you don't listen to rock music, and yet you and Eno are producing Devo in Cologne.

Yes. Firstly, I like their music, and then meeting them had a lot to do with it. I found them very interesting people, very much in the same sort of conversational pattern as Brian and Fripp, but an American equivalent.

I felt there was an awful lot of enthusiasm in what they thought they could enter into eventually. The theory of their potential is very strong. I don't think it's fulfilled at this particular moment. You really should go and see them live.

I don't think I'm particularly interested in their basic premise of de-evolution. I just quite like their music and their lyric composition.

"Jocko Homo" reminds me a bit of "The Chant Of The Ever Circling Skeletal Family" off "Diamond Dogs."

Yes, I like that piece of music, it was good. Actually, some of those pieces off that album would've been quite in place with some of the things I'm doing now, I think. The intro, sans poem, was a very interesting piece of music.

I would like to treat the Overture From Tannhauser in a similar fashion to the way I treated "Bewitched, Bothered And Bewildered." "Diamond Dogs" was a hard sort of album to live with at the time, but it does mature, doesn't it, and gains potency with time?

I don't like a lot of my albums. A complete album it would be hard for me to say I like. I like bits and pieces. A bit of it works exceedingly well, and a lot of it only works.

You prefer to make them and put them out very fast, don't you?

Yes, absolutely. I don't like too much premeditation.

I've heard that you use a peculiar system of notation for the musicians.

I draw the music, the shape that it should look like. I have to draw the feeling because I can't explain it. The musicians who have worked with me have now learned the language. It's very contributive music.

The last two albums have been a curious mixture of disco funk and New Music, haven't they?

Yes, it's still there, isn't it? I mixed up the bass very high, of course, and did very extraordinary and naughty things to the snare drum sound over the last two albums as well. I wanted the snare drum to disorientate.

I was so incredibly bored with the drum sound one hears, especially the American drum sound of the last four, five years: the big, heavy, upfront bass drum, the make-it-sound-like-a-wooden box that's been there ever since "I Can Hear The Rain."

I said, it doesn't cut anymore. So we fooled around with the drums, and found that when we treated the whole drum kit it started to get back to a sort of psychedelic sound, and so we picked out different drums and treated them all individually.

We found that corrupting the snare drum definitely put the whole thing out of focus with the normal perspective of how drums have sounded.

How did you come up with the idea of what I think you called at one stage "plastic soul": the music of "Young Americans" and "Station To Station"?

Mm, had a lot to do with where I was staying, and at that particular time it was New York and Philadelphia. I thought, I don't write soul music but I do enjoy this. I also wanted to keep messing around with my lyrics as well, which are very un-soully.

So I juxtapsoed the two: very un-soully lyrics over very soul-influenced music. It's always taking something and just twisting it. It's a very constant way of working that I have, really.

In those terms it's predictable, in that I will take something, look at it, and then say, okay, now let's just bend it out of focus and see what that does to our very comfortable positions. A little bit of unease.

You've never experimented with reggae, have you?

No, I don't like it very much. I got rather biased against it. . . . I heard an awful lot of it when I was a kid, and I heard even more of it when I was a teenager of the ska and bluebeat variety, and it rather unfortunately—I know it's terribly bigoted—but I find it very hard to come back into liking it again. It still doesn't move me. Maybe I just ain't got rhythm!

Going back to plastic soul, how did you come up with "Fame," for example?

It was, in fact, Carlos' riff to "Footstompin' " **(Carlos Alomar has been Bowie's guitarist for several albums.)** I wanted to do "Footstompin', " and I said, "Carlos, that is such a good riff. I'm going to take it away from that song, and let's do something with that."

And then Lennon came in and said (Scouse accent) "that's f—— great, that! Worra great riff that is!" And then John stood in his spot and made sounds, and it sounded not unlike "fame."

You know, one often just makes sounds and those sounds become words, and then you think, "gotta word. Now out of that word let's create a subject and evolve that subject." Things often start like that.

Can you contrast that process with "Warszawa," say, on "Low."

Oh, on my part that was a quite positive idea to try and take a musical picture of the countryside of Poland. But I didn't tell Brian that. The procedure of that one was really quite simple.

I said, "look, Brian, I want to compose a really slow piece of music, but I want a very emotive, almost religious feel to it. That's all I want to tell you at this point. What do you suggest as a start?"

And he said, "let's go lay down a track of finger clicks." And he laid down I think it was 430 clicks on a clean tape. Then we put them all out as dots on a piece of paper and numbered them all off, and I picked sections of dots and he picked sections, quite arbitrarily.

And then he went back into the studio and played chords, and changed the chord as he hit that number, and went through his piece like that. And I did a similar thing on my areas. We then took the clicks out, heard the piece of music as was, and then wrote over the top of that according to the length of bars we'd given ourselves.

It sounds incredibly mathematical.

Oh yes, quite assiduously so. But each of those instrumental pieces was done differently—very, very differently—and that's what retains my interest on these albums.

How about "V-2 Schneider"?

No, that was more of an idea of a sequence. Except we turned the riff around in the beginning, purely by accident. I started playing the sax riff on the offbeat instead of the onbeat. Halfway through I thought, "Oh, I'm the wrong way round," but we continued through.

So now you get this extraordinary intro where it's all the wrong way round—beautiful! Impossible to write that—so I stayed with that and built it up from that wrong way round.

But I must say, that is why I'm so held to these albums: that each track is a whole different system of methods. It keeps me interested. It's incredible! And I'm still learning, every album I go in with Brian.

Now I've learned some of his methods quite thoroughly, and I'm fairly competent with them so I can utilise them on my own, but I'm still learning more from him.

Do you work more spontaneously?

No, he's spontaneous, but in a slow, methodical fashion. He allows accidents to slowly evolve, and I work very quickly. So Brian is probably in the studio for a far greater length of time than I am, because we often work separately—either of us will not be in the studio when the other is, so we don't hear what the other one is doing.

It sounds awfully . . . no , I don't care! It does sound, as you say, very mathematical and icy, but that doesn't defeat its ultimate musical impact. The impact is definitely an arrangement and presentation of some emotive force, and it does touch one.

Can you see a future in ambient records? You know, albums which say "this mood is Nostalgia, this mood is Sombre."

Oh, well, Brian and I talk quite seriously about the idea of writing music for having a bath to. Yeah, absolutely. The idea of very subtle emotive influences for various parts of one's activities during the day could become a feasible reason for buying music, not just the old one, the Sixties one, which is to buy to develop an identity with somebody else.

The cult figure thing will always, I suppose, have its place; but I think the idea of having environmental music—which, of course, when it first came upon the world scene, was called Muzak—that cliché of Muzak will become a very important archetype. It's not to be scoffed at.

At first I was furious when what we were doing was described as Muzak, but then I reconsidered and thought, "Well, yes, it does have roots in that somewhere along the line."

The ideas we're working in are so undefined at the moment, because they are relatively a new kind of idea for music—in the rock and roll field, anyway—that I find it very hard to analyse exactly what it is we're doing.

I think Brian is far better at analysing it. I still work very instinctively, and I'm still affected by environment, people, passions and whatever.

Are you going to play this music onstage when you tour in March?

I'm going to play a lot of the last two albums, a lot of it. Brian, of course, would love to be able to, but for reasons of his own he is not able to complete a long tour.

He's certainly going to do some one-offs with me, and they may very well take place on the next tour. (**This American and European tour finishes at the end of June.**) But I would imagine far more of them will take place on the last leg of the tour (**in Japan and Australia in the autumn**).

For two reasons. One of them is his own business, and the other is that he would prefer to play in places he has never been to before because he does not like stage work. But he and Fripp will be doing six performances with me. I could only work with them if it was the unit.

I am going to play some synthesizer, with Roger Powell, who's sort of with Todd Rundgren. Originally, I wanted Larry Fast. It will not be the same as Brian's, 'cause I would not expect anyone to reproduce somebody else's work, but I'll certainly expand the framework with which we worked.

Also, Simon House will be on violin, and Stacey Heydon on guitar this time, with Dennis (Davis, drums) and George (Murray, bass). Again, the reason Carlos will not be there this time is I was getting too confident with bands somehow. (Smiles ruefully.) It's the same story!

And so the biggest test I can give myself is to remove what is considered one of the essential qualities of the stage performance and rearrange things by bringing in a violin instead of another guitar, and a synthesizer rather than another keyboard, then see what happens when I try and play my same music with a band which is not built for it quite the same way.

I've got to have the element that surprises me else I'm not on the panic level button, which I've got to be to make it live. If it becomes too sheltered and precious, it shows like hell and looks self-satisfied.

So I'm in great anticipation of rehearsals. I've no idea what they're gonna bring. A bit worried, but very excited about working with new people.

You constructed no image, no persona, for the last two albums, presumably because the choice of subjects was so diverse. Does this mean that you've decided to stop such conjuring tricks?

Quite definitely for the time being. I have no enthusiasm for that anymore, quite honestly. A lot of that's died since leaving America. It got me into an awful lotta trouble. It mixed me up quite a lot. I began to think I was Ziggy. And then, of course, Ziggy began to merge with the others, and I wasn't quite sure whether I'd completely dropped the last one or not. Bits and pieces would keep creeping through though.

I'm intrigued by your role-playing. It's probably a bore to you now.

Somewhat, yes, but . . .

I'd like to read to you something that Pete Townshend said to me about you. He said that you've "provided almost an alternative reality, a fabricated stable image which people could react to, because he himself isn't stable, he is constantly in flux." I think he was talking specifically about Ziggy. How do you feel about that?

"Constantly in flux?" It sounds like I'm heading from that for a future as the Grim Reaper of the Avant Garde! (Laughs.) Yeah. . . . Artistically, of course, I'm in constant flux. As a person, a living organism, I think I'm becoming a lot more rational and composed emotionally as I get older, and I welcome the age I'm moving into with open arms.

But that period of incredible role-playing, of Ziggy Stardust and Aladdin Sane, you were emotionally unstable?

Oh yes, very much so. But I read in that Sunday Times article on Surrealism that somebody suggested all revolutionaries should be shot once they reached the age of 30, and I sort of see why, because one does become far more composed once one reaches that age.

But I do enjoy it. There's also a feeling, though, when one's in one's 20s, that it's got to be done in that time period, whatever the greatness is that that one feels is in oneself.

But one feels success is something a lot more to do with having a contentment with the way things are—not being apathetic towards them, but to not be quite so rational about things.

I recently decided to adopt the doctrine that a man reaches his most creative strength at around the age of 35. I've given myself another five years, ha ha.

You used to be given to contentious statements, like that grand one in the Playboy Interview that you wanted music to "return to the sensitivities of the working-class."

Mmm. There's always that appeal to me for making the obvious controversy. I mean, that was my Los Angeles era. Bloody awful. I was pretty fractured. I really wasn't in a fit state to have myself interviewed all that year.

No, I've always been very wary of defining myself or actually having some concrete standpoint 'cause it does tend to shackle oneself. And I still don't have a viewpoint. I'm just as open to suggestion as ever.

How about your advocacy of Nietzsche and homo superior?

They were used very much in defiance more than anything else. I had a period when I was very fond of flaunting suspicious points of view in front of people, merely for effect. I found that very rewarding.

It's hard to remain artistically illegitimate; it's so easy to become legitimate and Establishment. That becomes a cause: "how can I avoid that next?" I'd hate to become part of the accepted cultural set-up. You know, "that's it, nicely, in place." That's not what an artist wants to do.

Your incessant role-playing always led to criticism that you were more interested in style, in synthesizing styles, than content.

Yes, I think I am still, in a way, interested in synthesizing styles.

But not at the expense of content?

No, not at all, no. I think it's a very important mode of working. A style is the superficial arrangement of things as they are, and to juxtapose a few of these styles against each other produces some quite important artistic factors and results.

Do you read your press a lot?

Months and months later. I'm now reading the reviews of "Heroes." There's a wonderful one I've just read, another one of those "he's driven the last nail into his coffin." It goes on about "this record will never move off the counter" and "it has nothing to say—he's obviously completely lacking in any ideas any more."

Actually, I think it had the line in it, "he can't write a good song anymore!" (Falls about.) Damn right. I think it was American. But I've got to Texas now, and Texas seems to like it a lot. It's the first time it's happened to me in Texas.

But you see, the only way to remain a vibrant part of what is happening is to keep working anew all the time. For me it always will be change. I can't envisage any period of creative stability and resting on any laurels.

I think for what I do and what I'm known for it would be disastrous. So that's my predictability. Again, it's the elitist in me, but I find it very hard to consider that I am primarily still in pop or rock . . . though I'm not quite sure of what the definition of **being in it** is.

I mean, I would be the first to say that I am absolutely and completely out of touch with what young teenagers are thinking. I have absolutely no idea.

Not about punk?

Artistically, I can understand, yes. But I don't know whether a 14- or 15-year-old on the streets thinks the way I was thinking at that age. I don't know. I think it would be too much to expect that he would be thinking that differently.

By the same token, 30-year-olds think very much the way they've always thought, because I look at myself and say, yes, I was told when I was 30 that I would be a lot mellower that I was at 25. And I am, and it's a fact.

Yes, punks are supposed to be oppressed by the past and figures like you and, more so, the Stones and the Beatles.

Yes, yes, I think that's the point: now music for me is not an expression of generation anymore. I think that has changed. That's a very important point. I was, when I was younger, writing for a particular generation, and I considered it my generation.

Now I have widened my interest in music to not making a statement of a particular generation, but it's a statement of the emotive forces that one feels in particular environments. It's no longer an age thing with me, it's a place thing, and place applies to any age.

So it's music for all ages, one wants to fall into, but it's not confined anymore to the generation that used to be interested or, indeed, hopefully is still interested in what I've got to say.

Although, actually, we are going through an incredibly important era. I think the Seventies will have the same chaotic appeal to future generations as the Twenties do to us, to a certain extent.

I hope it doesn't foreshadow another holocaust, as that decade did.

Well, yes. But I don't think I'll limn that one anymore. It became a bit of a torch in my earlier period.

Of course, we have now entered the Aquarian Age, which is supposed to have terrible consequences.

Enormous. It has always been cited in the past as being the age of unbelievable chaos. And, of course, Halley's Comet comes round in '88. It all falls in place with the more factual, scientific ideas that are going around.

But I've dropped enormous clangers on that before, so I'm not gonna even start on it. A little knowledge can be quite dangerous—or can be put to great effect if it's used only artistically. If it's used artistically a little knowledge can be very symbolic of how people are thinking.

And how about your professed knowledge of politics?

I have absolutely no interest whatsoever. Never have had, probably never will.

You were needling us all again?

Very definitely, yes.

You have no interest in the political situation in Germany, for instance?

The kind of interest one has if one lives in a foreign country. But may I live and die an artist! Through the ages, though, a lot of artists have used those very spiky little things just to get people at it.

We're not going to see a flesh and blood re-run of Peter Watkins' Privilege, then?

(Laughter.) No, no.

Because the movie was terrible, anyway.

But have you seen it recently? Much, much better than when it was made. It is really worth seeing, and I loathed it when I first saw it. I saw it again a couple of months ago—on Kenyan Airways, I think it was—and it is quite amazing.

Do look at it, and then remember that horrendous gig I did in London years ago—I think it was the retirement gig at Olympia. An enormous arena. And it was all so fanatical and quite horrendous-looking.

It was a cliché at the time, but now it makes a lot more sense, though not for what we thought it was about at the time.

You and Jean Shrimpton as the President and First Lady.

I think not, I think not. I think we've passed along that way once.

THE FUTURE ISN'T WHAT IT USED TO BE

Angus MacKinnon | September 13, 1980, *New Musical Express* (UK)

David Bowie has had a respectable acting career. The part of messianic alien in his 1976 entrée *The Man Who Fell to Earth* might have been a little obvious, but he was good nonetheless and he subsequently distinguished himself across material ranging from heavyweight (*Merry Christmas Mr. Lawrence, Basquiat, The Last Temptation of Christ*) to trashily entertaining (*Absolute Beginners, The Hunger, Labyrinth*). This interview was conducted as Bowie was preparing to transplant his lead role in *The Elephant Man* from the regions onto Broadway. He speaks of it as his "first piece of legitimate acting."

As well as his thespian activities, he also talks of music. Following the completion in 1979 of his "Berlin Trilogy" with *Lodger*, he was preparing the release of *Scary Monsters (and Super Creeps)*, probably the last Bowie album on which there exists a (positive) critical consensus. One startling thing that comes through here is the fact that, at a point where Bowie had long been established as a great artist, he is still stricken with doubt about his abilities. Even more startling in retrospect is his admission that his loss of audience since his Ziggy Stardust superstardom has hurt him financially. His next album, *Let's Dance*, was three years away, but it would mark for many of his fans the start of his "sell-out."

This feature is a grand throwback to the heyday of the *NME*, when articles could roll on for fourteen thousand words, the sky was thick with first-person pronouns, and a writer felt he could assert he knew intimately a man whom he had met only in the context of a promotional interview. Notes: for "*The Origins Of Consciousness In The Dawn Of The Bi-Camaral Mind*" by "J.P. Haines" read "*The Origin of Consciousness in the Breakdown of the Bicameral Mind*" by "Julian Jaynes."
for "Neu" read "Neu!" —Ed.

Only its pretentious facade and brash neon hoardings distinguish the otherwise nondescript exterior of Blackstone Theatre from its surroundings in downtown Chicago. Its mirrored foyer gives access to a surprisingly spacious and comfortable auditorium that faces a wide, deep stage.

Walls and ceiling are in a restrained neo-classical style, and only the chill rush of air-conditioning reminds you that this is not the West End— that and the fact London audiences are extremely unlikely to see the performance the Blackstone is currently hosting: David Bowie starring in the American National Theatre and Academy production of New York–born and bred playwright Bernard Pomerance's *The Elephant Man.*

The Elephant Man was premiered in London at the Hampstead Theatre in 1977, has won several awards, played both on and off Broadway and recently enjoyed another London run with Paul Scofield in the leading role of John Merrick, the grotesquely deformed so-called Elephant Man from Leicester who was rescued from a sad and sorry life as a Victorian freakshow attraction by the eminent surgeon Frederick Treves and who was subsequently lodged at the London Hospital in Whitechapel from 1886 until his death at the age of 27 in 1890.

Although it takes as many liberties with Merrick's genuinely pathetic story as does David Lynch's forthcoming but very different film on the same subject, Pomerance's play is a concise, fast-moving and compelling piece of theatre, by turns deathly serious and archly amusing, and one that places heavy demands on its lead player.

Merrick's physical abnormalities were extensive. His head was huge, egg-shaped and some 36" in diameter, his face terribly distended and dominated by a gaping, salivating maw of a mouth, his body draped with pendulous folds of skin that were themselves covered in foul-smelling, cauliflower-like fungoid growths, his right hand and arm a useless, unwieldy lump; only his left arm, its almost feminine hand and his sexual organs were left unscathed.

As a result it would be impractical if not impossible for the actor playing Merrick to hobble about the stage for some two hours encased in some sort of second skin that realistically depicted such ravages, and so Pomerance resorts to dramatic artifice. The audience is soon made aware of Merrick's disabilities by the device of having Treves show a series of slides taken of the Elephant Man when he was first admitted to the London.

At this point in the play a curtain is pulled back to reveal a spotlit

Bowie wearing nothing but a loincloth and standing with his legs apart and arms outstretched. As Treves dispassionately enumerates Merrick's afflictions, so Bowie amplifies the gist of the surgeon's lecture by gradually straining himself into the crumpled stance he will, one short scene excepted, adopt for the remainder of the play. This brief sequence of mime is astonishing enough, but there's better to come.

As well as having to adopt the Elephant Man's crippled gait, Bowie is obliged to speak in an odd, high, fluted voice out of the side of his mouth, which in turn he has to violently contort. The character is also denied any degree of facial mobility since Merrick's own face was rendered effectively static by its peculiar bone structure, and so Bowie must rely on eye and head movements to express emotion, something he manages with unsettling conviction.

Bowie succeeds in extracting a dramatic maximum out of the part and more significantly perhaps, he appears to have won the confidence and support of what is a very distinguished professional cast, one that he will leave behind him when he re-opens the play on Broadway in September. I can only add that I found Bowie's performance deeply affecting.

Merrick (whose real name was Joseph not John; Treves himself made the mistake) was by all accounts a remarkable man who possessed great intelligence and sensibility beneath his horrifying exterior. Both these faculties blossomed after he was taken into the London, and are dwelt on in some depth by the play. To be able to portray the first outward stirrings of this unusual mind encased in its shell of literally rotting flesh is no mean task in itself, made doubly difficult since *The Elephant Man* depends entirely on the ability of the actor playing Merrick to constantly project the man's awareness of his own predicament or, as Bowie puts it, his "newness" of mind and "physical vulnerability."

That Bowie manages as much and more in what is his first 'legitimate' role in the theatre is, to say the least, impressive—especially in the light of his last, excruciatingly hammy appearance on screen in *Just A Gigolo*. Time and again *The Elephant Man* hovers precariously between drama and melodrama, between tenderness and mawkishness, but Bowie's evidently absolute immersion in the part of Merrick enables him to express every nuance that Pomerance intended. As Dan, a hip black Bowiephile from

New York who's passing through Chicago on business, remarks to me after Thursday's show, "the play's the thing. It really doesn't matter who is Merrick as long as he's good—and yes, Bowie is very, very good."

Despite long-distance interference from Barbara De Witt, who is nominally in charge of Bowie's press worldwide and who calls from Los Angeles to tell me that I will find myself in "a one-hour situation with David," and despite the incompetence of RCA's Chicago office, who can only play me five tracks of "Scary Monsters" and who drone on imbecilicly about Bowie's "incredible creative input," photographer Anton Corbijn and I arrive at the Blackstone early Thursday evening. We have both met Bowie briefly after the play the previous night, but our impressions were at best fleeting.

We go backstage and are again ushered into Bowie's cramped dressing room. Anton asks if he can take pictures during the interview, but it is firmly rebuffed by Bowie: "I never allow it. Never. I find it *most* distracting." Exeunt Anton and Coco Schwab, Bowie's enigmatic personal press assistant, a helpful but reserved girl who has worked with Bowie for the past six or seven years, travelling with him wherever he goes, and who adopts a distinctly protective attitude towards the man.

Bowie grins a lot, looks extremely well and, lighting the first of a virtual chain of Marlboro, settles back opposite me adopting a suitably expectant but nonetheless commanding air. Almost shaking the Cola out of a paper cup with nervousness, I broach the vexatious matter of De Witt's time limit on the interview.

Bowie seems understanding of my position, but unimpressed by my banter. I've never met him before but I rapidly appreciate that he is not to be crossed. I begin to suspect that if he felt so inclined he would simply stop proceedings by elegantly stalking out of the room.

His good eye fixes me for an instant, he pulls deeply on his cigarette then, as if suddenly resigning himself to my presence and the obligations it entails, he replies with surprising hesitancy: "The thing is, you see, that— well, the reason why I haven't given any interviews in recent years is simply because I've become, I think, very private. Also, *(pause)* to be honest I really don't think I've got that much to say. But why don't we just start and see how it goes?"

I mumble assent and we begin. Bowie's earlier self-assurance seems to desert him occasionally during the 40-minute interview. If I ask him straightforward factual questions, he replies promptly enough. But if I touch on more sensitive areas, he becomes extremely evasive. He'll either, infuriatingly, agrees with everything I've said, divulge so much (not much) before deciding some psychological Rubycon is about to be crossed and changing the subject or simply answer me with a question of his own.

Bowie laughs frequently, sometimes because he's amused but more often because he's only too well aware of what Ian MacDonald later describes to me as the "double vector" of our conversation. In other words, Bowie laughs whenever it occurs to him that he's said or admitted something in a private encounter that is being recorded for public consumption. It's as if with this reflex reaction he can somehow shrug off the momentary anxiety he feels at having, perhaps, given too much away.

Talking with Bowie makes me more than usually aware of the manifold absurdities inherent in the interview process. Why should Bowie tell me anything at all? He has little to gain and much to lose by doing so. We're total strangers compelled by our respective positions and professions to confront each other for a ludicrously short time. For all Bowie knows I might just want to run for home and then tear him limb from limb in print. Mutual confidence and trust are understandably not easily won in such situations.

But if Bowie does worry on this score, he needn't. I make a conscious effort to steel myself against his gushing charm, an attribute he can and indeed does call on at will with both men and the small crowds of the merely curious and fanatically adoring that greet him every night at the Blackstone's stage door, but I still find myself liking the man; he's in fact surprisingly *sympat*.

Although one of the most profoundly amoral people I've met, Bowie is nonetheless hamstrung by an acuity of self-awareness that constantly threatens to bemuse or even overwhelm him. I really don't think he likes himself very much at times—and Bowie is extraordinarily introspective. His hyper-active mind resembles an entropic vortex that pulls a bewildering succession of variety of ideas, interests and influences into its orbit, arranging and then disarranging them at lightspeed. Concentration on any one thing for any length of time must pose him serious problems.

Bowie is also, or so it seems, painfully insecure. This is not something he flaunts in the hope of earning sympathy, but more of a compulsion. What he calls his "old re-examination programme" evidently entails continual reassessment and often comprehensive re-writing of his past, an intensive form of self-therapy which in turn forces him to be forever redefining the motivations and behaviour of the various characters he has created and whose mantles he has adopted.

In this respect Joseph Merrick is no exception to the rule. The sheer pathos of the Elephant Man's existence obviously entrances Bowie and so Merrick—or rather elements of what Bowie perceives Merrick to be—will undoubtedly merge imperceptibly in the man's mind with all the other self-analytical data already accumulated there by the likes of Ziggy. To that extent, nothing's changed. Bowie always has and probably always will "blame" his characters for his own more irresponsible or, in his view, otherwise inexplicable actions. This exaggerated, almost hapless identification with what are really no more than sub-personalities of himself will presumably continue to provide Bowie with some very necessary degree of solace.

It is of course something that most of us periodically catch ourselves at, but Bowie's past insistence on giving such characters concrete form by shining them through the distorting prism of the image-obsessed rock medium has meant that he's developed the faculty to an extreme degree, and thereby totally bamboozled himself in the process. In fact Bowie has externalised so much of himself so often that he seems virtually incapable of confronting fundamentals. When I eventually ask him why he thinks people continue to find him interesting, he backs off with an immediate disclaimer that he'd never even try to answer such a question. Small wonder then that he finds it so hard—and yet so absorbing—to make mental ends meet.

A "weak" person in the pejorative sense of the term Bowie most certainly isn't though—a more wilful individual I can't imagine. But given the complexities of his mercurial temperament—this a dark, deep pool from which I will draw no more than a glassful or two in the hour and a half I spend with him in Chicago—it becomes almost superfluous to have to point out how inconsistent he is and how often he bluntly contradicts himself.

Which doesn't mean that nothing Bowie says can ever be taken at face value—far from it—but merely that it's never any more or any less than what happens to cross his mind at a particular moment. The point's been made on every occasion Bowie's given a substantial interview, but its validity has, I'm convinced, increased rather than decreased with time—as, I feel, has Bowie's pronounced ability to phrase what he says in such a way as to utterly disarm his interviewer; he's uncannily adept at telling you exactly what he thinks you want to hear.

So much for psychoanalysis—when it's all dripped and dried Bowie must speak for himself.

MACKINNON: How did you come to play the part of Merrick?

BOWIE: Very simply. I saw the play just after Christmas. I wanted to see it on off-Broadway before it got all glossed up, but I wasn't in America at the time. So I saw the thing, liked it as a piece of writing and for myself I thought I would have loved to have the part if it had ever been offered to me—but it hadn't been.

And that was the last I thought about it until February of this year when I was back in New York recording the "Scary Monsters" thing. Jack Hofsiss the director approached me and asked me if I would consider taking over the role at the end of the year (on Broadway).

I wasn't sure if I liked the idea. I wondered if he'd seen me perform or if he knew anything about me. But then he told me about my concerts and things, so he had indeed seen me—or if not then he had a great script-writer. I thought that as long as he directed me I'd be quite willing to take the chance. It's the first piece of legitimate acting I've ever done per se. So I thought I might as well. It's a very complex and difficult role, but if I was going to jump in anywhere, I might as well jump there.

Did you know anything about The Elephant Man himself before you saw the play?

Sure. A lot of those strange freak stories appealed to me in my teens and then stayed with me—everything from hairy women (laughs) to people with 15 lips. I read all that stuff avidly and of course I did my homework on Merrick.

It must have been a rather unsettling experience for you. The last time

you encountered audiences as closely as you do here must have been back in the Ziggy days.

Yes, it makes on[e] suddenly very aware of how one's body and one's facial expressions function. It's—you do feel you're being scrutinised to an unbearable extent. It's not that pleasurable actually.

But I think that was the first thing I had to fight. After we'd finished rehearsals and opened in Denver I was furious with myself on the first night that the thing that was preoccupying me during the performances was how people were adjusting or relating to my body movements and that I hadn't been considering the character at all. It took a good week to shake that feeling off and become interested and involved onstage with Merrick.

I suppose the obvious thought must have crossed your mind that people were coming to see the play simply because you were in it.

Yeah, but I also knew that if I hadn't been successful within the first 15 or 20 minutes, then they'd have got up and started leaving because it's not the kind of part you can fuck about with, frankly. You've got to be credible. You've got to be a believable Merrick or it all falls to pieces.

Especially as the full extent of Merrick's deformities is measured through the other characters' reaction to him. It's their faces that register the shock and fright and fascination whereas, although you have to imitate Merrick's crippled walk, you are pretty much as you are—with no make-up to speak of and certainly no folds of fungoid skin.

Absolutely. You've got to be forthcoming with some kind of physical vulnerability, to show that you have a sharp but "new" mind—new inasmuch as Merrick hadn't been in a situation where he could take advantage of the quite excellent mental process that he had. He had never been involved in that kind of higher society before. So in those terms it was a new mind, encased in this terrible grotesqueness. And you have to imply all that at once. It's a terrible burden.

What about the physical aspects of the role—the walk, the way you have to speak out of the side of your mouth, and so on?

I didn't find that any problem at all. I went back into mime training during rehearsals and I had to use the pre-imposed exercises before and after performances to get myself into and out of it. One's spine can be damaged very badly. I had one night of excruciating pain when I didn't do the exercises. I've been to a chiropractor every now and then just to check I'm not putting my spine out of place. It's quite possible to do that, especially if you sit down in that position. You hear a click and think that's it. That was also frightening for the first week, but you learn just how much pressure to use and when to lay back a bit.

You must have explored the character in some depth by now. Merrick mirrors people; they all have their own preconceptions about him.

"We polish him so that he may better reflect ourselves," as it's later stated.

Yes, and that struck me as a role you might possibly relish.

It's certainly one in which I can see strong parallels with other kinds of folk that I've tried to develop. Yes (*insistently*), after you—you had a line of thought there.

I've lost it.

(*Laughs*) OK, we'll backtrack a bit. Yeah, studying Merrick. On a pedestrian level the first thing I did when I was told I actually had the part a couple of weeks before rehearsals started . . .

It was a very fast move. I had to make up my mind immediately I was told, so fortunately it didn't give me time to get cold feet. I think if I'd had a couple of months to think about the part I would definitely have got cold feet—over little things like could I project that far in a theatre without a microphone, stuff and nonsense like that. When it comes to the crunch those things are really important.

But I didn't have the chance; I had to say yes or no within 24 hours. I think they knew that as well. I think that Hofsiss knew that if I'd had time to think about it I would have dropped out. He was very clever psychologically in forcing me to face an issue like that.

So presumably you'd finished working on "Scary Monsters" by this time?

Yes, I was biding my time and was quite set to go back to the East or something. Then Hofsiss came to see me . . .

So anyway the first thing I did was to go to the London Hospital and see what's left there. The real letdown was seeing the bloody church which he built. The real thing he made—in fact he gave it to Mrs. Kendal and she donated it back to the hospital—was a penny plain and tuppence coloured thing that the nurses actually cut out for him; all he did was bend it up and stick it down. I was really disappointed that it wasn't a little wooden structure that he had patiently and tenderly carved by hand.

But that liberty in the play is justified, isn't it?

Oh yes, since one has to see that the purity Merrick was developing is evidenced in real form by the church that he was building. It's a good idea to hang onto the old church as a symbol—and also of course his enraptured idea of what heaven was going to be like and that he would be saved.

There was no doubt about it in his mind. Even though God does these terrible things to man and sits back and waits for them to ask for forgiveness . . . despite that, Merrick was prepared to believe in heaven, because of Jesus, not so much because of God.

In fact Merrick's very like the central character in that Werner Herzog film *The Enigma Of Kaspar Hauser*. That particular part was played by someone called Bruno S whom Herzog just found on the streets and who demonstrated that same sort of "newness" of mind. You know, like Merrick he has that capacity to swing between what seems to be the height of naivety and incredible, unnerving insight in the course of one remark. It's like Herzog really believes that children are it, that they understand much more than adults and that growing up and gaining experience just destroys the power and the subtleties of their thinking.

It's really such a used idea. I think it still captures the public's imagination now for the same reason that the original Elephant Man captured the Victorians' attention—because he looked funny. But what the play is actually doing is shoving that pure "new" spirit into the middle of sordid society and then seeing what sort of juxtapositions you get.

On the one hand you've got the play having a dig at Victorian notions of morality and of helping or "improving" people, and on the other there's this peculiarly English thing of fascination with the grotesque, something that you can trace all the way back to, say Elizabethan bear-baiting, and further.

Absolutely. There are also, I must say, elements of the same thing in *The Man Who Fell To Earth*, although in that instance the purity of the character was corrupted.

You took the words out of my mouth. Thomas Jerome Newton is partly that corrupted innocent and partly—well, he's obviously the creation of a very high level of technology and he can use that same technology very efficiently when necessary. So he's charming, appealing and yet quite ruthless.

Yeah, he has this hi-tech emotional drive. He discards people and their values all the time. Actually though, it's a false illusion of purity and in that sense it's very Nic Roeg. Sorry, Nic, I love you but. There's such a corruptness in Nic's thought, one that (*pause*) . . .

That reached its zenith or nadir, depending on how you look at it, with *Bad Timing*.

I saw it, I saw it. Wait for the next one. He starts it off at Christmas on Haiti. It's about voodoo and if any of that crew come off that island alive I'd be very surprised. Nic is always presenting something that is none too clear but which seems superficially to be everything that one's first impressions would have it be.

You know, pure spirit comes to earth, and they fuck it up. In fact, it's nothing of that kind. There's this insidious lie going on throughout the film; Newton is a far better person at the end of the film than he was when he came down. He's actually found some sort of real emotional drive; he knows what it is to relate to people, and what the effects of all that on him are is secondary. When he first comes down, he doesn't give a shit about anybody.

I've always seen Roeg as something of a fatalist, and sometimes a pretty demonic one at that.

I find him more like Puck. I would far more work with Roeg than, say Mr. Anger (*Kenneth Anger, author of "Hollywood Babylon"*).

There is, you see, a great purity in Nic's own thought. It's convoluted, but it's there. There's an enormous struggle going on in his own mind. It's very tense; he asks himself *why* he wants to create things, to make films. He knows though that he's undertaking some great magic—I'm wary of saying spell, but it's some kind of ritual thing when he's making a film. I mean, knowing the man it's very hard to look at the film (*Bad Timing*) without going back and feeling involved with him again. It's such a personal film.

But talking about *The Man Who Fell To Earth*—I got the impression that Roeg had been very dictatorial with you, that he'd very much said that it was *his* film, that he had a very definite idea of how he wanted you to appear in it, that he really didn't care whether you had any interesting ideas about film-making or not—those things could be discussed off the set but if anybody was going to channel them into the film it was going to be him.

Absolutely correct, all the way down the line. There was no—no, very little essence of myself. I think the only freedom I was given was in choosing how the character would dress. That was it. That was the only thing I could claim at all, that I chose my wardrobe and that I put in again—I had to—that Japanese influence, something that I felt had something to do with my very weak analogy between spacemen or a spaceman and what Westerners regard the Orientals as: an archetype kind of concept.

But *you* say there was very little of you in the film, whereas I'd say that there was as much David Bowie or whoever as we're ever likely to see of you on film. I thought that you weren't only at times physically naked but at others metaphysically so as well.

Yes, I agree there too, strangely enough. There are few directors who have the kind of discipline over actors that Nic has and who can then pull out more of the actor by doing that.

In *The Man Who Fell To Earth* you were almost, as it were, non-acting, just sublimating yourself to what you call Roeg's discipline, whereas in

Just A Gigolo **you were obviously trying to act very hard and the result were abysmal, truly appalling.**

Yeah, the film was a cack (*laughs loudly*), a real cack. Everybody who was involved in that film—when they meet each other now, they look away (*covers face with hands, laughs*).

Yes, it was one of those. Oh well, we've all got to do one and hopefully I've done mine now. I think the great failure on my part for becoming involved in that particular venture was my acceptance of the director (David Hemmings) as a person rather than actually bothering to consider what the script consisted of—or rather didn't consist of, since it contained absolutely nothing—and also what experience the guy had had as a director.

I love Hemmings. He's a terrific fella, and I fell for that. He's wonderful and a *great* talker (*laughs*). Listen—you were disappointed, and you weren't even in it. Imagine how we felt. Really, it was such a shame. I can only say that David and I are still great friends and we know what we did. We'll never work together again. Friendship was saved, if nothing else.

Fortunately it's been so long now that I don't feel so uptight when I talk about it, but the first year or so after I'd made the thing I was furious, mainly with myself. I mean, oh God, I really should have known better. Every real, legitimate actor that I've ever met has told me never to even approach a film unless you know the script is good. If the script isn't any good, then there's no way a film is going to be good.

Back a bit—what about the music you wrote for *The Man Who Fell To Earth*?

Well, only one piece survived and became "Subterraneans" on "Low." I really can't remember the details, but there was a great row—not between Nic and I because we kept apart from those areas; I didn't want to row with Nic. It was a production row I had with British Lion, a couple of er, unusual people who were putting the thing together.

I was under the impression that I was going to be writing the music for the film but, when I'd finished five or six pieces, I was then told that if I would care to submit my music along with other people's . . . and I just said "Shit, you're not getting any of it." I was *so* furious, I'd put *so* much work into it.

Actually though, it was probably as well; my music would have cast a completely different reflection on it all. It turned out for the better and of course it did prompt me in another area—to consider my own instrumental capabilities, which I hadn't really done very seriously before. The area was one that was suddenly exciting me, one that I never really considered would. And that's when I got the first inklings of trying to work with Eno at some point.

I had the impression that several of the songs on *Station To Station* were quite strongly linked lyrically to *The Man Who Fell To Earth*: "TVC 15" and "Word On A Wing," for instance, and also but more indirectly "Wild As The Wind" and "Golden Years."

"Word On A Wing" I can talk about. There were days of such psychological terror when making the Roeg film that I nearly started to approach my reborn, born again thing.

It was the first time I'd really seriously thought about Christ and God in any depth and "Word On A Wing" was a protection. It did come as a complete revolt against elements that I found in the film. The passion in the song was genuine. It was also around that time that I started thinking about wearing this (*fingers small silver cross hanging on his chest*) again, which is now almost a left-over from that period.

I wear it. I'm not sure why I wear it now even. But at the time I really needed this. Hmmm (*laughs*), we're getting into heavy waters . . . but yes, the song was something I needed to produce from within myself to safeguard myself against some of the situations that I felt were happening on the film set.

At the end of my review of "Lodger" I said rather flippantly that I thought you were ripe and ready for religion. That album seemed so desperate, so disparate, just a snapshot collage of journeyman melancholy; God seemed to be just about all you had left.

(*Laughs*) Yes, I can understand that, but I think you were probably post-period there. It had already hit me. There was [a] point when I very nearly got suckered into that narrow sort of looking—no, finding the Cross as the salvation of mankind around the Roeg period.

That whole period stretching through to '76 was probably the worst year or year and a half of my life in the old re-examination programme.

I imagine Berlin must have knocked a lot of that stuffing out of you.

Oh yeah, it was [the] best thing that could have happened to me. I'd come out of the American thing with (*pause, sigh*) smashed ideals inasmuch as I'd found that the ideals I did have weren't worth a shit anyway, that I was too willing to jump from point of view to point of view without taking into account the consequences of anything I was doing, just breaking out of the American cocoon. And so yes, Berlin was definitely the best place I could have gone.

At least "Low" and "Heroes" both had a certain emotional consistency, although it was sometimes a very distraught, withdrawn and perhaps cynical one. At least you were—well, looking at things again, or maybe for the first time, as opposed to just staring at images or reflections.

Yeah, looking at things, but with not that much conviction about whether I'm right or wrong about what I'm seeing. I think those three albums helped *me* to appreciate that my make-up is generally much more of a microcosm of what society is than me standing back and saying "This is what society is about."

Before, up until the '76 period, I was far more of the opinion that I had some kind of definite viewpoint on how society was made up and what it represented. But now I'm feeling like a society in myself, so broken up and fragmented that it's best just to throw me into the (*pause*) . . .

Into the ring? But isn't all that just the belated arrival of some sort of maturity, some realisation that you were fallible?

It was. To use a cliche—and why not?—it was . . . some kind of maturity.

Which brings us to your rather extraordinary means of arrival at Victoria Station in late '75. I was very perturbed by that: the black Mercedes, the handsome blonde outriders and everything. I was there (*at which point Bowie laughs briefly, as if embarrassed*) and I came away

thinking you were some sort of fascist maniac. The incident has never been very satisfactorily explained; I just thought you must have consumed an enormous amount of cocaine in Los Angeles (*Bowie chuckles broadly*). I mean, that *Rolling Stone* interview with darkened room, the black candles and the bodies falling past the window, and then seeing the *Cracked Actor* television film of the "Diamond Dogs" tour at around the same time—it all convinced me and a lot of other people that you'd flipped completely, wanted to take over the world or had some such equality idiotic, megalomanic gameplan.

(Still laughing) No, I'm sure none of that helped in the least.

So what *were* you up to then?

Well, actually, Victoria Station *(long pause)* . . . now this you're not going to believe, but everything else you're saying is absolutely correct. I had indeed been bombed out for quite long time.

This was all an escape plan heralded by a couple of friends of mine—I won't say who they are—who helped me get out of America and get back to Europe, whatever. That whole "Station to Station" tour was done under duress. I was out of my mind totally, completely crazed. Really. But the main thing I was functioning on was—as far as that whole thing about Hitler and rightism was concerned—it was *mythology*.

I was in the depths of mythology. I had found King Arthur. It was not as you probably know because . . . I mean, this whole racist thing which came up, quite inevitably and rightly. But—and I know this sounds terribly naïve—but none of that had actually occurred to me, inasmuch as I'd been working and still do work with black musicians for the past six or seven years. And we'd all talk about it together—about the Arthurian period, about the magical side of the whole Nazi campaign, and about the mythology involved.

All that stuff was flying around, buzzing around the skies. I could see it. Everywhere I looked there were these great demons of the past, demons of the future on the battlegrounds of one's emotional plain (plane?) and all that . . . I was in a haze of mythology. Mixed up too of course were my own fucking characters. The Thin White Duke—throwing him, it was like kicking him. There was *such* an addictive thing about what was happening there that actually being able to ride that particular storm I was able to send a lot of those demons back to their—well, wherever it is they live.

Altogether, none of it is something to be dealt with unless you're in a particularly stable frame of mind.

Yes, the temptations to draw all the wrong conclusions are too great. But you can always notice these thing surfacing into the cultural mainstream. I mean, the number of books you'll find in the "Occult" racks of, say, Smith's these days about the Third Reich and its supposed occultist tendencies.

Oh God yes, I know it all . . . ghastly stuff.

Yes, and there's more and more of it now. They're even writing pulp novels on the subject, that connection between Arthurian literature and legend and the Reich. There's James Herbert's *The Spear* and Duncan Kyle's *Black Camelot*: the SS and their Grail castles, very subversive and dangerous material, you know.

Yes, I know. Only too well. It's *so* insidious—and of course the first thing that happened to me when I got to Berlin was that I really had to face up to it, because all the people I had as friends there were naturally extreme leftists.

Suddenly I was in a situation where I was meeting young people of my age whose fathers had actually been SS men. That was a good way to be woken up out of that particular dilemma, and start to re-function in a more orderly fashion—not totally ordered, but you know . . . yeah, I came crashing down to earth when I got back to Europe.

And Los Angeles, that's where it had all happened. The fucking place should be wiped off the face of the earth. To be anything to do with rock and roll and to go and live in Los Angeles is I think just heading for disaster. It really is. Even Brian (Eno), who's so adaptable and quite as versatile as I now am living in strange and foreign environments, he couldn't last there more than six weeks. He had to get out. But he was very clever: he got out much earlier than I did.

Alright, so we have this sort of manic destabilisation in L.A. and then re-adjustment in Berlin, up to a point at least. But there again at the

end of "Red Money" on "Lodger" there's that line about "*responsibility, it's up to you and me*"—whereas in "Up The Hill Backwards" on the new album there's more than a suggestion of admitting defeat, or if not that then implying that there's bugger all you or I or anybody can do about the state of things.

Well . . . admitting it? I don't actually agree with that viewpoint, you see. To digress completely for a moment—I still adopt the view that music itself carries its own message, instrumentally I mean. Lyrics are not needed because music does have an implicit message of its own; it makes its case very pointedly. If that were not the case, then classical music would not have succeeded to the extent that it did in implying and carrying some definite point of view, some attitude which presumably can't be expressed with words.

That's why I'm furious you didn't get to hear the album because the lyrics taken on their own are nothing without the secondary sub-text of what the musical arrangement has to say, which is *so* important in a piece of popular music. It makes me very angry—and I'm not saying you're doing it at all—when people concentrate only on the lyrics because that's to imply there is no message stated in the music itself, which wipes out hundreds of years of classical music. Ridiculous.

If that's the case then I suppose I'd better concentrate on what I've heard and seen. The "Ashes To Ashes" video is very striking. Did David Mallet (who made the three "Lodger" videos) direct that?

That's my first direction. Well, no, I'll cross with him there. The other three that were done for "Lodger" were co-directions inasmuch as I gave David complete control over what I wanted put in there. But this one I story-boarded myself, actually drew it frame for frame. He edited it exactly as I wanted it and has allowed me to say (adopts Edward Heath voice) *publicly* that it is my first direction. I've always wanted to direct and this is a great chance to start—to get some money from a record company and then go away and sort of play with it.

Those recurring images of the astronaut, they're very reminiscent of H.R. Giger's sets for Ridley Scott's *Alien* film.

Yes they are, and intentionally so. It was supposed to be the archetypal 1980s ideal of the futuristic colony that has been founded by the earthling, of what he looks like—and in that particular sequence the idea was for the earthling to be pumping out himself and to be having pumped into him something organic. So there was a very strong Giger influence there: the organic meets hi-tech.

There're an awful lot of clichéd things in the video but I think I put them together in such a way that the whole thing isn't clichéd—at least inasmuch as the general drive of the sensibility that comes over is some feeling of nostalgia for a future. I've always been hung up on that; it creeps into everything I do, however far away I try to get from it. It does recur and it's something I have to admit to and I can't . . . and that's obviously part of what I'm all about as an artist (this said with uncharacteristic assertion).

Now I tend to go with it rather than escape from it because it's obviously an area that, even if I refuse to face it, does interest me. The idea of having seen the future, of somewhere we've already been keeps coming back to me.

Do you extend that to believing in the possibility of cyclic civilisations?

No, not on that kind of simplistic level. I don't . . . I think I work even more these days from dream sequences.

But then surely you're acknowledging some sort of wellspring of the collective unconscious? It's hard to think straight about this kind of thing—I mean, is it all down to *2001*-type interference? You know, *They* came from other worlds to give us knowledge, and so on.

(*With sudden enthusiasm*) Have you ever read a book called *The Origins Of Consciousness In The Dawn Of The Bi-Camaral (?) Mind*? It sounds an awful title but it's really a very easy book to read. In fact it's an extraordinary book written by a guy called J.P. Haines (?) which suggests that at one point the mind was definitely of a schizoid—no, a dual nature and that the right hand passed messages through to the left side of the brain, and vice versa. It's written in a very academic manner, but it's highly interesting.

I related to that tremendously because I've often had that feeling very strongly with myself that . . . well, it's like what Dylan said about the tunes are just in the air. I still believe in that kind of naive approach to writing. I leave the cerebral stuff to the Enos and Fripps of this world. Because I'm far more tactile in my approach to what I do, I think it's probably why we work together so well.

We could go off at a tangent and talk about the vagaries of human intelligence for hours, but it doesn't look as if we've got the time. But thinking about Eno and Fripp—I used to like most of what they did on their own records a lot, but now have my doubts about all this endless conceptualising. I just don't think it ultimately delivers in most cases; Fripp's "God Save The Queen/Under Heavy Manners" album struck me as a prime example—some of its theory was fascinating, but much of its practice, of what actually appeared on the album was unremittingly dull. The same, I felt, went for Eno's "Music For Airports."

I must say I like working with Brian a lot, but I think this happens to conceptualists: they often have the seeds and germs of truly revolutionary ways of doing things, which I believe Brian does.

I really think he's one of the brightest minds I've met in this particular area, although of course he's duplicated many times over in the field, in the so-called more serious world of painting, where you can find a conceptualist for every square yard. But there are few in this business and Brian is definitely one of them, and he has moments of true genius. I think some of the music on "Another Green World" was really, for want of a better word, transcendental. I dare say we'll be working together again.

Some more specific points—this question of Major Tom reappearing in "Ashes To Ashes"... he seems to be a fairly indestructible character. Why does he continue to interest you?

Again, the sub-text of "Ashes To Ashes" is quite obviously the nursery rhyme appeal of it and for me it's a story of corruption. It's also about as subversive as one can get in popular music terms inasmuch as I would love to get a record played by the BBC containing the word "junkie." I thought that was quite successful (*grins*). There's not much you can do these days; we're all such a blase, worldweary lot (*laughs*).

But if one can make anything more serious out of it all other than that it's The Further Stories Of, it's that when I originally wrote about Major Tom I was a very pragmatic and self-opinionated lad that thought I knew all about the great American dream and where it started and where it should stop.

Here we had the great blast of American technological know-how shoving this guy up into space and once he gets there he's not quite sure why he's there. And that's where I left him. Now we've found out that he's under some kind of realisation that the whole process that got him up there had decayed, was born out of decay; it has decayed him and he's in the process of decaying. But he wishes to return to the nice, round womb, the earth, from whence he started.

I guess it's that simple. I really don't think there's anything more insidiously perverse about the thing at all. It really is an ode to childhood, if you like, a popular nursery rhyme. It's about spacemen becoming junkies (*laughs*).

What about the new, simpler version of "Space Oddity"?

That came about because Mallett wanted me to do something for his show and he wanted "Space Oddity."

I agreed as long as I could do it again without all its trappings and do it strictly with three instruments. Having played it with just an acoustic guitar onstage early on I was always surprised as how powerful it was just as a song, without all the strings and synthesisers. In fact the video side of it was secondary; I really wanted to do it as a three-piece song.

Are you story-boarding the other two videos for "Scary Monsters"?

Oh yes, now I've started, no one will stop me. Also another thing I've come up with over the last six months are my first stoned-out video tapes that I did in 1972 on black and white reel to reel, which are *so* exciting, and some later ones I did after "Diamond Dogs."

In those I recreated the set for "Diamond Dogs"—this was in the Pierre Hotel in New York—and I built three or four-foot high buildings out of clay on tables. Some were standing up, others were crumbling and I took the camera and put a micro-lens on it, zooming down the streets in between the tables.

I tried animation out and had all these characters; the whole thing is so bizarre I'm going to put that together and put it out as a cassette. And as it's silent—there's a few bits of strange music on it but nothing much else; mainly I used the "Diamond Dogs" album as a backing track . . .

You know, I wanted to make a film of "Diamond Dogs" *so* passionately, *so* badly; I really wanted to do that, I had the whole roller skating thing in there. We had no more cars because of the fuel problems—which was super stuff to look back on and say yes, I thought that then—and these characters with enormous, rusty, sort of organic-looking roller skates with squeaking wheels that they couldn't handle very well. Also I had groups of these cyborgy people wandering around looking so punky it's going to be a lovely tape to put out. I want to write some new music for it though: a piece of music accompanied by a sort of strange black and white vision.

Because "Diamond Dogs" is certainly a retro-active sort of idea, one that seems to work much better after the event.

Now there's a certain quaintness in some of its arrangements that pieces it into the '70s as an artefact of the time.

Chopping and changing a bit, tell me about "Fashion" and the first part of "It's No Game," both of which I have heard.

The Japanese lyrics to the first "It's No Game" are exactly the same as the others, although "Part 1" sees a more sort of animal approach on my part. Also, repeating me parrot fashion but in Japanese is a young Japanese girl friend of mine who says the lyric in such a way as to give the lie to the whole very sexist idea of how Japanese girls are so very prim. She's like a Samurai the way she hammers it out. It's no longer the little Geisha girl kind of thing, which really pisses me off because they're just not like that at all.

And "Fashion"? You mention "the goon squad"—fascism?

No, not really. It's more to do with that dedication to fashion. I was trying to move on a little from that Ray Davies concept of fashion, to suggest more of a gritted teeth determination and an unsureness about why one's doing it. But one *has* to do it, rather like one goes to the dentist and has the tooth drilled. I mean, you have to have it done, putting up with the fear and the aggravation. It's that kind of feeling about fashion, which seems to have in it now an element that's all too depressing.

But that's hardly surprising when so many kids are leaving school today and not being able to find jobs, is it? If that is the case, then you're going to make bloody sure you have a good time down the disco or wherever.

I don't know, you know. The American disco I went to in the early '70s in New York when it was supposed to be the hot new thing that was sweeping the city—well, I never felt that grim determination that one feels now. There is that. Yes, I must say I did feel it when I was in London. I was taken to one extraordinary place by . . . Steve Strange? God, what was it called? Everybody was in Victorian clothes. I suppose they were part of the new new wave or the permanent wave or whatever . . . *(enter Coco making throat-slitting gestures)* . . . it's the Valkyrie *(laughs)*. We'll have some more time but I'll have to keep it to a minimum.

As we finish, I protest to Bowie about this "minimum," I overstate my case to Bowie, and he suddenly snaps "Alright, alright, don't *sell* it to me, Angus. I don't need anybody to *sell* me anything." I retire in confusion and, convinced that I've aged years in less than an hour, make my exit.

Friday afternoon finds Anton and I awaiting Bowie and Coco in a small, seedy bar opposite the Blackstone. They arrive on time and Bowie, sharing Anton's delight at having found Sinatra's "That's What God's Face Looks Like" on the jukebox, agrees to the photographer's request to do a session there and then, but not without first consulting Coco.

The bar's proprietor, a Chicano with knife scars criss-crossing the left-hand side of his face and neck, looks on in amazement.

We move to the theatre and on a whim Bowie suggests we do the interview onstage. I agree and so we heave table and chairs into position. The contrast with the claustrophobic dressing room couldn't be more complete. Whereas yesterday Bowie and I fenced tensely at each other, today we both seem much more at our ease. For my part I have noted down some dozen simple, factual questions and when these are dismissed, I plan to freewheel.

Bowie seems positively expansive. It's as if we're both convinced we have the other's measure.

As it transpires, the interview's very informality belies the way it progresses. Much to my surprise, after initial evasions Bowie begins to discuss himself with very little prompting and answers off-the-cuff questions I'm quite prepared for him to ignore altogether. Or so it seems.

On reflection it occurs to me that wondering whether or not Bowie is being as straightforward and comforting as he appears to be is pointless, just as to depict him as the archetypal manipulator-chameleon who invariably vanishes behind a verbal smokescreen of his own making is both fatuous and unfair. Suffice to say that, soon becoming quite oblivious to our surroundings, Bowie and I talk intensively for some 35 minutes. If our conversation doesn't follow a very logical course, that's only because most conversations don't but, since this one had a peculiarly insistent flow, I've left it unedited, intact.

Why did you choose to do a Tom Verlaine song ("Kingdom Come") on the new album?

That particular cut, it was simply one of the most appealing on his album. I'd always wanted to work with him in some way or another, but I hadn't considered doing one of his songs. In fact Carlos Alomar, my guitarist, suggested that we do a cover version of it since it was such a lovely song.

It's about the notion of grace. Did that influence you at all?

Yes and no. The song just happens to fit into the scattered scheme of things, that's all.

Why did you release two more versions of "John, I'm Only Dancing"?

Only because we dug them up and the beat version was something that never got on the "Young Americans" album. It seemed so right at the time and RCA wanted to put it out, and I agreed to it fully. It was just some more material that was held back there. I've still got lots of things canned like that which I'd like to release, things like "White Light White Heat" with the Spiders.

Do you have complete control over what RCA put out under your name?

Oh no, they've put out things without my approval. "Velvet Goldmine" is the one that immediately springs to mind. That whole thing came out without my having the chance to listen to the mix; somebody else had mixed it—an extraordinary move.

But haven't you recently re-negotiated your contract with RCA? Surely you can put a stop to that sort of thing?

No, I most certainly haven't. We're miles away from that and shall just have to see what happens.

There were rumours that RCA weren't very happy with "Lodger."

That's true. They weren't happy with "Low" either. At the time the one comment I received from them was "Can we get you another pad in Philadelphia?", so that I could do another "Young Americans." That was the kind of attitude I was having to cope with.

Does that appeal to you, making another "Young Americans"-type of album?

I don't know. You see, my own needs were satisfied within that area in the '73/'74 period, when I was staying as much as I could there, crashing down with people in either Philadelphia or New York. I spent an awful lot of time in that kind of environment.

Leaping about a bit—

That's alright, I'm in the mood.

"Red Sails" from "Lodger"—was the Neu influence there intentional?

Yes, definitely. That drum and guitar sound, that especially, is quite a dream. The moments of difference though, they came from Adrian (Belew, Bowie's guitarist at the time) not being played Neu; he'd never heard them. So I told him the atmosphere I wanted and he came up with the same conclusions that Neu came up with, which was fine by me. That Neu sound is fantastic.

You seemed at one time to have a fondness for using rather hysterical lead guitarists: Earl Slick, Ricky Gardiner and then Belew.

Well, that's a contrivance of my own. What I do is, say, use four tracks for a recorded solo and then I cut them up, knock up a little four-point mixer clipping the solos in and out. I give myself arbitrary numbers of bars in which they can play within a particular area, and go backwards and forwards from one track to another. So yes, the effect is somewhat histrionic.

Moving on again to "Teenage Wildlife"" on "Monsters", is it addressed to anybody in particular?

I guess . . . no, if I had my kind of mythical younger brother, I think it might have been addressed to him. It's for somebody who's not mentally armed.

To cope with what?

The shell shock of actually trying to assert yourself in society and your newly found values . . . I guess the younger brother is my adolescent self.

And who are the "*midwives to history*" who put on "*their bloody robes*"?

(*Laughs*) I have my own personal bloody midwives. We all have them. Mine shall remain nameless. For the sake of the song they're symbolic; they're the ones who would not have you be fulfilled.

You still seem to be quite concerned with giving advice to younger people.

I think that more and more that advice is given to myself; I often play questions and answer time with myself, however momentarily. I don't seriously think I could offer anybody else any advice at all. It would be about as profound as (*chuckles*) Alfred E. Neuman (*"Mad's" late cover artist and humourist*). It's just not my thing, maaann.

Obvious questions which I suppose I'm obliged to ask—what do you think of Gary Numan and John Foxx and all the other little "Diamond Dog" clones?

I only have opinions on them because I've been asked about them; I never had any before. I've already been asked once about Numan over the last month.

Foxx—I think he gives himself a wider berth; I think there's more diversity in what he does and could do.

Numan? I really don't know. I think what he did—that element of "Man Who Sold The World" and "Saviour Machine"-type things—I think he encapsulated that whole feeling excellently. He really did a good job on that kind of stereotype, but I think therein lies his own particular confinement. I don't know where he intends going or what he intends doing, but I think he has confined himself terrifically. But that's his problem, isn't it?

What Numan did he did excellently but in repetition, in the same information coming over again and again, once you've heard one piece . . .

It's that rather sterile vision of a kleen-machine future again.

But that's really so narrow. It's that false idea of hi-tech society and all that which is . . . doesn't exist. I don't think we're anywhere near that sort of society. It's a enormous myth that's been perpetuated unfortunately, I guess, by readings of what I've done in that rock area at least, and in the consumer area television has an awful lot to answer for with its fabrication of the computer-world myth.

Those lines from "Ashes To Ashes" spring to mind: "*I've never done good things/I've never done bad things/I've never done anything out of the blue.*" You seem to be saying that you're not prepared to judge your own achievements. Do you feel any—how shall I put it?—guilt about having helped propagate the sort of delusions we're talking about?

Well, how did you define those three lines?

Like many of your lyrics, they're infuriatingly ambivalent (*at which Bowie grins*). They could be referring to the Major Tom character specifically or—well, to put it another way, I can accept that in your career there has been more than a certain amount of calculation, which I think you've probably exploited in retrospect. That's to say you've claimed you planned A, B and C—

Yup.

(*Pause*) Whereas in fact you may well have planned D, E and Z. But it worked, and you've been very fortunate in that respect. I don't know, I

tend to believe that more often than not people's morality is completely screwed when they assume positions of public prominence, and that audiences presume a lot, too much perhaps, of those in whom they invest so much commitment.

I agree *(pause)* . . .

So would you dissociate yourself from that statement?

(Sigh) No, not really. Those three particular lines represent a continuing, returning feeling of inadequacy over what I've done. *(Bowie absently traces a finger around his mouth then proceeds, choosing his words very carefully)* I have an awful lot of reservations about what I've done inasmuch as I don't feel much of it has any import at all. And then I have days when of course it all feels very important to me, that I've contributed an awful lot. But I'm not awfully happy with what I've done in the past actually.

So what would you include amongst your positive achievements?

The idea that one doesn't have to exist purely on one defined set of ethics and values, that you can investigate other areas and other avenues of perception and try and apply them to everyday life. I think I've tried to do that. I think I've done that fairly successfully. At times, even if only on a theoretical level, I've managed that. As far as everyday life goes, I don't think so . . .

I have this great long chain with a ball of middle-classness at the end of it which keeps holding me back and that I keep sort of trying to fight through. I keep trying to find the Duchamp in me, which is harder and harder to find *(laughs)*.

Why should middle-classness be a problem? Isn't that kind of exaggerated class consciousness a peculiarly English affliction?

Yes, of course, and a class consciousness is a very great wall of contention with me, always getting in my way.

What is it that you feel then, you should have "suffered" more for your art or something?

Oh no, not at all. Not on that level. I just keep finding my vision gets blinkered and becomes narrowed all the time. I'm continually trying to open it up and break it down and do shattering things to it—and that's when it becomes dangerous, I suppose.

But don't you understand your own creative faculties any better now than when you started writing? Doesn't some at least of the more critical attention you receive in the media help you in that respect?

I don't know, you see. There are few magazines or newspapers or television programmes that will deal with me on the same level that your paper would for instance. In the majority of the media—there I'm completely stifled. I have been for years. I have never been anything other than Ziggy Stardust for the media en masse.

And yet even that—well, it's a ghost of your own making. When you toured and recorded what became the "Stage" album, for example, the first part of the show was old songs, very old songs. I suppose I overreacted, but I must admit I did feel a vague sense of betrayal.

Really?

Yes, because I'd been impressed by "Low" and "Heroes" at the time, although I feel differently about them now. But I just felt you were very consciously trying to recover your old audience again—a move that seemed to cancel out the validity of the newer material. Altogether I was naive enough to think it was a bit of a cheap trick.

I think it was rather to do with two ideas that I felt strongly. One was that I actually wanted to play the "Ziggy" album from top to bottom, from bottom to top, one to nine, because I suddenly found it again an enjoyable piece of music to listen to, having not done it for quite a few years on stage. So there was pure personal enjoyment value in there. On the other hand, I'm only too willing to admit to the number of people who come to see me to hear a lot of those old songs and without any hesitation I'm quite willing to play them. I will also play the things I'm doing currently. But I have absolutely no qualms about playing older things of mine that people like.

Do you have any plans to tour?

Yes, next spring. I say this every time and I hope it happens—I want to play smaller places. I think this, the play, has helped a lot; it encourages me to work in smaller environments.

At the same time Broadway is beckoning. After all, "Scary Monsters" can be used as a very convenient crutch. It's a new Bowie album and there hasn't been one for some time, therefore it will probably sell well enough with or without you touring. Are you or would you be tempted by the prospect of taking another part on the stage or perhaps another film lead?

At this time, as we talked yesterday about my 32 Elvis Presley movies contained in one, I wouldn't jump at the first thing that came along by any means. No, whatever it was, it would have to be a script that had the same kind of power as *Elephant Man*.

You give the impression that by becoming involved in the play and the part you've proved a lot to yourself.

Oh yes, I was well surprised that I was able to do this successfully. My confidence was at a very low ebb on opening night. I was terrified actually.

And you must have also proved to yourself that you can exist quite satisfactorily outside of the rock sphere—

I've been doing *that* for a long time *(laughs)*, since '76 in fact.

Not so satisfactorily as now.

For me completely so . . . oh, but you mean on a public level?

Yes.

Ah well, maybe not then.

Obviously music continues to interest you, but you skim quite a bit across its surface—an African influence here, a Japanese influence there. Do you ever feel you're in danger of misrepresenting some of the cultures you're very fond of?

I don't think that by taking a Japanese or an African emblem or motif I try to represent them at all. I would have thought it was pretty transparent that it was me trying to relate to that particular culture; not in my wildest dreams would I think I was trying to represent them.

But relating to what end? To your own satisfaction?

Because I've been there. Because it was there, rather. It is no more than . . . it does get back onto the sketchpad basis for songs for me. Often. And I guess that "Lodger" was the sketchpad of all of them.

Do you feel you're too old to be writing rock songs anymore?

I don't know how much of it is rock anymore. Music then? I don't think I'm too old to be writing the music I write either. (Laughs) That was an extraordinary thing to say. I mean, good God, when was the last time I wrote a rock song? Can you remember? I'm damned if I can.

It depends. Place one of your recent albums against one of Van Halen's and we're obviously not talking about the same sort of thing.

Well, *there* you are. I don't think I would try to revitalise the same area of energy and sensibilities that, say, Ziggy had. I wouldn't attempt that again, because I haven't got that same positivism within my make-up anymore. I mean, the very juvenile sort of assertiveness and arrogance of that period. He said modestly (*laughs*). I can't write young.

But you address yourself to the young—what about "Because You're Young" on "Monsters"?

I think repeatedly that having got a nine-year-old son that's an area where I can try and talk to an age group that I've been through.

Do you think any of your audience have grown with you, so to speak, all the way?

Not necessarily. My audience has diminished remarkably over the years.

Does that bother you?

No, not at all.

Does it bother you financially?

Yes it does. On those terms doing something like this is not something one does for the kind of money that rock and rollers can charge. And also of course I've never made any money on tours. Ever. Ever.

Why do you think people continue to find you interesting?

That's for you to answer. I'd never even try to answer that.

Because you don't want to?

Because I don't want to, and I don't want to because I can't. That's something that I would really have no interest in trying to find out. I think I would far prefer to spend more time on finding out if I am still interesting to myself, if I still feel, if I still relate, if I still have any capacity for understanding where I am within the very tight, very small area of society that I physically live in.

That for me is more interesting. If I can then broadcast my own doubts through my pieces of music, however that's related to by an audience, that's quite honestly where the responsibility for me stops. I can do no more than write about how I feel about things or how I . . . what dubious kind of thoughts I have about where I am and what I've done.

Your saying all that makes you seem quite er, vulnerable, quite unsure of yourself. But can you draw up any sort kind of moral guidelines for your work? Do you feel that somebody like yourself who's exposed to public scrutiny has any kind of responsibility in that way?

I don't think it's up to the one single person. It becomes a collective responsibility. Because, like it or not, whatever I do or say is going to be interpreted in a fair or unfair manner by disparate elements of the media.

So the responsibility is not mine alone and I do have to consider what I should contribute and then hazard a guess at how it will be dealt with. As I say, I'm still referred to over here as the orange-haired bisexual. Now that is what I am here. Period. Zilch. There's nothing else.

After all *(laughs)*, if ever there was a country of stereotypes and icons, this is the one. If you don't fall radically into some confinement or department, then they will stab away until they find something that is so super-ficially concrete that it will become the flag that they will wave.

Or the box to bury you in.

Absolutely. Far more so than in England or Europe generally. The other people who tend to do that, much as I like them, are the Japanese; they come up with -isms as well.

But there the process is in reverse, Japan having been actually and cul-turally invaded by America.

Oh sure, and of course there's a great anti-American thing there.

What is it that continues to fascinate you about Japan?

For me it's a physical representation—or I can read it in terms of that—of great new modern advances precariously balanced against an old, kind of mythological way of thinking and being.

Does the outward theatricality of the old Japanese way of life appeal to you? I mean, like the *Go* player who lives his whole life by the rules of the game he becomes so expert and accomplished at as he grows older—the definition of that selfless sort of freedom being that the more you subordinate yourself to a particular discipline, the freer you are.

Oh yes, very much. It appeals to me on the surface but it's something I can't handle myself (*laughs*). Yes, it's wandering back and looking at something that I felt would have a place in my life at one time. That kind of thing . . .

By which you mean what?

When I was flirting around with the ideal of Buddhism, which was also a set of values and disciplines that have to be adhered to in a strict form. At that time I had some idea of my way, or my potential, with nature . . . and I wished to confine it. What does Merrick say about truths? That they're "restriction, governance and punishment" (*laughs*). It's that self-flagellation element again in me . . .

Doesn't it also have something to do with the idea of the typically cul-

tured but dissatisfied Western man feeling envious of the "simple" truths of, say, a rigorous Eastern religion? Don't you feel that at all?

Yes, I do, I do. It's not infrequent that I wake up on a chilly morning and wish that I was in Kyoto or somewhere and in a Zen monastery. That feeling lasts for well over five or six minutes before I go and have a cigarette and a cup of coffee and (*laughs*) go for a walk round the block to shake that off. That idea of being controlled by an aesthetic set of values does recur with me.

I still have a pipe dream that when I'm an old chap (*the "p" deliberately over-stressed*) I shall go off to the Far East and smoke opium and go out in a sort of euphoric, cloudy bliss.

Would you be reincarnated?

I think I'd have to be (*laughs*)—many, many times.

What would you want to become?

What I might want to be and what I might become are two very different kettles of *poisson (laughs)*. Let's see, what would I want to be? Good God . . . well, it wouldn't be Lou Reed (*loud laughter all round*). But . . . probably a rock and roll journalist.

Well, I wouldn't want to be David Bowie.

(*Laughing*) No, no one's reincarnated as David Bowie. I'm quite positive of that.

Back to this middle-classness though—can you expand on what really bothers you about it?

I guess it restricts my thinking . . .

In what particular ways? Morally, aesthetically?

Aesthetically. Morally I've never had too much—I sort of approach things in quite a barbarian fashion when it comes to morals. It's more to do with aesthetic values for my own writing. What I write is so inadequate.

Compared to what? The writing of people you admire?

Compared to a Genet. Yeah, I do put myself against other writers and find my sensibilities thwarted and rather dulled and that . . . angers me.

Is it that you're annoyed because you're so busy filtering other influences that you feel you might actually not be expressing yourself at all? Or is it that you feel there's no essence that is David Bowie that can suddenly rush through? Maybe you think that people like Duchamp and Genet had some kind of incredible mainline that just thrust them forward regardless?

I think that I have a mainline, but I couldn't define it. Again, I wouldn't wish to; there's a danger in trying to define that one thing. There's also a particular spirit value that I find very difficult to articulate and I guess that's my, my mainline as you put it.

But it comes and goes, it hides, it gets lost and it reappears, rather like a stream that you come across when you're walking through a wood. You see it sometimes and it sparkles and then it disappears. And that makes me angry when it disappears *(here Bowie's tone becomes distant, abstracted, almost as if he's talking aloud to himself)*. And I should be happy about that because it's the natural way of things—but when it does disappear, which is known I think as a dry-up, then that is the most frustrating feeling of all.

I get repetitive feeling that . . . *(Coco appears in the auditorium; Bowie suggests we talk for another five or ten minutes)* that . . . come back, come back *(he gestures with his left hand, as if plucking something out of the air)*.

Streams disappearing—

Yes, I get the repetitive feeling that it is—and this somebody else's statement, I know—that the worst joke God can play is to make you an artist, but only a mediocre artist. And that happens, you get that kind of feeling. And one can get *so* despondent and melancholy and *(lowering his voice, almost choking the word out)* bellicose. And, boy, do I get bellicose.

But can't someone in your privileged sort of position afford to indulge himself in a little breast-beating?

(Genuinely astonished) Do you *really* believe that?

No, of course not. You're just as entitled to be nagged by self-doubts as anyone else; it was a leading question.

Really though, I think the greatest problem comes in wondering why I think that any of what I write should be of any import to anybody. And that's something I find more and more—that my contribution isn't enough.

But that's a problem of your own making.

Oh, quite. That dissatisfaction, it's an old quandary that all writers come across all the time. It's certainly nothing new; it seems to follow the integral feelings of most writers.

Perhaps your uncertainty and self-doubt are in fact your leading edge?

It *seems* to be so. It seems to be my one focus. Uncertainty? Yes, if there's one thing I've contributed, it's a great dollop of uncertainty *(laughs)*. For better or worse.

There again, artistic certainty can be boring, as some would say it's been in Dylan's case since he "found" God.

Although I must say I can see, I can feel exactly what brought that about.

Talking of other people who possessed a strength of purpose you find wanting in yourself, have any particular models? I don't necessarily mean in terms of their lifestyles.

No, I understand perfectly what you're saying. No, I think I'm very happy with the problems that I have in my own way of living. Day to day is very enjoyable for me and has been for a couple of years now, although I must admit that at one time my lifestyle was far over and above what anybody would sensibly inflict on themselves. But at the moment it's a rush, and it's really very enjoyable. Growing up with my son is one of the greatest enjoyments that I have.

But on an aesthetic level—no, *no (conclusively)*, I'm quite happy with my lot as a writer. I would really be nervous if I didn't have the uncertainties and the problems that I do have. I would dread feeling that complacent.

But do specific media-related problems frustrate you? "Scary Monsters" was finished months ago and still isn't released. Does that kind of thing annoy you, that lack of immediacy in communicating to your audience?

Oh God, yes. That sort of thing is just horrendous. Obviously I've already got a backlog of stuff I want to record, which I guess I'll start doing after Christmas. But I think it only becomes a drag for reasons of personal satisfaction, because the material isn't disposed of, swept out of the way so I can get on with something else.

But as far as the actual songs themselves are concerned, I don't think they're written with any particular timespan in mind. For me I don't think it would really matter whether they'd been released two years ago or two years forward. I think they're pieces of music I could listen to anytime. But I have to take that into consideration these days when I record something, as to whether or not I would want to listen to it again in a few year's time.

I try not to write as immediately as I once used to. There was a time when I was very keen to write songs that had a very definite edge to them, like all of "Diamond Dogs" comes over in a completely different light. It still has a validity, a strong one, but at the time and for a couple of years after it felt as if it was firmly slotted into that particular period. I had a thing about trying to write every year about that year, but I've loosened up now, I think . . . (*Coco appears at the foot of the stage pointing at her watch*)

Got a last one?

Any message for the folks back home?

Oh God, don't you dare.

Only kidding.

After I've stopped the tape, Bowie and I surface as if from deep trance. He asks if he can look at my copious but unused notes.

"It's a bloody thesis!" he exclaims.

"Well, what did you expect?"

"But don't you think I'm entitled to make similar preparations of my own?"

"Of course," I reply, "but it never happens that way, does it?"

"Shame really. I must say I wasn't looking forward to this at all, but have been pleasantly surprised at how it's gone."

Outside the theatre the inevitable limo arrives and, rather ridiculously, accelerates briskly away from the deserted sidewalk.

David Bowie is an intelligent, articulate and fascinating man who is still writing messages to himself and sealing them in bottles. It's an obsessively private process that for obvious reasons he offers up for public scrutiny. Whatever he may think or feel, Bowie has done both good things and bad things. He has also done a lot more of the blue than he may ever surmise.

Unsuspectingly I'm sure, Bowie positively leaks loneliness; it wraps itself around him like a clammy shroud. But the man is driven, and it's surely no accident that on "Scary Monsters" he sings Tom Verlaine's "Kingdom Come" with such unguarded passion:

"Well I'll be breaking these rocks until the kingdom comes,
And cuttin' this hay until the kingdom comes.
Yes I'll be breaking these rocks until the kingdom comes.
It's my price to pay until the kingdom comes."

Such is the alternately frustrating and rewarding lot of the long-distance creative person and such is David Bowie's typically reflective portrait of himself the artist as a now not so young man. You must make of both whatever you will.

THE FACE INTERVIEW

David Thomas | May 1983, *The Face* (UK)

By 1983, David Bowie had been around long enough as a recording artist to find himself being interviewed by journalists who had idolized him as children. David Thomas of British style bible *The Face* was one such person ("I used to hero-worship him").

Interestingly, '83 was the year that, for the first time, many of his former disciples started to feel disillusioned with Bowie. A purported $17.5 million-deal with EMI America saw Bowie begin to make music of a pedestrian and crowd-pleasing nature hitherto unimaginable for him. Or as Bowie puts it herein, "I'm quite happy to find myself involved with . . . clichés at this time." It certainly worked: Bowie was transformed by that year's *Let's Dance* album from a middle-ranker into a global star.

Although Bowie was both raking in cash and losing touch with his muse, he wasn't losing touch with reality. When asked by Thomas the crime that offends him most, his answer could have come straight out of the mouths of The Clash.

Some context to a couple of references: in "Kooks," Bowie's *Hunky Dory* paean to his son (variously known as Zowie, Joe, and Duncan), the narrator promises to throw his child's homework on the fire if it gets him down; George Underwood is the former Bowie schoolmate who, courtesy of a playground fight, is responsible for Bowie's mismatching pupils.

Note: for "Nick" read "Nic" (Roeg). —Ed.

David Bowie arrived back in the spotlight on a wet morning in March. He was using Claridges Hotel as his base for interviews and a press conference to announce his British tour dates, but he didn't appear to be staying there. Cabbies will tell you he still has a house in Chelsea. Bowie had a ruddy tan, having just returned from filming the "Let's Dance" video in Australia. He revealed at the press conference that he had spent the past year there and in the South Pacific. "I can afford to live a traveller's life now," he beamed, "but without the baggage of rock'n'roll." He seemed at ease in his Armani suit and looked much fitter than the emaciated white figure of old, lending credence to his claims of rising at 6:30 and going to bed at ten every day. With two films—*The Hunger* and *Merry Christmas, Mr. Lawrence*—set for release this year plus a new album co-produced by Nile Rodgers of Chic and a world tour beginning this month in Frankfurt, Bowie is going to need his new vitality. He need not, however, worry about ticket sales—over 100,000 applications for the London dates were received within a day of the box office opening! Nor are finances a problem: for one concert this summer in California promoted by Apple founder Stephen Wozniak where Bowie will headline over Stevie Nicks and John Cougar he is said to be getting over a million dollars. David Thomas met Bowie a few days after the press conference. He reports that Bowie's face still looks remarkably unlined, although it has become stronger with age (he is 36 years old). He was in good humour for the interview and his only apparent vice was a strong need for Marlboro cigarettes. Like all good actors, noted Thomas, he has a very attractive voice; regardless of what he's saying, he sounds sympathetic. They spoke for an hour, and Bowie was in the mood to say a great deal . . .

David Thomas: I was very impressed with the way you handled the press conference. They always seem to be like bearbaiting—do you enjoy them?

David Bowie: It's an extraordinary experience. I'm not at all fond of that situation, but *(smiles)* I was willing to give EMI every cooperation. We are . . . new to each other.

Was the move from RCA the cutting of the final link with a long drawn-out past?

It was just a question of non-cooperation with each other by the end of that contract. It was a ten year experience; just a weeny bit too long. And the turnover of personnel at RCA was just so absurd that it was no longer possible to have any kind of . . . there was no continuity.

At the moment, it seems to me, the climate is riper for the kind of work that you're doing, particularly in America where the kids who copied you have, ironically, opened up the market.

Absolutely, that has happened. Unfortunately, now that I've dropped synthesizers I suppose I'm going to have to start finding a new avenue for myself.

To go back a bit: the first time you ever crossed my path was when I was 13—I was exactly 13 when Ziggy came out . . .

Ouch! *(laughs)*.

. . . and I remember seeing "Starman" on Top of the Pops and thinking that it was something totally different. Were you aware of the effect that that was going to have?

I was incredibly excited by it at the time. The band and I—well, the band reluctantly—but I was very aware of how extraordinary the whole thing must have looked from the outside. And I felt very happy and excited about it because I thought, "This really is new." As though new was the be all and end all. When you're first entering into rock'n'roll, that's what you really want.

But why was it *then* that it all happened? You'd had "Space Oddity," but apart from that you'd been going for years and years as David Jones and then suddenly—bang! Why then?

I think it was because I was changing the entire context of English rock. It just felt so radical—completely against everything that was happening at the time with the denims and the whole laid-back atmosphere and the hardest thing out was Heavy Metal, I suppose.

There was T. Rex . . .

But there again Marc and I were . . . there was a bunch of us. For myself I was just very fortunate in terms of making the bigger impact before a lot of the others. But of course there was Roxy and so on, and we'd all been gigging around, aware of each other and aware that we all had almost the same idea of what kind of impression we wanted to make, and that was a throwback to art-school rock, I suppose. It was just, sweep out everything that was old and just be anti everything that's been before.

Ironically, now you're talking about putting content back in place of style . . .

Yeah.

But actually that empty artfulness is something that could be laid at your's and Bryan Ferry's doors.

(*Laughs*)Not for the first time, probably! Yes, that's a little demoralising in a way, that the changes I make are seen as being artful, in terms of *that* kind of artful—like the Artful Dodger or something.

Perhaps it's just that by the time that they're copied, they're copied as a pose.

For me it's just a question of finding there's little steam left in the last thing that I did to keep me happy as a writer. I'm not . . . even as a painter I would also flip about from one style to another, or change from oil to acrylics or suddenly just want to do little miniature watercolours. I've never explored anything to the point where it could be my life's work. I was never that kind of artist. And the same in music or rock, it was far more encouraging to me to find that when you are an artist you can turn your hand to anything, in any style. Once you have the tools then all the art forms are the same in the end.

You said at the press conference, talking about the pressures of that period, that you had a very low opinion of yourself, that your self-esteem was very low. What did you mean by that?

Actually, on reflection my opinion of myself at that time wasn't very low. I think it was far too high. I found that I had put myself into a situation where everything that I was doing and saying, in terms of my own personal life was inconsequential or a non-sequitur. And I brought it upon myself because I had cocooned myself and put myself in that Los Angeles scene, and now I'm just very surprised, knowing myself, that I allowed that to happen.

I remember reading interviews with you that gave the impression of

there being no continuity between your inner self and what you happened to be saying.

Yes. I mean, as an artist I was picking up on things in the air and writing them down. And then I would, in my very stoned state, intellectualise on those things afterwards, which was an absolute mistake, for an artist to intellectualise about his own work. But I didn't have the facility . . . I was completely fractured as a thinker.

There was that Charles Shaar Murray remark about wondering whether, if you peeled all the characters off David Bowie, there'd be a real David Bowie there at all.

That's right, and that became a concern of mine. That's why I pulled myself back into Europe.

One thing that's always interested me . . . if you look back at old photos, or old album covers, what do you think when you see yourself on, say "Pin Ups"? What do you think about the guy looking back at you?

(*Laughter*) I think, "Good Lord, how can you live looking like that!" I think that visually the whole thing was an awful lot of fun. It's almost Dada-esque. Everything about it was so unreal. I'm really quite proud of all that. But it's well and truly over. I find it hard to connect with it any more. I can't relate to it any more. I can't conjure up the enthusiasm I must have had for it all at the time. I can't even see how I could have been that enthusiastic about it. It's rather amusing. I think for my own survival as a person I've become fairly objective and detached about it.

Again, I noticed at the conference that the one thing you didn't answer was when somebody asked you about the '76 tour and your remark at the time about Britain being ripe for civil war. And there was the salute from the back of the Merc and so on. When you look back at that, or the famous Michael Watts interview on the cover of *Melody Maker,* what do you think of the person who said those things? Do you agree with any of them? Did you believe them then?

I almost had an antenna. I mean I did have an antenna. I still do, I think, for the angst of the times, or the zeitgeist. The zeitgeist is the best word.

The atmosphere I feel very strongly, wherever I am. And I felt those things in the air. That whole thing about the Nazi stuff was just prior to the real emergence of the National Front in England, and I just felt it. I was totally unaware of that situation taking place in England, because I hadn't been in England in years. I felt it and then, as I say, because I was so fragmented and broken up it seemed to fall in with my own ideas of the mythological Arthurian Britain, which I was incredibly interested in—the Englishness of the English and all that. And it just seemed to make sense at the time. It was more the mythology than the actualisation, or the formation of such a horrendous thing as the new Nazi Party. By that same token, now I look back and I think "How incredibly irresponsible." But I was in no state to be responsible. I was the least responsible person that I can imagine at the time.

Have you ever actually had therapy or some kind of mental treatment? There seems to have been a point in your life at which you took responsibility for yourself. (He nods in agreement at the last sentence.)

No, I must say that I've always been incredibly wary of therapy. I was just given the resolve by a couple of friends of mine to leave the States. I mean I walked through the '76 tour blind. I must say, I don't remember a thing.

They were very alienating shows to watch.

I definitely was without feeling. It was almost zombie-like on that tour. And then I just ensconced myself in Berlin, in the apartment I had there.

Were there friends there?

Yes, my PA was the most important person—Coco Schwabe. She just gave me a series of dressing downs. I mean, it was almost a question of, "Come on! Snap out of it!" (laughs) It really worked like that, and it did work. I did also, as much as I could have; I had a positive approach to wanting to get better.

Didn't you have a heart attack at one stage?

No, never. That was delightful, but untrue. It was very romantic, but I've got a very sound heart!

And then, on "Low" and "Heroes," there was a progression from that

terrible negativity on "Low" to the feeling that there might be some sort of hope or purpose to it all.

Yes, and that arc is continuing with what I'm doing now.

It was noticeable by the '78 tour—the difference between you then and in '76 was astonishing. It was friendly show.

I was feeling pretty good with myself by that time. I felt I was getting quite on top of the situation. And now I've had these other few years of respite and I've had time to make up my mind about whether I want to continue with music in any way, shape, or form.

Do you consider yourself to be "a musician," in the sense of a guy who picks up a guitar and plays for his own pleasure?

For this last album I have been. It's the first time that I've fallen into that role for a long time, where I've actually sat down and written songs on the piano. I guess I'm a composer rather than a musician.

You made a remark in your press conference about moving back to "helpful music." What do you mean by helpful? I mean, I know what I get out of Van Morrison, or Otis Redding, or whatever . . .

Exactly, that's it. That's the feeling. It's an emotionally uplifting experience, rather than an emotionally disturbing experience, which I'm quite good at producing. But for me, it's giving me no satisfaction right now to have those disturbing experiences. There's a slew of disturbing experiences to put oneself through without having to write them and create them to create a disturbing experience. I need to write music that puts things very, very simply on the line, to take note of very obvious problems and put them into a one-to-one relationship.

It's love and life and death, in the end.

It is. It's as cliched at that. And I'm quite happy to find myself involved with those cliches at this time. There's not a small amount of truth in cliches. They spring from some eternal truth.

Do you feel more settled in yourself, as it were in accepting the basic

rules of life? Because one might not necessarily have thought that from the early albums.

No. Absolutely. It was quite the thing to break every rule. To find out what happens when you break the rules. And what happens is that you create a chaotic situation. Musically it can be very interesting to break the rules, but I think that now popular music has moved somewhere out of just being music.

It seems to be going through a very mannerist phase now.

Yes.

That disturbs me, because the things that have ever been at all valuable about pop music have been the guts (*strong agreement from DB*), whether it's been Sam Cooke, or Otis, or Pete Townshend, or whoever . . . and now it just all seems to be hairstyles.

It's definitely going through a silly stage, but I think it's a short-lived one. Again, I can only relate it to me personally, and what I need to do is to be able to hear my songs and find some resolve in them.

Who are you singing to in "Let's Dance"?

It's an imaginary person, really . . . I wish I could say . . . I think at the moment because there's no constant companion in my life or a great love, or whatever, the only great affection that I live with, on a day-to-day basis, is with my son. I think he's been a pivotal reason for why I'm writing about such a two-way relationship thing.

How old is he now?

He's 12, so he's at that very interesting age.

Would you still sing "Kooks" to him?

Oh yes, he's heard that. He used to hear it and just think it was lovely, but now he plays it to me when I make him do his homework (*roars with laughter*). He says, "Just a minute, Dad. Do you remember writing this?" I think he thinks it's quite sweet and funny. There's incredible love between us. I think that's the important thing. And really he's opened me up to wanting to think about the future.

He travels with you but you seem very careful to keep him out of the public eye.

Absolutely.

It's one of the classically difficult things to grow up the child of somebody famous.

It really is, yes, it really is. He's not really been involved in the music thing at all. He's brought up for the majority of the time in Switzerland, and my lifestyle is such that I'm rarely in contact with that thing any more, so he's seen as little of it as I have over the past five or six years, which is a very healthy thing. The thing that we both have done a lot is travel. We both travel an enormous amount. Which for him has been such an advantage.

It must also enable you to get away from the kind of situations where you are David Bowie, famous star.

Oh, absolutely. I just don't have this. It's not something I've done for years. The only time I'm really confronted by all that is when I'm doing something public like *The Elephant* Man, or whatever. Even my recordings are done in a very leisurely and "real" way.

Does your son remind you of yourself as a child?

Yes, very much so. Except he's not as shy as I was. He's far more gregarious than I ever was.

When you were a kid growing up, did you have any awareness of what lay ahead? Did you have either a burning ambition, or a feeling of being different from your friends, or any inkling of what lay ahead?

I had every inkling. I knew from when I was about my son's age now exactly what would be happening to me; that I was going to do something very important. I didn't quite know what. At the time I thought I was going to be a great painter, but that changed in my teens.

What did your friends think about that?

I never told anybody. I never told anybody that I was going to be important. There was one other person in my class at school I thought was going to be more important than me *(laughs)*. His name is George Underwood, and I think indeed he is more important, but he hasn't been recognised as such. But I really thought that it was my task to do something important and make a statement about something or other.

Did your parents understand that attitude?

Yeah, I mean I talked to them later about it. Never when I was 12 or anything. It almost seemed sort of wrong to think like that. I wasn't very forthcoming with anybody.

Are you more forthcoming now?

Much more.

Who do you talk to now? Do you have close friends?

Yes, I have a circle of friends that are, again, far removed from this profession, who are writers and painters generally.

So the woodcut exhibition in Germany that you've been invited to contribute to—is that almost more of a concern of yours than the fact that you're playing a series of concerts?

No, I think that's a temporary delight. I've never done anything publicly before with my paintings or any of my artwork. I think I'm just delighted to have been asked to be included in it. There are some wonderful artists around, but actually not many working in woodcuts.

You've had stuff of yours in tour programmes before, haven't you?

Yes there was a Mishima painting I did. Or was it Iggy Pop? Iggy asked me whether I'd let him have the portrait I did of him for the back of his book, but those are the only two that I can think of.

Do you still carry a travelling library around with you?

How did you know about that?

Because when I was a teenager I think I read every single story that ever appeared on David Bowie.

Good Lord. Do you know I took—this is very funny—when I went to see Nick Roeg for the film *(The Man Who Fell To Earth)* down in New Mexico, I took with me hundreds and hundreds of books. It was one of those things where I was (chuckles) . . . quite awful. I was trying to find a book for Nick to refer to on alchemy or something. And I had these cabinets—you're quite right it was a travelling library— and they were rather like the boxes that amplifiers get packed up in, and I was going through all these books and they were pouring out all over the floor—there were just mountains of books. And Nick was sitting there watching me and he said, "Your great problem, David, is that you don't read *enough*." And I didn't even think it was funny until months later. I was so sort of gung-ho that I really thought he was serious. And I felt so depressed and I thought, "What else should I read?" It didn't occur to me at the time that it was a joke. I don't travel with those books any more! Although I must say that because of that period I have an extraordinarily good collection of books.

Was that a compensation, perhaps, for having left school quite young and not going to college or anything?

Yes, I mean, I always continued with my own self-education, sometimes in the wrong areas. I'm still an avid reader. I read continually. I'm never without a book. I much prefer the company of a good book to a television programme, unless the television programme is really good.

Did you see the one on Nick Roeg the other day?

I had it taped. Is it good?

Yes. I wasn't in the best mood to see it, having gone through a spate of fairly heavy awareness of mortality for the past few months, and then to see a programme about Nick Roeg was . . . We were talking about all those cliches. He deals with them on such an immediate level. He just socks you. You can't escape.

Absolutely. There is a very strong alchemy in his movies. They are magical. You come out winded from the experience of working with him. He is an old warlock. But I'd work for him again, any time. I'm prepared for him now. That's . . . ooh . . . *(laughs)* . . . no, maybe I'm not fully prepared for him, but I'm better prepared for him now than I was then.

What are you reading at the moment?

Oh Lord . . . *Setting The World On Fire* by Angus Wilson. What else have I just read? Theroux's thing, *The Mosquito Coast* and there was something else . . . *The Rose Of Tibet,* can't remember who the author was.

Do you read two or three books . . .

. . . at the same time? Yeah. And they're all open somewhere.

Your film *Merry Christmas Mr. Lawrence.* . . . Personally I'm looking forward to that much more than *The Hunger*.

So am I, and quite rightly because *Merry Christmas Mr. Lawrence* is a much better film.

Also you're not being asked to be a freak or an elephant man, or a spaceman—just a straightforward human being. Are you confident of your own ability to act a character which is not in any way . . .

I'm really happy with my performance in it. Yes, that was a very good role to have been offered. It was tremendous. It has also made me become very enthusiastic about my possibilities as an actor if I really want to pursue that. I've been more drawn to wanting to direct. I do find it very boring, generally, acting. Probably because I'm not convinced that I'm any good at it. I think that being a typical Capricorn, if I'm not good at something I'm very reluctant to do it. You sort of go away and practise until you're quite good at it and then you say, "Oh yes, I can do that!" It's very much a Capricorn trait.

The other Capricorn trait, of course, is the survival and the hard work—that no matter how fucked-up you are the job does get done somehow.

Yes—are you a Capricorn?

Yes.

Ah, yes . . . and shyness is another thing with Capricorns I've met. I think they're basically incredibly shy people. In a social situation I'm absolutely at a loss. I loathe parties because I always feel so uptight. I never know what to say. I sort of hang about on the edge. My remedy used to be to get absolutely stoned.

The other thing is that if people see your picture taken at a party that gives the impression . . .

That one spends one's entire time doing that. That's right.

How do you lead your life in Switzerland? What are you like in the morning?

I felt very odd saying this the other day, but I *was* asked. I actually do get up at 6:30 in the morning.

There were a lot of disbelieving hacks at that point.

I know, I know, but I do get up at around 6:30. Funnily enough on this trip I've been getting up around three o'clock in the bloody morning. I just cannot get to sleep at the right time. It's all gone. By five in the afternoon I'm finished. Apart from one night I just can't stay up past nine. . . . I get up about 6:30 and I generally go for a walk. I live in the woods. And then I spend most of the morning writing. Either just notes or, well, I've been playing around with the idea of a musical stage presentation other than a rock show . . .

Which has been quite a longstanding ambition—there was the *1984* idea.

Yes, I know, well I've kind of got down to it now and it's looking quite good. I carry on a fair amount of letter writing to friends in various parts of the world and get all that kind of stuff done. And often it's been the ski season when I'm at home, so I spend the majority of my afternoons skiing. That's when I'm not making films or recording or doing stuff like this. Day to day I don't think there's ever really two days the same.

Are you someone who has treasured possessions. If I was Roy Plomley doing Desert Island Discs, what would you take?

My library *(laughter)*. I think that's about the only thing. I'm very acquisitive when it comes to books. I think that's the main thing. When I'm relaxed, what I do is read.

The other change in your circumstances over the past few years has been the move towards taking care of business for yourself. Was there a terrible shock when you woke up at the end of Mainman and found the cupboard was bare?

Well, yes. I mean, that was most discouraging. But I've put my business very much in order, and I am healthily well-off.

The situation with "Let's Dance" is a bit similar to the Stones' position with "Some Girls." EMI must be hoping it's going to break you back into the American market the way "Some Girls" did with the Stones.

Absolutely. The kind of enthusiasm they've shown is peculiar for me. I mean, I've never had that kind of thing shown to me for years.

Is that anything to do with the extremely large sums of money that have been rumoured . . .

Rumour, they remain!

Presumably you're not going to say what the true figure was.

Oh Lord no!

Does your back catalogue sell? Do people go back to catch up on things that were too much for them when they first came out?

No, that doesn't happen to me much. Although I met a couple of fans the other day. I went to EMI to do something or other and met them. And they had "Diamond Dogs," and had only just found it. They were fifteen or sixteen years old or something. And I found that delightful. I just wondered if they'd—I guess they'd just have to—think of it in a contemporary situation. But I don't know how the music seems to them. Does it sound new-ish?

Well, those albums were so much a product of their times.

Absolutely, they don't have that longevity. They're not classic statements that go on through the years. They are like polaroids. You can divide up the last ten years in those albums.

Yes, I remember, we all used to rush out, buy them on the first day they came out, play them rotten for six months and then . . .

. . . That was it. Exactly. They did work like that. They were very immediate.

Whereas I found "Let's Dance" much less immediate. But the more I listen to it the more it grows.

That's exactly the quality I wanted to bring into my music at this stage of my life. I want something now that makes a statement in a more universal, international field.

That's also true of the re-recording of "Cat People." The first version has that standard Moroder sound and hits you very hard straight-off, and when I heard the new one I thought, "He's fucked up a good song." But then I heard it three or four times and it made sense.

Yes, I took the instruments away. They're not quite so integrally important to the music on this album. It's far more just a very simple base to put the lyrics and the melody on. They don't weave quite such a magic spell over the construction of the lyrics, or lend an ambience to the lyrics. They get the chords right and that's about all I wanted to do.

What about the band that you're working with now?

There's Stevie Ray Vaughan—he's on guitar. And Carlos Alomar I've got back in from the old days. I like working with Carlos. The simple reason is that he knows all my songs, and it's far easier having a member of the band who knows everything. He knows every arrangement.

I was quite sorry to see the old rhythm section go.

What, George (Murray) and Dennis (Davis)? Well, George is now living in Los Angeles on a permanent basis and doesn't seem to want to be involved with music. And Dennis Davis—because I can't give him work, I can't expect him to hang around for five years or whatever—has gone with Stevie Wonder. He's done at least half the tracks on the last two or three Wonder albums and he's doing all the tour work now.

There were stories of you taking piles of old Stax soul singles to listen to before the sessions for "Let's Dance."

No, actually the stuff I was listening to before "Let's Dance" was much older than that. I didn't actually take things to the studio. I'm the best audience for music when I'm working on something else. When I'm working on a film I find I really listen to music. When I'm writing music something awful happens. I start analysing everything I listen to; I can't listen to the radio. Anything that I hear on the radio I immediately take to pieces and find all its influences—where it came from, exactly how they constructed the thing in the studio, what equalisation they put on the drums. That's awful—you know what I mean?

That's the curse of professionalism.

It really is—it's such a drag.

Once people get into the music business they hear the sound first, and the music second.

I hate that, and I find it very hard to be an audience. But when one's going off to the South Pacific, or something, you think, "Well, what tapes shall I take?" And I thought that the only things I could really take that I wasn't going to pull apart, were things like the Alan Freed Rock 'n' Roll Orchestra and Buddy Guy, Elmore James . . . I'm trying to think of all the stuff that I took . . . Albert King, Stan Kenton—I took a lot of Stan Kenton. I took them because I wanted something to listen to that I wasn't going to get bored with. Something that I could play over and over again. You know, when you're in the jungle and you've got half an hour before they do a lighting set-up and you're not going to write or read. And that was the only stuff that I could actually listen to more than four or five times. And when I was listening to it on the island I started thinking, "Why is this stuff so good? Why does it stand up to continual play, and is that something that I want to do?" I won't say that I've succeeded, but I feel as though I'm on the right track.

Will the stage show reflect that? Is it going to be much more of a straight musical show, or will there still be a strong performance element.

There's a very strong performing element. A gig used to be referred to as a date, between . . . you know, audience and performer. Between is the key word. I want it to have much more of a relationship backwards and forwards.

But that's always been your greatest gift—to stand on a stage and not do very much, but draw everybody in. Have you always been aware of that ability to communicate?

Yes, there's a physical vocabulary that's used on stage. I have Lindsay Kemp to thank for that. He taught me such a lot about keeping movements to the minimum, but making every movement important.

Is it strange looking out and seeing your past—little groups of people dressed up like Ziggy or Thin White Duke clones in the audience?

Yeah. I'm picking up bits and pieces of clothing for the next tour, and I've found something that I used to wear that is absolutely right now! I'm not saying what it is, but I guess if the audience go through their wardrobe before they come to the show they might pick on the right thing (laughs).

Do you have any sense of rivalry with other artists or other people?

I used to have a very strong rivalry—we were almost like sparring partners—with Mick (Jagger). But that's mellowed out over the past few years as we've realised, I guess, that we've established everything that we thought we wanted.

When was the last time that you were really angry?

(*Long pause*). That's an interesting one . . . we're not going to talk about RCA. I think that was my biggest anger over the last few years. I can't remember exactly the last time I was angry. That seems to have been another emotion I've always been able to control. I probably should let fly a bit more, but I don't. I'll take any amount of . . . I find everything so transient that it doesn't really bother me. But the one thing that I do remember getting specifically angry about was RCA's reaction to the "Low" album. I went into incredible anger first and then depression for months. I mean, it was really awful the treatment they gave to that album and their reaction to it. It was hideous, because I knew how wrong they were about it. They had obviously lost every idea of what modern music was all about, because that was . . . in any other context it was a super piece of writing. It was just great.

Do you still have your fear of flying?

No, I've been flying constantly for the past five years.

How did you get over that?

It just seemed so idiosyncratic . . . so stupid. It's much safer flying than it is driving and I drive a lot. The first time I flew was for Iggy Pop. There was no way that I could get to do his tour. There were no ships going and I didn't want to let him down. That was the first flight I took after all that time, to go and be a pianist.

What was the first flight like?

It was wonderful! It went extremely well. I've now been in the cockpit quite a few times and I think that anyone who is scared, if they were to sit in on both take-off and the landing, I think they'd feel a lot better about it, I really do. Although I've been in a cockpit a couple of times with some American pilots and I've absolutely freaked that these guys have been given that authority. Some of the cowboy pilots bring those things down like broncos. *(Puts on broad Texan accent)* They say, "Jesus, what a night I had last night," and I think, "Oh, my God!"

One final, idiosyncratic question. What do you think is the worst crime that could possibly be committed? What is the crime that offends you most?

(Another long pause) Seeing a man humble himself in his capacity as a worker to somebody else, and having to have that accepted as a given situation.

Seeing other people take shit.

Yes, I think that really is a crime, a continuing crime, that probably is the cause of more social problems than just about anything else.

And with that our formal conversation ended, apart from a brief discussion along the lines of "the worst flight I ever had" and a cheerful farewell. Bowie has a reputation, or has had in the past, for telling interviewers exactly what they want to hear and flattering them into thinking that their suppositions are more accurate than they may actually be. Not once in our conversation did he disagree strongly with anything that I said. It has also been said that anything he says at one moment may not be true the next. At the very least he has tremendous surface charm, and at best he struck me as a man who had been through some extremely bad, dangerous and distorted times and come out the other side, if not unscathed, then a great deal wiser for the experience. In the days when I used to hero-worship him, he probably wasn't worth it. But I'd say he deserves one's admiration now.

SERMON FROM THE SAVOY

Charles Shaar Murray | September 29, 1984, *New Musical Express* (UK)

This interview is much better than the album it was intended to promote.

In September 1984, Bowie followed up his successful-but-empty *Let's Dance* album with *Tonight*, a motley collection containing two new Bowie songs bulked out with cover versions, half-hearted collaborations, and exhumations of stuff he'd never previously felt merited a place on his albums. An artistic low-tide mark, it was the sort of meaningless product of which it had previously seemed Bowie was incapable. The impression of a lost artist was confirmed by Bowie's reasoning for releasing the record: "I wanted to keep my hand in" is hardly the noblest creative impetus.

The blurb to this *New Musical Express* double-pager carried the proud boast that it was the only official interview granted by Bowie on a visit to Britain. One suspects that this was due to Bowie being nervous about the work being subjected to too much critical scrutiny, although that didn't stop the artist stooping to fishing for compliments from his interlocutor ("What did you think of the album, by the way?"). It also seems significant that his chosen audience was Charles Shaar Murray, a man known at the time for his undiscriminating partiality to Bowie's work, as caustically noted in the paper's letters page at the time.

Murray was pliant. He describes *Tonight* herein as an album "with a dizzying variety of mood and technique" of which he "approved heartily." Even Bowie is more honest on that score, acknowledging that his music is currently "staid." However, Murray's journalistic integrity seems to compel him to elsewhere inject an ambivalence about the health of Bowie's art (see the comment about the possibly illusory nature of Bowie looking like he knows exactly what he's doing and where he's going).

Murray also elicits some interesting comments from Bowie about the process of composition, the lack of the confessional and the political in his songs, his thoughts on organised religion, and his observations on the rapidly changing racial situation in his home country as exemplified by a new musical movement. —Ed.

The week before Carnival: London is gasping like a beached fish. All along the Strand is sweat and dust and air hanging heavy with the promise of coming thunder, but the foyer of the Savoy is a world away from the oven of Trafalgar Square just a couple of minutes down the road.

Cool and dark and marbled, it has something of the hallucinatory ambience of a mirage: step inside and you almost expect it to disappear, leaving you back on the blazing pavement.

In the tea room, with its vaulted ceilings and tromp l'oeil murals, an almost perfect insulation exists. Outside, the miners' strike could boil over in open insurrection: Maggie Thatcher could declare martial law and no one inside would even notice. No one speaks above the polite murmur; the walls seem to swallow sound, filtering and smoothing anything which would upset the equilibrium.

The Savoy is the next best thing to being underwater.

At three in the afternoon, a blue Mercedes pulls up outside and David Bowie walks briskly and decisively through the foyer and into the tea room, his destination a table tucked inconspicuously away to one side of the staircase. Bowie moves everywhere like that, with the calm and determined air of a man who knows exactly what he is doing and where he is going at any given moment. Whether this is actually the case is another matter entirely.

He is wearing—starting at the ground and working upwards—blue shoes, black slacks, a studded belt, a white shirt with a spidery black Picasso print and a crucifix on a neck chain. He is suffering from a summer cold brought on by a sweat-soaked day's filming in the sweltering confines of the Wag Club in Wardour Street where a guest appearance on a US MTV gala had been laid down the previous week.

The principal items on Bowie's agenda are the release of "Blue Jean," his first new single of '84, a highly unorthodox video based around the song and directed by the young British film-maker Julien Temple (who directed The Sex Pistols' *Great Rock 'N' Roll Swindle* movie and has since become the cutting edge of radical style and content in the pop video racket), plus "Tonight," a new album with a dizzying variety of mood and technique.

Bowie arms himself with a fresh pack of Marlboros, a pot of decaffeinated coffee and a sandwich and settles down to explain why—after the numerous exertions of 1983, a year in which he released his best-selling

"Let's Dance," starred in two feature films and toured the world—he made an album this year in the first place.

"I suppose the most obvious thing about the new album," he begins, "is that there's not the usual amount of writing on it from me. I wanted to keep my hand in, so to speak, and go back in the studio—but I didn't really feel as if I had enough new things of my own because of the tour. I can't write on tour, and there wasn't really enough preparation afterwards to write anything that I felt was really worth putting down, and I didn't want to put out things that 'would do' so there are two or three that I felt were good things to do and the other stuff . . .

"What I suppose I really wanted to do was to work with Iggy again, that's something I've not done for a long time. And Iggy wanted us to do something together. We're ultimately leading up, I hope, to me doing his next album. We've been talking about it for a year or so and we've got him off the road. He's not on the road now and he won't be going back on the road for a while."

The star-crossed Iggy Pop—James Osterberg in civilian life—was one of Bowie's early heroes. His group The Stooges were the last word in late '60s Detroit dementia, and Pop's blistering, demonic stage act was a primary source of inspiration for Bowie's own characterisation of Ziggy Stardust. When his own career took off, Bowie sought out Iggy and signed him to his then management company Mainman, who in turn signed the band to CBS, for whom Bowie mixed Iggy's "Raw Power" album.

The association didn't work out, but the two remained in contact, reuniting for two enormously influential 1977 albums "The Idiot" and "Lust For Life," both of which combined Bowie's production and melody lines with Pop's scarifying lyrics and vocals.

Bowie's massive 1983 hit "China Girl" was drawn from "The Idiot," and now "Tonight" revisits two more songs from this period: the title tune and the savage "Neighbourhood Threat," as well as including two new collaborations by the pair and another song from Iggy's past, "Don't Look Down," written in collaboration with guitarist James Williamson.

"I don't think touring was having a good effect on him, particularly on his writing. He wasn't getting any done. He's always had an incredibly loyal following, but that's not really enough. Living continually from one gig to the next just made him feel that he was falling out of time, because he had no time to write anything any more: it just seemed to be a question of getting from Akron to Philadelphia and doing the rounds; I think 'China Girl' helped him out a lot that way, and now he's writing quite prolifically. Hopefully, we should be able to mull through about 30 or 40 songs by the time we come to record.

"I think more than anything else I write the musical side of the new songs; we worked very much the way that we did on 'Lust For Life' and 'The Idiot,' and I often gave him a few anchor images that I wanted him to play off and he would take them away and start free-associating and I would then put *that* together in a way that I could sing. Rather than write straightforward songs, he would do collective imagery, and we'd rearrange things from there."

So it's nothing as simplistic as Iggy becoming your lyricist?

"No, not at all. I think it worked out around 50/50 lyrics on most of the songs, but Jimmy's work stands out most obviously on 'Tumble And Twirl' (a surging, Afro-tinged snapshot of Bali and Java). "I think that's obviously his line of humour. The lines about the T-shirts and the part about the sewage floating down the hill . . . we had a holiday after the tour, Jimmy and his girlfriend Suchi, Coco and I—we went to Bali and Java, and in Java particularly the very rich oil magnates of Java have these incredible colonial-style houses with sewage floating down the hills into the jungle.

"That stayed with me, and watching films out in the garden projected on sheets. It felt so bizarre to sit there in the jungle watching movies at the end of the garden through monsoon weather with rain pouring down. Images of Brooke Shields . . . it was quite absurd."

"*I like the free world,*" sings Bowie in "Tumble And Twirl," a line less ironic than might at first be thought.

"I guess those circumstances make one quite fond of the 'free world' because a country like Java or Singapore is quite most definitely *not* free.

"There's an extraordinary split between one class and another, far more exaggerated than any class system in the West. If I had the choice between Singapore or Java, I'd pick England! That's what I meant by that line, but when put in a musical structure these things take on a life of their own—as we know from past experience!"

Two of the Iggy tunes—"Tonight," which is a duet with none other than Tina Turner, and "Don't Look Down"—receive reggae treatments, which is something of a surprise, because Bowie's only previous dabble with ital beats came on "Lodger's" "Yassassin," and Bowie stated at the time that he hadn't penetrated reggae and intended to leave it alone. What changed his mind about Jah Music?

"I think it was the drum machine!" He laughs loudly. "I was trying to rearrange 'Don't Look Down' and it wouldn't work. I tried it every-which-a-way. I tried it jazz-rock, I tried it as a march, and then I just hit on an old ska-sounding beat, and it picked up life. Taking energy away from the musical side of things reinforced the lyrics and gave them their own energy. I think working with Derek Bramble really helped a lot, because he played proper reggae bass lines . . ."

Derek Bramble is Bowie's newest collaborator, the former bassist with British pop soulsters Heatwave and more recently musical partners to ex-Linx frontman David Grant. Bowie was introduced to Bramble's work by his London PR Bernard Doherty, was intrigued and got in touch. Bramble made the album's reggae tunes possible, because most Americans can't play reggae to save their lives.

"I'm sure Dennis Davis won't mind me saying this" (Davis, now with Stevie Wonder, was Bowie's drummer from 'Young Americans' through to 'Scary Monsters') "but when we did 'Ashes To Ashes,' that beat was an old ska beat, but Dennis had an incredibly hard time with it, trying to play it and turn the beat backwards, and in fact we worked through the session and it wasn't turning out at all well, so I did it on a chair and a cardboard box and he took it home with him and learnt it for the next day. He really found it a problem. I've found that with American drummers, more so than with bass players. Where Derek can succeed is that he will leave a lot of spaces. He's not scared *not* to play a note. Omar, I must say, didn't have a problem."

Bowie's drummer for the new album is Omar Hakim, who featured on a couple of the "Let's Dance" tracks and who replaced Peter Erskine in Weather Report in the same shake-up wherein Victor Bailey replaced my man Jaco Pastorius.

"What did you think of the album, by the way?"

I tell him that I approved heartily, except for the rather iffy version of The Beach Boys' "God Only Knows." He chuckles a trifle defensively.

"Really? Oh—I knew you were going to say that."

However, the reinterpretation of Chuck Jackson's "I Keep Forgetting" is masterful.

"Oh good! Oh, you liked that! I've always wanted to do that song . . . I think that this album gave me a chance, like 'Pin Ups' did a few years ago, to do some covers that I always wanted to do. 'God Only Knows' I first did—or tried to do—with Ava Cherry and that crowd The Astronettes when I tried to develop them into a group. *Nothing* came of that! I still have the tapes, though. It sounded such a good idea at the time and I never had the chance to do it with anybody else again, so I thought I'd do it myself . . . it might be a bit saccharine, I suppose."

Bowie's reinterpretation of "Tonight" itself, apart from transmuting the song into reggae, changes the context considerably by omitting Pop's hair-raising prologue, which establishes that the song is being sung to a lover in the throes of a heroin overdose.

"That was such an idiosyncratic thing of Jimmy's that it seemed not part of my vocabulary. There was that consideration, and I was also doing it with Tina—she's the other voice on it—and I didn't want to inflict it on her either. It's not necessarily something that she would particularly agree to sing or be part of. I guess we changed the whole sentiment around. It still has that same barren feeling, though, but it's out of that specific area that I'm not at home in. I can't say that it's Iggy's world, but it's far more of Iggy's observation than mine."

Did you play on the album yourself?

"No, I didn't. Not at all. I very much left everybody else to it. I must say, I just came in with the songs and the ideas and how they should be played and then watched them put it all together. It was great!" He chuckles to himself. "I didn't work very hard in those terms. I feel very *guilty* about it!

I did five or six pieces of writing and I sing a lot, and Hugh Padgham (the engineer) and Derek put the sound together between them. It was nice not to be involved in that way."

It makes quite a change from the period between "Low" and "Monsters."

"Yes, I couldn't have been more dictatorial about it. . . . I feel that period coming on again now we've had a refreshing bash with other people's songs and other people playing the way they want to play. I feel I really want to do something probably with no more than myself and two other people, and build up tapes again. I haven't done that for such a long time.

"But I've got to a point that I really wanted to get to where it's really an organic sound, and it's mainly saxophones. I think there's only two lead guitar solos on it. No synthesisers to speak of, though there are probably a couple of *twing* sounds or something. It's really got the *band* sound that I wanted, the horn sound."

Funnily enough, the album's opener "Loving The Alien" feature some ah . . . ah . . . ah backing vocals that are reminiscent of Anderson's "O Superman."

"No, that's Philip Glass actually, more reminiscent of 'Einstein On The Beach,' but maybe Laurie was thinking also of something from that."

Both of the Bowie solo compositions from the album "Blue Jean" and "Loving The Alien" are astonishingly dissimilar to each other.

"Aren't they just! 'Blue Jean' reminds me of Eddie Cochran." He sings the opening lines of Cochran's "Somethin' Else" under his breath and follows it with the *"She's got evreh-thang"* line from "Blue Jean." "It was inspired from that Eddie Cochran feeling, but that of course is very Troggs as well. I dunno . . . it's quite eclectic, I suppose. What of mine isn't?

"Somebody once said—who was it? It's terribly important—that Harry Langdon, the silent comedian, cannot be taken on his own; you have to put him alongside that which went on around him, like Buster Keaton and Harold Lloyd and Chaplin. He can only be seen by reference, and somebody said that about me, which is probably very true. I kind of quite like that, actually, that you can't take me on my own. You can only use me as a form of reference!"

He bursts into such hearty laughter that *people actually start looking round.*

"Don't ask me! The older I get, the less I know about what I'm doing!"

Regaining composure, he continues, "I think this'll be the last album where I'm involved in this kind of thing. There's a particular sound I'm after that I haven't really got yet and I probably won't drop this search until I get it. I'll either crack it on the next album or just retire from it. I think I got quite close to it on 'Dancing With The Big Boys'—the Bowie/Pop collaboration that closes the album and occupies the B-side of 'Blue Jean'—which got somewhere near where I wanted it to be. I think I should be a bit more adventurous. That was quite an adventurous bit of writing in the sense that we didn't look for any standards. I got very *musical* over the last couple of years; I stayed away from experimentation. It's not helpful sometimes, although it's a good discipline.

"I really got into that: trying to write musically and develop things the way people used to write in the '50s, but in 'Big Boys' Iggy and I just broke away from all of that for the one track. That came nearer to the sound I was looking for than anything. I'd like to try maybe one more set of pieces like that. Whenever anyone asks me what the next album is going to be like, I invariably reply 'protest' because I have as little idea as anybody what comes next.

"I'm terribly intuitive—I always thought I was intellectual about what I do, but I've come to the realisation that I have absolutely no idea what I'm doing half the time, that the majority of the stuff that I do is totally intuitive, totally about where I am physically and mentally at any moment in time and I have a far harder time than anybody else explaining it and analysing it. That's the territory of the artist anyway: to be quite at sea with what he does, and working toward *not* being intuitive about it and being far more methodical and academic about it.

"*That's* what produced the last two albums. I'm not sure how comfortable I am with that any more. It was fun for these two albums, but I'm not sure that I want to do that again."

Over the last few years, Bowie has performed a remarkable about-face from the solipsistic concerns of his early work and has concerned himself with the precise nature of the world that he finds around him, and the kind of world into which he wants his son to grow up. This "un-typical" concern has, however, manifested itself more through the visual imagery of the "Let's Dance" and "China Girl" videos than through any blatant pronouncement, which is probably just as well, since the political activities and statements of pop stars are generally devalued by the general received notion of entertainers as privileged cranks and eccentrics.

Despite his off-the-cuff remarks about "protest," Bowie has shied away from the overt-statement, but he stills feels that his responsibility exists.

"What one ends up doing, I think, is charity work, which is very interesting. I think it's because you start doing things quietly and low-profile rather than doing something excessive in one's writing. It's because I'm terrified of all forms of musical writing in the popular music idiom just getting *crunched* within days of release in terms of any political significance or any social statement they might make. It just becomes a T-shirt too fast. I often adore and appreciate the sentiment, but I'm just so unsure of myself in that area. I'm never sure how much real, physical manifest good it can do, whereas I know that if I do *this* for *such-and-such* a charity then that's a physical accomplishment that can do something manifest."

Last year, at the end of the British leg of the Serious Moonlight tour, Bowie put his act where his mouth was. With one show at the Hammersmith Odeon, he raised £90,000 for the Brixton Neighbourhood Community Association.

"In songwriting, I feel all at sea with that; I'm not sure where my place is with all of that. My writing for so long has been to do with the surreal that I don't even know whether I could take *myself* seriously as a writer of didactic statements. I'm not sure that as a writer I'm succinct enough to give it a wholeness."

Last year you used to quote John Lennon: *say what you mean, make it rhyme and put a backbeat behind it* . . .

"Yes, I know, and John was so excessively good at that, but the things I end up doing are done on a far quieter basis. Also having a lot of money is very problematic for changing things . . ."

People often don't take millionaire socialists like Ray Davies and Pete Townshend seriously.

"I know, and so it's best not to be one, but I take them very seriously. I take Pete very seriously. He's absolutely committed to his way of life and the expression of what he believes. Pete's quite right: it makes a lot of sense for people in the so-called artistic professions to become involved in areas that they are knowledgeable about.

"I think that unless one has a *penetrating* understanding of the social issues of the time it's very dangerous to get involved in other areas where one might be misled by forces who would take you off the path. It's very important not to be led, and in political areas I think it's very dodgy for a lot of artists—including myself—who have only an understanding of the topsoil of the political and social system to declare themselves under any political banner.

"But I tell you one thing that's very interesting for me, coming back to England only periodically as I do, to see what happened with the 2-Tone music of a few years ago, to see how that black and white/together thing has now become a given in popular music here. That is incredible, and it's happened quite fast. That has made a difference, and it has said something socially and promoted, particularly for a lot of younger people, the idea of being *together* with another sex and another race. To put that against 1972, it has become a different world over here. Now *that* is something to get excited about."

Bowie himself has led integrated bands for the last decade, but it hasn't always been easy.

"Back in '74 it was something of an effort. Going to play in the South was something of an effort for my band. It wasn't a pleasant experience going down to Atlanta in those times: we had to just hit and run, play and get out as fast as possible. Socially it was just a no-no; it wasn't pleasant for them and likewise to a lesser extent it wasn't pleasant for me to see them being insulted . . ."

As Bowie wrote in "It's No Game": *"to be insulted by these fascists is so degrading . . ."*

"Yes, it was very much like that. I don't think that much has changed. We only played a couple of Southern gigs last time, Houston and Dallas . . . but things have changed, yes they have. It's changed a lot, especially in those big cities in Texas. I wonder what it would be like playing Florida now . . ."

The song from the new album that deals most strongly with the pleasures and pains of the struggle for unity is the album's opener "Loving The Alien." It also approaches subjects Bowie has never tackled before: religion and history.

"It really doesn't fit in there very much, does it? That was the most personalised bit of writing on the album for me; not to say that the others were written from a distance, but they're a lot lighter in tone. That one was me in there dwelling on the idea of the awful shit that we've had to put up with because of the Church. That's how it started out: for some reason I was very angry."

You don't normally hear people wearing crucifixes making remarks like that.

"I know . . . this"—he fingers the crucifix around his neck—"is strictly symbolic of a terrible nagging superstition that if I didn't have it on I'd have bad luck. It isn't even religious to me—I've hardly even thought of it as a crucifix, anyway, probably because it's so little. The most obvious lie or cover-up I can think of is through education . . . at the time of writing the song I was reading a book called *The Jesus Scrolls,* and the conclusion of that book is that Jesus died at the age of 70 at Masada and wrote a scroll himself, which is currently in the hands of the Russians, who are holding it over the Catholic Church. Actually I read that a long long time ago, around '75—it was a real Los Angeles book, but it really stayed with me. The crunching thing about the Church is that it has always had *so* much power.

"It was always more of a power tool than anything else, which was not very apparent to the majority of us. I never thought about it as . . . as a child it was just going to church and listening to the choir and hearing the prayers, and it was never really made apparent how much weight they carried. My own father was one of the few fathers I knew who had a lot of understanding of other religions. He—this is an abuse of the word—'tolerated' Buddhists or Muslims or Hindus or Mohammedans, whatever, and he was a great humanitarian in those terms. I think some of that was passed on to me, and encouraged me to become interested in other religions. There was no enforced religion, though, he didn't particularly care for the English religion—Henry's religion. Oh God!

"'Alien' came about because of the feeling that so much history is wrong—as is being rediscovered all the time—and that we base so much on the wrong knowledge that we've gleaned. Now some historian is putting forward the notion the whole idea of Israel is wrong and that it was in fact in Saudi Arabia and not in Palestine. It's extraordinary considering all the mistranslations in the Bible that our lives are being navigated by this misinformation, and that so many people have died because of it, and all the power factions involved . . ." Bowie sighs.

"I don't know . . . just like everything else, it's just a song of images. I can't ever see any cohesive view point in my songs.

"It's a fortunate thing in music that so much of the subconscious comes through with the melody and the placement of a particular word on a particular note. For better or for worse, the information is inherent in the *song*, not in the writer or his intentions or even in the lyrics. It's probably my strongest point that I write evocatively in terms of musical and verbal expression. When I put the two together it can be a powerful format, and I'm just starting to rediscover that again. I think that's what's giving me the bug to be a bit more adventurous in my writing again.

"Recently I've used an *accepted vocabulary,* as Eno would say. I think because I was starting to feel sure of myself in terms of my life, my state of health and my being . . . I have relapses, as we all do, but I feel on the whole fairly happy about my state of mind and my physical being and I guess I wanted to put my musical being in a similar staid and healthy area, but I'm not sure that that was a very wise thing to do. I don't know.

"I never bloody know."

The room is filled with the languid strains of celebrated ditties from the past few decades of the collective unconscious. A neatly attired man has walked to the piano in the centre of the room and commenced tickling it. The piano does not seem to mind. The conversation moves neatly to the subject of movies, including a couple of things that are *not* happening, like the alleged score that Bowie was described as contributing to a forthcoming adaptation of our old friend Mr. Orwell's *1984* featuring John Hurt as Winston Smith and the late Richard Burton as O'Brien.

"No, I'm not doing that. There was talk of me doing that at one time, but I don't have enough time. I've seen bits of it and I think it's a fabulous movie. Really, *really* good."

Then there was the small matter of a role as the villain in the next Bond movie, a role allegedly (ho ho) previously declined by Sting.

"Absolutely out of the question. Yes, I was offered that. After Sting? I rather think it was the other way about. I think for an actor it's probably an interesting thing to do, but I think that for somebody from rock it's more of a clown performance. And I didn't want to spend five months watching my double fall off mountains."

Predictably enough, Bowie has a keen interest in and strong views on the British film industry.

"I like to believe that it's going through one hell of a shake-up. I think we've got some great young film-makers, I really do. I think the guy that I'm working with, Julien Temple, is really a very perceptive and ambitious young film-maker and I think he's going to end up doing something quite remarkable. *The Great Rock 'N' Roll Swindle* wasn't faultless by any means, but it was rejuvenating, and I think his plans for his own film *Absolute Beginners*"—adapted from Colin MacInnes' classic '50s novel, scored by Gil Evans and featuring Paul Weller, Keith Richards and Ray Davies in supporting roles—"should do a lot for young British film-making. It feels essentially *London:* but London not in a passé way. The excitement of London, which has never been featured properly.

"I mean, there are so many stories of young America and young New York."

America has indeed monopolised the '50s to the point where it's hard to believe that there ever *was* a '50s anywhere else.

"For instance, he deals with the '50s black riots in Notting Hill, and that's an area which has never been treated on film. That's an extraordinary thing to have even dug up; so few people remember that it even happened. He's got a very good chance of carrying it off. I'd love to do a feature with him because we've enjoyed working together tremendously. I've never ever put so much into someone else's hands in terms of making videos."

Temple, on the other hand, says that he's never had so much input from the performer on a video before.

"I think that what for me feels like handing stuff over to somebody else as a responsibility for other people still seems very much like a collaboration, but that's only by past reference. I was completely protective with everything I did, so for me loosening up on some aspects and letting Julien decide what camera shots should be used is for me passing the responsibility over.

"It's a bit like the album: for me, that was like standing back; having the courage to admit that other people have their own ideas on what should be done and that I shouldn't be so graspingly self-opinionated about what's best, not granting other people the respect that they deserve as musicians or whatever job that they have. It's taken me an awful long time to get to that point. I feel much easier working on a collaboration basis now.

"In film-making, I'd love to do a collaborative thing with someone like Julien. I don't think pop videos are very interesting, and I don't think video's going to go *anywhere*. Firstly, nobody's doing it on video. Forget videotape. It's all being done on celluloid. Video's out the window. Nothing ever happened to video; it's like the quadrophonic sound system, which just stood up and went down again. There are so many innovative people in video, but they'll never be accepted by the majority and never accepted on network television. The experimental videos will be as well received as experimental movies were, like *Eraserhead*. It'll have about that much impact.

"As far as video is concerned, the video format—stuff that gets called video and goes on television—I know the music channels in the States want to open up. They don't know which way it's gonna go themselves. I think we're coming to a revitalisation of the '50s short; that's the only direction it's going in. I know what I'd like to do with it; which is to start making full-scale movies for television. What standard or quality they are is dependent on the people who put them together.

"The thing that we've just put together is more like a '50s short than a video, the music takes a back seat—more or less. It's a piece in the film. The first thing that EMI are going to have to do is put subtitles on it, because there's so much dialogue that it won't mean a thing if it's shown in Germany or Spain or France without them. The talkies—I think we're into the talkies. The format of 'Blue Jean' is of a small talkie, and that's the emphasis.

"I think what is going to work is getting our finance out of record companies and video stations to make movies rather than the film industry. The producers in the video market are keener to make movies than the movie people: it's as simple as that, and some of us are taking *full* advantage and trying to make movies through this other channel, this new system that's developing."

Bowie's own current taste in movies—current movies, at any rate—includes John Schlesinger's forthcoming feature *The Falcon And The Snowman.*

"It's the story of two young American guys who sell secrets to the Russians. It's Tim Hutton and Sean Penn giving the performances of their *lives,* but I don't know how it will be received in the States given the current political climate. It's very objective, though one feels *great* sympathy for the two boys. It's a magnificent piece of film-making, the best Schlesinger movie I've seen in years."

Another current favourite is Wim Wenders' current release *Paris, Texas.*

So what does Bowie, the arch-trendsetter, think of current London fashion? He finds it considerably less impressive than, say a Wenders movie or a good book.

"I think it's *silly,*" he declares defiantly, and then snorts with laughter. "But it looks like fun. I can see that they derive an awful lot of pleasure from it, but I can't take it seriously. I don't think it expresses very much."

What, big white T-shirts with things written on them?

"God, I hate those damn things, I really hate them. That's why I had my Ernie character in 'Blue Jean' wearing a RELAX T-shirt!"

Bowie can afford to grin at the vagaries of frivolous youth. As he approaches his 38th birthday, he is securely enthroned as one of the pop racket's most dominant individual presences. He is a consistent innovator and experimentalist who nevertheless maintains a massive hold on the pop mainstream, and his career as an actor is just beginning. He has a huge and devoted audience which nevertheless not only refuses to demand that he stay with a winning formula but which virtually insists that he follows his own instincts and desires. He is the '80s incarnation of the dashing English gentleman about the arts, reassuring and unsettling his public simultaneously. He is as established as an artist can get in this racket.

And yet . . .

Does Bowie think pop is at its best when it's dangerous, when it's something subversive and weird and unlike the harmless consumer durable we know and love today?

"It's very interesting to hear Julien talking about 'the old days' when he thinks back to The Sex Pistols. You mention '77 and he says 'Oh, in *those* days, it was so dangerous then!' Well, it's not so far off, is it? If things are as cyclic as they're supposed to be, then it's bound to come. I didn't get the full brunt of all that, because it was just the period when I was settling in Berlin, so it came from a different direction there and it didn't have the full wrath and anger of what happened in England. For me it's all just footage and I can't feel the same thing.

"I really regret missing out on that. I wonder how I would have received all that. I'd love to have seen the dialogue on television and all that, and the feel of the clubs at that time . . . of *course* that's a much healthier climate. Of *course* it is."

Could you see yourself contributing to another major upset?

"In rock, I think it's very hard for . . . after the initial point of view that you put forward, unless you're capable of adopting more than that initial statement, it's hard to come up with another that has that same kind of force that the first one did. For me, the early '70s period was the thing that gave me my opening. I don't think I would ever contribute so aggressively again . . .

"The interesting thing about rock is that you never think that it's going to go on for much longer. Then when you find that it has . . . I'm 37 going on 38 and I find myself thinking, 'I'm still doing it!'

"So you're re-defining it all the time. The whole animal of rock keeps changing itself so fast and so furiously that you just can't plan ahead. I've got absolutely no idea. I've got two or three anchors: to do some more work with Iggy and to try and write something for myself that is extraordinary and adventurous.

"Those are the only things in music that I *know* I'll be doing in the future . . ."

BOYS KEEP SWINGING

Adrian Deevoy | June 1989, _Q_ (UK)

"I've never been worried about losing fans," states Bowie in this _Q_ magazine feature.

Unlike with any other major rock star, this could be read as something other than bluster. When Bowie told Cameron Crowe of _Rolling Stone_ in February 1976, "I really, honestly and truly, don't know how much longer my albums will sell. . . . And I really don't give a shit," it was just before he launched into his "Berlin Trilogy" which seemed designed to alienate anyone who'd ever loved his records for their polish and relative accessibility.

Adrian Deevoy's question about whether the artist had any concern about losing fans was prompted by Bowie having, following his album _Never Let Me Down_ (1987), subsumed himself into Tin Machine, his first-ever exercise in musical democracy. This feature was the band's inaugural ensemble interview.

Some will discern something significant in the fact that Bowie is reported as being extremely nervous about the reception to the playback of the album. Certainly it seems almost heartbreaking to read his optimism about his new project—which he states to be a way out of a trough he'd lately gotten himself into—in light of its actual deafening mediocrity and subsequent poor reception. Meanwhile, when Bowie is asked to continue his interview tradition of championing current favorite artists and responds with the grisly, self-stroking comment, "It's very nice to be able to say Tin Machine is my favourite band," it seems the antithesis of the anti-showbiz sentiment inherent in the famous don't-give-a-shit quote.

For his part, Deevoy says, "Imagine my shock when he played me his new art-metal endeavours at nosebleed volume. Imagine my bemusement at still rather admiring that album, and its smart architect, a quarter of a century later." —Ed.

"I'm David," says David Bowie blushing slightly and extending a moist hand. "I'm not looking forward to this one bit."

We are standing in the control room of a recording studio three floors above the reverberating music stores and palm-slapping huddles of between-gig musicians on New York's West 48th Street. Positioned solemnly around David Bowie are his own three musicians, collectively called Tin Machine: the softly spoken lead guitarist, Reeves Gabrels, wearing a denim shirt and an expression of mild distress; the wisecracking drummer Hunt Sales, his raven-black mess of hair wound up in a combination of bandanna and cloth cap and his feet encased in a stout pair of tartan bedroom slippers, and his brother Tony Sales, a lean, lantern-jawed bass player dressed all in black and sitting cross-legged and silent on the floor.

The Sales brothers first worked with Bowie 12 years ago when they provided the spunky and swaggering rhythm tracks for Iggy Pop's Lust For Life album. Gabrels met him last year when they both joined the dance group La La La Human Steps to perform a ballet—Gabrels wrote the music, Bowie rather woodenly cut a classical rug—at London's ICA.

"You wanna see 'em all together," Bowie's American press agent had enthused prior to entering the studio, "joking and funnin' like bands do!" He too, however, is now looking rather sullen and apprehensive having, no doubt, registered the worrying absence of all activities light-hearted.

The root of all this concern is the reason why we are here. For David Bowie has decided to hold what Americans have come to call a "playback"—the airing of a previously unheard record in the presence of a (in this case very) select few. And now he's regretting it. Perched uncomfortably on the arm of a sofa, he pensively strokes a newly nurtured beard in a slow, downward motion as if willing it to grow. The blond meringue-like hairdo that has sat uncertainly atop his head for the last few years has been trimmed down to a more sober mousey arrangement. Similarly his clothes have made the painless but significant transition from flamboyant to "classic." Today David is wearing a fine maroon shirt and dark tie with dapper charcoal trousers and brown suede shoes rakishly buckled at the side.

These are suddenly put into action as he jerks to his feet. Snake-hipped and devoid of any discernible backside, he walks, in small, delicate steps, across the studio floor and returns clutching a sheaf of papers. "These are the lyrics," he grins sheepishly proffering the sheets. "There's probably a few mistakes. I haven't proofread them yet." He settles once more on the studio settee and nods to the album's producer, Tim Palmer—whose previous achievements have included works by The Mission and The Cult—who, in turn, moves to the vast, flickering mixing desk.

"Shall we have Side One?" enquires David Bowie, lighting a Marlboro.

Of course, this situation could prove uniquely embarrassing should the album—as Bowie's last two LPs, Tonight and Never Let Me Down with their blustery pomp, cod-reggae "treatments" and twaddlesome lyrics have intimated—turn out to be a whimpering artistic failure. Indeed, because of these two records, the latter promoted by the ludicrously overblown Glass Spider tour, Bowie's career had reached an impasse so sticky it necessitated a hasty reacquaintance with the drawing board. His last convincing album was Let's Dance, in 1983.

Track one, side one of this soul-scouring exercise is now cannoning out of the French dresser-sized studio speakers. It is, mercifully, quite splendid. The sound is raw, hysterical and crackling with life. Reeves Gabrels's decidedly non-vegetarian guitar—bringing immediately to mind the words, Jimi and Hendrix—screams, crunches and collides with the big, bare drums and rolling bass. Bowie shrieks and snarls and sings of "beating on blacks with a baseball bat," "right wing dicks in their boiler suits" and "savage days." Then as abruptly as the track started it ends.

The room is oppressively quiet. Not a solitary word is spoken. Bowie stares ahead hard at the wall in front of him, resting his chin on the steeple formed by his hands. Tony Sales flashes a quick smirk from the floor and the second track begins. Toes begin to tap, Bowie mouths some words and twitches his head in tiny, tense movements and reaches, once again, for his cigarettes. By the time the fourth track is under way, either confident that his album is being well received or exhausted by the almost electric intensity in the room, Bowie slips out into a side room where, through a small window, he can be seen playing pool with a bespectacled Oriental youth. Upon closer inspection, his partner turns out, bizarrely, to be Sean Lennon. By some strange—positively *surreal*—coincidence, the next song to blare forth is a powerful rock revision of Working Class Hero, during which Bowie re-positions himself on the edge of the sofa and Sean Lennon sits on the other side of the studio glass, tinkering with a guitar.

After 28 minutes, side one crashes to halt. Reeves cracks a joke about the album being "pastoral mood music" which is completely ignored. "Side Two?" suggests Bowie.

Tim Palmer complies and more of the same fills the room. This time, between the great surges of guitar and harsh vocals there a few tender moments: an English-accented song about finding religion at a bus stop; a racy number which expresses the desire to "tie you down, pretend you're Madonna" and a touching heavy metal love song. As the album finishes there are audible sighs of relief and Bowie cracks a huge wide-mouthed grin, laughs lustily and stubbing out his sixth stress-relieving cigarette says, "Of course, the CD comes with two extra tracks."

The ordeal over, Reeves, Hunt and Tony repair to a side room with tumblers of mineral water to discuss their new venture. The much-promised "funnin'" commences immediately in musicianly good spirits. "Is it too late to re-do all the guitar parts?" enquires Hunt innocently.

Ever the dramatist, Bowie appears a minute or so later and extravagantly mops his brow. "Phew!" he says. "That was like having an argument with your girlfriend in front of a crowd of people. Did you feel like that? It was, *Honey! Not here!* It was very much that feeling. This was really traumatic for us inasmuch as it was the first real listening session we've had. It was like, This is it. It's only now I'm starting to think, Well, what is the reaction to it going to be like? It's really like exposing yourself in a way. It's been an incredibly insular experience making it, almost tunnel vision at times. Finally breaking it open to other people—it's *uncomfortable.*"

When asked, en masse, in their first interview as Tin Machine, what's the best part of being in a group, they launch into a bout of excited badinage, giving a good indication of how the next couple of hours will shape up.

"For me," says Bowie, "it's the element of surprise that I get from the other guys. They surprise me all the time, mostly by what they say. It's quite gang-like in that there's a kind of buoyancy."

"Oh *yeah,*" says Tony, adopting Bowie-like sincerity. "This is like *one big happy family . . .*"

". . . with child abuse!" shouts Hunt triumphantly.

"There's a lot of love," deadpans Reeves.

"That's right," agrees Tony. "It's a unity. A unit."

Bowie feigns confusion. "A *eunuch*?"

Q: What do you think the main criticisms of the record will be?

Bowie: There's going to be a whole bunch of people who'll say it's just not accessible. I guess it's not as obviously melodic as one would think it would probably be. I don't know. *We* don't know. But *(adopts the voice of a children's television presenter)* I think the little house knows something about it. *(Laughs at his fellow band members' blank faces).* That's the problem working with bloody Americans, they don't get half your references!

Q: Is this a brief indulgence or a long-term project?

Bowie: There'll be another two albums at least. Oh, yes, this will go for a while. While we're all enjoying playing with each other so much, why not? The moment we stop enjoying it, we're all prepared to quit. I'm so up on this I want to go and start recording the next album tomorrow.

Q: The sound is, in parts, rather extreme. Are you worried about losing fans?

Bowie: I've never been worried about losing fans. I just haven't bothered to put that into practice recently. My strength has always been that I never gave a *shit* about what people thought of what I was doing. I'd be prepared to completely change from album to album and ostracise everybody that may have been pulled in to the last album. That didn't ever bother me *one iota*. I'm sort of back to that again . . .

Q: What would you recommend people do while listening to the LP?

Bowie: Don't drive! I was listening to the roughs and I was just *glued into it*. I just put my foot down and had gone 15 minutes past the studio before I realised where I was. It's a demanding album. There's no compromise. It *demands* your attention.

Q: Do you feel more at ease with this record than any of your recent recordings?

Bowie: Oh absolutely. I . . . it's hard without sounding phony. I *love it*. This, for me, is kind of like catching up from Scary Monsters. It's almost dismissive of the last three albums I've done. Getting back on course, you could say.

Q: Was it basically a relinquishing of control?

Bowie: It was really throwing myself into a group format which is something I haven't done . . . for ever really. Even in The Spiders it was what I said went. I was young, I was going to burn the world up and you do think that when you're that age. But to have other members of the band making decisions was . . . *really difficult! (laughs)*

Q: Can you be a tyrant?

Bowie: Less and less as I've got older. But I was born to have opinions.

Hunt: Man, he's got a reputation. The whip's in the other room . . .

Bowie: *(Shouts jokingly) Look, I know what I want!*

Q: When was your most tyrannical period?

Bowie: What, the desperate vision? Let me see now. It was pretty bad—although in a slightly different way—around Ziggy Stardust. There was just no room for anything else. I had to—at least in *my mind* I had to—hum a lot of (Mick) Ronson's solos to him. It got to the point where every single note and every part of the song had to be exactly as I heard it in my head . . .

Reeves: I'm shattered! Did you really do that?

Bowie: No, no, that's not true of say, Man Who Sold The World which was very much Ronson. But say the more melodic solos that Ronson did, an awful lot of that was just me telling him what notes I wanted. But that was cool. He's very laid-back and he'd just go along with it. He was happy to be playing. I didn't know any other way anyway. No . . . I did. That is what I had to do. I knew what I wanted, you know? *They* didn't know what I wanted.

Q: Is it ever embarrassing bumping into people you've thrown out of groups or "let go" in the past?

Bowie: I never threw anyone out of my band. *Never.* I've never had a permanent band. Being a solo artist, you're in a funny position because I hire guys for eight months or a year and that's the parting of the ways at the end of that. I still see some of them, Carmine (Rojas) and Carlos (Alomar) and I was with Slicky (Earl Slick) last year. But it's their life. The only real band thing which, I guess, at the time, was a bit nasty was The Spiders. That was because they wanted to remain doing what we were doing and I didn't. I was going somewhere else and they didn't want to go. They were quite happy to play Jeff Beck covers. But I knew what I wanted the band to do. I still do, it's just that no-one takes notice any more! I get shoved around—Go and put another tie on, David!

Q: Were there arguments during the recording?
Bowie: There were disagreements.
Reeves: But not actually about the music.
Bowie: There was that strange period of feeling each other out in Switzerland. Did you sense that? It was in the first week. Once we'd decided to go for it we went to Montreux, because we could all get away from the shit that we were up to our necks in and go and be alone while we decided how we'd work together. And for the first week there was this kind of . . . sparring.
Reeves: No, not sparring. I'd not met Tony and Hunt at this point and I'd heard that they had weird attitudes and everything.
Tony: The only weird attitude we had was *you*, buddy!
Reeves: When I first got there, Hunt has got a knife on his belt and he's wearing a T-shirt that says, "Fuck You, I'm From Texas." So I think, Oh *shit*. And whenever I played something they'd say, No, you play it like this, kid. And after a week of being a nice guy—walking that fine line between ignoring what people were telling me and being gracious about it—I did it how I wanted.

Q: How determined were you that the project worked? Was it something that you would easily have given up?
Bowie: I was desperate that it worked. I wanted it to happen very badly. After a few days I was very nervous that it might not work out. Then everyone sorted themselves out, got over their emotional jet lag . . .

Q: What would you have done if it hadn't come off?
Bowie: I don't know. I really don't know actually. Wept . . . *at least*. But I can't even think of a hypothetical situation. I definitely would have reversed what I'd been doing some way or another. I had to for my own musical sanity. I had to do something where I felt more involved and less dispassionate. I had to get passionate again. I couldn't keep going the way I was going. It was shit or get off the pot.

Q: Your last two LPs—Tonight and Never Let Me Down—weren't terribly good, were they?

Bowie: Mm. I thought it was great material that got simmered down to product level. I really should have not done it quite so *studio-ly*. I think some of it was a waste of really good songs. You should hear the demos from those albums. It's night and day by comparison with the finished tracks. There's stuff on the two albums since Let's Dance that I could really *kick* myself about. When I listen to those demos it's, How did it turn out like that? You should hear Loving The Alien on demo. It's *wonderful* on demo. I promise you! *(laughs)*. But on the album, it's . . . not as wonderful. What am I meant to say? *(laughs)*.

Q: What have the other band members thought of your career over the past five years?

Bowie: Oh, that's not fair. Get *outta* here! *(laughs)*. Oh God.

Hunt: Listen, I like David. On a personal level, I like him . . .

Reeves: He's a beautiful cat, right?

Hunt: But, man, those albums. I dunno. And the Glass Spider tour? Well, I didn't go and see it but I saw it on TV and . . .

Bowie: But, Hunt *(slips into music hall straight man mode)*, I thought you never missed any of my tours . . .

Hunt: . . . I never miss any of your tours. I never go see 'em, so I never miss 'em . . .

Bowie: Boom boom!

Hunt: But I didn't like Glass Spider. I mean that. Seriously. I thought it was a bit beneath you. That's my opinion. I don't need to sit here and say that I love something I didn't think much of. I watched it thinking, *This is the guy who did Spiders From Mars.*

Bowie: What he's saying is he hasn't listened to anything of mine since Spiders From Mars!

Reeves: But Glass Spider was cabaret. A lot of critics said . . .

Bowie: Yeah, critics. Give me your personal opinion.

Reeves: If you want my personal opinion you'll have to ask my wife. But it seemed to me it was about entertainment more than music. I went to see a soundcheck in Chicago and that was better than the show.

Q: It was a very hammy show, wouldn't you say?

Bowie: To come to its defence, I liked the video of it. But I overstretched. I made too much detail of . . . Oh *Christ*. Next question!

Tony: He's beginning to roast!

Bowie: There was too much responsibility on the last tour. I was under stress every single day. It was a decision a second. It was so big and so unwieldy and everybody had a problem all the time, every day, and I was under so much *pressure*. It was unbelievable.

Q: How did you cope with the stress?

Bowie: Badly. I just had to grit my teeth and get through it which is not a great way of working. I admit, I overstretched and put too many fine details into something that was going to be seen *(indicates tiny figure with his finger and thumb)* this big. Serious Moonlight worked much better because they were much broader, bigger strokes yet there was detail work as well. There were facial moves. I mean, *why bother?* It was only for myself really. It was so great to burn the spider in New Zealand at the end of the tour. We just put the thing in a field and set light to it. That was such a relief!

Q: The lyrics on the Tin Machine LP are very brutal. There's a lot of quite violent imagery. Is there any particular reason for this?

Bowie: Lummee. I didn't realise they were that brutal. I wouldn't really like to say why that is.

Reeves: There was a lot of resistance on our part to him going back to a lyric and re-writing what was essentially gut-writing.

Bowie: I'd not thought of that. That's it! I hadn't even thought about that. That's true. They were there all the time saying, Don't wimp out, sing it like you wrote it. Stand by it. I have done and frequently do censor myself in terms of lyrics. I say one thing and then I think, Ah maybe I'll just take the edge off that a bit. I don't know why I do that. I'm English. Maybe I just felt it was a bit impolite or something. I don't quite know where that comes from but it's almost like something somewhere in me doesn't want to offend. I've always been like that.

Q: Have you made lyrics deliberately obscure in the past. Dressed ideas up?

Bowie: Dressed them up? No. Watered them down. But certainly over this immediate period I simply haven't been allowed to. Reeves is quite correct and that's quite an insight for me. They didn't let me re-write. The lyrics were my first kind of feelings when the stuff was coming out. I just got it down as fast as I could. Do you know a guy came up to me on the street the other day and said, Do you like pussy cats? And I said, Yes I do but my name isn't Cats!

Q: Boom boom
Tony: *(Laughs)* Oh, Jesus . . .
Bowie: No, seriously, the words just went straight down on to the canvas as it were . . .
Reeves: I hate to bring Art up . . .
Bowie: Art does a good job. Paul was the wordsmith but Art could sing 'em and make you cry. He would if you stuck him on a wall anyway!

Q: There's a couple of lyrics that leap out. Could you explain them? The line in the song Pretty Thing—"Tie you down, pretend you're Madonna."
Bowie: *(Laughs)* Hey, we were hanging out with Sean and he told us a few things! You know what I mean? Nah. It's a throwaway. I was just trying to think of a . . . it's such a silly song anyway.

Q: Do you think Madonna will respond?
Bowie: Respond? Oh . . . who cares? Really?

Q: Whose idea was it to cover Working Class Hero?
Bowie: I think that was mine. That's always been a really favourite song of mine. I like that first John Lennon album a hell of a lot. I think all the songs are really beautifully written and, again, very straight from the shoulder. There's an honestly in the lyrics there. And that particular song, I thought, would sound great as a rock song. It seemed very *worth* doing.

Q: What does Sean Lennon think of it?
Bowie: I think he likes it a lot. He's followed this album almost from the start, from the second week. He's a big Reeves fan.
Tony: Reeves was giving him guitar lessons while we were putting tracks down.
Bowie: Ah. Sweet.

Q: One song, Bus Stop, you sing in a very English accent. Why has your singing accent always changed so much?

Bowie: The song felt so English. It's almost vaudeville. I don't know if the others feel very American or whatever by comparison but that felt very English.

Q: Do you still feel English?

Bowie: Well I spend so little time there. I haven't really been in England since 1973. I don't really know much about it. I go in there once a year or, actually, sometimes not at all. When I was living in Berlin I wasn't going into England at all. I stayed in Berlin for two and half years without moving out. I mean, my present day knowledge of England is based entirely on what I read. But in terms of atmosphere it's just a blast every time I go in for three or four weeks.

Q: Does it get sepia-tinted? Good old Blighty.

Bowie: Not really.

Q: Do you miss the humour?

Bowie: Yes. *(Stony faced)*. That's something that stays with you. Always. *(laughs)*.

Q: Presumably you've heard Lou Reed's New York LP. What do you think about the way his writing has developed in relation to your own?

Bowie: I think Lou writes in a much more detached manner from me. Lou's the kind of guy who sits back and watches what's going on and takes notes. He's very New York. I feel he could have been a feature writer of some kind if he wasn't a musician. He'd write these little essays and they'd go in New Yorker or maybe something a bit punchier like Bomb magazine. He's a natural journalist. He's almost become a kind of musical Woody Allen. The writer, the observer, the Samuel Pepys of New York.

Tony: Don't you think he's become a caricature of himself?

Bowie: No, I just think as he's growing older he's becoming the writer that he was probably always going to become. A short story writer. He writes in the narrative form very clearly. For me there's still a lot of symbolism or instinctive or emotive lyric writing—I don't know where it comes from— that explains the way I feel or the atmosphere I'm in. There's a couple of lines in Crack City on this album—*They'll bury you in velvet/And place you underground*—which had intent. The drug dirge—and this is not a slight on Lou because Lou is clean—the sound that one associates with that particular lifestyle is very much personified by the early Velvets. I had hoped that I gave that away in those two lines.

Q: Have you listened to much Velvet Underground lately?
Bowie: No. I'm too old for that *(laughs)*. That was 1971!

Q: It certainly sounds as if you were listening to Jimi Hendrix prior to making this record.
Bowie: Jimi Hendrix is definitely in there. That new Rykodisc stuff is exceptional *(an American CD release, Live At Winterland)*. The clarity of vision that the man had. It's just fabulous. Trying to catch things mid-air. I guess I re-discovered Hendrix, Cream, Neu, Can—all the Berlin period bands—Glenn Branca *(noisome electric guitar orchestrator)*. Me personally—not so much these other guys—spent a long time with my old albums. Heroes, Lodger, Scary Monsters, Low to push myself back into why I was writing.

I had been doing that anyway before we got together. I wasn't enjoying myself as a writer and performer again. I get that periodically. I think every writer and performer does. Inevitably what happens—and it happens every time—is that one goes back to what one considers one's roots are. For me that was the people I used to listen to whether it be Syd Barrett, Hendrix or whatever and the stuff you did yourself that you knew was really good. You listen to it again and think, Where has that state of mind gone? Why aren't I thinking in those terms anymore—thinking that I should be pleasing myself first and foremost, and then if somebody else likes it, great. But I'm not going to be happy if I'm not happy.

I love those albums, you know. I think I've done some great albums. In 20 years, generally, what I've made is stuff I'm *so* happy with and I'm *so* glad I've done it. I think I've made some *fabulous albums*. I've got to be honest. I love it. I love my stuff. And I get so shit-headed and angry when I hear stuff that I haven't done my utmost on. I couldn't possibly articulate what happened when I listened to those albums but it creates . . . an atmosphere.

Q: Did you take any drugs while you were making the album?

Hunt: A lot of LSD, right?

Bowie: Lox, Salmon and Danish *(laughs)*. No, we didn't take drugs. We've all been around the block and we all have different perspectives than those we had 10 years ago as to what we want to do with our lives. We've watched ourselves screw up our lives in the past and—why waste the time—we just want to do what we're doing and enjoy it for what it is.

Tony: We know better now. We weren't in the pursuit of destroying ourselves while we were recording. Our forum of hanging out was not at a dealer's house or at the bar.

Bowie: We were hanging out in the parking lot! Sitting on comfortable chairs.

Q: What, in contrast, do you remember about making Low?

Bowie: I was a very different guy by then. I mean, I'd gone through my major drug period and Berlin was my way of escaping from that and trying to work out how you live without drugs. It's very hard. *(Turns to Tony)* You know that period?

Tony: I remember that period. I tried to figure the same thing out.

Bowie: You're up and down all the time, vacillating constantly. It's a very tough period to get through. So my concern with Low was not about the music. The music was literally expressing my physical and emotional state . . . and that was my worry. So the music was almost therapeutic. It was like, Oh yeah, we've made an album and it sounds like this. But it was a by-product of my life. It just sort of came out. I never spoke to the record company about it. I never talked to anybody about it. I just made this album . . . in a rehab state. A dreadful state really.

Q: Why did you choose to go to Berlin?

Bowie: Well the whole reason for going there was because it was so low-key. Jim (Iggy Pop) and I—we were both having the same problems—knew it was the kind of place where you walk around and really are left alone and not stopped by people. They're very blasé, there. Cynical, irony-based people and it's a great place if you really want to try and do some soul-searching and find out what it is that you really want.

Q: Does listening to Low bring back uncomfortable memories? Do you sweat when you hear it?

Bowie: Yeah, I do. It brings it all back instantly. It's a great piece of work but you certainly feel the shivers and the sweats again.

Q: What are the band members' favourite Bowie periods?

Reeves: Aladdin Sane, Station To Station.

Hunt: I like Ziggy Stardust and the Spiders.

Tony: I'm there with Ziggy Stardust too. It made such an impact. I really dug Ronson and the bass player. Who was that bass player?

Bowie: Trev. Trevor Bolder. Trev's still working. He's with Uriah Heep, isn't he?

Reeves: It was a great period—1970 to 1973—because you could go to school with a green streak in your hair and say, Fuck you, I look like David Bowie.

Bowie: My biggest up was when I met Mickey Rourke for the first time and he said (*unspeakably poor Mickey Rourke impression*), Oh man, in 1973, man, I was dressing just like you, man, I had green hair and stack-heeled boots and leather trousers. And I'm trying to see Mickey Rourke wearing all this gear. I said, *You were a glam-rocker?* He said, Yeah, man, in Florida nobody had seen anything like it! I found that absolutely great. I felt so encouraged by that. A guy like that and it was a major part of his life.

Q: That must happen a lot—people relating periods of their life to the different stages in your career?

Bowie: It does and . . . it's lovely. No, it really is lovely. Ever so nice. If it meant something to someone, that's great. Even if you looked like shit in eye-shadow (*laughs*).

Q: What will Tin Machine be like live?

Bowie: When it happens it will be in what I guess you'd call a fairly intimate situation. We've already done one gig. We showed up at a club in Nassau where we were recording and did four or five songs. We went down to the club and just did 'em.

Reeves: We weren't announced, we just walked up on stage and you could hear all these voices whispering, That's David Bowie! No, it can't be David Bowie, he's got a beard!

Q: So the gigs will be very pared-down affairs?

Bowie: Non-theatrical. Definitely. Just a six-piece horn section and a trapeze artist!

Q: What will you look like?

Bowie: You're looking at it. We're wearing it!

Hunt: I might change these socks.

Bowie: And Kevin Armstrong will be playing. He's been involved from the start. Kevin was originally in the band I used at Live Aid. That's where he came from. He'll play rhythm guitar because I tried but my rhythm guitar just isn't good enough.

Reeves: Oh come on, you just want to run around and pull girls out of the audience.

Bowie: There you go *(laughs)*. I don't want to be rooted to a microphone.

Q: Will it be a big change not doing an over-the-top theatrical stage production?

Bowie: But it's only really been like that for the last couple of tours. Before Let's Dance the last theatrical tour that I did was Diamond Dogs, which was 1974. Everything in that period afterwards, like the Young Americans tour was pretty basic. It was just like a white soul band thing. It was very image-oriented. There was (David) Sanborn on saxophone, Luther Vandross on backing vocals and all that. It was a hell of a band but it wasn't very theatrical. It sounded great and it was going for that white soul feel. And then the Station To Station tour was a bunch of lights but we didn't do anything. I walked around rather haughtily, a lot of the lights went *(opens and closes hands)* like that a lot. It was very white and black. It was about non-colour schemes. So really the theatrical things have been since Let's Dance. From '74 to '83 they weren't really *theatrical*.

Q: Have you listened to very much hardcore?

Bowie: Thrash metal I *love*. Or speed metal. It's actually been around America for a while. It kicked off in about '78 or '79 in California. It's become the California sound in a way. Now New York has picked up on it. Actually, I say I love it, it depends who the band are.

Q: Do you still keep your eye on what is happening in Britain?
Bowie: Not really. I've heard a lot of stuff that comes out of England. I've always known what's happening musically. Nothing has really excited me for a while. What is happening there at the moment?

Q: Hardcore, deep house, various types of world music, Morrissey is still very popular . . .
Bowie: Oh *he* isn't bad. I think he's an excellent lyric writer. I've never been able to come to terms with his melodies. I'm a sucker for an old-fashioned melody and I find his very disparate. They tail off a lot. But I think his lyrics are absolutely superb. One of the better lyric writers that England—and it's *very* English—has produced over the last few years. I don't know much about his image or what he's about because I've never seen him live but I like the records.

Q: In interviews you used to name-check particular groups that you were listening to at the time—Psychedelic Furs, The The, Screaming Blue Messiahs. You were almost championing them. Is there anyone this time?
Bowie: It's very nice to be able to say Tin Machine is my favourite band. It satisfies everything I want out of music at the moment. Being where I am, where I'm from, my age, Tin Machine is everything I want to hear. And that's the first time, in a long, long time that I've been able to say that.
Reeves: It's pinstripes and Purple Haze.
Bowie: It's what? Pinstripes and Purple Haze? That's brilliant. Can I say that?
Reeves: Sure.
Bowie: Incidentally, have I told you, it's pinstripes and Purple Haze! (*laughs*)

———————

The interview having reached a satisfactory conclusion, David Bowie rises and shunts his tie knot neckwards. He enquires nervously about the safety of flights in and out of Britain. "Why are they having those delays?" he asks with all the paranoia of a true flying phobic. "Are the delays as long as you hear or is that just airline propaganda?" When he learns that one flight was held up on account of a faulty wing he turns red in the face, sits down again and clutches his head and says, very quietly, "No, no, not the bloody wing!" Then, remembering his promotional duties he stands, shakes hands and delivers his parting shot.

"You know I was playing the album at home," he says confidentially, "and my son (Joe) who's 17 and listens to rap, heavy metal, The Smiths and hardcore said, Is that *you*, Dad? God, *that's* more like it!"

TIN MACHINE II INTERVIEW

Robin Eggar | August 9, 1991

This interview with Tin Machine took place in Dublin when the band were publicizing their second album, which unfortunately had a title as unimaginative as its contents: *Tin Machine II*. It was released in the wake of Bowie's Sound+Vision tour—or what is referred to herein as the "farewell tour" in reference to Bowie's claim that it would be the last time he would perform his old songs.

This verbatim transcription of the interview has never previously been published. It provides an amusing and sometimes illuminating picture of a group interacting with each other, even if the all-for-one spirit rather quickly unravelled in the face of the album's failure to crack the US Top 100.

Says Eggar, "Eighteen months earlier I had interviewed Bowie just before his Sound+Vision Tour. Then, he had been uptight, nervy, and defensive. This was a different man, relaxed, cracking jokes, putting on silly voices. It was categorically a group interview, with all the banter one expects from musicians who respect each other. It never needed to be said but everyone knew that Bowie was still the first among equals and time was to prove the guy who said 'I just sing the songs mate' was playing another of the myriad personalities of his career. But Bowie's strength has always been that he believes in what he is doing when he does it."

The discussion starts with talk about Dublin, the album's first single, and its video. —Ed.

David Bowie: Here they are really laid back, you don't get fan build-up. The foot at the end of the video is for film buffs, as is the guitar slicing the moon. They are film puns on two other Spanish films made in the twenties.

Reeves Gabrels: We deferred to Victory in London about releasing a different single in the UK than the States. We just make it. We'd stand by any track as a single.

Hunt Sales: We make it, they market it. It was finished after ten to eleven months. After our first two to three week tour we went into the studio and came up with about twenty-five to thirty-five songs. Shortly after that David embarked on his solo thing, his farewell tour, but on his breaks we worked on the record here and there.

Bowie: Before the farewell tour, I thought we had finished the second album. Everyone knew it all had to be put on [the] back burner until I had finished the commitment to Ryko. It is hard to just sit on it. In the breaks from my tour we went back and did more tracks. We did "One Shot" with Hugh Padgham. It was an ongoing process until March this year until we settled on the right tracks and then mixed them.

How did you hook up in the first place? Originally it seemed a one-off project.

Tony Sales: The inception started fifteen years ago when Hunt, David, and I worked with Iggy Pop on *Lust for Life*. We went out and did a tour with David on keyboards, then we did a further tour with Iggy Pop. At sound checks the three of us would jam around and we were having fun with some other pieces of music that either David or we had written. We'd just mess around. We liked playing together. It was different stuff. We never talked about getting a band together. We figured we'd run into each other and play a bit more. Time passed. Over the years we've seen each other and hung out. Three years ago I ran into David in L.A. and he told me he had been working with this great guitar player. He said, "Why don't we get together and throw some ideas around?" Hunt, David, and I got together in L.A. and two weeks later we were in Switzerland, where we met Reeves for the first time.

Gabrels: My wife worked on the Glass Spider Tour in America.

Bowie: She stepped in to do press at the last moment. She was a friend of a friend and came in for the last couple of months. I'd met Reeves because of Sarah working on the tour. He used to be there, this polite quiet guy, and we'd talk about art. I didn't realize he was a musician. He was Sarah's husband, a painter by early training. Then Sarah gave me a cassette near the end, saying, "You must listen to this; it's my husband's work."

I said "Great," but I didn't think much of it because you get given a lot of cassettes on tour—three or four hundred—but I do play them. When I got back to Switzerland, I started going through everything. I put his on and I couldn't believe the guitar playing. I couldn't believe this guy played like that. To look at him you'd think if he did play guitar it would be Spanish classical. Certainly not . . . oh, I can't put a description on it. I was more than impressed, so I called him up and asked if he'd like to come over.

I'd received a request from Édouard Lock, of the Canadian dance troupe La La La [Human Steps], who were going to do a performance in London for the ICA [Institute of Contemporary Arts] to stop their roof falling in, and asked if I would write the music. It was a perfect opportunity to work with this new guitarist I'd met. So we got together and we used machines to do the bass and drums. Then it dawned on me that people who actually played like those machines—it was so thunderous and heavy— were Hunt and Tony. Within thirty-six hours of them flying in, we had recorded the first track off the first Tin Machine album. It decided us we wanted to do the same things along the same lines.

There was a lukewarm response to the first Tin Machine album . . .

Bowie: Not among us. We were the greatest fans. It's still on my turntable. I think it's the best album of that year. I don't usually like my own records to that extent. I think the first Tin Machine album is a cracking classic. I really love it. It has a really interesting sound, the desperateness of four people trying to get their point known to each other. These guys had never met Reeves before. There was a lot of sparring going on. The music was the only cement between all of us.

The second album is a lot more interior?

T. Sales: The band had been together long enough to play live. The first album's chaos is a document of a band that's just got together.

How do you fit in?

Bowie: I sing the songs, mate. This is the first time I've not been the headline name in twenty-five years. Absolutely. It feels great.

Is it first among equals?

Bowie: You'd better ask the others.

H. Sales: David is the only one who knows how he feels, but in the studio we cut thirty-six tracks in six weeks. It just kept snowballing. A couple of times we finished and David would say, "I just want to try a couple of things" and we'd say, "No, we just laid it down, that's it, that's the groove." We nudged him—

Gabrels: Maybe bullied him a little bit.

Hunt: —and he played along.

Always?

Bowie: I'm in a band of very strong-willed people. Everybody gives opinions but nobody gives orders. We've reached a consensus of what and where we'd like to do.

H. Sales: He's not a complete pussy, but then none of us [are]. It's often a case of who's the strongest today.

Gabrels: Given David's history at the point where we came together, the band has made itself obvious as a band. That it felt like a band, looked like a band, smelt like a band, so it must be a band. Because of David's standing in the pop community, he had to be the one to acknowledge it. As much as the rest of us felt it was a band, the weight of that fell upon David. That addresses the first among equals thing. He had an ongoing high-profile career with or without the band. It was David's call.

T. Sales: There is just so much prestige can do. The rest of us are self-supportive by our own contribution. Without David we still survive. We've been around twenty-something years. David had some things to sift through, a juxtaposition of where he was coming from.

Gabrels (to Bowie): I don't want to speak for you.

Bowie (to Reeves): I can tell. You shouldn't have to explain.

How did you feel about being put on hold for the Sound+Vision tour?

T. Sales: We weren't put on hold. David told us of certain commitments he had and we were very communicative about that with him. We got time to do other projects.

Bowie: It was frustrating. Especially for me, because I was and still am so excited about the band.

In my opinion the Sound+Vision Tour was disappointing. It felt as if your heart wasn't in it.

Bowie: Yes my heart was in the Sound+Vision tour. I don't agree with you overall. It was one of the best solo tours I've done in years, the simplicity of design, the way it treated arenas, was among the most successful I or any other artist have been involved in.

So you didn't just do it for the money?

Bowie: Of course I did, but that doesn't defeat or diminish the effort I put into it. Anything of that size, you have to be aware of the kind of money you can make from it and I'd be a fool not to have done it.

T. Sales: We should point out that you didn't just do it for the money.

Bowie: That's immaterial, because nobody takes those things seriously anyway. As far as my creative input, I brought everybody I really adored into the team including Édouard Lock to work with conceptualization of what the tour would look like, and Adrian Belew and his band, who are some of the best musicians in a small band available today. Apart from those here today, for this is the ultimate band. It was socially one of the most enjoyable tours ever. The people around were so giving and generous.

T. Sales: That is assuming we'd want to go around backing up David Bowie on David Bowie songs. There was talk of doing it. After playing with Reeves and doing that record, we decided we wanted to do this, to shift gears and go and back up David. Well I'm a fan of David. I'm certainly behind his stuff.

Bowie: I'm a fan of yours, Tony.

T. Sales: But I'm behind Tin Machine more.

You've switched labels from EMI to Victory Records.

Bowie: This album deal we have is for one album for this band. I won't sign with any label as a solo artist right now. What we were very assiduous about was finding a label that only wanted Tin Machine, not David Bowie, because that was no use to us. Victory have shown nothing but enthusiasm for what we want to do. We don't want to be obligated to go into a studio to make another album if we weren't getting on with each other musically. This band only lasts as long as we are enjoying it. We will not be pushed into any other position. If it is all collapsing around us, nobody wants to be forced into that position. Tin Machine is absolutely the only focus of my musical energies at the moment. Certainly for the next year I won't be doing anything as a solo artist.

Take everything as it comes. If we still love each other at the end of the tour there will be a third album. But it is not a good thing to forecast. We might end up like Guns N' Roses meets the Who: at each others' throats. I doubt it. We're not playing the rock 'n' roll corporate game where our every movement is scheduled for the next ten years.

T. Sales: We play together because we like doing so. If someone else likes it . . . great. We can either do it or not.

Bowie: We only want to be with [a] company who are one thousand percent behind us. We don't want to suddenly find we are slipping into a David Bowie posture again. I've had enough of that, so have we. They have to bear that, too.

T. Sales: With the first label, I don't think they were best pleased. When we got together, it was just to see what happened. Out of that came a band that might have turned into his record, a Reeves solo record . . . It was obviously a band record.

Gabrels: We write all the songs together in various formats and David does most of the lyrics with Hunt.

Bowie: Hunt does some of the lead vocals on this record, ["Sorry"] and "Stateside." On the tour, he's singing more. It is evolving at its own pace, which is exciting. You just don't know where this band is going, which in this day and age is very refreshing.

Gabrels: Unlike the way it seems with Guns N' Roses, we spend time apart, doing whatever interests each individual member of the band, which makes it more interesting when we get back because everybody hopefully will have picked up new interests.

Bowie: Everybody has their own families, so we are not living in each other's hip pockets where it becomes incestuous when everything starts to spiral and sound the same, it's one singular shared experience most of the time. That's not a great thing for creativity.

What do you like to do in your time apart?

Gabrels: I read. I'm a music guitar junkie. I'll play with friends of mine in Boston I played with for ten years before Tin Machine. I stay active. Do soundtrack stuff. I'll paint and draw and do that stuff. Most of my friends are either hard news journalists or engineers, lawyers or local musos. It's a different existence. They might think I'm strange because I'm not strange, the popular myth of the rock musician. There are a lot of people who try to kill themselves trying to live up to it. We've got most of their names crossed out in our address book. I don't feel any desire to live a lifestyle other than the one appropriate to me, than to someone's concept of what a muso does.

People assume that we don't do the laundry, wash your dishes, and clean your cat box. Suddenly a little dove comes down and takes all that away. It's not like that. When I play with my friends, it's the same as it ever was: just couple of amps.

H. Sales: I play in Orange County hardcore clubs, in Tijuana clubs, funded my own band in lounges around L.A. I work in Texas with a new band Geffen signed that nobody wanted to work with because they'd actually have to work with them. I've seen this with producers: they'll come and work something out with [the] band.

That is not the way we make our albums. It was one of the reasons for going to Australia. There's a sad scene with Joe Perry saying if I want to be a rock musician, I'll go play in a bar in Cambridge—there's hardly anywhere to play, so he's obviously been out of the circle for a while. I'm a rock 'n' roll entertainer.

Bowie: I cannot imagine a situation where we would let [in] anyone who is not intimately concerned with the creative process. I couldn't stand to have that, a suit sitting there.

T. Sales: I have three children, so I am responsible for three little lives.

Bowie: Us three (laughs).

T. Sales: Seven, eight, twelve. And thirty-seven—their mother. I'm an actor as well. I do some TV things in L.A. I've done a dozen commercials for Pepsi, Polaroid. I did a Norwegian chocolate thing called the Blues. I don't put everything I have into the acting avenue right now, but it is a calling for me. I'm concentrating mostly on being a father. I'm a mature guy. I'm not a seventeen-year-old dreamer anymore. I like what I do.

Bowie: I'm still a seventeen-year-old dreamer. I did a movie before Christmas called *The Linguini Incident* with Rosanna Arquette, the first comedy I was offered—other than *Absolute Beginners* which was comedy by default. I do believe Julien [Temple] to be very talented and one day [he] will pull it all together to make a full-length movie that has a continuum to it. At the time, his weakness was dividing it into cameos. If you take any four-minute segment it looks great, but the cohesiveness was lacking because the quantum leap from five-minute videos to a full-length feature was lacking. He's working on his next one, which is a performance job, not special effect, so I believe he'll come through. He does have the ability.

Other than that, I did a piece for John Landis for a TV series called *Dream On*. He just started the new series and he directs the first episode and a sub director comes in for the rest. The first one of the new series was with myself, Sylvester Stallone, Tom Berenger, and Mimi Rogers. It also is a comedy. I play an arrogant prick of an English film director based on somebody we all know.

[In] *The Linguini Incident* I was a conman. It was Richard Shepard's debut movie, far more of a New York than an L.A. movie, sort of comedy Scorsese area thing. It was dark but some of it was hysterical. I was quite happy. I'm not going to do that much longer because I'm going to direct my first movie next year. I finished the script this year; it goes into the second draft next month. I go into pre-production in March to April and start shooting in August. I won't be in it and all else is secret.

You previously said there'd be no more films.

Bowie: How silly of me. If it's not received as any good I'll never make another movie. But I might be a genius [in it].

The scripts were so incredibly funny, I couldn't stop laughing. I love working with Landis, he's a very funny man. Working with Tim Pope lends itself to having fun. He's an incredibly eccentric man, very funny guy. He hid the cameras behind two-way mirrors so the only one we saw was the one I'm playing with. It was an odd atmosphere. We didn't know when he was shooting and when he wasn't. He makes videos the way we make records.

Tin Machine II is a lot more cohesive than your recent work. The inclusion of a Roxy Music cover—"If There Is Something"—harkens back to Ziggy days.

Bowie: It is our recent work. To take the wind out of those sails, the Roxy Music track was done for the first album, the second track we made, and we included it to show the cohesiveness of what we were doing then and now. We did it because after "Heaven's in Here" we were so exhausted that we didn't have it in us to write another song so we used an old song to show how we as a band would approach someone else's material. We also did "Working Class Hero" on the first album. When we were mixing this album, I remembered we'd done the Roxy song, pulled it out to see how it sounded. We really got off on it.

It's a very cohesive band because after the first record there has now been a two-year process, including playing live, be it only twenty shows. Playing live is when you understand it as a band. Certainly with waving the flag of playing live music it's going back twenty years. Sometimes we can be absolutely dreadful on stage; other nights I don't think there is a band to touch us. That is the exciting part, because we don't have machines or samples, or loop tracks, stuff like that behind us. That's the excitement of live music. We're not going to achieve mediocrity every night. Up and down continually. That is one of the things you got from seeing live bands: you never knew whether Cream were going to be happening, if they were playing as a unit or fractured, or whatever.

When we first played with Iggy, that was part of it. As musicians, we enjoy that process. That's where real music-making comes in by virtue of changing the songs every night. Because of Hunt, I never know where it's going to go. We might want to end it and it doesn't, or vice versa.

T. Sales: Most of our recordings are one take. It happens the first time. If you start changing it here and there, manipulating it, it becomes a whole other form, not the band.

Bowie: We've never played a new song through more than twice. If it doesn't work, it doesn't get recorded. It has to work almost immediately or it's not the song for us.

Gabrels: References to Cream aside, in a way this [is] a new breed of band. There are few other around like this. We're not twenty-year-old old kids in their first band. I'm thirty-five. I'm the baby of the band. I'm always quick to point that out.

Bowie: We're all adults.

Gabrels: We all share common life experiences. Instead of living in each other's pockets for five years like other bands do, we kind of parallel each other and intersect at the band, which affects the way we play. Kids may not like it.

What does your son Joe think of Tin Machine?

Bowie: Frankly, he thinks it's the best thing that I've been involved in for a long time. But then again, he likes Cream and Jimi Hendrix. Like most of the guys his age, he's totally into mid-sixties bands. And rap. Black American music and English mid-sixties bands with his particular crowd. That is where it's at—and some Mancunian stuff.

T. Sales: My eight-year-old son loves rap. He had to have a Walkman so he could rap at the breakfast table. He's also into Tin Machine, The Cure, all different kinds of stuff. At his age I wasn't into as much varied stuff. But there wasn't that choice. The stimulation of MTV, the peer stuff at school, the shaving of the heads—they are doing that at eight years old. In a way it's frightening he has an earring and he's eight years old, whereas I put a needle through my own ear. With the influx of crack dealers onto the school playgrounds, kids are strung out at twelve years old. It's a strange time. It's epidemic.

Bowie: At the moment, that is an American phenomenon. It hasn't taken England by storm the same way. God yes, I worry about drugs among my children. It's not a pleasant life at all. God forbid it should ever happen to any of our children, my immediate close circle of family and friends. We've all lost friends to drugs. One can't do anything about it. One only has control of one's own life.

H. Sales: I don't take drugs.

Bowie: Exactly. The same with me. Life by example is the only thing to do. We've all gone through it in the past. It's okay for me to explain all my experiences to anyone who cares to ask me, which I have done frequently. One uses one's life and one's negativity. It shouldn't just be put under the carpet, and something that shouldn't be talked about like our parents did.

T. Sales: My eight-year-old son isn't seeing his father drinking and frugging at home. He sees rock 'n' roll on TV, Guns N' Roses and all that sort of stuff . . .

Bowie: We should really get off them because we're not that close to them. Get off their case. They're a handy band to use but . . .

[He is interrupted by a general swell from the band.]

Bowie: A lot of that drug culture thing is because it's an exact mirror of what they saw the Rolling Stones do.

Gabrels: You have to allow the artist to speak his mind about what is important. If you don't agree, that is a healthy thing because there is room for debate. You have to hope that people realize the responsibility they have. Some of it is because they are in the middle of it and lack an overview.

Bowie: When I see an artist propagating the use of drugs as a good life-style, one wonders and hopes that when the drugs kill him the example will be even better, frankly. You don't feel your feelings when you're on drugs. You're just feeling numb. When you stop doing drugs or when you stop drinking, that's when you feel feelings and then you've got to deal with them and if you never learned to deal with them then, boy, watch out.

The cleaning-up is a whole different ballgame. That's danger, if you want to end up black and blue in the morning, that's the time. Instead of just blue.

You think, "Fuck it I'm not worth anything at all. I'll be somebody else." When you can't be somebody else easily and you take drugs to be somebody else, anybody else. When you're real young you don't say, "When I grow up I want to be a junkie." You kind of drift into that later on. That's horrible. So I've heard.

If music is going in cycles, you seem to be riding the right wave.

Bowie: Be careful of your similes. Be careful of that axe, Eugene. An artist needs what he feels is missing in the atmosphere, that was missing in my life. It was a natural gravitation with a number of musicians who have subsequently formed the kind of band that we're endeavoring to. We need it. Things come out of need in life as in art.

T. Sales: I would not encourage my kids to do any one thing. I would encourage them to do something they had a drawing to. If it were negative I'd try to tell them, but you can't tell kids anything. I was into music as a kid. I'd go to sleep listening to doo-wop bands and I wanted to be a singer. My parents said if you don't get good grades you won't go anywhere.

Bowie: Joe's going to college now, studying liberal arts and communications. He has no idea of what he wants to do. I always knew. I was in the unfortunate position of locking myself into what I wanted to do when I was eight years old. Now I don't quite know what I'm looking for, but I'm on a street with no name—as we're in Dublin.

T. Sales: When I started I wasn't aware of what an A&R man was.

Gabrels: I think one should point out that if you are successful, it's a combination of Sweet Smell of Success and Spinal Tap; if you're not successful it's more like mopping floors, so you have to love the act of making music, because that will make the act of mopping floors worthwhile.

T. Sales: If I had known beforehand that being in rock 'n' roll meant spending a lot of time by yourself in unfamiliar rooms, a lot of hours with people who weren't particularly there, a lot of time traveling, a lot of time packing, that's not very attractive. But the music attracted me. The whole romantic idea that all entertainers do is show up, play, get paid, have the women—that's bullshit. Only Chuck Berry does that.

Gabrels: At least you're traveling, going to places you might not have done before. You have a lot of time to read, you can educate yourself. Every major city has museums and galleries.

H. Sales: And Burger Kings.

Bowie: We do visit museums.

T. Sales: Most musos sit in hotel rooms and drink. They get to try every brand of everything in the world.

Bowie: I love traveling as least often in an airplane as possible. I'll put up with it. I adore it. I'm still pretty into Indonesia. I would really like to go to India. I never went in the sixties because I thought it was full of hippies. I looked like one for a couple of weeks but my heart wasn't in it. I'd like to go there. Burma is terribly intriguing.

"Shopping for Girls" is about the child prostitution in North Thailand. Reeves's wife did a story on it. The song came about because we were talking about it one evening. I'd been to Thailand and witnessed the same sort of thing going on. Approaching that as a subject was pretty hard because one didn't want to make it a sensational kind of thing. It was hard to stop it being finger-wagging so it ended up as pure narrative.

What about your changing relationships?

Bowie: How's your love life, Dave? [laughs] I saw a double-page article in an English newspaper which purported to be an interview with Iman talking about me. I'd read something very similar a few years ago. Could it have been a cut-and-paste job? I haven't proposed to her. We have no plans to get married and we're very happy together. That's the only access to my private life you're getting.

Gabrels: We've all proposed to her, that's why it's safe.

Bowie: My main interest is here and now. Tour starts in October and ends in February, with a Christmas break. Europe, America, Japan, and probably Australia. We did talk about doing Indonesia, Bali, and maybe Delhi, Jakarta.

In the past it was a situation where people worked for me. This is where we work for each other. We split all the money four ways.

Gabrels: I try to keep more of it than the others but they're sharp.

H. Sales: In the beginning it might have been better if there were some salaries because with that you have all the expenses.

Bowie: The band is totally self-sufficient. It works for itself. It's not me funding the band. It's not my hobby. We all have a quarter commitment to the bills that come in.

H. Sales: I don't work for anybody. I haven't done that since the last mistake that was Iggy. At the time I didn't consider I was working for him, which was probably why the band was good.

Bowie: These guys know me so well they wouldn't give a shit about working for me.

H. Sales: This is a band in the truest sense. Whatever he's got from his past, he can have. There are no expectations whatsoever. Very nineties. I hope so. The nineties are the sixties upside-down.

Bowie: I love being full of potential. Before *Let's Dance* I had always felt quite happily balanced on the edge of mainstream popular music. I loved the money, but full establishment acceptance meant that I started to strangle myself artistically.

In the past I was a much more isolated person and one of the strongest things about this band is that we have a lot of common experience. We're all of a certain age, we're all divorced. At one point that was going to be our name: Four Divorced Men or Alimony Inc.

H. Sales: The only thing that makes us different from other bands is that the lead singer's a millionaire, but that's where it stops.

Bowie: Image is just a soft-option word for somebody who's not afraid of going through his changes in public. My changes are really on my sleeve. Tin Machine has style but it's not fashionable.

"ONE DAY, SON, ALL THIS COULD BE YOURS . . ."

Steve Sutherland | March 20 and 27, 1993, *New Musical Express* (UK)

Although plenty are able to do a takeoff of his quivering, mannered, Cockney-inflected vocal style, there is no instantly recognizable Bowie musical signature. Yet spotting his fans among recording artists is not difficult. Gary Numan, Echo & the Bunnymen, Joy Division, The Smiths/ Morrissey, and Pulp have little in common except certain things that mark them out as people who once spent hours in their bedrooms poring over the artwork of *Ziggy Stardust* or attended concerts with a lightning flash painted on their adolescent faces: affected delivery, esoteric lyrics, archness, quasi-disdain for conventional rock instrumentation, toying with androgynous imagery, or a combination thereof.

To that list of obviously Bowie-influenced artists can be added Suede, whose debut album appeared in the month of lead vocalist Brett Anderson's *New Musical Express*–arranged meeting with the man who was patently his musical godfather. Bowie's solo comeback album *Black Tie White Noise* came out the following month. This duologue between successive generations of men as pretentious as they were talented sprawled across two issues of the paper. During it, Anderson even helpfully explains one of the devices he has lifted from Bowie: "octave lower vocals."

Bowie provides some interesting family detail in the second part of the article, talking frankly of his mentally unstable half-brother Terry, who committed suicide in 1985. Peculiarly, Bowie refers to him as his "step-brother." Even more interesting is the fact that the feature contains what must be the most in-depth exploration of gay and bisexual themes in any Bowie interview.

A measure of the depth of Bowie's talents compared to those of many of his disciples is that, since this interview was published, his legend is undiminished, while Anderson has had a spotty career following his grand entrée.

Note: for "Night Flights" read "Nite Flights." —Ed.

PART ONE

It happens like this: Suede are about to release their debut album and, as fate would have it, one of Brett's biggest heroes, David Bowie, is about to release an album of his own about a week later.

Now, considering Suede are widely reckoned to be crucially influenced by the glam scene that Bowie invented in the '70s, and seeing as Bowie's forthcoming "Black Tie White Noise" LP is widely rumoured to be a return to some kind of sassy form after about a decade in the wilderness, it seemed a damn good idea to get them together.

So I compile a Suede tape for Bowie—I occasionally send him tapes; he likes to keep in touch. I include the first two singles and some bootleg stuff, and wait. Bowie usually writes back to say thanks but no thanks. This time it's different.

"Of all the tapes you've ever sent me, this is the only one that I knew instantly was great," he tells me later. Bowie agrees to the meet. I inform Brett, who's been kept in the dark up until this point because I didn't want to disappoint him if it didn't come off and I didn't want to give him enough time to get cold feet if it did.

We meet on a dull afternoon at a studio in Camden that Bowie has hired for the specific purpose of playing Brett his new LP. Brett is nervous, Bowie assured. They do photos together. Bowie has brought along a contact sheet of a photo session he did with William Burroughs in 1973. Today Bowie is dressed just like Burroughs was—grey suit, white shirt with a thin, dark stripe, and a fedora. Brett is dressed like Brett, in what the tabloids have taken to referring to as his "jumble sale chic."

"Tell you what, I'll be Bill and you be me," Bowie says to Brett. It helps break the ice.

Photos over, we retire to the studio where Bowie plays us some of his new album. He jokes about the tracks I won't like in advance. He's right every time. There's a great, hard-edged Eurodance number called "Night Flights," a crappy, campy cover of Morrissey's "I Know It's Going To Happen," something weird called "Pallas, Athena" in which Bowie's voice is treated beyond recognition, going on and on about God being on top of it all. "I don't know what the f— it's about," he admits.

We laugh and drink tea. Brett compliments Bowie on the way he's messed around with his sax sound and Bowie bemoans the purist snobbery that surrounds the instrument. "It's great when you don't know what you're doing," he says. "Like when Lennon told the orchestra to play from the bottom note to the top note for 'A Day In The Life.' He didn't know what an insult that could have been to those guys." Bowie tells us what a thrill it was to work with Mick Ronson again and Brett goes off for a piss.

"Doesn't he look like a very young Jimmy Page?" Bowie asks. "Page played on some of my early sessions. He must have been six years old! Hahaha. Brett looks just like him. Believe me, I'm really accurate. Especially when he smiles . . ."

Brett returns and Bowie plays us one last track. It's "Looking For Lester," a racy jazz instrumental with Bowie getting off playing with trumpeter Lester Bowie. He admits the title cheekily emulates Coltrane's "Chasing The Trane."

Then the track finishes and Bowie precludes any embarrassment about getting down to the interview by immediately launching into a long and elaborate question about Postmodernism. He starts with Picasso stealing the native form from the Ethnological Museum in the '20s and expands it through the recent history of Western art until he arrives, somewhat flamboyantly, at his point.

"Your playing and your songwriting's so good that I know you're going to be working in music for quite some time," he says to Brett. "But how aware were you of how deeply you were involved in the chord progressions of . . . well, actually not specifically me at all; you're far nearer Roxy Music."

Brett, visibly relaxed by not having to make the running, replies that he has always been quite bored by Postmodernism as an idea: "We never wanted to trigger off any political or cultural things in anyone's mind by alluding to the past, like Denim or people like that. That's too theoretical. It's just that lots of the things from that period, lots of the devices, strike a chord with me emotionally rather than mentally. Lots of things that we rip you off for like . . . well, specifically like the octave lower vocals and things like that, I just love what it does to the song; how it makes it darker.

"But half the time people say we sound like somebody that I won't even have heard. Like, I haven't heard one song by . . . what's his name?

Joe Brown? Y'know, the Cockney Rebel bloke, apart from 'Come Up And See Me' but everyone keeps saying we steal from him."

Bowie: "Oh him . . . I wouldn't even claim to have heard that if I were you! Hahaha! When Steve sent me your tape, I listened to it with an open mind because, although I'd heard of you, I hadn't actually heard you before. And I thought, 'Well, it's supposed to be a '70s thing' but I got over that within seconds. I was very aware that there was a very bright set of minds working and your writing abilities are really very mature. I wonder, are you apprehensive that there are bands like Denim around?"

Brett: "Yeah, completely, because you start getting put in the same bucket and it's just a coffin really."

Bowie: "In our day," he says, a little reluctantly, and with some sense of resignation, *(he goes into theatrical cock-er-nee)* "we used to 'ave to make do wiv stack 'eel boots . . . No, actually, looking back on it, we were a very odd little genre because, to knock out The Sweet and all that, there was actually only a very few of us working. What became known as glam or glitter rock wasn't a movement at all, musically. It was very limited. On this side of the Atlantic there was myself, Roxy, Bolan and, to a certain extent, Slade, I guess."

Brett: "You didn't feel part of a gang then?" Bowie shakes his head. "So it's only that people like Suzi Quatro came along and started ripping you off that, in history's eyes, makes it seem like it was a scene. I think people get it wrong when they talk about 'Bowie, T-Rex, blah blah blah.' I always thought of your gang as much more you and Iggy and Lou Reed, people who were just thinking rather than . . ."

Bowie: "Yes, well that actually became my outfit, but I always put myself in with the English . . . and with the New York Dolls to a certain extent but never with people like, say, what's his name? Elizabeth Cooper. Hahaha! Alice Cooper were just a rock band who wore mascara. I don't think they even tried theatricality until they saw the English bands. It felt to us that they were more Frank Zappa than part of this kind of compunction to parody rock and make it very vaudeville or whatever it was that some of us were doing."

Brett: "Did you feel as though, at the time, you wanted to run away from it altogether?"

Bowie: "What d'you mean, with the advent of Suzi Quatro and Gary Glitter and all the rest? Yes, it actually became a sense of embarrassment, iconically. I mean, in my feather boas and dresses, I certainly didn't wanna be associated with the likes of Gary Glitter who was obviously a *charlatan*."

NME: They're running this *Sounds Of The Seventies* programme on TV just now and most of the glam rockers look like old pub rockers who'd chanced upon a third or fourth bite at the cherry. Y'know, like Shane Fenton reinvented himself as Alvin Stardust. They looked like beerguts in make-up, which isn't how I remembered it at all. Nostalgia just ain't what it used to be.

Bowie: "Very true. But we were very aware of it at the time and we were very miffed that people who had obviously never seen *Metropolis* (*Fritz Lang's ground-breaking silent sci-fi film about industrial society gone mad*) and had never heard of Christopher Isherwood (*the author of* Cabaret) were actually becoming glam rockers."

NME: Brett, do you think you've learned from what happened to people like David and to other icons from other eras? Do you spot the pitfalls and try to avoid them?

Brett: "No, I'm never that conscious of it. The only thing I'm really wary of is of things getting cartoonised, but that happens to anyone who's any good—you get misinterpreted and what filters through lacks all the subtlety of the original."

Bowie: "That's true and, way back then, I think I kidded myself that I didn't wanna be stereotyped because it would lock me into one kind of image that would be very hard to break away from if ever I wanted to start doing other things. But now I see it differently. Now I wonder if, in fact, the reason I didn't want to be stereotyped is that it would force me to actually examine what it was that I wanted out of my life. Now I have far deeper psychological reasoning for a lot of my actions in the early '70s which, at that time, I explained through the machinations of being in the rock business and what one needed to do to not be caught like a moth under the searchlight. But you're not in that position yet where you've been pinned."

Brett: "Oh there are people who want to pin us."

Bowie: "Before the first album comes out! That's awful! That's a fast event horizon if ever there was one!"

Brett: "Well, that's the media for you. Pinning only happens when people can only see one side of you because that's all they've been shown. That's why it's so necessary for us to play live because, when everyone's so critical and you're under such a microscope, it's necessary to actually go out there and be quite honest about it. I'd never wanna appear like a media fabrication, which I'm sure lots of people think we are. Premeditated is one thing we're completely not. We do what we do quite naturally."

Bowie: "Ah, therein lies the difference. That's where we vary. I may not have had any real understanding of why or how but what I was doing was a fabrication . . ."

Brett: "But the important thing is the ultimate product, and if you create something great out of premeditation, then that's fine. That was one of the greatest things that came out of the whole dance thing: the reaffirmation that it's the end product that matters. Dance music had the whole punk ethic—y'know, dispense with the musicians because it's the record that's made in the end that matters. I'm quite a believer in that."

NME: But you can't deny that you both inspire adulation because your fans respond to something that they believe is your personality being expressed through your music. When David said that he was making fabricated records—ie, inventing personalities—and when Brett says he makes his records naturally, they do, in the end, amount to the same thing. It's the character that people respond to. When Tin Machine got panned, it was because David just wanted to be one of the lads, one of the band, an ordinary bloke. And people didn't want that. They wanted a star. We need our heroes. We need people to stand out, to be individual, because we can't. And with Tin Machine, David was absconding from his duty.

Brett: "It's funny that, when David started Tin Machine, it was at the start of the cult of non-personality and the whole Manchester thing, when the star of the alternative press was someone called Ian Brown, y'know, the blankest name in the world. And everything was geared towards being mates. Maybe you were just feeling the times . . ."

NME: Well, that's what people always say about David Bowie, that you react to the zeitgeist like a chameleon. Compare "Black Tie White Noise" to, say, Bryan Ferry's new LP, "Taxi," which is just an old crooner doing cover versions, and it's obvious that it's important to you to matter. That your artistic pride won't let you rely on your reputation. I mean, to make this album in the middle of Tin Machine projects is another statement of your individuality. You still won't be pinned down and, whether it's for selfish reasons or not, it seems to me that the way you behave is somehow synonymous with what Brett is always saying in the press, that we should speak out against the facelessness and sloth indicative of artistic cowardice.

Brett: "I agree. David, did you have quite a romantic self-image before you started? Did you have an image of yourself as an individual star?"

Bowie: "I think I had an image of myself more as an artist somehow; an artist who would work through the medium of entertainment somehow or other only it never became clear until I actually put together the whole Ziggy Stardust concept. Everything up until 1970 now seems to have been a learning period for me. I just put myself through every possible situation I could, just to see what would happen to me and what kind of taboos I could mess with, just to see if it meant anything."

Brett: "No-one had ever really messed with anything before, had they? I mean, there'd been stars but, y'know, Elvis Presley was the biggest star and he never wrote his songs and he would always just state that he was just a singer."

Bowie: "Yeah, and it's strange that, when I broke a rule, it really produced an awful lot of hostility. I mean, when I was going through my bisexual stage in the early '70s, and then it became quite apparent to me eventually that I was heterosexual, I never disclaimed my messing around with bisexuality. But the fact that I wasn't gonna be a spokesman for the gay community really produced a lot of hostility. It seemed like, 'Well, how about guys like me then, guys that sorta try it out for a few years? Where do we actually fit in? Us who aren't gay; us who are straight but just wanted to find out?'"

Brett: "You're not allowed to be like that."

Bowie: "Exactly. Everybody wanted me to be either one thing or the other or definitely bisexual or definitely this or definitely that. And I found that quite disturbing. Even some of my own friends who were gay, afterwards, it was like, 'Oh, you really sold out, you let us down, you were just a fraud'. Well, trying out bisexuality is not being a fraud, what it is is trying out bisexuality. That's what it is."

Brett: "And just because you express yourself bisexually artistically, it doesn't necessarily have anything to do with what you're like personally. I don't think it actually matters what you do personally because you're just one individual in the world but, when you make a record, you speak to millions of people and that's so much more important. It's like when you get fan mail from people wanting you to solve their problems. You're not a psychiatrist. People should gain strength from your records, not from you individually as a person."

Bowie: "Yeah, people just won't let you diversify. So . . . hey, let's diversify! I find the whole banner-waving of AIDS over people's lives scary. I mean, I would hate to be a 14-year-old now and believe that there was no way that I was ever gonna be able to try and find my orientation if I was at all confused; that I was already a victim, already a prisoner. We're almost being told. 'Hey, forget about sexuality, it no longer exists. You can't do anything apart from meet one person and stay with that person for the rest of your life.'

"I go against the flow of, 'Oh, you mustn't mess around any more.' I think that's bullshit. Of course you've gotta take every possible precaution you can, but for us to feel our sexuality is crushed at this point could become the greatest impotency-bringing factor of the whole civilisation because it's going to produce incredible psychological nightmares with people, especially young people. Young people are almost being told that they will never have the fun that everybody else had for the rest of history and, ha, just hard luck."

Brett: "Hence nostalgia."

Bowie: "Yes, absolutely. And, of course, it's starting to build this huge anti-gay thing and, until they find a cure for AIDS—which I have no doubt they will—I think anti-gay campaigners will have a heyday. And I think we should be aware of all this, aware that you should keep pushing the walls because so many breakthroughs were being made in the '70s whether people want to admit it or not. We now look back and, because some of those experiments went wrong—specifically the ones with drugs—that doesn't mean that all the experiments were negative. The Dionysus-style energy we have of being and doing, that's what makes us human beings, that's what gives us the advantage over every other living energy form, and it is right and our need to be continually pushing the boundaries of what we believe our existence means. And there are people who are telling us we shouldn't be doing that. It's terrifying!"

NME: People are suspicious of people like you, people in showbusiness, talking like this. They're always looking for the angle. Like, the thing people say about your bisexual period is what a great gimmick it was.

Bowie: "Well, talking personally, I had been bisexual for many years before I made that statement but, yes, it was perceived like that and, yes, I found out I wasn't truly a bisexual but I loved the flirtation with it, I enjoyed the excitement of being involved in an area that, up until that particular time, had been perceived as a social taboo. That excited me a lot."

NME: And now Brett is being accused of flirting with ambivalent sexuality to titillate us into buying his records.

Bowie: "That's enough these days! Hahaha! In the dangerous '90s, you even talk about it and you'll get beaten with a big stick."

Brett: "That really pisses me off because the reason people might think I flirt with it is because I use it in my songs. But I use it in my songs because I don't wanna write about boy-meets-girl. I sometimes write my songs from a gay point of view regardless of whether I am gay or not because I think there's certain segments of society that have been horribly underrepresented in pop music. That's why I write like that. It's not a desire to be deliberately commercially viable or deliberately difficult for any profitmaking reasons or anything like that. It's because I truly feel that even some gay men tend to play the game and that bothers me quite a bit."

NME: So what you're saying is that, in 1993, sex is even more taboo than it was in the '70s? I suppose that goes some way to explaining why Madonna managed to whip up so much publicity with her Sex book.

Bowie: "Well, it looked like the outtakes from a Helmut Newton session but the action itself was so confrontational that I was very impressed with it. I'll definitely go against the usual opinion about her. We don't have to say any more that she exploits the situation—we know that, OK. But I think the action that she made in doing that at this particular time is very adventurous. It almost doesn't matter what she thought she was doing. Divorce the action from the personality and that was an extraordinarily courageous and adventurous thing to do. In a way, more things like that should probably happen to fight the tide of repression."

NME: If you'd thought of it in the '70s, would you have done it?

Bowie: "Yes, I probably would. But the thing is, I didn't take photographs of it. I did it! Hahaha! Tony Defries (*one* of *Bowie's old managers*) never thought of it, obviously. Otherwise I'm sure all those hotel shots would have been out everywhere. Hahaha! No doubt they probably will be one day."

Brett: "What it actually achieved is commendable because everyone should be completely aware of their sexuality no matter what it is. But what bothers me with Madonna was that it was so Athena, so bland."

Bowie: "Sure, but I'm not sure people are aware that they have every right to demand from themselves their true sexuality any more. If a guy or a girl feels that they're gay, they're probably thinking about how they're gonna hide it these days rather than, 'Let me go and find out if I really am.' They daren't even think about it now. They're being told not to think about it. I expect a campaign coming out soon to say, 'Make Youself Straight' and 'Learn Monogamy Right Now' and 'The First Girl That You Meet, That'll Be The Only Girl In Your Life.' That's how it used to be! Hey, you got a girl pregnant, you married her."

NME: And this sort of thing forces the gay community to become more radical which, in turn, alienates it even further from what is perceived as the mainstream.

Bowie: "Exactly. No doubt we'll get the little pink triangles eventually. One rather well-known television political commentator suggested they all have their backsides tattooed with numbers! In all seriousness! This was a respectable person. That's the scariest part. He's taken seriously."

NME: OK, so we all agree that Brett has the right to be ambivalent about his sexuality in his songs and we agree with David that a person has the right to be ambivalent with his or her own personal sexuality, but doesn't that also apply across the board? For instance, David, you've covered Morrissey's "I Know It's Going To Happen" on your new album. I don't know if you're aware that he's been ostracised recently for his ambivalent use of the Union Jack at his concerts. It has been decided that Morrissey does not have the right to be ambivalent about race and that he should make a statement regarding whether he is or is not a racist. Are we not beating him with the same stick?

Brett: "No. The difference is, the way I speak about things is in a positive way and I think the way he's speaking about certain issues of racism is in an intentionally negative way. Therefore, I think we need to know the reasons behind it."

Bowie: "I have to be careful here because I'm not quite sure what he said. But what I believe he said is that blacks and whites will never get on. I think that's the general tone of it. So I guess the adult approach is to say, 'OK, let's take his question and figure out for ourselves our own answer to that. Will they get on? Won't they get on? And why?' He is just posing a question so there is an argument that it's perfectly OK for him to just pose that question.

"He's not giving us facts either way or giving us his feelings on the matter. Surely it would only be really negative if he were to say blacks and whites will never get on because it's obvious that one is superior to the other."

NME: I think his silence is more sinister than that. I'm suspicious of his motives. He's never, to my knowledge, committed one altruistic act in his life so I don't know why he should start now.

Brett: "He's said other things in the past about how reggae is vile and hang the DJ and other things with all these connotations but, the thing is, he might actually be one of the most generous people that's ever lived. I don't know if it's true but, by making himself a target, he might actually be trying to mend some gaps and build some bridges. I mean, he must know that he's making himself a target because he's not stupid and, by having criticism directed towards him, he might actually be doing some good. It might just be possible that he's thinking that."

NME: Oh come on! He's just luxuriating in playing the misunderstood, the martyr, and damn the consequences.

Bowie: "I must say I found him charming the couple of times I met him. When he heard my version of 'I Know It's Going To Happen' (*which, according* to *Brett, is, "very '50s,* very *Johnny* Ray"), it brought a tear to his eye and he said, 'Oooh, it's so-o-o grand!'"

NME: I've been suspicious of him from the start. All those bedsit anthems about wallowing in misery didn't seem to be helping anybody achieve anything. He was just making himself an icon on the back of other people's inadequacies and I don't find that in any way admirable.

Bowie: "Tell that to Samuel Beckett. Or John Osborne."

Brett: "David, what were you thinking about with The Thin White Duke? You were accused of similar things at the time and you were flirting with similar right wing symbolism."

Bowie: "Yes, I certainly was. I wasn't actually flirting with fascism *per se*, I was up to the neck in magick which was a really horrendous period. All my reading in that particular time were people like Ishmael Regarde, Waite and Mavers and Manley and all these sort of warlocks. And, y'know, it was all the secrets of the cabbalistic practices and all that, an intense period of trying to relate myself to this search for some true spirit. And I thought I was gonna find it though reading all this material.

"I didn't get into Crowley by the way, because he uses too much Greek. I'm always very suspicious of anybody who says they're into Crowley because they'd better have a pretty fair handle on Greek and Latin otherwise they're talking bullshit."

Brett: "You mention him in 'Quicksand.' "

Bowie: "Yes . . . Haha! Caught out! Well that's before I tried reading him. Hahahaha! That's when I had his biography in my raincoat so the title showed. That was reading on the tube. The irony is that I really didn't see any political implications in my interest in the Nazis. My interest in them was the fact that they supposedly came to England before the war to find the Holy Grail at Glastonbury and this whole Arthurian thought was running through my mind. So that's where all that came from. The idea that it was about putting Jews in concentration camps and the complete oppression of different races completely evaded my extraordinarily f—ed up nature at that particular time. But, of course, it came home to me very clearly and crystalline when I came back to England."

Brett: "Do you think, again, that you were picking up on the zeitgeist with the whole punk thing happening?"

Bowie: "I don't know because, over in Los Angeles, where all this was happening for me, I had absolutely no idea what was going on in England so, presumably, if the swastika was becoming a motif in the London punk scene, it was synchronistic. I was certainly unaware of it."

Brett: "Your antennae seem to be subconsciously in tune with things sometimes. Lots of movements in your career seem to be in tune with things that are happening that you might not be consciously aware of."

Bowie: "Yes, unnervingly so. At times it rather reminds me of the South Seas tribe that saw an aeroplane going over and then built a wooden model of an aeroplane in their forest hoping for that god to come back again. They had the shape of the aeroplane absolutely perfect but had no idea what it was. Y'know, sometimes I felt a lot of what I did was rather like that. I built models of the things that I didn't fully understand."

NME: It's interesting that you talk about it in the past tense. Do you not work that way any more?

Bowie: "Well, no. By virtue of the fact that I don't do drugs. I think that probably has a lot to do with the fact that I now have some idea of where my rationality comes from."

Brett: "D'you think you miss anything through not doing drugs?"

Bowie: "No, not at all, because, looking back, 'Low,' 'Heroes,' 'Lodger' and 'Scary Monsters' were all virtually drug-free . . . I won't say they were completely drug-free because I was still climbing out of it, but it wasn't anything like the kind of drug situations that I was going through, starting with 'Diamond Dogs' and through 'Young Americans' and 'Station To Station.' I think probably my best work came out of that late '70s period when there was virtually no drugs. . . ."

Brett: "How did you actually manage to keep a grip during the darkest depths of it?"

Bowie: "Well, I didn't."

Brett: "You were pretty prolific for someone so deeply into drugs."

Bowie: "D'you know, there are alcoholics that can keep the pretence of real, normal existence, clinging on by their fingernails, and nobody around them will ever suspect how deeply their problem goes? I think a lot of it was like that. I think I held on by my fingernails. I really did. Especially by 'Station To Station.' I look back at photographs of myself in those days and I just can't recognise the same person. It was extraordinary that I made it through. And the two or three times that I overdosed and actually came out of it . . . y'know, I'll never understand how I allowed it to become two or three times! Why the first time wasn't, 'That's it,' I don't know! But you just don't."

NME: Did you glean anything positive from it at all?

Bowie: "Um . . . I would have to feel so irresponsible in saying that I did. Possibly . . . but the chances of being able to dip into it just enough to get the positive stuff and then step out are so stacked against you that I would never in my right mind advise anybody to try it. Y'know, that's the trouble—it's like having this huge great oyster with this pearl in the middle and you could get the pearl but you do risk having your arms snapped off. Well, do we do it or not? I would suggest that possibly the best thing is just to not bother."

NME: And yet people continue to revere f—ups. We all know Jim Morrison grew into a great fat, wasted jerk and yet people steal his gravestone.

Bowie: "Well, we don't see enough photographs of the stupid fat berk lying in his bath tub, we only see him moody and handsome. It's the same with Dean. The youthful expression goes that he lived too fast and died too young. Well, maybe if more photographs were published of him after the car wreck . . .

"I think we are just led to believe by the mythology of drugs that, if we take them, we shall be put in touch with the secrets of the cosmos, that we shall have this straight line to knowledge of what it's all about. And it's just not true. I know from my past that I used drugs in such excess that I probably obliterated any chance of getting anything useful out of the situation at all apart from maybe these quick insights.

"One of them was this thing of only living in the moment. When I was heavily into coke, I couldn't remember two minutes past and I certainly didn't think about the future. I really felt as if I was only existing in the now and, because of that, there was this separation from personality and it was so totally focused into the moment that you felt you had a godlike insight into what was going on. And the feeling of no past and no future gave you a weightlessness of insight and perception.

"But I also remember there were times when I occasionally got near that when I was doing meditation back in the late '60s. It's just harder work and drugs are the quick passport to nirvana. You can get it on acid. You can get it on coke. You can get there quicker and you don't have to do all the hard labour of actually having to meditate and all that boring stuff, y'know? Learn a language instantly. Hahaha! It's like those little books on

Learn Japanese In A Week. You learn how to ask all these questions yet God forbid anybody should answer you in Japanese 'cos you won't have any equipment to understand what they're talking about!"

NME: But the people who buy Brett's records, the drugs that some of them come into contact with are likely to be very different from what you were taking in your days. Cheap crap that really f—s 'em up.

Bowie: "Yes, I must say it was good stuff in my day. In the giddy heights I was operating in, we had what was called pharmaceutical coke which is this extraordinary, sparkling medicinal stuff . . ."

Brett: "I think that's why Ecstasy became so big, because for lots of people it was the first drug that was actually like how people imagine drugs to be. When I first started taking drugs when I was young, you took something like coke and were left wondering what the big shit was all about."

Bowie: "It was probably an awful lot of talcum powder."

Brett: "But the first time you take Ecstasy, it's a completely different story. You think, 'This is the most amount of happiness that anyone's ever had since . . . Julius Caesar.'"

Bowie: "Well, I've heard from the people I know who still take drugs that the kind of purity that was around 20 years ago just doesn't exist any more."

NME: Listen to us! Drugs ain't what they used to be!

Brett: "Club culture's completely changed it all really. People don't take drugs how they used to at all as far as I can tell. I mean, drugs used to be used in a much more experimental way, it was a mental thing, whereas now people use them for an almost animalistic return. Y'know, you go to a club and you take Ecstasy which is quite an ugly thought to me. I wouldn't really wanna do that."

Bowie: "I know somebody who was with Aldous Huxley (*author of* Brave New World *and* The Doors Of Perception) when he died and it is absolutely true that he took acid as he was dying. Isn't that extraordinary? He went out tripping. That's real belief! That really is using yourself as a guinea pig and there's an element of that in wanting to be in music as well. Using yourself as a guinea pig is terribly seductive—what can I do to myself and how far can I go before it starts to have an adverse effect on me? How far can I go and get the delights of this thing before it starts turning nasty? The trick is knowing when to stop. Hahahaha!"

PART TWO: ALIAS SMITHS AND JONES

"There's quite a bit of you in this one . . ." Brett is at the tape deck, his back to us, about to play a rough mix of an as-yet-untitled track from the forthcoming Suede LP. Bowie puts his hand to his mouth, checks that Brett can't see him, and sniggers.

The track plays. Bowie closes his eyes and mock-swoons at the voluptuous chorus. He compliments Brett on his vocals and lyrics. "That's brilliant," he says. "The poignancy of the everyday is very apparent in your work."

Brett smiles: "Well, I'm bogged down by the everyday, so it feels like I should write about it."

"And here they come, the boys from Suede, dignifying the lot of the working man . . ." Bowie has adopted the plummy accent of a Second World War newscaster. "In their long shorts, with their shovels on their shoulders, they're ready to dig the trenches for the good of the English folk. Hooray, we say. Hip hip hooray."

"I always aim to take a small statement and make it elegant," laughs Brett. "The point is to actually speak to other people. I never actually do things for myself at all. Thoughts are essentially quite useless for me unless they're broadcast in an acceptable way.

"That's the great thing about Morrissey—loads of people have thought those thoughts before, his thoughts weren't particularly groundbreaking in any way, but the fact that he actually managed, for the first time, to express them to the general populous instead of being an elitist philosopher or just a writer that spoke to a few people, the fact that he actually managed to put those thoughts within an easily palatable art form; that's what was great about him."

Bowie: "And he did it asexually. So many of Morrissey's songs are very asexual. There's not a sexual bait to them, even if he talks about sexual situations. I think people are quite happy to take their grey anguish from a band like the Velvets or, at the moment, Nirvana, because it's got great dollops of sex attached to it. But he neutered it to an extent and that seemed kind of unfair or something. I think that maybe produces a lot of hostility toward him."

Brett: "Were you into The Smiths, then?"

Bowie: "I thought they were good, yeah. I got to like The Smiths more and more as it went on. I wasn't an immediate fan. I must say that I was disturbed to find out that the Pixies had broken up. That was the band that I thought was gonna happen in a big way, and I was a bit miffed when Nirvana came along using the same musical dynamics; y'know, keeping it way down for a verse and then suddenly bursting out with the volume on the chorus. And, of course, Charles was far better lyrically. His lyrics were fabulous. It feels like so many of the bands now are Johnny-Come-Latelys. There's a huge bandwagon. It's opened the gates to mediocrity."

Brett: "But anything good does, doesn't it?"

SS: *I guess there's a whole generation of little Suedes* on *their way as we speak. And the irony of that is that you've got people who stand for individuality being copied. Instead of following the credo—be yourself, do something different—they just waggle their bums and rip their shirts.*

Brett: "That's the whole horror of the music business generally though, isn't it? The visionless people who inhabit the music business are always looking for copies of bands that are now being successful and never actually looking for anything that's truly got any worth."

Bowie: "And boy, is the word 'business' applicable to the American situation right now? I mean, never, ever, has it become such a career-oriented option. It's light years away from how it felt in the early '70s. It really grinds 'em out. I mean, nobody believes in bands, works with them, promotes them. It's such a ruthless, ruthless business."

Brett: "That's why the independent scene should be championed. It's true that sometimes independent is just a byword for untalented but, on the other hand, there's a certain life to it that doesn't exist within the Sonys who just plough it out. The funniest thing is you get these comical bands who are like major label ideas of what indie bands are. I mean, have you heard this band The Lemon Trees? They're just MCA's idea of what an indie band is."

Bowie: "Ah, didn't they do Simon & Garfunkel's . . .'"

No, that was Lemonheads.

Bowie: "Oh, Lemonheads, That's right."

Same thing, though. What a crappy record that was. What a crappy thing to do.

Bowie: "Yes, I honestly don't get that at all."

Do you pity *Brett that he finds himself working now as opposed to, say, in the '70s?*

Bowie: "Yeah. For most new bands starting up it must be a f—of an uphill climb."

Brett: "It is very stifling when there's so much emphasis on producing the goods. I mean, you could never have done something like 'Low' if your band were starting now. You'd have just been dropped, because people wouldn't have known what it was. But now, in hindsight, it's seen as completely ground-breaking."

Bowie: "Yeah, We'll be listening to the first Tin Machine album in a few years and re-evaluating that, I'm sure. Hahaha!"

I take it that you've never been in the position of having an A&R man come into the studio to tell you that maybe the backbeat shouldn't be like that?

Bowie: "Never! Absolutely not!"

I bet Brett has to put up with that sort of thing, though.

Brett: "Yeah, and that's why you have to be shrewd in deciding who you work with. That's why we signed to an independent in this country, so we don't have that kind of interference, because in the end the artist does know best, otherwise it just becomes a product."

Bowie: "I can't imagine what that must feel like. I was advised, though. When I delivered 'Low' I got a telegram offering to pay for me to go back to Sigma Sound in Philadelphia to do another 'Young Americans.' They just couldn't accept 'Low,' they couldn't understand it. That's when I knew it was over with that particular company. And that's why it's so psychic that I should come back to Arista, within the RCA association, for this album. In my mind, it's almost as though I lost 'Let's Dance,' 'Tonight' and 'Never Let Me Down' and, if I was putting together sets of albums, I would go 'Low,' 'Heroes,' 'Lodger,' 'Scary Monsters,' 'Black Tie White Noise.' It kinda slots in there in feel. And, of course, my last album with RCA was 'Scary

Monsters,' so the EMI years are this misfit that kinda got in there somehow. Maybe this is the album that Nile Rodgers and I did make in 1983, and there's been this timewarp ever since!"

Maybe the fact that so many people said Tin Machine were crap gave you your attitude back? Maybe that was the edge you needed to start fighting for your music again, and maybe that's what gives the album its strong sense of purpose?

Bowie: "Funnily enough, I think working with Tin Machine was a confidence-builder, because I lost my confidence during the '80s and I was quite willing to use the stand-in of indifference. I always look back on those two albums after 'Let's Dance' as being indifferent; I purposely didn't get very involved with them. Now I listen to 'Never Let Me Down' and I wish I had, because there were some good songs on it, but I let go and it became very soft musically; which wasn't the way I would have done it if I had been more involved."

When I heard that this album was inspired by your wedding to Iman (two pieces were specifically composed for the occasion), I feared it was gonna be soft as shite.

Bowie: "Yeah, I know: 'He'll probably put Iman on the cover. Oh, she's gotta be in the video.' Hahahaha! I knew what people would think when they heard I was going back in to work with Nile. But I was thinking, 'I hope this doesn't turn into another 'Let's Dance,' and that probably drove me even harder. It is a very personal album.

"'Jump They Say' is semi-based on my impressions of my step-brother and probably, for the first time, trying to write about how I felt about him committing suicide. It's also connected to my feeling that sometimes I've jumped metaphysically into the unknown and wondering whether I really believed there was something out there to support me, whatever you wanna call it; a God or a life-force? It's an impressionist piece—it doesn't have an obvious, cohesive narrative storyline to it, apart from the fact that the protagonist in the song scales a spire and leaps off.

"There's also a personal reason why I cover Cream's 'I Feel Free' on the album. One of the times I actually went out with my step-brother, I took him to see a Cream concert in Bromley, and about halfway through—and I'd like to think it was during 'I Feel Free'—he started feeling very, very bad.

. . . He used to see visions a lot. And I remember I had to take him out of the club because it was really starting to affect him—he was swaying. . . . He'd never heard anything so loud; he was ten years older than me and he'd never been to a rock club, because jazz was his thing when he was young. He turned me on to Eric Dolphy . . .

"Anyway, we got out into the street and he collapsed on the ground and he said the ground was opening up and there was fire and stuff pouring out the pavement, and I could almost see it for him, because he was explaining it so articulately. So the two songs are close together on the album for very personal reasons.

"So much of this album comes from a more emotional plane than I'm wont to generally show about myself. It's a very emotionally-charged album. There's a lot of jumping into the unknown about it. Maybe a lot of my negative things have surfaced on this album, that's why it's got such a saccharine ending. It's called 'The Wedding Song,' but it should have been called 'The Wedding Cake,' because it really is all icing with a couple on top."

The title track's the hardest thing Bowie's done in ages, and it transpires it was inspired by the LA riots. Bowie and Iman returned from Italy to LA the day the verdict of the Rodney King trial was announced.

Bowie: "We were standing on the roof of our apartment block, hand-in-hand, looking out at these fires starting up everywhere. And they were close! It was unbelievable. If it hadn't been so frightening, you could have looked out and said, 'Cor, dunnit look like *Blade Runner*?' But we thought, 'Oh shit, we're in this' and we did the same thing that everybody else did— we got in the car and went down the supermarket and started buying food, because we didn't know if we'd be able to get out of there for a few days.

"And I stayed up all night the second night because they were getting quite close to our block."

What were you going to do if they came knocking?

Bowie: "I had my car keys, I had some money and I had my jeans near the bed, and I was gonna quickly get dressed and get outta the building in case it went up."

Brett: "You should've told 'em you were born in Brixton!"

Bowie: "That wouldn't have helped. Hahaha! And I don't think showing 'em my wife would've helped either. They'd have just said, 'Well, you're both to blame. You're the problem!' Hahaha! It was terrifying.

"It really did feel like a prison where people had been imprisoned unfairly on no trial and no evidence, and that they'd just had enough. This was like the last insult by the guards and it was like, 'I don't care what you think, we're gonna f—you up!'

"And Clinton had better do better than he's doing at the moment. He'd better actually have some policies, because everybody's depending on this administration to resurrect this wave of hope and, if all that morale just dissipates—which is what's happening it the moment—all hell's gonna break loose over there."

How come you namecheck Benetton in 'Black Tie White Noise'?

Bowie: "Because I thought it was dodgy when Spike Lee did a thing for them. Y'know, I felt that reading about race relations through Benetton adverts was almost an insult. But then again, we're presuming that any statement made has to be altruistic. I mean, what actually has the most validity; altruism or opportunism? I wonder . . . I mean, because of the humanisation and dignifying of black athletes, are Nike doing a better job at promoting race relations than, say, the administration?

"Everybody loves Magic (Johnson), everybody loves those guys now, primarily because Nike made people of them and showed them as personalities rather than saying, y'know, 'All black guys are good at basketball.'

"It cut through all that and presented them as real, living human beings who think and have their own opinions, and it's very successful and very seductive and, yes, of course it sold loads and loads of Nikes. But has it done something else also, in terms of race relations?"

Spike Lee does get people's back up though, doesn't he? Maybe he's not the best spokesman . . .

Bowie: "Hahaha! Well, not the best spokesman from a white perspective. 'Shouldn't we have a more altruistic spokesman up there for the black people?' Y'know, they can have any damn spokesman they want! We don't have a say in it. We're far too keen, as white liberals, to suggest to black people how they should improve their lot. I don't think they actually wanna hear it anymore. They've got their own ideas of how they can improve their lot, and they couldn't give a f—what we think. They don't want our advice. Actually, they're pissed off every time we advise them now, us goody goody liberals."

We argue about homophobia and sexism in black music for a while, good-naturedly getting nowhere. Then I ask Brett if he can imagine being in Bowie's position, a dozen or so albums down the road?

Brett: "No, I think it's a bit dangerous thinking like that. Once you've got too clear a sense of your path, you lose a bit of your spark."
But do you have an idea of what you want to achieve?
Bowie: "To make a difference I bet."
Brett: "Just really a track record. That's it. To be a thorn that you can never really get out. Crawling off somewhere and having a comfortable lifestyle doesn't really interest me at this point. Right now I don't particularly want to live in comfort or in particular personal harmony or anything like that, because I think that would be quite an unhealthy thing at this stage."
Bowie: "What! Yeah, well let me tell you, my son . . . hah ha haha."
Brett: "Go on, dad!"
Bowie: "Well, you're going to give up a lot, you really are."
Brett: "I'm willing to give it up, though, I really am."
Bowie: "You are at the moment, but believe me . . . haha . . . Oh dear, I don't like this bit at all. Hahaha. Um, you see, it works like this . . . I presume you don't have children yet?"
Brett: "No, I don't."
Bowie: "Well, you see, I do. I have a son, and one of my major regrets is that I just wasn't there for the first six years of his life. And that is a continual source of guilt and regret, because I really should have been there, and he really should have been able to expect that I would he there for him. But you don't know that you're giving all that up when you're going through it. It's only in hindsight that you think, 'Wow! I really let go of some serious relationships along the way. If only I'd known.' It's true when they say you

sacrifice a lot as a musician. And it's generally out of selfishness. You see something and you go for it. But you don't realise that until much later."

Brett, are you saying that you're deliberately avoiding relationships?

Brett: "No, I'm not deliberately avoiding them, but I'm very wary of them. I don't feel there's any space in my life for those sorts of things. It's nothing to do with not having the time, it's actually to do with realising that creativity comes through tension and, as soon as you get too comfortable, it all goes."

Isn't that a recipe for loneliness? Won't you wake up one day and think, 'I've achieved all this but what the f— for?'

Brett: "Maybe, but at the moment it doesn't really matter to me. The thought of loneliness doesn't really bother me. I don't feel I'm some sort of Morrissey. I've always had really good friends that I've always relied on; I've always had a lot of people in my life. I've never been a sad case. I've always been too much inclined to the other side of life if anything, to having a good time . . ."

Bowie: "'Friends I've always relied on' . . . There's a giveaway, young Brett. Hahaha."

Brett: "You a prophet of doom or what?"

Bowie: "No. It's just that I've never heard a young artist say, 'Well, I want a fairly balanced life. I don't want the work to actually take over my private life' . . ."

Brett: "You want it to take over, you want it to occupy your dreams and everything. That's the whole point. Otherwise it wouldn't be any good."

Bowie: "Yeah, and that's why you do have to remain empty of relationships and all those things. But you're always the loser in the end. You must be aware of that."

Brett: "I am, yeah."

Bowie: "It sounds very pretentious, but that is the sacrifice one makes. You do sacrifice a lot of real, honest, internal psychological safety by doing what we're doing. You end up as some sort of emotional casualty because you learn how to keep relationships away from you. And breaking that habit suddenly becomes very hard. You suddenly realise at some point that you don't have the equipment for creating relationships; because you've never utilised it, you don't know how to do it. You've lived your life learning how to not create relationships that will tie you down to anything or anybody. And there you are, at a certain age, thinking, 'Wonder how you get to know people and develop something?'

"Art is a burden isn't it? Hahaha!"

Brett: "Oh it is!"

Bowie: "Genius is pain. Oh, dear me."

It's time to part. Brett is due back in the studio. Bowie has another engagement. They swap phone numbers and Bowie promises to come and see Suede play live the next time he's around. The original plan—that I should interview Bowie separately for an hour about his new album—has gone out of the window. We've used up all our time and more. "That was too much fun," says Bowie.

Later, Brett tells *NME*'s John Mulvey: "It was just great. I was really shitting myself, much more than when I go onstage, 'cos it could have been really dreadful, it could have completely changed my point of view about a whole section of my life . . . which would have been quite grim. I imagined coming back and smashing up all my Bowie records, but he was actually one of the nicest people I've ever met . . . just so, so charming.

"He came in and he smelt beautiful, that was the most important thing. He smelt of Chanel—but not poor person's Chanel. He wafted in in a suit. It was just like *Jim'll Fix It!*"

STATION TO STATION

David Sinclair | June 10, 1993, *Rolling Stone* (US)

In 1993, Bowie took David Sinclair of *Rolling Stone* on a memory tour of his old London haunts. He found many of them unrecognizable or gone, but also found evidence that he'd left his mark on the culture—not least because some passersby instantly recognized him. Surreally, they remained unfazed, as if characters from one of his more arch song tableaus.

As well as sharing his bliss at his newly married state, Bowie helpfully clarified that famous "I'm gay" comment of two decades previous: apparently he'd always, in fact, been a "closet heterosexual."

Recalls Sinclair now, "Bowie did a lot of work himself on this piece. He dug out old diaries, figured out our route and the various stopovers himself, and supplied his own chauffeur and car. He seemed to be on a mission to exorcise a few ghosts. He got emotional several times during the day: on stage at the Hammersmith Odeon—it was bitterly cold—and, later, talking about Mick Ronson (who was desperately ill and died a couple of weeks later). It was one of the most gratifying interviews I ever did. I felt like I was watching his life flashing past in front of my eyes."

Note: the resumption of Tin Machine activity Bowie mentions herein never happened. —Ed.

In a dingy alleyway in Soho, London's notorious red-light district, David Bowie stops in front of a doorway. Uncertain of whom or what he will find on the other side, he pushes a buzzer.

"Yes," says a voice on the intercom.

"Hi," says Bowie. "Did this used to be Trident Studios once upon a time?"

"Indeed so, a long time ago," comes the voice from inside.

"This is David Bowie. I used to record here. Do you think I could come in for a second?"

A moment's pause. The door swings open. Bowie walks in. Directly in front of him is a short flight of stairs, and filling virtually the entire wall on the landing, halfway up, is a massive print of . . . David Bowie, as photographed on the set of *The Man Who Fell to Earth*.

"Well, it's nice to feel you've left a mark," Bowie says, as various surprised people emerge from their offices to form an ad hoc welcoming committee.

> *Time—He's waiting in the wings*
> *He speaks of senseless things*
> *His trick is you and me, boy*
> —"Time" (1973)

In London, on a cold spring morning, Bowie is on a voyage round his past, revisiting the old haunts of the 1970s and reviving memories of a period of English rock when the brilliance of his work, indeed the very fact of his ambiguously gorgeous presence, eclipsed all other stars.' But this trip down memory lane, like his new album, *Black Tie White Noise,* is no idle exercise in retro indulgence, more a timely celebration of a legend that has become reenergized by the latest turn of the fashion wheel.

After a long period of artistic and popular decline, Bowie has emerged like a man reborn. At the peak of his powers, of course, he reinvented himself on a regular basis, but this is something different.

To say that his career went cold in the 1980s would be putting it mildly. While his lackluster post–*Let's Dance* solo work eroded his standing in the mainstream, his detour into pregrunge, one-of-the-lads rock & roll with Tin Machine left even his hard-core fans at first baffled and then resentful.

Two things have happened since then. One: Bowie has relocated the mother lode. Returning with his first new solo album in six years, he has picked up where 1980's *Scary Monsters* left off. Out has gone the guitar-based rock; in has come a gleaming new set of dance-track rhythms and keyboard-based arrangements redolent of his best work on albums like *Station to Station* and *Heroes* but with a new jazz dimension reflected by the contributions of trumpeter Lester Bowie and by the singer's own valiant efforts on saxophone.

Two: The 1970s have suddenly become hip. Here in England, the era of Bowie's greatest vitality and influence is providing the unlikely template for the latest music and fashion trends of 1993. A new generation of writers, artists, musicians, designers and fans is going back to take another look at that most glamorous, decadent and frequently reviled of decades.

So it is that Bowie has set off to see for himself the physical remains of his past, to remind himself—now that everyone else wants to know—of where exactly the bones are buried. Hence the unannounced arrival at what used to be Trident Studios, the place where he recorded *Hunky Dory* (1971), *The Rise and Fall of Ziggy Stardust and the Spiders From Mars* (1972) and most of *Aladdin Sane* (1973) with in-house producer Ken Scott.

In those days it was a sixteen-track studio with a state-of-the-art reputation. It eventually closed in 1984, and now the building has been split into separate floors. Of the actual studio where *Ziggy Stardust* was recorded, the four walls remain but not much else. It is now used by an audio-video production company specializing in dance records. A couple of amplifiers and an old bike are stacked in a corner. There is a bit of blue screen set up at the back, and most of the walls are covered with a sort of tatty felt underlay. It all looks a bit run-down.

Not like it was in July 1968, when it was the first studio in London to boast a functioning eight-track recording machine. The Beatles came here to record "Hey Jude." In the early 1970s, Elton John, Supertramp, T. Rex and Queen were regulars here. And in 1972 it was on this very spot that Bowie and the late Mick Ronson shared production duties while Lou Reed recorded *Transformer*. (Ronson, a frequent Bowie collaborator, succumbed to cancer on April 29th, just three weeks after the release of *Black Tie White Noise*.)

"Lou loved Soho, especially at night," Bowie says. "He thought it was quaint compared to New York. He liked it because he could have a good time here and still be safe. It was all drunks and tramps and whores and strip clubs and after-hours bars, but no one was going to mug you or beat you up. I think it's got quite respectable now, but in those days it was very twilight."

Bowie is shown around the former Trident premises by several of the building's current occupants. Somebody asks him for an autograph, a memento for his eighteen-year-old son, who is just getting into Bowie's music. Bowie, who writes left-handed (even though he does everything else right-handed), scrawls a suitable message, the pen gripped close to his platinum wedding ring. He checks the date and finds it is Saint David's Day (March 1st).

"Do you ever have the impression that you were twenty years ahead of your time?" the man asks.

"Oh, Lor," Bowie says with a sigh. "Well, only when there's a revival. Obviously, we were having a very exciting time. There were a bunch of us that knew we were on the wave of something that would be the dominant sound of the 1970s. I don't think it was quite clear what exactly it was at the time. But it took us over rather than us taking it over. There's a kind of *Zeitgeist,* and if you're capable of plugging into it. . . . I don't know what happens, but I really believe that the fabric of your music starts to reflect what society is feeling. Music is usually well behind what society is actually thinking, and it's those odd times when you catch up that it really becomes invigorating."

In the London of 1993 fashionable society is once again thinking of the 1970s. The capital is in the grip of a massive retro craze focused squarely on the period that for many years was derided as the decade that taste forgot. As *The Face,* the U.K. style mag, put it: "If the Seventies were all about having a good time and trying to get your 'look' together with no money and no decent hairdressers, then the Nineties is looking pretty similar."

Many established artists have blatantly echoed the 1970s in recent months. Morrissey, whose last album, *Your Arsenal,* was produced by Mick Ronson, parodied a T. Rex sleeve for his Marc Bolan–influenced single "Certain People I Know." The Abba revival, kick-started last year by Erasure, has become a full-blooded mainstream phenomenon. Abba's *Gold* is lodged in the British charts, along with Mike Oldfield's *Tubular Bells II,* Neil Young's *Harvest Moon* and Pink Floyd's *Dark Side of the Moon,* which reentered the Top Ten in March, exactly twenty years after it was first released.

Meanwhile, a new wave of bands has plugged into the spirit of the early 1970s to create something more than mere revivalism. Primal Scream, which won the prestigious Mercury Music Prize for its album *Screamadelica,* makes no secret of its admiration for Mott the Hoople. Saint Etienne has located the interface between 1990s and 1970s pop kitsch and elevated it into a minor art form. Denim's album *Back in Denim* is littered with references to the Osmonds and glitter. And the Auteurs have released a superb debut, the audaciously titled *New Wave,* which combines songwriting in the great English tradition of Ray Davies with lyrics that create the sort of mythical world and strange personas that Bowie himself created with *Ziggy Stardust.*

Towering above all of them and about as plugged into the *Zeitgeist* of 1990s rock as possible is Suede, the London four-piece outfit that has unapologetically raided the Bowie–Ronson song book for inspiration, yet created a mood and a style that are all its own. The band's debut album topped the U.K. charts in April. But in a twist of fate that illustrates Bowie's almost supernatural sense of timing. Suede's massive-selling record was knocked off the top slot by *Black Tie White Noise.*

With his fey mannerisms, ambiguous sexuality and magnetic star appeal, Suede's singer, Brett Anderson, is virtually Bowie's alter ego of the 1990s. But far from stealing Bowie's thunder, Anderson, through his hero worship of Bowie, has given a vital boost to Bowie's reputation, especially among a new generation of fans. The joke in London media circles is that Suede is really just an invention of Bowie's record company, the band's mission to pave the way for Bowie to make a suitably spectacular comeback.

> *Time may change me*
> *But I can't trace time*
> —"Changes" (1971)

"It's a bit disappointing in some respects to look back, because there was actually no 'scene' as such in the early Seventies in London," Bowie says as his car travels east, past the splendor of the Houses of Parliament, across the Thames at Westminster Bridge and through Elephant and Castle into the shabbier environs of the East End.

"If there was supposed to be something like a glam-rock scene emerging, it seemed to be happening only within three or four disparate bands,"

Bowie says. "There was no club or area that became the focus for our particular kind of music. We worked very much on our own, in isolation from each other. There was Roxy Music, myself, Marc Bolan [T. Rex] and it really is hard to think of anyone else who was actually doing anything very much between 1970 and 1973. I guess Eno was still doing a lot of stuff at the RCA [Royal College of Art]; he was probably still going backwards and forwards from being a conceptualist to being a rock star. In the States you had the equivalent of bands like the Flamin' Groovies, the New York Dolls and to a lesser degree Alice Cooper."

The car travels south down the Old Kent Road. Looking out of the window, Bowie points to a pile of rubble on a building site. "That used to be a pub called the Bricklayers Arms," he says, "which was one of my earliest constant gigs in the Sixties. There's another one further down here called the Green Man. They were very, very tough venues; real heavyweight South London kids. We were still doing a lot of R&B stuff, Marvin Gaye, 'Can I Get a Witness,' that kind of thing. But you had to be pretty tight to keep their interest. It was a good honing ground for young bands."

The car pulls up at a pub called the Thomas à Becket, and Bowie steps out into a bitterly cold wind and a flurry of rain. He is dressed in a waisted black frock coat, trim black trousers and an immaculate pair of black brogues. He wears gold-rimmed spectacles, which give him a rather severe look, although at forty-six his lightly tanned and fabulously sculpted features remain enviably intact. A woman hoots her horn, giving him a big grin and a thumbs up as he crosses the road. Bowie responds in kind.

The Thomas à Becket, established 1787, is a three-story building where Bowie and the prototype Spiders From Mars began rehearsing in 1970. The rehearsal room was on the top floor, above a boxing gymnasium, with the pub itself on the ground floor.

In those days Bowie's band was called Hype and was made up of Ronson (guitar), Tony Visconti (bass) and John Cambridge (drums). They all lived together at Bowie's residence in a large Victorian town house called Haddon Hall, with a baronial staircase and a circling gallery at the top of the stairs that served as a communal dormitory. It's since been demolished.

The Thomas à Becket is still standing, but although it remains a pub, its doors are firmly shut this lunch time. Bowie stands on the pavement outside as the traffic thunders past. The gym is still there, and through the upstairs windows he can see men working out with skipping ropes and punching bags.

"This was a major training ground for a lot of South London boxers," Bowie explains. "We were very impressed that Henry Cooper [the British heavyweight champion who floored Muhammad Ali in 1963] started his career here as well. The embryonic Spiders really put their sounds together up there, always expecting that Cooper would walk in at some point so we could get his autograph."

Nowadays, of course, it's Bowie who gets plagued for his autograph, one of the few things that he finds irksome when he's out and about. In general, he seems perfectly at ease moving around town in a chauffeur-driven, beige Mercedes. There is no fuss or celebrity entourage.

"The only time I have people with me is when I'm on tour or doing something that has got a high profile for some reason or other," Bowie says. "Otherwise, I much prefer to be on my own. I find that if you put a pair of glasses on and you don't play it up, you can travel around very easily. I've always been suspicious of people who say they need entourages, because you don't. In fact, that's when you're going to get problems. I remember walking in Hollywood with Eddie Murphy, who I like very much as a guy, but every time we took five paces down the street, there'd be this sound of about forty footsteps following behind us. It was impossible."

> *Staying back in your memory*
> *Are the movies in the past*
> —"The Prettiest Star" (1973)

Back in the heart of town, Bowie has arrived at a tiny cul-de-sac called Heddon Street, tucked away off Regent Street. He gets out of the car a little uncertainly and starts walking toward an alleyway at the end, mumbling: "We're gonna have to suss this out a bit. . . . Everything's gone, obviously. There was a photographer up here called Brian Ward, I think it was this building here, and outside the building there was a phone box . . ." There is indeed a phone box, a squat, modern blue job. Suddenly, the realization dawns. This is where the photography for the cover artwork of *Ziggy*

Stardust was done. But of course it's all changed. For one thing, the sort of big, red enclosed phone box in which Bowie posed for the shot on the back of the sleeve is a thing of the past.

A woman walking up the street toward her office greets Bowie with a genial smile. "They took your phone box away, isn't it terrible?" she says. Whatever Bowie may say about wearing glasses and keeping his head down, his is still a face that few people fail instantly to recognize. The woman informs him that the photographer has moved on and so has the company, K. West, under whose sign Bowie stood with his foot up on a rubbish bin twenty-one years ago. Amazingly, the old light above the doorway is still there, but the famous sign was auctioned off as part of a sale of rock & roll memorabilia. At home, Bowie has got hundreds of photographs of fans who have sent him pictures of themselves with their foot on a dustbin under the K. West sign.

"It's such a shame that sign went," Bowie says. "People read so much into it. They thought K. West must be some sort of code for *quest*. It took on all these sort of mystical overtones.

"We did the photographs outside on a rainy night," Bowie continues. "And then upstairs in the studio we did the *Clockwork Orange* look-alikes that became the inner sleeve. The idea was to hit a look somewhere between the Malcolm McDowell thing with the one mascaraed eyelash and insects. It was the era of *Wild Boys,* by William S. Burroughs. That was a really heavy book that had come out in about 1970, and it was a cross between that and *Clockwork Orange* that really started to put together the shape and the look of what Ziggy and the Spiders were going to become. They were both powerful pieces of work, especially the marauding boy gangs of Burroughs's *Wild Boys* with their bowie knives. I got straight on to that. I read everything into everything. Everything had to be infinitely symbolic."

Driving back to Soho, Bowie spots various landmarks. Selmer's music shop on Charing Cross Road was where he bought his first saxophone. Turning onto Wardour Street, he points to a tall building on a corner where Pete Townshend used to live in the top flat. "I always envied him for living right bang in the heart of London," Bowie says. "The nearest I got was Oakley Street in Chelsea, just around the corner from Cheyne Walk, where Mick Jagger lived. Indeed, that was when I first got to know Mick."

At the next stop, yet another pile of rubble awaits. DANGER DERELICT SITE—TRESPASSERS WILL BE PROSECUTED is the only sign now marking the spot where the celebrated Marquee Club once stood.

"I played here a lot in the 1960s, always as a support act," Bowie says. "And I came to see a lot of acts here, because all the American R&B artists would usually open here. But then when the 1970s came, it was falling out of favor a bit. It picked up again during the punk era, but it had a really soft period when it was mainly holiday makers and tourists from abroad that were going to it."

Bowie did utilize the Marquee in late 1973, however, to record a show for American TV called *The 1980 Floor Show*. It featured a ragbag of material from *Aladdin Sane,* one or two *Ziggy* numbers and a preview of a couple of songs that were going to be on *Diamond Dogs*. The whole highly costumed affair was, according to Bowie, "shot abysmally." Among the guests were the Troggs doing "Wild Thing" and Marianne Faithfull dueting with Bowie on a version of "I Got You Babe." Bowie was dressed as the Angel of Death and Faithfull as a decadent nun.

"She was wearing a nun's habit with no backside and black stockings," Bowie says with a chuckle. "I've got that clip at home, and it is fantastic. But they wouldn't show it in America. It was felt to be beyond the pale. Madonna, eat your heart out!"

> When the kids had killed the man
> I had to break up the band
> —"Ziggy Stardust" (1972)

"After 'Ziggy' happened it was just work, work, work," says Bowie. "And for the first time you realized what you were going to be giving away. You realize that you're not going to have any kind of private life, and you're not going to be able to wander down to a club. Well, you don't *think* that you can. Actually, time proves that you're wrong. It's not worth giving up all those things to become a popular artist. Fortunately, I learned how to get back into circulation again."

The car speeds westward, down Cromwell Road toward Hammersmith Odeon, the scene of Bowie's final gig with the Spiders From Mars.

The venue has recently been renamed the Hammersmith Apollo, and the stage has been extended at the front, but otherwise it remains the same 3500-capacity theater in which, on July 3rd, 1973, Bowie made his fateful announcement: "This show will stay the longest in our memories, not just because it is the end of the tour but because it is the last show we'll ever do."

Standing at the front of the stage, Bowie now repeats the statement to the rows of empty seats. His feet clomp noisily on the boards, and in the cold, deserted atmosphere the words take on a ghostly ring. Pulling up a wooden chair, he casts his mind back to that strange period of his life when reality and fantasy were becoming increasingly blurred.

"To this day I'm really not sure if I was playing Ziggy or if Ziggy was exaggerated aspects of my own personality," Bowie says. "A fair amount of psychological baggage was undoubtedly coming out through the character. Because I felt awkward and nervous and inadequate with myself, it felt easier to be somebody else. That was a relief and a release. And that feeling of not being a part of any group of people. I always felt on the fringe of things rather than being a participant. I always felt I was a wallflower of life. So it really got a bit complex. Because once you lay these little patterns out for yourself, it's very hard to retrace the steps and see how far you've got yourself immersed in all that. And when drugs came along, that really added to the brew to the point that it was inescapable that I was committing huge psychological damage to myself.

"I started on the drugs at the end of 1973 and then with force in 1974," Bowie continues. "As soon as I got to America, *pow!* It was so freely available in those days. Coke was everywhere. It was just impossible to get away from. Because I have a very addictive personality, I was a sucker for it. It just took over my life, but completely, until late 1976, '77, when I got myself over to Berlin—the smack capital of Europe, ironically—to clean up."

In her book *Backstage Passes,* Bowie's ex-wife Angie describes him during this period as "a friend-abusing, sense-mangling, money-bleeding, full-fledged Vampire of Velocity. Like coke addicts long before and after him, he'd learned to travel far and fast, to keep his mind spinning in tight circles even when standing perfectly still, to arrange an existence almost entirely devoid of daylight, to assume a worldview of paranoia. . . ."

Bowie greets mention of Angie with a show of complete uninterest.

"The reason that we got married was for her to get a work permit to work in England," he says, "which really wasn't the basis of a good marriage. And it was very short, remember. I mean, by '74 we rarely saw each other. After that she would drop in or drop out for a weekend or so, but we were virtually living our own separate lives. There was no real togetherness. I think the one thing that we had in common was Joe [their son, originally named Zowie, born in 1971]. He's what became the signpost toward me retrieving my sanity. I saw how he'd been emotionally neglected, and we started to develop a father-son relationship around '77, and since that point he's been under my custody constantly."

Leaning forward in his chair, Bowie pulls another Marlboro from its packet. He is a heavy smoker. The flame from his lighter flares momentarily beneath his face, and he shivers slightly as the cold of the deserted theater begins to take a grip.

"Joe has been blessed with a nonaddictive personality and has no truck with drink, drugs, smoking or anything," Bowie says. "It's just not part of his life. I think he likes himself in a way that I never did. He doesn't feel that he has to change his personality or lose his personality in quite the same way I felt I had to escape myself and the responsibility of my own feelings of inadequacy.

"I didn't love myself, not at all," Bowie continues. "Ziggy was a very flamboyant and theatrical and elaborate character. I wanted him to look right, and I spent a lot of time looking in the mirror, but it wasn't me I was looking at. I saw Ziggy. I think I'm vain, but I hope I'm not narcissistic. We all have our own feelings about what we look like. I like to dress well, but it's not something on which I felt my reputation should be built. I always held great store by my writing abilities. That's my strength, whether it's songs about me or about some fictional character, that's what I do best."

Every time I thought I got it made
It seemed the taste was not so sweet
—"Changes" (1971)

Be that as it may, there is no doubt that a vital element of Bowie's peculiar talent has been his ability to filter his thoughts and writing through a kind of psychological prism provided by characters like Ziggy, Aladdin Sane and the Thin White Duke. Taking his cues from the visual arts—sculpture, painting, dance, mime—of which he has long been a knowledgeable admirer, Bowie has instinctively recognized and accepted that presentation is an integral part of his art form. It was when he lost his feel for presentation that he stumbled and fell.

The 1980s kicked off with the biggest success of his career, *Let's Dance*. Produced by Nile Rodgers and released in 1983, it was a worldwide smash that hoisted Bowie into the international first division. But the view from those Olympian heights was not as clear as it might have been.

"I fell foul for the first time, wondering if I ought to be writing for the audience as opposed to me," Bowie says. "Should I try and duplicate the success of *Let's Dance,* or should I keep trying to change with every album? It was a real quandary. In the end I didn't lose the songs, but I lost the sound. There are some really good songs on *Tonight* [1984] and *Never Let Me Down* [1987], and I literally threw them away by giving them to very good people to arrange but not being involved myself, almost to the point of indifference."

Bowie's cure for this indifference was to find a new way of triggering his creative enthusiasm. For the first time, at least since the early 1960s, he threw himself into a democratically organized band situation. The result was Tin Machine. But here was a role and a presentation that his fans simply would not accept. In trying to sell himself as part of a bona fide, four-way democratic group. Bowie came up against a mirror version of the credibility problem faced by stars associated with groups trying to carve a solo career. In the same way that gifted performers like Mick Jagger, Roger Daltrey, Roger Waters and Jon Bon Jovi have all failed to establish themselves as solo acts with anything like the success of their respective bands, Bowie simply wasn't convincing as a member of a group.

Then there was the music. Quite unlike the suave synthesizer soul of *Heroes* or the mainstream white R&B of *Let's Dance,* the raw, scathing, bruising noise of the first Tin Machine album, released in 1989, was greeted by many Bowie fans with shocked disbelief. It was in many ways an inspired piece of work that neatly prefigured the grunge explosion, even if the band did guess wrong about the suits.

Bowie is unrepentant about the project, which he describes as "a dreadful commercial failure, but an artistic success." The band plans to reconvene toward the end of the year to record a new album, and Bowie professes himself at a loss to understand why the band has attracted such a virulently adverse reaction, especially in Britain.

"It doesn't seem to be England's cup of tea at all," Bowie says. "People seem to have a job seeing me in a band context. Judging by some of the antagonistic letters we had, it's almost as if I'd let the side down. Very strange. Maybe it's because it has no further abstractions than just being a band that's making music. It didn't have anything more to it. There's no real personality driving it, no theatrical statement.

"But it's not as if it was out of the blue and I'd never been involved with that kind of music before," he continues. "Ziggy and the Spiders were a hard-rock band, maybe not as experimental. I think the fact that I was much better known than the others was a real big obstacle. A lot of the flak seemed to be saying, 'Why has he dropped back into their anonymity?' We did make a big effort at the beginning to try and change people's minds, but we gave up after a while."

And the idea of having the other members adopt the role of backing band was ludicrous. "The Sales brothers would never accept having another boss," Bowie explains. "They are far too stubborn and aware of their own needs. They're not in the market to be anybody's backing band, either of them. You do not fuck with the Sales brothers, or Reeves [Gabrels]."

Oh no, not me
I never lost control
—"The Man Who Sold the World" (1970)

The way in which Bowie has shaken off the chorus of discontent that Tin Machine generated, swatted his detractors like so many flies and reemerged to surf a fresh wave of critical acclaim and public adulation with *Black Tie White Noise* will go down as one of the great Houdini-like tricks in the history of rock & roll.

Coproduced by Nile Rodgers, also the architect behind *Let's Dance*, the new album succeeds because instead of searching for a new role to play, Bowie has finally found the emotional strength necessary simply to be himself.

Artistically, he declares that he has not been so satisfied with the outcome of an album since *Scary Monsters*. "I listen to this album all the time," Bowie says, "which is always a good sign. With all due respect to Nile, I didn't listen to *Let's Dance* that much. It wasn't all me. It was a lot of Nile. On the first side particularly, I was really letting Nile run with it. This time when I went back in with Nile, I thought, 'Not again.' So it was very much *my* album that we made this time, and Nile contributed to it, as opposed to Nile doing everything and me just suggesting we get Stevie Ray Vaughan in or whatever. That's probably why it's so identifiably me."

According to Rodgers, Bowie was "a lot more relaxed this time than he was at the *Let's Dance* sessions, a hell of a lot more philosophical and just in a state of mind where his music was really, really making him happy."

Which is not to say the sessions were straightforward. Anything but. As far as Rodgers is concerned, *"Let's Dance* was the easiest record I've ever made—three weeks total; *Black Tie White Noise* was the hardest—one year, more or less."

Not the least of Rodgers's worries during recording was Bowie's saxophone playing, which is featured more on this album than on all the rest of his catalog put together. The instrument has always been crucial to Bowie's creative process. He uses it to compose his melody lines. But in performance, Bowie's fiercely untutored style can be a little jarring to the technically trained ear.

"I think David would be the first to admit that he's not a saxophonist in the traditional sense," Rodgers says with a wry chuckle. "I mean, you wouldn't call him up to do gigs. He uses his playing as an artistic tool. He's a painter. He hears an idea, and he goes with it. But he absolutely knows where he's going, because he damn well plays the same thing over and over again until I say, 'Well, I guess he hears that.' It's what you might call accidentally deliberate."

But more important than such technical considerations has been the mood swing that has enabled Bowie once again to become fully engaged with his music. His new-found willingness to examine himself more openly and reconnect with his past has resurrected his career. *Black Tie White Noise* is without doubt the most personal album he's ever released.

"I think this album comes from a very different emotional place," Bowie says. "That's the passing of time, which has brought maturity and a willingness to relinquish full control over my emotions, let them go a bit, start relating to other people, which is something that's been happening to me slowly—and, my God, it's been uphill—over the last ten or twelve years.

"I feel a lot freer these days to be able to talk about myself and about what's happened to me, because I've been able to face it," he continues. "For many years, everything was always blocked out. The day before was always blocked out. I never wanted to return to examine anything that I did particularly. But the stakes have changed. I feel alive, in a real sense."

After sitting among the shadows of his past on the Hammersmith stage for the better part of an hour, Bowie is ready to move on. The temperature has dropped uncomfortably, and he moves briskly toward the stage door, thanking the man who let him into the building with a courtesy that seems to come naturally. He is far more solicitous of those around him than stars with half his status, and it is one of his most disarming characteristics. The car heads off to a nearby hotel, where Bowie thaws out over peacock soup and a cheese sandwich.

A sizable chunk of the new album was inspired by having to sit down and write the music for his wedding to the model Iman last year. The album's opening cut, "The Wedding," is a beautiful, mystical instrumental piece with haunting Middle Eastern cadences, which reappear toward the end of the album with lyrics as "The Wedding Song."

"I had to write music that represented for me the growth and character of our relationship," Bowie explains. "It really was a watershed. It opened up a wealth of thoughts and feelings about commitment and promises and finding the strength and fortitude to keep those promises. It all came tumbling out of me while I was writing this music for church. And I thought: 'I can't stop here. There's more that I have to get out.' For me it was a tentative first step toward writing from a personal basis. It triggered the album."

> *I could fall in love all right*
> *as a rock & roll star*
> —"Star" (1972)

"I'd never been out with a model before," says Bowie, "so I hadn't even bargained on the cliché of the rock star and the model as being part of my life. So I was well surprised to meet one who was devastatingly wonderful and not the usual sort of bubblehead that I'd met in the past. I make no bones about it. I was naming the children the night we met. I knew that she was for me, it was absolutely immediate. I just fell under her spell.

"Our romance was conducted in a very gentlemanly fashion, I hope, for quite some time," Bowie continues. "Lots of being led to doorways and polite kisses on the cheek. Flowers and chocolates and the whole thing. I knew it was precious from the first night, and I just didn't want anything to spoil it."

This must have been something of a novel situation for Bowie, having to adapt to the pleasures (and rigors) of a monogamous relationship. "It's an incredible source of comfort to me," he says. "In fact for three years before I met Iman, I was engaged to another girl, so I find [monogamous relationships] very, very pleasurable. It excites me. I absolutely adore it. I've gone from the extreme promiscuity of the 1970s to a changing set of attitudes in the 1980s and hopefully to some sense of harmony in the 1990s."

Would he be so promiscuous if he were a young man now, in the 1990s?

"No, I don't think so," Bowie states. "I don't know. From my understanding there's still a lot of experimentation going on, so maybe I would. I did throw caution to the winds to an extreme point in the 1970s, so maybe I would now. I don't think people should experiment; let me *try* and be responsible, I think it's not the period to experiment, but I don't think people should hide from their orientation.

"I think I was always a closet heterosexual," Bowie continues. "I didn't ever feel that I was a real bisexual. It was like I was making all the moves, down to the situation of actually trying it out with some guys. But for me, I was more magnetized by the whole gay scene, which was underground. Remember, in the early 1970s it was still virtually taboo. There might have been free love, but it was heterosexual love. I like this twilight world. I like the idea of these clubs and these people and everything about it being something that nobody knew anything about. So it attracted me like crazy. It was like another world that I really wanted to buy in to. So I made efforts to go and get into it. That phase only lasted up to about 1974. It more or less died with Ziggy. I was only really adopting the situation of being bisexual. The reality was much slimmer.

"I wanted to imbue Ziggy with real flesh and blood and muscle, and it was imperative that I find Ziggy and be him. The irony of it was that I was not gay. I was physical about it, but frankly it wasn't enjoyable. It was almost like I was testing myself. It wasn't something I was comfortable with at all. But it had to be done."

> *They called it the Prayer,*
> *its answer was law*
> —"Saviour Machine" (1970)

"Unfortunately, I didn't really know Freddie [Mercury] that well at all," Bowie says. "I'd met him about two or three times in all those years. I found him very witty, quite bright and indeed very theatrical. So I don't know the ins and outs of what he had to live with or what happened to him. I do have a lot of gay friends, and I know the pain of losing friends through AIDS. Unfortunately, I lost one just after the Queen concert [the memorial concert for Freddie Mercury at Wembley Stadium in April 1992]. His name was Craig, a New York playwright, and he'd actually slipped into a coma the day before the show and died two days after it. Which was why I said the Lord's Prayer that night."

Bowie's flair for drama notwithstanding, the gesture left many people surprised. "Yeah, they probably were," he says, "but it wasn't for them." Part of the surprise was that Bowie has never been known as a particularly religious sort of person. "I'm not. I'm spiritual," he says. "I've never bought in to any organized religion. But now I have an unshakeable belief in God. I put my life into his hands every single day. I pray every morning.

"My friend Craig was not a Christian," he continues, "but I thought that prayer the most appropriate inasmuch as it's not . . . it's a prayer about our Father, not so much about Christ. For me, it's a universal prayer. I was as surprised as anyone that I'd said it at that concert. But I was pleased that I'd done it."

The image of Bowie as a coldly calculating, European iceman who keeps his feelings buttoned down as securely as his shirt collar became fixed at around the time of *Station to Station* (1976) and the return of the Thin White Duke. And yet it is an image that now could not be further removed from reality. Bowie is actually a highly emotional person, which may go some way to explaining his behavior at the Mercury concert.

One of the less remarked but most highly charged performances at that show was Bowie's reunion with his old sparring partner Mick Ronson, together with Ian Hunter, for a rousing version of the old Mott the Hoople hit "All the Young Dudes" (a Bowie composition).

It was an especially poignant moment given that it was to be Ronson and Bowie's last live performance together. Mention of this almost brings tears to Bowie's eyes.

Still desperately ill, Ronson had been hanging on through sheer force of will. "The doctors tell me I shouldn't be here now," Ronson said from a London recording studio shortly before his death. "But I don't go to the doctors for chemotherapy or anything anymore. I just put one foot in front of the other, and the next day is the next day, and you do your best. I've still got so much to do."

Ronson contributed to *Black Tie White Noise,* playing on a drastically revamped version of Cream's "I Feel Free." Like Nile Rodgers, he noticed Bowie's incredible vigor and enthusiasm throughout the sessions. "I hope David's album does well," Ronson said. "He's put everything into it. I speak to him often. He sounds so positive."

At the end of his day's sightseeing, Bowie is in a reflective mood.

"I've never done that before," he says. "It was quite extraordinary, despite the fact that most of the things I went to see were either closed or pulled down. It puts into focus just how much time has passed. I actually made a list the other night of the bands that were coming up on the circuit during the time of Ziggy, Bolan and Roxy Music. This was the competition: Lindisfarne, Rory Gallagher, Stray, America, Juicy Lucy, Peter Sarstedt, Thin Lizzy and Gnidrolog. It really was a long, long time ago."

BOYS KEEP SWINGING

Dominic Wells | August 30–September 6, 1995, *Time Out* (UK)

It's significant that in the period straddling the end of the sixties and the start of the seventies, David Bowie devoted much of his time to the Beckenham Arts Lab, a collective which, as well as music, explored and championed painting, poetry readings, light shows, street theater, dance, and puppetry. His interest in forms of artistic expression outside music has only increased over the years, with him becoming involved in painting, sculpting, and wallpaper design.

The following joint *Time Out* interview with Bowie and Brian Eno was nominally for the purpose of promoting Bowie's new album *Outside*. It developed more into a three-way conversation that touched on pretty much all of Bowie's nonmusical artistic endeavors, as well as his (and Eno's) thoughts on art's often un-straightforward relationship to its audience.

Recalls Dominic Wells, "David Bowie was (and still is) my idol. So becoming editor of *Time Out* magazine in 1992 presented a dilemma: to meet him, all I had to do was give him a cover feature; yet how could I when our readers thought him a has-been? For an entire decade he had seemingly lost his way. When his reunion with Brian Eno on *Outside* rekindled that spark of genius, I fought for the chance to interview them jointly for the cover. We had a wonderful hour-and-a-half's discussion about art, philosophy, and the roots of creativity. Try doing that with Miley Cyrus or Rihanna.

"All the same, I have never felt more nervous before an interview, especially since I knew I would have to ask him the question: 'So, David, how does it feel to be thought such a tosser?'"

Note: for "Stone Love" read "Soul Love." —Ed.

The first thing that happens when I finally meet David Bowie is I break his arm. Almost. As I shake his hand, too hard, a resounding crack sounds from inside his elbow. He doesn't seem to feel it, but it's alarming all the same when his limbs are as achingly thin still as when Candy Clark carried him, bloody-nosed and unconscious, down the hotel hallway in "The Man Who Fell To Earth."

It's an Oedipal moment: Bowie is the only pop star to have visited my dreams (I was hitch-hiking, he pulled up in a black stretch limo, we chatted amiably about Japanese culture), the only one I've pinned to my wall—not counting Debbie Harry, where the attraction was purely hormonal. As with an astonishing number of my peers, my golden years were played out to a Bowie soundtrack. The likes of Suede worship him, and Nine Inch Nails, with whom he's touring in September. Hell, he used to date Slash's mum, and read the six-year-old future Guns N' Roses axeman bedtime stories. Always more than a pop star, Bowie introduced me to the films of Nic Roeg through "The Man Who Fell . . . ," the works of Kahlil Gibran through "The Width of a Circle," Nietzsche through "Oh You Pretty Things" ('Gotta make way for the *homo superior*'), pop art through "Andy Warhol," Jean Genet through "Jean Genie," and performance art through "Joe The Lion." The mime, admittedly, I could have done without.

"Let's Dance," in 1983, was the turning point—his first album to be of the times rather than ahead of them. Since then, barring small upwards blips such as "Blue Jean," he's lagged pitifully behind. The last of the six times he graced a *Time Out* cover was for "Absolute Beginners" (oops!) in 1986. Then there was his reciting of the Lord's prayer at the Freddie Mercury tribute; the wedding photos in *Hello!*; the desire to be considered an artist, my dear; the Laura Ashley wallpaper . . . And that's what makes me nervous as I sink into a sofa: not so much meeting the man of my dreams, but the very real possibility of finding him a complete prat.

The omens, at least, are good. After disappointing years of collectively wishing each album will be the one which, if we all just *believe*, will finally resurrect him like some suited, superannuated Tinkerbell, it's official—there is a God. Brian Eno, back with Bowie for the first time since the "Low"/"Heroes"/"Lodger" trilogy, has worked the same magic as when he turned U2 into one of the greatest rock bands on earth. "Outside" may require a few hearings; it may, at 75 minutes, have a few tracks you would skip; but it is Bowie's best for 15 years—and he knows it. After *TO*'s cover shoot, having larked around like Piglet to Eno's Eeyore, Bowie flounces out declaring: "And they said I was history!"

Indeed he was; but now once again his playground is the future. "Outside," if you'll bear with me, is a "concept" album. Nathan Adler, art detective, is investigating the grisly murder of a 14-year-old runaway by an artist or artists unknown: "The arms of the victim were pincushioned with 16 hypodermic needles . . . From the last and seventeenth all blood and liquid was extracted. The stomach area was carefully flapped open and the intestines removed, disentangled and reknitted, as it were, into a small net or web and hung between the pillars of the murder location, the grand damp doorway of the Oxford Town Museum of Modern Parts." Bowie plays several characters, aged from 14 to 78. Musically too, it spans several generations of Bowie's old muckers: Mike "Aladdin Sane" Garson on piano; Carlos "Station To Station" Alomar on rhythm guitar; Reeves "Tin Machine" Gabrels on guitar; Erdal "Buddha Of Suburbia" Kizilcay on keyboards and bass; and David "Lodger" Richards as engineer. The result is an extraordinary fusion of sounds, rhythms and nations that plays like an updated cross between "Lodger" and "My Life In The Bush Of Ghosts."

For the moment, however, it's impossible to get in a question about it: I have arrived in the midst of a discussion about satellite TV (which Eno strangely does not possess), and Bowie inquiring about some Polish film-maker whose name Eno cannot remember. They make a good double-act, this diminutive duo of rock intellectuals, these laughing gnomes. Brian Eno (anag. Brain One), often referred to jocularly as The Professor—by virtue of his balding dome, measured lecturing tones and generally planet-sized mind—has recently become one for real, at the Royal College of Art. David Bowie (anag. Ow, I Bed Diva) is dapper, goateed, relishing his new role as English gentleman-artist. Only the pen in his breast pocket strikes an incongruously nerdish note. His mismatched eyes are indeed disconcerting (though you wouldn't know it from our cover, thanks to blue contact lenses): as Desmond Morris would tell you, the one that is permanently dilated says to your subconscious, "You're fascinating, I want to sleep with you"; the other, contracted, signals, "You bore me, worm."

And does Angus Deayton's Bowie parody on 1981's "Heebeegeebies" LP—"I think I'm losin' my miiiiind/I'm disappearin' up my behiiiiiind"— still apply? I found the pair not just fiercely articulate, but fun and unaffected in a way quotes on paper cannot properly convey; but decide for yourself as we limber up for a rambling discussion about art, Burroughs cut-ups, cutting yourself up and, oh yes, their new album.

David Bowie: Could I just ask you first, do you mind terribly if we also tape this? Just for our own usage.

Dominic Wells: *So you can sample me and stick me on your next album?*

DB: Actually, it is likely. I nearly sampled Camille Paglia on this album, but she never returned my calls! She kept sending messages through her assistant saying, "Is this really David Bowie, and if it is, is it important?" (*laughs*), and I just gave up! So I replaced her line with me.

Brian Eno: Sounds pretty much like her.

So: how did this album come about?

DB: A pivotal moment for us was actually at the wedding.

BE: It's absolutely true, that's where we first talked about it.

DB: I was just starting the instrumental backings for the "Black Tie, White Noise" album and I had some of them, just as instrumental pieces at the wedding, because it was written half around the idea of the marriage ceremony. Brian at the time was working on "Nerve Net," and we realised that we were suddenly on the same course again.

BE: That was quite interesting, because it was the wedding reception, right, everybody was there, and we started talking and Dave said, "You've got to listen to this!" He went up to the DJ and said, "No, take that off, play this."

DB: And then we both rushed off to our individual lives knowing it was almost inevitable we'd be working together again. Because we both felt excited about the fact that neither of us was excited about what was happening in popular music.

It seems strange that on your last album you went back to Nile Rodgers, with whom you had your greatest commercial success ("Let's Dance"), and now you're going back to Brian . . .

BE: With whom you had your least commercial success!

. . . With whom you had some of your greatest critical successes.

DB: Funnily enough, the things I said to Nile were much the same things that Brian said to me: look, we're not going to make a stereotypical follow-up to "Let's Dance." I'd just come out of the Tin Machine period, which was a real freeing exercise for me, and I wanted to experiment on "Black Tie." I love doing a hybrid of Eurocentric Soul, but there were also pieces like "Pallas Athena" and "You've Been Around" which played more with ambience and funk. Then there was an interim album for me which was very important—"Buddha Of Suburbia."

BE: That was the one I got really excited about. In fact I wrote you a letter saying this record has been unfairly overlooked. I felt because it was a soundtrack, as usual people were saying, "Well it's not real music then, is it?" It's so incredible to me that the critical community is so unbelievably restricted in its terms of reference.

I went to the "Warchild" exhibition at Flowers East [where Eno persuaded dozens of rock stars to auction off their art works for Bosnia], and you made a very good little speech about that. And in fact my magazine was one which had printed a snide, snipy little thing in Sidelines.

BE: Yes, I remember that. Do you, David?

DB: Which snide was this? Ha ha. I've had at least a couple in my life.

BE: It was, "If these people are so concerned why don't they give their money over instead of just massaging their already enormous egos."

DB: I remember that line! Yes, but it's perfectly understandable. It's a very British thing, isn't it?

The same's true in America, isn't it?

BE: No. You're allowed to take pleasure in, enjoy and actively even benefit from the act of helping somebody else. Here, if you want to help somebody else it's got to be directly at your own cost.

DB: It's got to have a halo attached.

But it's not just the charity, is it? It's an assumption that rock musicians shouldn't be doing art, shouldn't be acting and shouldn't be writing books.

DB: It's like saying journalists shouldn't be doing television shows—which in some cases is probably very true!

BE: In England, the greatest crime is to rise above your station.

DB: There are more and more people moving into areas they're not trained for, especially in America. I've just been doing this film with Julian Schnabel ["Basquiat," in which Bowie plays Andy Warhol], and he's making movies, having just made an album . . . I think that's fantastic.

What's the album like?

DB: It's Leonard Cohen meets Lou Reed. Lyrically, I think it's really good.

A good dance record then?

DB: Ha ha. I think it's as good as a lot of other records that came out that week. Not as good as others that came out that week.

BE: One of the reasons it's possible now is that for various technical reasons, anybody can do anything, pretty much. I can, sitting in my studio, put together records with basses and drums and choirs, or I can put together a video in a similar way. So the question then becomes not, 'Do I have the skill?' It's not an issue.

DB: The skill hasn't been an issue in art for 50 years. It's really the idea.

Damien Hirst once said something to the effect that if a child could do what I do, that means I've done it very well.

DB: Picasso said, I think, when someone said to him a child of three could do what you're doing, he replied, "Yes, you're right, but very few adults."

I think he said: "It took me 16 years to paint like Raphael, but 60 years to learn to paint like a child."

BE: Einstein said, "Any intelligent nine-year-old could understand anything I've done; the thing is, he probably wouldn't understand why it was important." That's the other side of that coin: to be free and simple and child-like, but able to understand the implications of that at the same time. To be Picasso is not suddenly to become a three-year-old child again, it's to become someone who understands what's important about what the three-year-old child does.

It says in the blurb about your album that much of it was improvised, and that Brian would hand out cards to different musicians saying things like: "You are the last survivor of a catastrophic event and you will endeavour to play in such a way as to prevent feelings of loneliness developing within yourself"; or: "You are a disgruntled member of a South African rock band. Play the notes they won't allow." Is that to strip everything down, remove everyone's preconceptions and start again from scratch?

BE: There are certain immediate dangers to improvisation, and one of them is that everybody coalesces immediately. Everyone starts playing the blues, basically, because it's the one place where everyone can agree and knows the rules. So in part they were strategies designed to stop the thing becoming over-coherent. The interesting place is not chaos, and it's not total coherence. It's somewhere on the cusp of those two.

The rhythm is very strong throughout the album. That's what holds things together . . .

DB: Something we really got into on the late-70s albums was what you could do with a drum kit. The heartbeat of popular music was something we really messed about with.

BE: And very few people had done. It was, "Right, bass and drums, get them down, then do all the weird stuff on top." To invert that was a new idea.

I did a lot of walking around with the album playing on my headphones, and often you would get noises from the street—a bicycle bell, beeps from bus doors—and wherever they came in the songs, whatever noise it was, it fitted right in, you could absorb it into the song and it would work because the layers were so strong you could add anything on top.

DB: The great thing about what Brian was doing through much of the improvisation is we'd have clocks and radios and things near his sampler, and he'd say find a phrase on the French radio and keep throwing it in rhythmically so it became part of the texture. And people would react to that, they'd play in a different way because these strange sounds kept coming back at them.

BE: Yeah, and he was doing the same thing lyrically. We had a thing going where David was improvising lyrics as well; he had books and magazines and bits of newspaper around, and he was just pulling phrases out and putting them together.

DB: If I read some off to you, some of them you'd find completely incomprehensible.

I did try that in fact. I read the lyrics sheet out loud and thought, "He's gone off his rocker." Then when I heard it with the music, it made sense.

DB: Exactly. There's an emotional engine created by the juxtaposition of the musical texture and the lyrics. But that's probably what art does best: it manifests that which is impossible to articulate.

If an English student, on a poetry course or whatever, sat down and tried to analyse your lyrics, would they be wasting their time?

DB: No, because I think these days there are so many references for them in terms of late twentieth-century writing, from James Joyce to William Burroughs. I come from almost a traditional school now of deconstructing phrases and constructing them again in what is considered a random way. But in that randomness there's something that we perceive as a reality—that in fact our lives aren't tidy, that we don't have tidy beginnings and endings.

So you'd be very happy if I and another journalist had different ideas of what the songs were about?

DB: Absolutely. As Roland Barthes said in the mid '60s, that was the way interpretation would start to flow. It would begin with society and culture itself. The author becomes really a trigger.

In rock music, the lyrics you hear are sometimes better than they turn out to be. In one of your early songs, "Stone Love," a line I adored was "in the bleeding hours of morning"; I finally got the lyrics sheet and discovered it was "fleeting hours of morning," which is much more prosaic.

DB: That's right. For me the most fascinating thing was finding out after years that what Fats Domino was singing was nothing like . . . I'd gained so much from those songs by my interpretation of them. Frankly, sometimes it's a let-down to discover what the artist's actual intent was.

You've now got a computer program, apparently, to randomise your writing. But you've been doing cut-ups since the '70s, inspired by Burroughs.

DB: As a teenager I was fairly traditional in what I read: pompously Nietzsche, and not so pompously Jack Kerouac. And Burroughs. These "outside" people were really the people I wanted to be like. Burroughs, particularly. I derived so much satisfaction from the way he would scramble life, and it no longer felt scrambled reading him. I thought, "God, it feels like this, that sense of urgency and danger in everything that you do, this veneer of rationality and absolutism about the way that you live . . ."

It's a drugs thing as well, isn't it? When I was a student and took lots of drugs, suddenly all kinds of things would make sense that otherwise wouldn't; or rather, you'd see connections between things you otherwise wouldn't.

BE: That's what drugs are useful for. Drugs can show you that there are other ways of finding meanings to things. You don't have to keep taking them, but having had that lesson, to know that you're capable of doing that, is really worthwhile.

DB: But you know, I think the seeds of all that probably were planted a lot earlier. Think of the surrealists with things like their "exquisite corpses," or James Joyce, who would take whole paragraphs and just with glue stick them in the middle of others, and make up a quilt of writing. It really is the character and the substance of twentieth-century perception, and it's really starting to matter now.

BE: What I think is happening there is it removes from the artist the responsibility of being the "meaner"—the person who means to say this and is trying to get it over to you—and puts him in the position of being the interpreter.

DB: It's almost as if things have turned from the beginning of this century, where the artist reveals a truth, to the artist revealing the complexity of a question, saying, "Here's the bad news, the question is even more compli-cated than you thought." Often it happens on acid I suppose—if I remem-ber!—you realise the absolute incomprehensible situation that we're in. . . . *(Bowie, who has been gesturing with dangerous animation, knocks an ashtray full of chain-smoked Marlboros on to the carpet)* . . . like this kind of chaos! *(Eno kneels to sweep up the ash and butts from Bowie's feet.)* Why are you doing that, Brian? That's immensely big of you.

BE: Just so you can finish your sentence.

DB: I didn't need to. I illustrated it! *(Hilarity)* The randomness of the everyday event. If we realised how incredibly complex our situation was, we'd just die of shock.

(There follows a good 20 minutes of discussion about Bosnia; how morality is an outdated concept which should be replaced simply with the law; and how sex and violence are not gratuitous, but forces our human nature com-pels us to explore.)

There's a lot in the short story that accompanies your album about artists who indulge in self-mutilation: Chris Burden, who had himself shot, tied up in a bag and thrown on to the highway and then crucified on top of a Volkswagen; Ron Athey, an HIV-positive former heroin addict who pushed a knitting needle repeatedly into his forehead until he wore a crown of blood, then carved patterns with a scalpel into the back of another man and sus-pended the bloody paper towels on a washing line over the audience. You seem to have this morbid fascination. It's also the most literal expression of the old idea that art can only come out of suffering.

DB: Also it has something to do with the fact that the complexity of mod-ern systems is so intense that a lot of artists are going back literally into themselves, in a physical way, and it has produced a dialogue between the flesh and the mind.

BE: Yes, it's shocking suddenly to say, in the middle of cyberculture and information networks, "I am a piece of meat."

And is shock also a necessary part of a definition of art?

BE: At some level I think it is, yes. It doesn't have to be only that kind of shock.

DB: The shock of recognition is actually more what it's about, you know. I think that's what it does to me, anyway. That, for me, is Damien [Hirst], of whom I am a very loyal supporter, it's the shock of recognition with his work that really affects me; and I don't think even *he* really knows what it is he's doing. But what there is in the confrontation between myself and one of his works is a terrible poignancy. There's a naive ignorance to the poor creatures he's using. They're cyphers for man himself. I find it very emotional, his work.

Have you been collaborating with him?

DB: We did some paintings together. We took a big round canvas, about 12-foot, and it's on a machine that spins it around at about 20 miles an hour, and we stand on the top of step ladders and throw paint at it.

BE: You should see his studio!

DB: It's from a child's game; you drop paint on and centrifugal force pushes the stuff out.

You're on the editorial board of Modern Painters, *along with the likes of Lord Gowrie, and actually they're not so modern. You must be like the man in the HM Bateman cartoon, saying, "Actually, I think Damien Hirst is rather good."*

DB: The magazine is changing. But why write for, say, the *Tate* magazine, which is full of people already on one side of the argument? At least on *Modern Painters* there's a chance of opening up the magazine a little bit. I love the idea of combining some ideas from the Renaissance with ideas that are working now; not to make some kind of . . . editorial point, but because of the pure . . . fun of creating those hybrid situations.

A lot of people were shocked by you doing a wallpaper.

DB: Well, it's not very original. Robert Gober and a number of others, even Andy Warhol, did them. It's just part of a tradition.

You also had your first solo art exhibition recently. It must have been frightening to open up your work of 20 years to public scrutiny and to the critics.

DB: No, it wasn't at all.

Why not?

DB: Because I know why I did it. Ha!

BE: The thing is when you show something, or you release a record, you open it up to all sorts of other interpretations which don't belong to you any longer. I have millions of tapes at home I haven't released. I feel quite differently about those than if I put them out on to the market and suddenly there they are, filed in the racks, after the Eagles. Suddenly I imagine someone who isn't at all sympathetic, who's actually looking for an Eagles record, happening on mine, and I start to hear the thing through what I imagine are their ears as well. So by putting something out you actually enrich it, I think, and you enrich it for yourself. You get it reflected back in a lot of differently shaped mirrors.

DB: I was just a bit late. The reason I wasn't afraid, either, is I'm an artist, a painter and a sculptor. Why should I be afraid? Seemingly the only other thing I'm supposed to be afraid of is whether other people thought it was any good or not, but I've lived that life ever since I began, publicly, of whether I'm any "good" or not, for nearly 30 years, so that comes with the territory.

Does it hurt you if a lot of people are walking around London saying, "David Bowie, what a pretentious tosser"?

DB: I don't know of a time when it was never said, though. What's the difference? It's just a different colour overcoat. Not at all.

BE: You know for sure that in England, if you do something different from anything that you did last time, there is going to be a band of people who'll walk around saying you're a pretentious tosser but after a while you just have to accept (Bowie is laughing too), both of us just have to accept that we're good at what we do. The record proves it. We've both influenced a lot of things, and a lot of things that are going on can be traced back to what we did, as we would trace ourselves back to other people.

DB: The history of any art form is actually dictated by other artists and who they are influenced by, not by critics. So for me, my vanity is far more interested in what my contemporaries and peers have to say about my work. A lot of it just comes from pure pleasure, you know? I work because it's such a great way to escape having to work in a shop—to be a song-writer, and a musician and a performer and a painter and a sculptor—it's so cool to do all this stuff, I can't tell you how exciting it is. It really is great.

ACTION PAINTING

Chris Roberts | October 1995, *Ikon* (UK)

As with many interlocutors around the time of the *Outside* album, Chris Roberts of Britain's *Ikon* magazine found Bowie in loquacious form, and this time it produced an interview which ranged across post-modernism, acting, the coming new millennium, literature, and mankind's twentieth-century loss of faith in a higher being. As a special bonus, the artist even talks about music. —Ed.

I met him once before, four years ago, in LA, crazed sun blazing. So I've come, personally, to associate the David Bowie I interview, impersonally —as opposed to what David Bowie signifies to me—with rude health, cars, sumptuous hotel lobbies, pools, Sunset Boulevard. It feels great but it doesn't feel apposite. I tell him this, after a fashion.

David Bowie lights a cigarette, which is something he does well and often, making love with his ego, always crashing in the same car. The face that launched two-decades-and-counting of imitators cracks, in its own time, into a famous English grin. "I have moved since then," he says. "I haven't just sat here since you left."

White Duke, he speak the truth. Music, films, paintings and ideas in general are flying out of 49-year-old David Bowie at an alarming, charming, disarming rate. I try really hard not to use the phrase "renaissance man," and then I use it.

"God I'm scared of that word! Let's just say I'm taking the bull by the horns and expressing myself—by any means necessary. I can do it, so I'm gonna flaunt it. I'm really not very self-judgmental anymore. I feel, psychologically, in a safe place. It's publish and be damned, it really is."

The king, the very king, of artifice and appropriation, David Bowie was Ziggy, then Aladdin, then a better soul singer than any real one, then kind of German and frosty and depressed and coked-out, then a cheery skippy Live Aid person, and then fell, finally, out of vogue. Then he did the Tin Machine thing at precisely the wrong time in precisely the wrong suits. While all this was going on he was in films ranging from the sublime (*The Man who Fell to Earth*) to *The Linguini Incident*. Now he's releasing an album, *Outside*, which is, naturally, nothing like his last (the ambient *The Buddha of Suburbia*), or even the one before that (the sensible, poppy, *Black Tie White Noise*). While Suede have come and—some might say—gone, Bowie's undertaken yet another wild mutation. *Outside* is provocative, creepy, nasty, irritating, and, eventually, addictive. The first in a planned series of collaborations with Brian Eno, it documents, albeit abstractly, the fictional diaries of "art detective" Nathan Adler. Bowie's also working with Nine Inch Nails soon, and if he will design wallpaper for Laura Ashley we sure as hell can't stop him.

Early 1996 will see *Build a Fort, Set It on Fire*, a film by painter-turned-director Julian Schnabel about the late African-American painter Jean-Michel Basquiat, in which Bowie plays Pop Art guru Andy Warhol. I'm crediting you with the intelligence to keep up here. Also this year Bowie exhibited his own work (watercolours, sculptures, computer-generated prints) at the Kate Chertavian Gallery in Cork Street. I went to look at it one lunchtime with the girl who played the alien in the *Loving the Alien* video. A mad woman with teary eyes started shrieking at us for no reason whatsoever that we'd be sorry, very sorry, when David came along to sweep her away and make everything alright. We ran off, confused, but the mad woman chased us down the street. The best thing in the show was a picture of a star, called *Star*.

"I'm not content," Bowie said in 1972, "to be a rock'n'roll star all my life." In 1995 he is almost absurdly energetic. You have to interrupt him to get a word in edgeways. We talk about art, cinema, literature, music, computers, South Africa, ageing, religion, and *Boys from the Blackstuff*. He's very keen to discuss his friendships with Damien Hirst and Julian Schnabel, less keen to mull over the past. Without breaking sweat, and even while wearing a peculiar snakeskin shirt, he'll say things like: "When you've developed an art form that questions its own existence, you're left only with philosophy. Heh heh heh! Or so my son tells me!"

You have healthy debates with him (Joe, formerly Zowie, now 23 and a philosophy graduate) on such topics?

"Oh boy, you try and stop us. We can shoot the breeze; we can talk so much crap all night long. But that's one of the joys of parenthood, I've found."

Joe (The Lion) has influenced his groovy dad "in an obtuse fashion, I think." Watching him "getting into Cream and Dylan and Hendrix," Bowie Senior realised there was no eighties music of interest. "Apart from maybe the beginnings of rap, it was all rubbish. Paula Abdul had no bearing on his life. He'd had to go back to find something with musical depth to it. It kind of gives validity to what Lennon used to say—what were his exact words?" Bowie shifts into a faultless Scouse accent. "Say what you wanna say, make it rhyme, and put a backbeat to it."

As regards your new album then, one out of three ain't bad.

Bowie laughs uproariously. "Accessibility is not its keynote!" I am somewhat relieved.

"Pose the same question NOW to the younger generation and they'll say YES, there's a lot of music we'll take with us. Pearl Jam, Nirvana, NIN, Smashing Pumpkins.

"And in Britain, Tricky is wonderful, PJ Harvey is extraordinary. The context and atmosphere of it all is tremendous. I think rock music's got strong legs at the moment. It's really bloody exciting."

Here is what I think David Bowie's new album is about: WHAT IS ART? To someone like Bowie, or rather to someone who *is* Bowie, you can actually say that, say those three words with a question mark at the end, without being laughed at. He loves a lot of things but most of all he loves being taken seriously. Nobody expends this much effort on creativity, not when they've already scored as many been-there-done-that points as he has, without some unquenchable desire for acclaim, to defeat mortality.

How is your ego these days?

"Well, you know, I have enough vanity to be convinced that what comes out of one of my cut-up lyrics is only as good as the stuff that was put in in the beginning."

And so when you say WHAT IS ART? to Bowie, plain as that, he'll say, "It's either art or murder, ha ha! The strength in MY work is when there's as much room for multi-interpretation as possible. I've always had an orientation toward combining contradictory information. And just seeing what happens. Messing about with structures, taking them apart. Dismantling toys and putting the wrong bits back together. I would've been great in Japan making those Godzilla-type things that become tanks, I'm sure. I treat music in the same way; what happens if you put that note with that word, what effect do you get? Because of that, it has its own informational output, that's sometimes more, sometimes less than the two components. That's one of the fascinations of writing for me."

I ask if he seeks to confuse as much as to enlighten, and am given possibly the longest and most articulate answer in "rock interview" history.

"I don't think so. I think that we as a culture embrace confusion. We're happy to recombine information, we take event horizons incredibly fast. The generations—and I CAN use that plurally now—underneath me have an ability to scan information much quicker than my lot, and don't necessarily look for the depth that maybe we would. They take what they need for their survival, and their means to adapt to this new society.

"It IS the inheritance of Sixties, not only of what happened with the breakdown of the American Dream and the conflicts of that period, and the emerging pluralistic attitude towards society, but also of a spiritual loss. A realisation that absolutes weren't the law, weren't the thing that one could abide by. There's no absolute religion, no absolute political system, no absolute art form, no absolute this no absolute that. Things weren't black and white like we'd always been told (especially during the great stiff Fifties).

"There are so many contradictions and conflicts that when you accept them for what they are, when you accept that this IS a manifestation of the chaos theory that's been put forward, that it really is a deconstructed society, then contradiction almost ceases to exist. Every piece of information is equally as unimportant as the next."

Bowie glances at the TV for a second and I have to stop myself thinking I'm Nicolas Roeg.

"An OJ Simpson trial, one week's buzzword is 'the gloves didn't fit,' those few words were the news on it—and, say, something from a Middle East crisis, it could be 'the mother of all wars'—those two pieces have

EQUAL WEIGHT. There seems to be no disparity between them, it's all relevant and all irrelevant. When you get that lack of stress upon what's important and what isn't, the moral high ground seems to disappear as well. You're left with this incredibly complex network of fragments that is our existence.

"Rather than running away from it, I think the younger generation is learning to adapt to it. I'm very wary of calling them out for being—this is so often thrown at them—indifferent or ignorant or lazy or all that. That's bullshit, I think that actually they're in their own nurturing stage. It's not going to get any more clarified; it can only get more impetuously complex. There's no point in pretending: well, if we wait long enough everything will return to what it used to be and it'll all be saner again and we'll understand everything and it'll be obvious what's wrong and what's right. It's NOT gonna be like that."

Sorry, what was the question?

"So. The album deals with all that to an extent. That kind of . . . surfing on chaos."

Bowie gets a coffee and another Marlboro Light going, sprawls across his armchair like a confident woman or a happy cat. Some of his prints are on the wall. We're at the Chateau Marmont, where every ten minutes someone tells you "this is where John Belushi died." Keanu Reeves was in the lobby earlier. Later, Bowie will tell me something funny about actors, but right now the sometime editor of Modern Painters, who last year interviewed Balthus, is on paintings . . .

". . . on the other hand, I can revel in a Romantic or Renaissance piece. I can just fall away into a sort of euphoria over a beautifully-painted landscape or a wonderfully-executed sculpture. I have needs for all those things. I don't think one thing REPLACES the other. Consider the more positive aspects of post-modernism. I hope we get bored with the ironic stance it continually takes, because one of the better things about it is that it seems so willing to embrace ALL styles and attitudes . . ."

Do you feel like an elder statesman of sorts? Your hilarious press release says portentously: "It is only now, when he has reached his own mid-life, that Bowie can make music encompassing the point of young, middle-aged, and old."

He creases up, for the only time today, shaking his head, speechless.

Do you feel you've acquired significant wisdom?

"The old sage, har har har! Ah but you see I was playing 130 at 38, or something, in *The Hunger*. It comes easily to me now!

"I am now old enough—hurray!—to have a body of work, which is great. It means that I can dip in and pull out symbols and atmospheres and even processes and techniques that I've utilised before, and re-apply them in new situations. It's the basic maxim that if you take something out of one context and put it in another, it takes on a whole different set of meanings.

"So with *Outside,* placing the eerie environment of a *Diamond Dogs* city now in the Nineties gives it an entirely different spin. It was important for this town, this locale, to have a populus, a number of characters. I tried to diversify these really eccentric types as much as possible. Overall, a long-term ambition is to make it a series of albums extending to 1999—to try to capture, using this device, what the last five years of this millennium feel like. It's a diary within a diary. The narrative and the stories are not the content—the content is the spaces in between the linear bits. The queasy, strange, textures."

Bowie wants to stage all this as a piece of "epic theatre," hopefully with *Einstein on the Beach* director Robert Wilson, and with "a definite sensibility shift from when you went into the theatre. It'd probably be about five hours long, so you'd have to bring sandwiches."

The work sounds paranoid and ominous, whereas you personally, or as personally as I'm ever going to get to know you, seem exuberant . . .

"Oh, I've got the fondest hopes for the fin de siècle. I see it as a symbolic sacrificial rite. I see it as a deviance, a pagan wish to appease gods, so we can move on. There's a real spiritual starvation out there being filled by these mutations of what are barely-remembered rites and rituals. To take the place of the void left by a non-authoritative church. We have this panic button telling us it's gonna be a colossal madness at the end of this century. And it WON'T be. The biggest problem we'll have will be what to call it. Twenty-O-O? Twenty-O-Zero? Two Thousand? Well we lived through it; now what shall we call it?"

David Bowie openly admits that after the success of *Let's Dance* gave him a mainstream audience in the early Eighties, he hit a quandary. "I succumbed, tried to make things more accessible, took away the very strength of what I do." The Tin Machine period he puts down to "Reeves Gabrels shaking me out of my doldrums, pointing me at some kind of light, saying: be ADVENTUROUS again." When it's interpreted like this, it nearly makes sense. But not quite. "It did break down all the contexts for me. By the time it was over, nobody could put their finger on what I was any more. It was: what the fuck is he DOING?! I've been finding my voice, and a certain authority, ever since."

"The acting," chuckles Bowie, who has so much pop and so much art in his blood that it must be a riot in there, "is purely decorative. It's just fun, it really is. It's not something I seriously entertain as an ambition.

"The few things I've made that were successful were because I homed in on the directors, as they had something I wanted to know about. And just . . . curiosity. I wonder what Scorsese's like—well you'll find out, he's offered you a role. Right! With somebody like that you don't even question the role. You say—Scorsese? Yeah, I'm doing it.

"That's the impetus for me. Whenever I CHOOSE ROLES, it's usually a joke. I've now learned that my gut instinct is right—just go because you think the guy making it is interesting. And generally then I'll have a better time and be able to live with the end result.

"I find it really boring, actually."

Really?

"Yeah."

A lot of hanging around waiting?

"Yeah, I hate all that, y'know? I run out of film talk after a bit. People sitting around talking about what films they've just finished or are gonna be doing—the whole thing revolves around the INDUSTRY. People don't seem to have another life outside of it—you think: Christ, can't we talk about anything else except movies? Zzzzz. . . ."

Playing Warhol, who you once claimed not to be able to tell apart from a silver screen, must've been fun though.

"Yeah, that was great 'cos it was just ten days. I only had 7000 words, and once I got them in the right order, it was a doddle. I mean, a most challenging role."

Once he revs up however, he's full of praise for superstar painter Schnabel's directorial debut—"the first film about an American painter, and it's a BLACK painter. Not Pollock, or Johns, or de Kooning—although John Malkovich as Pollock would've been stunning."

This leads to anecdotes about a recent visit to Johannesburg ("accompanying my wife on a modelling gig") and the "fucking sensational" exhibition Africa 95, which comes to Britain soon. "I got very evangelical about it. It has no pretensions of grappling with philosophical problems. It's: can I eat? Can I stay in this house?

"They look on Basquiat as THEIR Picasso, who made it in a white world. I'm not sure even Julian realises the reverberations of his movie. It's an informal, poignant story of a tragic life. How by tacit agreement an artist and society endeavour to demolish the artist himself. His own addictions are so much a part of his downfall. But then that's one of the great occurrences of the day.

"If the film cocks up in the editing, I'll be so angry at him 'cos it's going so well. The performances are wonderful."

There follows a rather darling list of how well David knew the rest of the cast. "I've known Hopper, Dennis, for close on 20 years. Through good times and bad! And Gary Oldman I've known for maybe the last eight years. Chris Walken I've known FOREVER. And Willem Dafoe I worked with in the Scorsese movie, when . . . when he was Christ! Ha! He was hung up at the time."

You washed your hands of him.

"I did! Ha ha! Got tired of him hanging about."

In *The Diary of Nathan Adler or the Art-Ritual Murder of Baby Grace Blue*, a text which accompanies the new album, Bowie writes: "He didn't do much after that. I guess he read a lot. Maybe wrote a whole bunch, I suppose. You never can tell what an artist will do once he's peaked."

"I tend to steal from high art and demean it to street level," he smiles, apropos of nothing. "Brian [Eno] is the professor, and hasn't changed a bit in 20 years—he's STILL bald. Me, I'm the old limey queen."

We've done everything bar scuba-diving, so we may as well discuss books.

"I've always been drawn to stream-of-consciousness. Ever since I was a kid. I felt more familiar, had more empathy, with people like Jack Kerouac and Ginsberg and Ferlinghetti, and then Burroughs of course in the late

Sixties. There's a resonance in people like Thomas Hardy, that I appreciate, but I still find it hard work."

Plodding?

"Yeah. Y'know, I understand that it's of its times, and that there are nuances in there I should ponder over. I'm just not sure I have the time!"

Yeah, there's a lot of trees.

"I can read a LOT, mind you. On a good week I'll get through three or four books. We are by tradition a literary nation. As can be seen by the way we revile all visual arts! And I've inherited that great love of literature, I love being told a story, being shown new ideas.

"But what I like about the stream-of-consciousness writers is—it's the same reason why I would HOPE my audience likes MY work—that they belong to me more. There's more room for interpretation. In a Hardy book the parameters of the narrative and its sensibility are dictated by the author. You have to follow his plan and get into his world the way he wants you to. I prefer to be allowed more latitude; something I can USE.

"I don't know why I'm picking on Hardy. Jane Austen then. Alright, even later . . . who've we got at the moment? Oh, Amis, I can—well, he's just funny. Peter Ackroyd is great. There's a great mysticism in his work. Now who's somebody who's really stiff and hard work?"

You mean, like, a Booker Prize winner?

"Oh! Yeah! Of course! Oh dear. Anita Brook . . . Brook . . ."

Um, Brookner? *Hotel du Lac*?

"Yeah, I mean something like that I have a real problem with. It really takes the aesthetic high ground and it's all up there in that rarefied strato-sphere. I'm sure it's great art, but I can't USE it, it doesn't apply. It just shows me that woman has very well-honed sensibilities, and I'm very pleased for her. But I need art that actually enriches my life in a very personal way. Something that I can USE. Something that's FUNCTIONAL. And in its own way, interpretation is a function, it's a function of the psyche. And I kind of hope that's what my audience finds as one of the main things they can do with my . . . stuff. Ha ha ha!"

Fleetingly, when you're talking to him, or more likely listening, the shafts of sunlight shimmy a little and the eyes do something or his pro-file does something and you're thrown, your breath goes: wow, it's David

Bowie, who redirected the finest minds of my generation. He's still recommending books about Mapplethorpe and revelling as a raconteur as hints are being dropped that it's time for him to go make videos, and records, and films, and paintings, and CD ROMs, and things happen, and whoopee.

"Or," he adds enigmatically, "they could bury it under dust."

We'll interpret that David Bowie line as we wish. We always do.

THE ARTFUL CODGER

Steven Wells | November 25, 1995, *New Musical Express* **(UK)**

More than a decade before this feature was published, the old house style of *New Musical Express* had given way to a new breed of gonzo journalism and hard-left ideology. As such, by 1995 granting an audience to one of its contributors involved being veritably lectured by someone so passionate he could be imagined spraying spittle as he talked.

Such proved to be the case with Steven Wells. Although—as with so much *NME* journalism of the era—it could be argued that the piece says more about the writer than the subject, the feature is interesting for how Bowie is, for reasons other than the quality of his music, not an idol to the interviewer. Bowie's previous radical aura cut no ice for a certain kind of then-contemporary British left-winger.

Despite his hip-talking self-aggrandizement (or gonzo pseudo self-aggrandizement), Wells does make an interesting point: how in the early seventies Bowie managed to turn something which caused revulsion—his alleged bisexuality—into a selling point. —Ed.

So I walk in and here he is—The Zig!—sipping a pale pink cocktail from a gnome skull-shaped glass and munching lime green monitor lizard foetus-flavoured crisps.

He's got a teetering orange Mohawk, a *quo* decadent one-piece shocking-scarlet Lurex sexromper body-stocking (cut high on the skeletal hips) and silver glitter platform space-clogs. He's got this sort of massive yellow zig-zag tattoo on his face and he says (or rather, sort of hisses like a bad-ly-dentured Martian snake on cocaine): "Oh, you must be the funny little man from the *NME*," as he holds out his thin, white, triple-jointed fingers (with, of course, the very long purple fingernails sharpened to a point and dipped in diamond dust) for me to kiss. And I glazedly gaze up at him in slack-jawed awe and I say: "Hey, has anyone ever told you that you've got different coloured eyes?"

No, that's not what happens. What happens is I walk into a rather grungy East End photography studio all nervous and trembly because it's not every day that you get to meet the undisputed Alien Rock God Of Strange Sex Pop and . . . he's not there. There's just some unshaven tramp in a leper-skin grey Oxfam coat and £2.99 (from Halifax Market) sunglasses slouched like a sack of mouldy potatoes on the couch.

As I am staring at this human wreckage in disgust, this PR person sidles up and whispers in my ear:

"David's very jet-lagged and very, very tired. Do you mind if we start the interview now?" And then the penny drops and I realise that the dozing tramp on the battered ketchup'n'chip fat-splattered "grunge" settee is David Bowie. I'm confused. I mean, never mind "Is there life on Mars?," is there life in f----ing Whitechapel? I mean, talk about "the chameleon of pop"!

And then it dawns on me. He probably turned up looking very cool and *très groovy* after an all-weekend cocaine-flavoured, alcoholic jelly-gobbling, eyepatch-wearing and talking about "art" orgy with his mates Iggy, Noddy, Damien, Lou, Brian, Keef, Iman, Salman, Naomi, Alvin, Tarquin, Cecil and Claude. But the minute he walked into this genuine cockernee Britpop punk-rock shithole, his weird alien chameleon-like chemistry kicked in and he automatically blended into his new environment. Cool!

So David Bowie is absolutely shattered and in no fit state to do an interview. Tally ho!

I ask him did he watch that documentary on the telly last night about The Small Faces and isn't it weird how they used to be such skinny, shaggable pretty things and now they're all chubby and creased and old, but you, Mr. Dorian Gray, still look cool and thin and sexy (slurp slurp). I ask if he thinks that he'd have been half as successful at Pervy Rock God-dom had he had a bit of a chubby hamster-face like *moi* and he looks at me and says: "Heh heh heh! I dream about being chubby!" And not only that, but he says he's willing to swap bodies with me the minute that the technology becomes available. Cool!

A long time ago, when the sexy '60s crashed into the scary '70s, the young David Bowie went to bed looking like Johnny out of Menswear and woke up as a Peter Frampton-permed Buddhist art-student gibbering on about laughing gnomes. Then he went really mental. He started telling everybody that he was an androgynous spaceman and making records about cavemen dancing with spiders and left-handed Japanese cats (no, really) and dressing up in incredibly silly costumes. And the strange thing is (remember this is a time when the streets of England crawled with skinheads looking for "puffs" to kick to death) that while "dads" bit through the stems of their pipes and kicked in their black and white TV sets, foaming at the mouth and screaming "Enoch was right!", the "kids" said, "Bowie's cool! He's thin! He dresses like a twat and he's got different-coloured eyes and we want to be just like him." Bowie was like LSD in the water supply. *Plus* he made having bad teeth and ginger hair and singing in a funny cockernee accent dead cool and thus single-handedly invented punk rock. So I'm expecting *Bladerunner* meets Noel Coward and I get Compo from *Last Of The Summer Wine*. He chain smokes Marlboro Lights.

"I was smoking 30 red Marlboros a day and then I went on to the Lights and now I'm smoking 60 of them a day. Oh it's ridiculous! I'm really supposed to stop altogether, but I can't . . ."

Do you now worry about mortality? Every time you light a fag do you not picture yourself rotting on a cancer ward?

"No, I love death, the more of it the better, I think it's a good thing, heh heh heh!"

Have you read Allen Carr's *The Easy Way To Stop Smoking*?

"Oh yeah! I've read the book, I've played the tapes,—I've done the lot! I've been to a—sheesh!—a 'well-known-hypnotist'—that was embarrassing. About 20 minutes into the thing and I wasn't anywhere near under. I was just listening to him droning on and my arse really hurt. I mean my arse was really sore but I daren't move because it'd just embarrass the both of us because I'd pretended to be under for so long. I couldn't just say—excuse me, do you mind if I shift my arse?"

How much did it cost you?

"Nothing, he did it as a favour for a Rock God. Heh heh heh!"

Bowie has made some undeniably, indefinably, unarguably awesome pop music. Dozens of tracks that are so look-at-me manicured, so counter-jumpingly pretentious, so breathtakingly brittle, arse-achingly arty and dick-headedly daft that they still rattle and buzz around the collective pop-skull, and will do so for decades (because pop that isn't pretentious, brittle and daft simply isn't worth listening to).

Most of his '70s contemporaries are now either dead, stuck on the chicken-in-a-basket circuit or part of the hideously uncool 'aristocracy.' Bowie, however, despite some truly horrendous records and more than a few knuckle-suckingly run-from-the-room-screaming cock-ups (his recital of 'The Lord's Prayer' at the Freddie Mercury tribute concert springs to mind), has somehow managed to remain cool to such an extent that we, the Guardians At The Gate Of Cred, are willing to give his new album—"Outside"—a listen, whereas we just *know* that the next 15 Rolling Stones LPs (for instance) are going to be utter shite.

Why this should be I don't know, the bastard has let us down enough times. By rights, Bowie should be locked away in the dreadfully musty cupboard marked "Crap Dad Rock." Because—let's face it—most of you reading this weren't even born when Bowie was God, and, as you must be sickeningly aware as you listen to your ex-mod/hippy/punk parents blather on about how fings-ain't-what-they-used-to-be, *again*, the Grim Reaper has let rock'n'roll down badly. He cornered and kicked the crap out of Jimi, Marc, Kurt and Jim at exactly the right moment but he let scores of others get old, bloated, sordid and boring.

When that violent tide of millions-of-tongues-rammed-up-one-arsehole capital pop fame eventually and inevitably receded, Bowie was stranded high and dry—Johnny Nofriends stuck on a little island of Loopy-twatland. Suicide, choking to death on his own highly toxic vomit or the living hell of self-parody all became highly possible options. He retreated to Berlin with the equally mental Iggy Pop.

"I started making friends for the first time. I know it sounds strange but I didn't have many people to pit myself against and say, 'My life's not like theirs.' I didn't know anybody, I really didn't. I mean, Iggy was one of the few people that I sort of knew. We are still very cordial with each other but we have this certain wariness of each other—there was only a tenuous link between us at the best of times. I can't ever say we were bosom buddies . . ."

You don't go round his house and play Scalextric, then?

"HA HA HA HA HA HA HA HA HA HA! Cough! HA HA HA HA HA HA HA HA HA HA HA HA HA HA HA! Cough! HA HA HA HA HA HA HA!"

Do you like a bit of cheap sentimentality?

"I *thrive* on cheap sentimentality! I am a real crier!"

Are you a big *Little House On The Prairie* fan?

"Oh, I remember that. No, I never really got into that, but a well-crafted or, actually, even a rubbish film, if it strikes a note and I immediately understand the symbolic notion behind it. I am a very good audience."

Do you ever look in the mirror and go, "F---king hell! It's David Bowie!"

"HEH HEH HEH! I've gone long past that. I think the nearest I get to that is to try and get excited about myself. To tell myself that I'm really good. I've always had a problem with that . . ."

You lack self-confidence?

"Yes, terribly. Early on it was really important for me to try and believe that I was really, really great at what I was doing, um . . ."

Despite the fact that everyone's got their tongue up your bum?

"Yeah, yeah, I never bought into that at all. No, I always had a serious problem with my worth as an artist and, I guess, with myself as a person as well. Terrifically low self-esteem. Really, really diabolically low. You wouldn't believe it."

The "Tin Machine" period must have been hard, then, because no f---ker liked that.

"No, yeah, yeah, um, actually I enjoyed the hell out of it. I just loved it. I loved all the havoc it caused, heh heh! The fact that I could still cause that amount of hostility. I've been fortunate that nobody has ever been indifferent to me. The only indifference I've ever felt was in the mid-'80s when I did sort of 'indifferent albums' and I felt what it was like to be mediocre, y'know? In fact the irony of it is that both 'Tonight' and, er, the other one, I can't even remember, um, 'Never Let Me Down,' both taught me another lesson, that crap sells. Heh heh heh! Crap songs, really awful!"

Yet here you are, still looking thin and sexy and dead cool. Still got your credibility despite "Tin Machine" and some really crap albums. I mean, how many cool middle-aged white people are there in rock'n'roll? There's you, Neil Young, Iggy and Keef.

"HEH! Cough! HEH! HEH!"

Was "Tin Machine" you getting that embarrassing middle-aged rock star bit out of your system all in one go?

"Tell you what, you do me a favour, when you go back to your record player, try and find a copy of 'Tin Machine' and listen to a tune called 'I Can't Read,' listen to that one, will you? I don't ask you to listen to any of the rest, just listen to that one song because I think that song is one of the best I have ever written. I really do!"

Oooops! Time to change the subject. "Outside" (subtitled "The Nathan Adler Diaries: A Non-Linear Gothic Drama Hyper-Cycle") is sort of about a weirdo "art detective" living in a world populated by nutters who make aural-sculptures out of the bodies of 14-year-old girls and hammer knitting needles into their own heads and similar fun stuff. The recording sessions (with free-range egghead Brian Eno at the controls), saw each musician given a card which had something written on it like, "You are the last remaining member of a catastrophic event and you will endeavour to play in such a way as to prevent feelings of loneliness developing within yourself," or, "You are a disgruntled ex-member of a South African rock band. Play the notes they won't allow."

The end result is something of a cross between an early cyberpunk novel and an ambient remix of an LP by one of those mondo-horrorveggie post-grindcore industrial-spookster-headache bands but with serious arts A-levels. It is all utterly unfashionable—all horrifically post-apocalyptic we're-all-gonna-die BOO!ish and "clever" and millennialist mondo-futuro cosmopolitan—at exactly the time when young people's cool pop is about posh girls trying to shag you at college, admitting that you're an uncool nerd, riding Chopper bikes, smoking fags and being parochially dumb.

Put next to the witty, sly Kinksian slices of dry wit delivered by the likes of Blur, Supergrass and the simply awesome Pulp, "Outside" is a confused and confusing neo-gothic avant-garde-a-bleeding-clue-what-they're-on-about monster. It's like going into a fish'n'chip shop and being served some freakish, bug-eyed mutant anglerfish from the deepest depths of the Atlantic Trench when you've just gotten used to a diet of nice, safe, comfortable and comforting cod.

"Outside" has been backed up by interviews where Bowie has banged on at great length about how everything is going to the cyberdogs, about how the world teeters on the fracturing lip of an abyss which seethes and bubbles with a babbling stew of insane nanosecond factoidal soundbites—an increasingly senseless present and a soon-come utterly unravelled future of which, one assumes, only music like Bowie and Eno's and art like Damien Hirst's can make any sense.

So I'm reading this stuff on the tube and I'm listening to "Outside" on the headphones and I'm getting really spooked, scared to look up for fear of being brain-raped by images of my hard-wired fellow passengers injecting themselves in the eyeballs with smart drugs and engaging in art-terrorist acts which involve soldering irons, dead sheep and each other's genitals. Eventually, I pluck up the courage and look up and see the same old boring bastards in their boring clothes who think that "art" is nice paintings and all drugs are utterly evil, thank you very much. Jarvis Cocker's worldview nails these bastards down and slips drugs to their children. Bowie's seems completely incongruous.

"Was this on the London Underground?"

Um, yes . . .

"Mmmm, well, it really is endemic in the States. That really is a country committed to violence as a way of life. It's very scary over there now, much scarier than it was ten years ago. Not only the violence, the segregation is appalling. I don't think we've ever experienced anything like it in Europe. . . ."

Odd, isn't it, that that's true of a country which created the music we both make a living out of—the world's first multiracial, black and white music?

"There's also this denial in America that slavery ever took place. I think there should be a confrontation and there should be a museum of Black America."

I trawled through old *NME*s to research this article and I came across one piece about "Nazi chic," illustrated with a picture of you at Victoria station giving it the Nazi salute in your leather jacket.

"Actually, it was a woollen blouson."

You've apologised for that incident 100 times and yet you're now on tour with Morrissey, an artist who has also been hauled over the coals for allegedly flirting with dodgy far-right imagery and who, incredibly, has never felt the need to apologise or even explain his actions. How do you feel about that?

"I really don't know what his whole thing is. I'm not familiar with what he's been saying. In fact, that was one of the things I wanted to talk to him about. You tell me."

And so I do. I tell Mr. Bowie that what really pissed people off was the timing, that Morrissey, in what seemed like a fit of arrogant artistic pique, dismissed all criticism and denied the need for an explanation of his actions at a time when Turkish migrant workers were being firebombed in Germany, when an openly Nazi party were winning a council seat in Bermondsey and the "new" Nazis were cocky and confident enough to start roaming the streets looking for blacks and Asians to maim and murder. The parallels with Bowie's 1976 flirtation with fascism, at a time when the Nazi National Front (forerunners of the BNP) were reaping a real and frightening rise in popularity, are obvious.

"You can be very thick. I had this morbid obsession with the so-called 'mysticism' of the Third Reich. The stories about the SS coming over to England in search of the Holy Grail, that was the aspect of it that really appealed to me in my beleaguered and drugged state. Absurd as it may seem now, it just didn't occur to me that what I was doing had any relevance. My overriding interest was in Kabbalah and Crowleyism. That whole dark and rather fearsome never-world of the wrong side of the brain."

Do you believe that "magick" has any ability to affect the physical world?

"No, I think all those things merely become symbolic crutches for the negative. It was all an adolescent state of mind, even though I wasn't adolescent. I think drugs really perpetuate that adolescent state. Or can do, anyway, with me they certainly did."

Your interviews recently have emphasised the "art" nature of "Outside" and you've also talked a lot about "the spirit."

"I've just read this book by John Berger, *Ways Of Seeing,* and he goes on about how 'art' is really talked about with this 'fake religiosity.' "

Isn't it a bit daft to talk about "the spirit" post-Marx, Freud and Darwin? In a world where all intelligent people are atheists?

"I have a real *thrusting, rampant, spiritual* need. I can't become comfortable with any organised religion and I've sort of touched on all of them. I'm not looking for a faith, I don't want to believe anything. I'm looking for knowledge."

But why does it need to be outside of us? Aren't we fundamentally decent animals? One of the new Darwinists said something about how you could walk up and down the most violent street in New York and see a thousand acts of courtesy, caring and kindness before you saw one negative act. Isn't he right?

"I think there are lots of people who can live their lives on that level and on that platform and I am so envious of them. I can't do that. I'm perturbed by the idea of morality, of good and bad. I'm much more comfortable with the idea of illusion and reality. I get such moral drift—I've seen people killed with f---ing kindness and I've seen some negative situations actually turn out in a positive way and I find it all very confusing.

"More recently, I've been interested in the Gnostics. They aren't that different from Buddhists, really, in that they thought that God is within yourself, it's their idea that there's illusion and reality and the illusion part of it is what we perceive as reality in our conscious state. But, there again, it's just another codification. I don't think I could subscribe to saying that I was a Gnostic."

So we're not going to see you put out an album called "Laughing Gnostic"?

"No."

What about . . .

"HA HA HA HA HA HA HA HA HA HA! I like that. That's really funny! Well, you may now! HA HA HA HA HA HA HA!"

And bugger me if he doesn't nearly fall of[f] his stool. Funny bugger, Johnny Jet Lag.

You've talked a lot recently about modern youth "surfing on chaos," about them wallowing in a sort of semi-literate, plugged-in nihilism. Do you not think that you're exaggerating a bit? Isn't this akin to what people of a certain age said about the flappers of the '20s or the mods in the '60s?

"Well, firstly there's a psychotic difference between the American youth of today and the flappers—the germ of joy is absolutely missing from American youth. I wouldn't say it was nihilistic but there's a grim countenance over the youth, there really is. They go through a *grimly* day-to-day existence. There doesn't seem to be the bounce that I remember when I was the same age."

Don't you think that all this is merely it-were-all-fields-round-here-when-I-was-a-lad baby-boomerism? That this is just you getting older?

"HA! HA! HA! Well, no, I find that they are struggling with and producing their own culture and, of course, that's going to be excitingly different to ours by virtue of the fact that the world we're existing in now is a completely different world from when I was 16."

Like you had Timothy Leary and they've got Newt Gingrich?

"That's a decided concrete presence for them. I don't think they have the will or the ability to actually unscramble the overload of information that they get from day to day. Just little, simple things like reading. Like I know that a lot of my generation really did read. Everyone that I knew in that period read at least one book a month. The way they were accessing information was a lot slower, a lot more deliberate and to an extent a lot deeper—I'm not saying that was necessarily a good thing. They don't read in that way any more and that's not derogatory either, it's just the way that things are."

Um, how do you know all this? You've got a son at university studying philosophy for God's sake! Do you actually hang out with teenagers?

"Hang out? No, I can't say that I 'hang out' with teenagers. Yeah! Every move! HA HA HA HA HA! I pop down to the local youth club, I play ping pong every week! HA HA HA!"

You grew up in the '60s, the age of anything-is-possibilism, I think that punk, in a sense, was a continuation of that. People would look at a rock star like you and go, 'Yeah, I could do that, it's no big deal.' That seemed to get crushed to death in the '80s.

"Alright, I think that a lot of what could have been role models, for good or bad, are disregarded now. I think even the style of clothing reflects the same thing. I think there's a real searching, ruminating quality to this present generation that will explode, somehow, either in anger or great creativity or a wonderfully innovative way of dealing with a society which is completely and absolutely dysfunctional."

Did you see that documentary on TV about The KLF burning £1 million?

"I caught the last 20 minutes of it, I found it very confusing."

There was this bit where they took the suitcase containing the ashes of the money into an art gallery and asked the bloke there how much it was worth as a work of art and all the bloke wanted to know was—who was the artist who burnt it? Total bollocks or what? I mean if I play you a rock'n'roll record, it either rocks or it sucks, never mind who made it, right? And this is the problem that I have with your and Mr. Eno's talk about "art." I find it really puzzling because both you and he have already made great pop records, a form of late-20th Century art which is superior to "art" in every single respect.

"Well, it's more popular and it's more communicative and more accessible, but I don't think that that defeats our initial interests in the visual arts. I get so many seeds of ideas either from literature or the visual arts. I mean, I do kind of cross-pollinate all the time. In this country I think we're going through a renaissance in the visual arts. Look, just butt in if I'm going on a bit."

Well we are being hassled to finish . . .

"OK, back to Rock God! Back to Laughing Gnostic! HA HA HA HA!"

Both you and Mr. Eno have got chips on your shoulders, about being dismissed as working-class counter-jumpers who should stop trying to be arty because you haven't got the right breeding. My argument is that you shouldn't even try to embrace "art," that "art"—the whole Turner Prize fiasco establishment bullshit—is dead and that lumbering your music with "artistic" references is like tying a corpse to your back. How are we supposed to judge your record? Are we to say this record is a work of art because David Bowie is an artist?

"No no no!"

Or do we say does this record rock?

"Well, yeah, because if you didn't think that then there'd be something wrong with you because a lot of it just plain rocks, y'know? I mean Brian's a lot more fearful of the testosterone than I am. I LOVE it when it rocks, I love it when it has balls! I love it when it has big, hairy massive balls on it! But Brian is a lot more informed by minimalism and I am definitely not a minimalist. Layer it on! The thicker the better! Baroque and roll! No, but I agree there's got to be a primeval need to the music."

Who do you think is best qualified to judge your music?

"Oh Lord!"

Hang on, I haven't finished yet. You have got to choose between the Turner Prize Committee and Beavis And Butt-head.

"Oh God! Jesus! Um, well, you know something? Beavis And Butt-Head to see if it rocks and the Turner to see if it's well dressed, heh heh heh!"

You could always turn them around, you could stick the Turner mob on the couch and have Beavis And Butt-Head wandering around the Tate going "This installation, like, really sucks" or something.

"HA HA HA HA HA! Yeah, that's what Brian would do."

It is at this moment that the PR person swoops like an avenging angel of death and grabs Mr. Bowie by the collar and drags him off to do *Top Of The Pops*. Hopefully, my little talk with him has put him straight and we'll be hearing no more of this nonsense about art and religion and, who knows, maybe the next time he goes into a studio he'll not bother decorating it with "crazed colour pieces of fabric" and equipping it with "paints, charcoal, scissors, paper and canvas to give us something to fly on when not playing" and instead concentrate on rocking like a mutha.

Yes, thanks to *NME*'s timely intervention, it looks like David Bowie is back on course at last and that the soon-to-come "Laughing Gnostic" album will be his best yet.

So let's look at the old scoreboard:

QUESTION: Does "Outside" rock?

ANSWER: In parts, and enough parts for this to be David Bowie's best album in years.

QUESTION: Does the "concept" kick ass?

ANSWER: Nah! The Internetty, cyberpunky vibe is one tiny but crucial robostep behind the hipgeist—which unfortunate fact you can blame on huge-brained Messers B&E reading too many nerdy row-of-pens-in-the-top-labcoat-pocket big books and not enough slashing-edge New Wave Of Cyber New Wave (ugh) pulp fiction flick'n'flings like Manc novelist Jeff Noon's *Vurt* and *Pollen* (both awesome stuff).

With "art" you can make it up as you go along, but with pop you're either bang on the nail, just in front or f---ing nowhere.

QUESTION: Does it work as "art"?

ANSWER: Who gives a toss? . . .

NO LONGER A LAD INSANE

HP Newquist | January 1996, *Guitar* (US)

Although David Bowie is an artist who has given the impression of being as much—or even more—interested in artifice than substance, that beneath his chameleon and flashy exterior beats the heart of a thoughtful musician is demonstrated by the simple fact of the consistent excellence of his work. Accordingly, *Guitar* magazine felt he might have something interesting to say about the many people he had employed on that instrument during his by-now three-decade career. They were proven right.

   HP Newquist recalls, "In all the years I spent interviewing musicians, Bowie was one of the most interesting. Not only was he articulate, but he was engaging, erudite and funny. David had that rare quality—which I've encountered in only a handful of people—of immediately making the interview a conversation between two people instead of a question-and-answer session. His interest in all forms of music, and discussion of the creative process, set him far above the archetypal model of the bored and disaffected rocker."

   Note: to date, the world still awaits the intriguing collaboration with Jeff Beck that Bowie muses on herein. —Ed.

David Bowie is one of a handful of people who have directly influenced the course of popular music during their careers. It may even be safe to say that Bowie is the only musician who has been able to change the face of rock music more than once in his career. Through it all, he has been supported by some of the best guitarists in the business, many of whom rose to fame on the strength of their stints with David. With the release of *Outside,* his 24th album, Bowie has created yet another eclectic combination of guitar players. In this exclusive interview, Bowie reflects on the guitarists he has worked with over the past 25 years, starting with Mick Ronson and hinting at the possibility of a future collaboration with Jeff Beck.

How have you decided at different times which guitarist you wanted to work with?

I guess it's usually job-specific. Right at the very beginning, virtually when I started out, it was the Beck-iness of Mick Ronson that attracted me to his playing. At that particular time, I was looking for something. . . somebody who could work within the realms of the rock/rhythm & blues thing that I was doing but was just interested enough in what a guitar could do other than just deal with notes themselves. Mick sort of liked the idea of playing around with feedback and extraneous noises, to a certain extent; although not as much as some of the other guitar players that I worked with later on. But there was enough there to make it a little more adventurous than just the standard guitar. By the time I moved into the Berlin period [*Heroes, Low,* and *Lodger*] I was really much more interested in finding guitar players who were interested in the guitar as a sound *source*. It was really more a question of creating atmosphere rather than playing biting solos that showed off the virtuosity of the players. But to be that adventurous, they really need to understand the instrument very well—to really make something of what they're doing. It's the old adage of knowing the rules to be able to break them, which applies to Reeves Gabrels, and I must say, obviously, to Adrian Belew and Robert Fripp.

You have a history of dealing with eclectic guitarists that are frequently unknown before they work with you. Do you tend to just stumble on these guitiarists?

Yeah. [*laughs*]. I do. I'm just incredibly lucky. But then again, I kind of go out and see just about everything; there's not much that gets past me. I really like to know what's happening in this contemporary field of mine. I'm just a great fan of contemporary music. I catch every act as they come out, just to see what their attitude, what the chemistry, is all about. I thrive on a sense of competition. If I see something that's really, really good, I automatically say, "God, I can do better than that. . . ."

Robert Fripp was actually the only guitarist who was kind of a recognizable face when you were working with him.

Well, firstly, Fripp was brought to my attention—by Brian Eno himself—as somebody who'd he willing and probably interested in working on what Eno and I were working on. [Eno] said "Look, I've done such a lot of work with Robert, and he's really a collaborative spirit. He's somebody who can really get into what we're doing." So it really was Brian's nomination [*laughs*]. Fripp got very involved when we started. With Adrian it was simply [the result of] going to see a Frank Zappa gig. I was backstage, I was watching from the wings, and in between when he wasn't playing, he would come off into the wings and start talking with me. I think it sort of upset Frank a bit [*laughs*], because the guy was talking offstage for most of the show, and asking me what I was doing, if there was any chance to do something together, because he liked the way I was working, and all that. So that was sort of a gig meeting.

With Reeves, it was a very strange thing. Reeves I kind of got to know on the '87 tour, because his wife, Sara, became a stand-in publicist when our publicist was sick. So he was just like this guy that I chatted to a lot, he kind of knew a lot about art. We just seemed to have some common interests, you know'? But Sara gave me a cassette on the tour or maybe sent it to me shortly after the tour had ended, and I put it in my bag of stuff, like, "Oh. I'll do that when I get home to Switzerland." So I was playing through tapes and things that I got on tour, and I did come across Reeves' tape. It hadn't actually gotten through to me before that he was even a guitar player, and I was just blown away by the pieces that were on the tape. And I immediately phoned him up and asked him if he'd like to work with me on something, although I didn't quite know *what* at the time. But I was very excited by his playing, and I thought, "This is a real kindred spirit."

It was very exciting, finding him, because I was going through creative doldrums to a certain extent. I really was becoming quite indifferent to the idea of music. I was kind of getting more involved in visual arts again. I don't think I was at the point where I would have stopped writing music, but it was certainly almost taking a back seat. I have to credit Reeves with giving me the sense of adventure and experimentation. I really must. I mean, he kind of pulled me out of a hole with the formation of Tin Machine. It became a very freeing exercise—I hope for both of us. Definitely for me. It gave me the impetus to carry on doing what I again realized I like doing best, which was working in an arena that was more adventurous than what I had drifted into, sort of between '84 to '88, I guess. To me, that was a really dull, flaccid, lethargic period [*laughs*].

Reeves played on Outside *and is on the tour, but you also brought Carlos Alomar back in. Why was that?*
I just felt that the nature of some of the material that we're working with needed that very strong rhythmic element again. I guess I could have covered it with either samples or synth, but there's just something so complete about the way that Alomar handles it that I thought I would try the chemistry out. I didn't know how they'd get on together, and I'm always worried how personalities will work together. So I put Carlos in the studio with Reeves in New York when we were coming towards the end of making *Outside*, and Carlos worked on about five of the tracks as rhythm player, but I made sure Reeves was there at the same time. I saw that they were both big enough to sort of get on with each other, so that kind of clinched it for me, that I would have Carlos work within a band context again. And I think the combination of Reeves and Carlos is just terrific. They kind of automatically found their own positions within the band. I don't feel that there was a terrific rivalry. Maybe a sense of competition, but that's okay, that's great. In fact, it produces very good music.

How did Trent Reznor come into the Outside *picture?*
Brian and I virtually had nothing in store for us when we went into the studio. In fact, the band that I was actually quite taken with was three guys from Switzerland called The Young Gods [*See "Groundwire," Nov/95—ed.*]. I'd been aware of them previous to knowing about Nine Inch Nails. I thought they had some extraordinary ideas, by taking one chunk guitar riff and then sampling it, looping it, and having that as the consistent pattern through a piece of music. That became very much something that I thought, yes, I like that a lot, I'll try to employ that. They're quite something; I'd be very interested to see where they go.

But when I was made aware of Nine Inch, through interviews actually more than anything else, what fascinated me was the evolution between the first album [*Pretty Hate Machine*] and the second [*Broken*]. It was so speedy and mature in one album, I thought that was tremendous. It really made me aware that Trent was indeed somebody who was going to be around for a very long time. And something that is not noted with Trent is that once you get past the sonic information, the actual writing abilities are very well grounded. He writes very good bits of music. And as with most of the younger bands, there's nothing that goes past him; every era of rock is actually in there—even though it's in this guise of apocalyptic or postindustrial music. There's actually Beatles harmonies in there and all kinds of other things [*laughs*].

I wanted to do something a little more adventurous than possibly an artist of my . . . hmmm. . . I'm not quite sure what to call myself—I guess it's what an artist of my "fill in your own blank" normally would do. Having read that Trent was quite interested in my music from *Station To Station* on to *Scary Monsters*, obviously there was an empathy between the two of us. When Virgin Records called up to ask who I would tour with in support of this album, I thought that he'd be just great to work with. So I called Trent, and he'd just come off a tour. And he said he would love to tour with us as long as it wasn't any longer than six weeks, because he was pretty exhausted. So I was absolutely delighted that he agreed to do it.

Stevie Ray Vaughan was one guitarist you hired who really came into his own later on. How did you find him?
He was playing in the Monterey Jazz Festival. I'm not very good at years, but I suspect it must have been about 1982, the year before we started working together [*on* Let's Dance, *released in 1983—ed.*]. He was just a support act for some major band, with Double Trouble, and he just blew me away. He was just extraordinary.

You and he had a fairly well-publicized falling out after 1983's US Festival. Did you ever see him again after that?
I did indeed. In fact, just before he died, for about six months prior to his death, we got back together and got on so extremely well. We started going to each other's gigs, he'd come to see mine, and I went to see his, and we really started to buddy up. He changed an awful lot—he'd got a lot of the problems that he had earlier in his life out of his life. He just seemed to be so buoyant and enthusiastic, full of life. And his death was tragic, it really was.

You played all the guitars on Diamond Dogs, *which was fairly impressive given cuts like "Rebel, Rebel" and the title cut. Why did you choose not to use another guitar player?*

I think it was because I had what I thought might be fairly off-the-wall ideas. I was fairly shy and intimidated by other musicians in those days, especially musicians who I felt just were so far above me in experience and what they did. And I felt, God, I'll just try these ideas on my own because I'd be too embarrassed to ask other guitarists to do what I wanted them to do. I think that was the same period where Brian Eno was doing a similar thing and working on his own albums, because he also felt embarrassed about asking accomplished musicians to detune their guitars and things like that [*laughs*]. I was very naive then. But I got quite close to getting the sound I wanted on that album without using too many other musicians.

Are *there any guitarists that you'd like to work with, maybe those that already have their own reputation?*

I think maybe in the future, Jeff Beck. Jeff and I have, in fact, talked about doing a very special project at some point. I'd very much like to work with Jeff—I still think he's one of the most undervalued guitar players. I think he's absolutely extraordinary and I'd like very much to work with him.

A guy who's not actually known as a guitarist, but certainly wrote for guitar, is Glenn Branca [*see* Guitar, *Aug/95—ed.*], who I'd dearly like to work with. I'm not sure in what capacity, whether we'd kind of construct something for guitars—although Glenn has moved away from guitars, and he's working primarily with strings. I'd like to encourage him. . . . Maybe we could do a combination piece working with the idea of the string, and it could be guitar strings and gut strings as well. I'm such a big fan of his, and have been for quite a number of years. I think David Torn is also extraordinary, although I don't feel a need to have to work with him. I kind of feel that I know players that are in the same areas as David. Those needs have been fulfilled for me by the people I'm working with [*laughs*]. But the Branca and the Beck modes are something I would like to pursue, to really discover that.

FASHION: TURN TO THE LEFT.
FASHION: TURN TO THE RIGHT.

David Bowie and Alexander McQueen | November 1996, *Dazed & Confused* (UK)

On the cover of his 1997 album *Earthling*, Bowie can be seen standing—back to the camera—wearing a stylish frock coat with a Union Jack design. It was codesigned by him and Alexander McQueen, who dressed Bowie for his 1996 and 1997 stage shows.

In 1996, the year that McQueen was first declared British Designer of the Year, youth fashion and culture magazine *Dazed & Confused* allowed Bowie to interview fashion's wunderkind. The exchange shows that Bowie knows his sartorial onions—but also, interestingly, reveals that he takes fashion more seriously than does McQueen.

Sadly, McQueen took his own life in 2010.

Note: for "Arthur Hanes" read "Arthur Haynes." —Ed.

This conversation took place on the phone, as is always the case with my conversations with Alex. We have worked together for over a year on various projects and never once met. It's a beautiful Sunday afternoon and he is in the verdant green hills of Gloucestershire visiting at the house of his friend, Isabella Blow. Ring ring. Ring ring. Ring ring.

David Bowie: Are you gay and do you take drugs? (*laughter*)

Alexander McQueen: Yes, to both of them. (*more laughter*)

DB: So what are your drugs of choice?

AM: A man called Charlie!

DB: Do you find that it affects the way you approach your designing?

AM: Yeah, it makes it more erratic. That's why you get my head blown up shot. (*In reference to a Nick Knight photograph at the Florence Biennale.*)

DB: Well I once asked you to make me a specific jacket in a certain colour and you sent me something entirely different in a tapestry fabric, quite beautiful I might add, but how would you cope in the more corporate world?

AM: I wouldn't be in a corporate world.

DB: Even if you're going to be working for a rather large fashion house like Givenchy?

AM: Yeah.

DB. So how are you going to work in these circumstances? Do you feel as though you're going to have rules and parameters placed on you, or what?

AM: Well, yeah, but you know I can only do it the way I do it. That's why they chose me and if they can't accept that, they'll have to get someone else. They're going to have no choice at the end of the day because I work to my own laws and requirements, not anyone else's. I sound a bit like yourself!

DB: Unlike most designers, your sense of wear seems to derive from forms other than fashion history. You take or steal quite arbitrarily from, say the neo Catholic macabre photographs of Joel-Peter Witkin, to rave culture. Do you think fashion is art?

AM: No I don't. But, I like to break down barriers. It's not a specific way of thinking, it's just what's in my mind at the time. It could be anything—it could be a man walking down the street or a nuclear bomb going off—it could be anything that triggers some sort of emotion in my mind. I mean, I see everything in a world of art in one way or another. How people do things. The way people kiss.

DB: Who or what are your present influences?

AM: Let me think. I don't know. I think that's a really hard question because in one way, one side of me is kind of really sombre and the other side of my brain is very erratic and it's always this fight against the other and I choose so many different things. This is why my shows always throw people completely: one minute I see a lovely chiffon dress and the next minute I see a girl in this cage that makes her walk like a puppet and, you know, they can't understand where it's coming from because there are so many sides of me in conflict. But influences are really from my own imagination and not many come from direct sources. They usually come from a lone force of say, the way I want to perform sex or the way I want people to perform sex or the way I want to see people act, or what would happen if a person was like that. You know what I mean? It's not from direct sources. It's just sort of from a big subconscious or the perverse. I don't think like the average person on the street. I think quite perversely sometimes in my own mind.

DB: Yeah, I would say, from just looking at the way you work, that sexuality plays a very important part in the way that you design.

AM: Well, because I think it's the worst mental attitude. Sexuality in a person confines you to such a small space and, anyway, it's such a scary process trying to define one's sexuality. Finding which way you sway or what shocks you in other people and who accepts you at the end of the day when you're looking for love. You have to go through these corridors and it can be kind of mind-blowing sometimes.

DB: There's something a lot more pagan about your work compared, say, to Gaultier. Your things work at a more organic level.

AM: Possibly. I gather some influence from the Marquis de Sade because I actually think of him as a great philosopher and a man of his time, where people found him just a pervert. (*laughs*) I find him sort of influential in the way he provokes people's thoughts. It kind of scares me. That's the way I think but, at the end of the day, that's the way my entity has grown and, all in all, in my life, it's the way I am.

DB: Do you think of clothes themselves as being a way of torturing society?

AM: I don't put such an importance on clothes, anyway. I mean at the end of the day they are, after all, just clothes and I can't cure the world of illness with clothes. I just try to make the person that's wearing them feel more confident in themselves because I am so unconfident. I'm really insecure in a lot of ways and I suppose my confidence comes out in the clothes I design anyway. I'm very insecure as a person.

DB: Aren't we all? Could you design a car?

AM: Could I? It would be as flat as an envelope if I designed a car.

DB: Could you design a house?

AM: Yes, very easily, very easily.

DB: Do you paint or sculpt?

AM: No. I buy sculptures. I don't do it, I buy it. I buy lots of sculptures.

DB: Do you ever work in the visual arts?

AM: No, but I just did a show the other day. I don't know if you heard, but we did this show, it was on water and we did this kind of cocoon for this girl made of steel rods and it was in the form of a three dimensional star and it was covered in this glass fabric so you could see through it and this girl was inside it, but we had all these butterflies flying around her inside it. So she was picking them out of the air and they were landing on her hand. It was just about the girl's own environment. So I was thinking about the new millennium in the future thinking you would carry around with you your home like a snail would. She was walking along in the water with a massive star covered in glass and the butterflies and death-faced moths were flying around her and landing on her hand and she was looking at them. It was really beautiful. It threw a lot of people completely sideways.

DB: It's interesting how what you're talking about, is somewhere between theatre and installation.

AM: Well, I hate the theatre, I hate it. I used to work in the theatre. I used to make costumes for them and films, and it's one thing I've always detested—the theatre. I hate going to the theatre, it bores me shitless.

DB: Well, I'm not talking about a play.

AM: I know, but I just wanted to tell you that anyway! (*laughs*)

DB: **All right, change the word to ritual.**

AM: Yeah, that's better. I like ritual . . . (*laughs*)

DB: **Armani says, 'Fashion is dead.'**

AM: Oh, so is he . . . I mean, God . . .

DB: **Now you sound like Versace . . .**

AM: He's close to dead. I mean, no one wants to wear a floppy suit in a nice wool—the man was a bloody window dresser. What does he know?

DB: **Do you think that what he's really saying is that maybe . . .**

AM: He's lost it . . .

DB: **He might still be making an observation in as much as the boundaries are coming down . . .**

AM: Yeah.

DB. **The way fashion is presented these days is a quantum leap from how it was presented say, five to ten years ago. It's become almost a new form, hasn't it?**

AM: Yeah, but you know you can't depend on fashion designers to predict the future of society, you know, at the end of the day they're only clothes and that never strays from my mind for one minute.

DB: **Is the British renaissance a reality or a hype do you think? The world is being told that it's so. Through all strata of British life and from fashion to visual arts, music, obviously, architecture, I mean there's not one aspect of culture where Brits haven't got some pretty fair leaders, English designers in French houses, you know what I mean? It's like we're pervading the whole zeitgeist at the moment.**

AM: Being British yourself, I think you understand that Britain always led the way in every field possible in the world from art to pop music. Even from the days of Henry VIII. It's a nation where people come and gloat at what we have as a valuable heritage, be it some good, some bad, but there's no place like it on earth.

DB: But why is it we can't follow through once we've initially created something? We're far better innovators than we are manufacturers.

AM: Yeah, exactly. But I think that's a good thing. I don't think that's a bad thing. It makes you holy, it makes you quite respectable about what you do and the actual moneymaking part of it is for the greedy.

DB: So you're not greedy, Alex?

AM: I'm afraid I'm not. Money's never been a big object. Well, I mean I like to live comfortably, but I've been asked by this French fashion house how would I put on a show and I said, well, the sort of money these people buy these clothes for in this day and age, you don't want to flaunt your wealth in front of the average Joe Public because it's bad taste and with all the troubles in the world today, it's not a good thing to do anyway. I'm sure these people that have this sort of money don't feel like showing their face on camera, so I said it would be more of a personal show and people with this sort of money who do appreciate good art and good quality clothes and have these one-off pieces made just respect the ideal, not the actual chucking money around. They can do that anywhere.

DB: So when you are affluent, which I'm afraid is probably on the cards for you, how are you going to deal with that?

AM: I'd like to buy Le Corbusier's house in France . . . (*sniggers*)

DB: Here's a nice thing. What was the first thing you designed ever? Like when you were little or a kid or something?

AM: Oh I can't think that far back, but for my own professional career, it was the bumsters. The ones that Gail, your bass player, wears.

DB: Was there a point when you were sort of playing around with stuff, and when you used to dress up and go to clubs when you were a kid, and all that, where you would do original things?

AM: Actually, yeah. I would wear my sister's clothes and people wouldn't recognise it because I'd wear them in a male way. I did go round my street once in my sister's bra when I was about 12 years old and the neighbours thought I was a freaky kid, got dirty looks and all that . . . and you're talking about Stepney here.

DB: My father used to work in Stepney.

AM: Yeah?

DB: What age were you when you left home?

AM: 19.

DB: Did it give you an incredible feeling of freedom? Or did you suddenly feel even more vulnerable?

AM: I felt really vulnerable actually. Because I was the youngest and I was always mollycoddled by my mother, so that's why I turned out to be a fag, probably. (*laughter*)

DB: (*laughing*) Was it a clear choice?

AM: I fancied boys when I went to Pontins at three years old!

DB: Did you ever go on holiday to Butlins or Bognor Regis or Great Yarmouth?

AM: No, I went to Pontins in Camber Sands.

DB: Camber Sands?! I used to go there too!

AM: Oh my God!

DB: They had a trailer park with caravans . . .

AM: Exactly.

DB: . . . and next door to us we had a, at the time, very well known comedian, Arthur Hanes, who was sort of like a bit of a wide boy; that was his bit on stage, you know, and I used to go over and try and get his autograph. I went three mornings running and he told me to fuck off every day. (*laughing*) That was my first time I met a celebrity and I was so let down. I felt if that's what it's all about . . . they're just real people.

AM: Two memories on Pontins—one, was coming round the corner and seeing my two sisters getting off with two men. (*laughter*) I thought they were getting raped and I went screaming back to my Mum and I wound up getting beat up by my two sisters! The other one was turning up in Pontins when we first got here and looking out the cab window 'cos my family was, like, full of cabbies; it was like a gypsy caravan-load to go to these places, and I looked out the window when I got there and there were these two men with these scary masked faces on and I shit myself there and then in the cab! I literally just shit my pants! (*laughter*)

DB: Which comes to . . . who is the shittiest designer?

AM: Oh my God . . .

DB: Who is the worst designer?

AM: In my eyes?

DB: Yeah, in your eyes.

AM: Oh God, I'm open for libel here now, David . . .

DB: Do you think there's more than one?

AM: I think you've got to blame the public that buy the clothes of these people, not the designers themselves because it turns out they haven't got much idea about, you know, design itself. It's the people that buy the stuff. My favourite designer, though, is Rei Kawakubo. She's the only one I buy, the only clothes I buy ever for myself as a designer are Comme des Garçons. I spent about a thousand pounds last year (I shouldn't say that) on Comme des Garçons menswear . . .

DB: I've never paid, Alex! (*laughs*) Until . . .

AM: Until you met me! (*more laughter*)

DB: Until I met you! Yes, but I knew that you needed it!

AM: I did at the time! But I tell you what I did do when you paid me, I paid the people that actually made the coat!

DB: No, listen, you were so kind about the couple of things that I

didn't need that you actually gave me. I thought that was very sweet of you. You work very well in a collaborative way as well. I thought the stuff . . .

AM: I still haven't bloody met you yet! (*laughs*)

DB: I know, I think it's quite extraordinary that we've done so well with the stage things that we put together. Do you enjoy collaboration?

AM: I do, but the one thing you have to do when you collaborate is actually respect the people that you work with: and people have phoned me up and asked me to collaborate with them before and I've usually turned them down.

DB: Do your clients really know what they want and what is right for them, or do you usually have to dress them from the floor up?

AM: It can work either way and I don't resent either because, at the end of the day, I'm the clothes designer and they are the public. If you want a house built you're not expected to build it yourself.

DB: Here's a fan question. Who would you like to dress more than anyone else in the world and why?

AM: There's no-one I'd like to dress more than anyone else in the world, I'm afraid. I can't think of anyone who deserves such a privilege! (*laughs*)

DB: The sub-headline there! (*laughs*)

AM: Oh my God no, 'cos I'm an atheist and an anti-royalist, so why would I put anyone on a pedestal?

DB: Well it does draw one's attention back to your clothes and what you do is actually more important than anything else.

AM: Well, I think it would limit your lifestyle somewhat if you said your music is just for that person down the road.

DB: You just sort of hope there's someone out there that might like what you do.

AM: And there's always someone, I mean the world is such a big place.

DB: Yeah. Prodigy or Oasis?

AM: Prodigy. I think they're brilliant.

DB: Well, you haven't answered this one. I have to drag you out on this one. Armani or Versace? (*laughs*)

AM: Marks and Spencer. I'm sorry. I don't see the relevance of the two of them put together. Actually, they should have amalgamated and sort of formed one company out of both. If you can imagine the rhinestones on one of them deconstructed suits . . .

DB: What do you eat?

AM: What do I eat?

DB: Yeah.

AM: Well, I've just had a guinea fowl today . . . it was quite an occasion to come here. . . . It's such a lovely place and I love to come here. Bryan Ferry comes here a lot. It's an amazing place and it was built in the Arts and Crafts Movement by Isabella's husband's grandfather. It's on a hill in Gloucestershire and it overlooks Wales and everything. And my bedroom is decorated with Burne-Jones' Primavera tapestry—I always come here to get away.

DB: So this is your sanctuary is it?

AM: Yes, it is. Very much so.

DB: Did you ever have an affair with anyone famous?

AM: Not famous, but from a very rich family. Very rich Parisian family.

DB: Did you find it an easy relationship, or was it filled with conflicts?

AM: No, it: he was the most wonderful person I have ever met and I was completely honest with him. Never hushed my background or where I came from, and this was when I was only 19 or 20, I went out with him and I said to him whatever we do, we do it Dutch and he didn't understand what I said. He thought it was a form of sexual technique! Going Dutch!!

(*laughs*) I said it means paying for each of us separately. He thought it that was great, but he gave the best blow job ever! (*laughter*)

DB: How royal! Was it old money or was it industrial wealth?

AM: Long time industrial aristocratic wealth.

DB: Do you go abroad very much? I mean just for yourself, not for work?

AM: No, not really.

DB: So you really are happy in your home grown environment?

AM: I like London, but I love Scotland! I'd never been to Aberdeen before and I went to see Murray's friends in Aberdeen for the first time and it was unreal because I stepped off the plane and I just felt like I belonged there. It's very rare that I do that because I have been to most places in the world, like most capital cities in Japan and America, and you feel very hostile when you step off the plane in these places. I stepped off the plane in Aberdeen and I felt like I've lived there all my life. And it's a really weird sensation. I like more of the Highlands. My family originated from Skye.

DB: Are you a good friend, a stand up guy, or a flake?

AM: I'm afraid I have very few friends and I think that all of the friends I have, I can depend on and they can depend on me. I don't have hangers-on, and I'm very aggressive to people that if I read through 'em in a second, they've usually found the wrong person to deal with. So if you have got me as a friend, you've got me for life. And I'd do anything for them, but I don't really have associates that use me or abuse me, unless I ask them to! (*laughs*)

DB: Are you excited about taking over at Givenchy?

AM: I am and I'm not. To me, I'm sort of saving a sinking ship and not because of John Galliano, but because of the house. It doesn't really seem to know where it's going at the moment and, at the end of the day, they've got to depend on great clothes, not the great name.

DB: **Have you already formulated a kind of direction you want to take them?**

AM: Yeah, I have.

DB: **Is it exciting?**

AM: Yeah it is, because the philosophy is mainly based on someone I really respected in fashion. There's a certain way fashion should go for a house of that stature, not McQueen bumsters, I'm afraid.

DB: **My last question. Will you have time to be making my clothes for next year's tour?** (*laughs*)

AM: Yeah, I will. We should get together. I mean, I want to see you this time. (*laughs*)

DB: **We could put this on the record right now . . . are you going to make it over here for the VH-1 Fashion Awards? I can't remember.**

AM: When is it?

DB: **October 24th or something . . .**

AM: My fashion show is on the 22nd.

DB: **So you're probably not going to make it. 'Cos you know I am wearing the Union jacket on that. Because millions of people deserve to see it.**

AM: You've got to say, "This is by McQueen"! (*laughs*)

DB: **Gail will be wearing all her clobber as well.**

AM: Oh, she's fab!

DB: **Oh, she wears it so well.**

AM: I'd love to do your tour clothes for you again.

DB: **Oh, well that's great. I can't wait to be properly fitted up this time!**

AM: Yeah, definitely. But I've got to see you. I don't want wrist measurements over the phone, 'cos I'm sure you lie about your waist measurements as well! (*laughs*)

DB: No, not at all . . .

AM: 'cos you know some people lie about their length! (*laughs*)

DB: I just said I'd never lie about the inside leg measurement.

AM: What side do you dress David, left or right? (*laughs*)

DB: Both!

AM: Yeah, right.

DB: No. Yes. Well, maybe.

A STAR COMES BACK TO EARTH

Mick Brown | December 14, 1996, *Telegraph Magazine* (UK)

In this interview feature for the Saturday magazine supplement of Britain's *Daily Telegraph* news-paper, Mick Brown touches on pretty much all the bases in his précis of Bowie's career so far.

If he gets the year wrong with regards to Bowie's "I'm gay" declaration, we can forgive him for both the overall quality of the feature and the interesting personal anecdote he tells at the beginning that gives an example of how the shadow of a superstar falls onto an ordinary life.

Note: for "Rudolf Schwarzkogler" read "Rudolf Schwartzkergler." —Ed.

Throughout the Seventies, David Bowie did not have fans. He had acolytes, disciples, obsessives; teens and 20s who would buy every record, watch every move, copy his clothes, his haircuts—the upswept flaming bush of Ziggy Stardust, the soul-boy quiff of *Young Americans*—his attitude.

Tony, a student friend of mine, idolised David Bowie. Back in the late Sixties, before the world at large even knew who Bowie was, Tony had even met him once or twice. Bowie was living in suburban Beckenham at the time—an aspirant pop singer, dabbling in mime, *kabuki*, the visual arts—running an arts project, and a couple of times Tony was invited back to Bowie's home to hang out, smoke a joint or two and talk.

This was before Bowie recorded *The Man Who Sold The World*, the album that made his reputation. *The Man Who Sold The World* was notable for two things: its cover, which showed Bowie lounging on a chaise longue in a fetching silk dress, the first signal of the sexual ambiguity that would become his stock-in-trade; and its lyrics, which dealt explicitly with the thin line between sanity and madness, alluding to the history of schizophrenia in Bowie's family and suggesting, as the song had it, that Bowie, too, *"would rather stay here with all the madmen/For I'm quite content they're all as sane as me."*

Tony loved the *The Man Who Sold The World*, perhaps because it not only mirrored the madness germinating in his own mind, but also legitimised it. Sometime in the early Seventies, Tony was diagnosed as schizophrenic and admitted to a mental hospital. I visited him there once or twice. On the door of his room he had a huge poster of Bowie in his incarnation as Aladdin Sane—the flash of lightning zigzagging across a face that looked like a death mask. I could imagine Tony in his room, tuning into the poster, picking up his own scrambled meanings and messages—A Lad Insane. The poster was calling him, and one day Tony walked down the long driveway of the mental hospital and took a bus to Beckenham, to see Bowie.

It was tricky, but eventually Tony found the house. There was no reply when he rang on the doorbell, so Tony opened the gate to the back garden, smashed the kitchen window and let himself into the house. After all, David would understand.

Tony looked around; the G-Plan furniture and swirly patterned carpets weren't as he remembered—but, hell, Bowie's taste was ever eccentric. Tony was sitting in the front room, in front of the electric logfire, drinking tea, when the respectable suburban couple whose house it was eventually returned.

Tony was back on the ward within an hour.

Bowie had long since left Beckenham by then, of course, and probably long since forgotten Tony. It's difficult to place this correctly, but by the time Tony was smashing that kitchen window, Bowie was holed up in the Pierre Hotel in New York, a Rock Monster. He had rented two suites, at $700 a week, one for living in, the other transformed into a makeshift studio, where Bowie sequestered himself, making films of himself building scale models of the stage-set for his forthcoming nightmare-of-the-apocalypse *Diamond Dogs* tour.

"It's unbelievable," says Bowie, leaning forward on the sofa in the New York recording studio where we are talking. "I'm a real hoarder, and I actually came across this film the other day, and it's *so* funny.

"John Lennon was around at that time, and every now and then the camera catches sight of him in the background, sitting there with his guitar playing hits of the day and saying, 'what the bloody hell are you doing, Bowie? It's all so negative, your shit. All this *Diamond Dogs* mutant crap. Ha, ha, ha.'

"I loved John. I remember asking him once what he thought of glam rock and he said"—Bowie adopts a plausible Liverpudlian accent—"'It's just fooking rock and roll with lipstick.' Which was very succinct, but not all that accurate. Ha, ha, ha."

Bowie rocks back on his chair with laughter. He laughs readily. It's the first thing you notice. That and his immediate warmth. There is no hint of diffidence or reserve, no hint of mystery. Quite the opposite, in fact: the warm handshake, the south London mateyness, the air of breezy candour —all conspire to effect that great social trick of leading you to believe after five minutes acquaintanceship that you've known Bowie all your life.

This is unexpected because what we came to expect from Bowie in his heyday as a rock star was deliberate mystification. Better than anybody, Bowie understood the imperative of ambiguity and change in pop music— the fact that a moving target was harder to hit. In the Sixties "authenticity" had been the most highly prized commodity in rock music—a throwback to its roots in the "pure" form of the blues. Bowie's talent was for miscegenation, artfully appropriating avant-garde ideas and popularising them.

He also understood the power of sex in pop music. Mick Jagger flaunted effeminacy with the Rolling Stones; Bowie took it further, elevating the thrill of sexual ambiguity to a cri de coo-er!—"Oh you pretty things," he sang in one of his most popular songs, "Don't you know you're driving your mamas and papas insane."

Above all, Bowie's performance was predicated on the deployment of disguise, shifting through a series of theatrical identities and musical styles which, as much as they enthralled his audience, begged the perpetual question: who *exactly* is David Bowie?

This was a game that made Bowie the most consistently inventive rock performer of his generation, and one of the most successful—until he ran out of steam sometime in the mid-Eighties, when his touch appeared to desert him, and nobody much seemed to care who Bowie was anymore.

So who exactly is David Bowie now? He is 50 next month. The father of a 25-year-old son, Joe, by his first marriage. Married for the past four years to Iman, the former fashion model, who now runs her own cosmetics company. They have a home in Switzerland, where Bowie has lived since 1981, although he is as likely to be found working and travelling in New York, London, Paris and the Far East. (He has a passion for Indonesia.)

You might describe him as all-purpose art-dilettante. He makes records; he acts (most recently playing Andy Warhol in the film *Basquiat*, directed by his friend, the painter Julian Schnabel); he collects paintings (German Expressionist and British contemporary) and paints himself; he designs wallpaper; he sits on the board of the art journal *Modern Painters*, for which he also writes art criticism. He has described himself as "a mid-art populist and postmodernist Buddhist surfing his way through the chaos of the late 20th century," which may explain why a lot of people nowadays think that David Bowie's worst vice is pretentiousness.

In fact, what he is most guilty of is being carried away on a tidal wave of his own enthusiasm. Talking of Bowie's work, Brian Eno, his sometime producer and close friend, describes him as "a wild intuitive, which is to say he works from his own excitement a great deal. He's capable of really fast, brilliant tangents off into somewhere that you hadn't suspected."

The same might be said of his conversation. Bowie talks in great, voluble torrents, darting from one topic to the next, parenthesising and then parenthesising the parathenseses, as if he has too many ideas for one conversation.

Mention the phrase "German Expressionism" (which Bowie does quite often) and it's the prelude to a protracted lecture about Pabst and Fritz Lang, the Blaue-Reiter enclave and how, as Bowie puts it, "the homemade quality of German Expressionist theatre generated an emotional flamboyance which contrasted with the slick professionalism of American theatrical design." Want to talk performance art? Bowie will discourse at length on the artistic interest in bodily fluids, self-laceration, and the work of "the Viennese Castrationists," whose leader, Rudolf Schwartzkergler, he will tell you, "cut his balls off in performance, and died in an insane asylum."

What about the occult? "Nobody professing a knowledge of the black arts," says Bowie firmly, "should be taken seriously if they can't speak Latin or Greek. I know, I know," he sighs, long inured, one suspects, to accusations of, at best, autodidactism; at worst, not allowing anybody else to get a word in edgeways. "If I've got a new rave about something I'll just talk endlessly about it and I'll explain where it comes from and how it started . . . " If he had no artistic abilities of his own, he says, he would be "absolutely and perfectly satisfied to learn and teach."

The afternoon has already provided something of a guided tour around Bowie's current enthusiasms. We have met downtown, at the studio of Tony Oursler, an artist friend of Bowie's, whose speciality is creating "installations" consisting of video portraits that are projected on to fabric dummies. A distorted image of Bowie gabbling to himself was running in one corner of the studio, while Bowie bounded around enthusiastically, elaborating on his plans to incorporate Oursler's "talking heads" into his forthcoming stage performance as surrogate backing singers.

Leaving Oursler's studio, we have made a pilgrimage, around the corner, to a particularly vivid piece of street graffiti that has sprung up overnight, Bowie striding along Houston Street, oblivious to the stares of passers-by—"Hey, that's David Bowie!"—a small crocodile behind him: me; his PR person; his personal assistant, Coco; his minder. We have now journeyed back uptown (Bowie in a black limousine, me following in a taxi) to the recording studio where he has been working on a new album.

He is pencil-thin, dressed in brown drainpipe trousers, a striped athletic top, and a baggy black corduroy jacket, decorated with three flying saucer brooches—a sort of space-cadet's pun on flying ducks. His hair has made some strange, atavistic journey back to the flame orange upswept brush cut he was wearing in the early Seventies, accentuating the paleness of his face, the finely chiselled features.

He settles back on to the sofa, lighting the third in an endless chain of Marlboro Lights. "There have been periods in my life," he says, "when I have been so closeted in my own world that I would no longer relate to anybody. And I *do* love communication. These days more than ever I feel like a *very* social animal, which I wasn't at one time. And I love the freedom of it; I love the joy it brings. And I love the conflicts and the debates which go with being much more a fully active member of society."

There is something disconcerting about this peroration. It is almost as if you are hearing someone talking about rejoining the human race. It is likely that more biographies have been written about Bowie than any other pop star of his generation. Two more have been published to mark his 50th birthday. He has never collaborated on any of them. His joke is that he plans to publish them all under one cover as the ultimate unauthorised biography. "Then if it were really successful, I could sue myself and make a fortune."

In lieu of this, Bowie helpfully offers a handy, back-of-the-envelope sketch of his own life. This suggests that there have been two occasions when he has lost himself: the first—"emotionally and spiritually"—in the Seventies, when he became mired in drug-sodden isolation; the second, "artistically" in the Eighties, ironically, at the time of his greatest commercial success, when he ran out of creative steam.

The supposition underlying this thumbnail thesis is that Bowie has now found himself again, whoever "himself" might happen to be. Bowie has always had stories to tell about himself—not always truthful. In the Seventies, for example, he was fond of likening his early childhood in Brixton to the rites of passage experienced by young bloods on the mean and picaresque streets of Harlem; the truth was that by the time he was six his family had moved to the tree-lined, net-curtain twitching streets of suburban Bromley, and that his early teenage years were stultifyingly uneventful. The slightly eerie difference between his left and right eyes—the left pupil is so dilated that it resembles a tie-dye T-shirt—was variously attributed to alien origins, schizophrenia or molecular reconstruction through drugs: the prosaic truth is that he was once jabbed in the eye in a school playground argument over a girl.

These fibs are merely the usual tricks of the pop trade, of course, but Bowie's propensity for self-mythology went further, creating a series of alter-egos which enabled him to make a career out of an identity crisis. "I think my problem used to be that I was always shy and fairly awkward in social situations," he says. "All through my youth, I would use bravado and device—costume and flamboyant behaviour—in a desperate attempt to not be iced out of everything."

In other words, so you didn't have to be you?

"Exactly." Bowie stubs out his cigarette, and reaches for another. "It's interesting how you can do this at parties. In a simple family game such as charades; you see these incredible manifestations of personality come out of Uncle Bill or whoever when he's describing something in mime. That device allows you in an exaggerated form to display who you are. And I used a lot of those things."

His first public charade, the androgynous and unearthly Ziggy Stardust, was, in a sense, an artist's caricature of a rock star: glittering, outlandish, larger than life. It became a self-fulfilling prophecy. "Very much so," he leans forward, warming to the theme. "And I think I encouraged that. Having created this character, to then want to *become* him was incredibly tempting. And I was the first volunteer."

In some strange process of metamorphosis, Ziggy was taken over by the glam-rock icon Aladdin Sane, then the desiccated Thin White Duke, then the "white soul boy" of *Young Americans*, until the creator had lost sight of himself in the creations. "It's OK," says Bowie, "as long as you're really in control of the image, as a painter is, for instance. But when you're using *yourself* as the image it's never quite as simple as that. Because aspects of your own life get mixed into the image that you're trying to project as a character, so it becomes a hybrid of reality and fantasy. And that is an extraordinary situation. Then the awareness that that's not the real you, and you're uncomfortable having to pretend that it is, makes you withdraw. And I withdrew, obviously through the use of drugs, as well, which didn't help at all."

This sense of confusion reached its nadir in the mid-Seventies—what Bowie describes as "my first period of isolation"—when he was living in Los Angeles, leading a shadowy and largely solitary existence, enveloped in a cocoon of cocaine and messianic self-importance. A confusing period, he reflects. "I felt like I was involved in this insane one-man voyage that was just pulling me along."

The occult had made its way to the top of his reading list—the album *Station to Station*, that he recorded in 1976, was, he now says, a step-by-step interpretation of the Cabbala, "although absolutely no one else realised that at the time, of course"—which led, in turn, to "Grail mythology" and then to an unhealthy interest in the role of black magic in the rise of Nazism. "Being seriously involved in the negative," as he puts it.

This was the period when he was quoted as saying that "Britain could benefit from a fascist leader," and apparently declaring himself as a prospective candidate. In the end, the clouds of delusion and the clouds of cocaine were all too much. "I blew my nose one day in California," he once, memorably, recalled, "and half my brains came out."

He decamped to Berlin, where, on one occasion, he was seen in a cafe with his head in a plate crying "Please help me." "I was in a serious decline, emotionally and socially," he now says. "I think I was very much on course to be just another rock casualty—in fact, I'm quite certain I wouldn't have survived the Seventies if I'd carried on doing what I was doing. But I was lucky enough to know somewhere within me that I really was killing myself, and I had to do something drastic to pull myself out of that. I had to stop, which I did."

There is nothing particularly novel in this. The idea that the path of excess leads to wisdom was, of course, a required text for the Sixties. Reading Jack Kerouac's *On The Road* at the age of 15 was, Bowie says, an epiphanous moment. ("The only people for me are the mad ones, the ones who are mad to live, mad to talk, mad to be saved, desirous of everything at the same time, the ones who never yawn or say a commonplace thing, but burn, burn, burn like fabulous yellow roman candles. . .")

There is a time in any teenager's life, I suggest, when, consciously or not, they make the choice between staying on the rails and going off them. "Oh yes, and I chose the second course, definitely. I think I fundamentally opted out of a controlled environment—the workaday kind of life that I found repellent, that I just couldn't take seriously. I don't think I ever felt that life was very long. It was certainly no surprise to me that I got old. I don't know if that's a good or a bad thing, but I was always terribly aware of its finiteness, and I always believed that if we only have this one life, then let's experiment with it.

"We know what can happen—you can get a job, go to work, you can follow that line of perceived security. But I think there's a different kind of security, which is trusting to and living by a code, of almost drifting where the wind takes you. And I spent well into my 20s doing that—just throwing myself wholeheartedly into life at every avenue and seeing what happened. Taking drugs; being totally and completely and irresponsibly promiscuous . . ." He pauses, chuckling to himself. "To the best of my abilities. Just getting into situations, and then trying to extricate myself from them as they occurred."

Sexual experimentation was a part of that. His public "coming out" to *Melody Maker* as a bisexual in 1974 suggested either a bracing honesty, or a shrewd understanding of the shifting sexual barriers of the time—it was probably a bit of both. In any event, it was a *cause du scandale* which would hardly raise an eyebrow today.

His first wife, Angie—the rock wife from hell—an American model whom he married in 1969 and divorced (acrimoniously) seven years later, wrote her own book which gleefully recounted details of Bowie's orgiastic excesses and as much sensationalist claptrap as she could muster. She recently appeared on television accusing him of hypocrisy for having eventually declared himself resolutely heterosexual.

The truth is, Bowie suggests, that his bisexuality was merely a phase. "I was virtually trying anything. I really had a hunger to experience everything that life had to offer, from the opium den to whatever. And I think I have done just about everything that it's possible to do—except really dangerous things, like being an explorer. But anything that Western culture has to offer—I've put myself through most of it."

The conclusion that he eventually came to, he says, was that he is "not a particularly hedonistic person—I tried my best. I was up there with the best of them. I pushed myself into areas just for experiment and bravado, to see what would happen. But, in the final analysis, it's not really me."

What he now recognises, he says, is that the peregrinations through drugs, hedonism, experience—the road of excess—were all part of "trying to recognise what the spiritual life is within myself, and how to identify it." He pauses, mindful that he is broaching an area that some people would regard as "awfully hippie trippy."

As a teenager he was drawn to Buddhism. For a year he studied under a Tibetan lama and says that at one time he contemplated becoming a monk, "until my teacher told me I wasn't born to be one. But so much of what first appealed to me about Buddhism has stayed with me. The idea of transience, and that there is nothing to hold on to pragmatically; that we do at some point or another have to let go of that which we consider most dear to us, because it's a very short life.

"The lesson that I've probably learnt more than anything else is that my fulfillment comes from that kind of spiritual investigation. And that doesn't mean I want to find a religion to latch on to. It means trying to find the inner-life of the things that interest me—whether it's *how* a painting works, or exactly *why* I enjoy going for a sail on a lake—even though I can't swim more than 15 strokes."

I wondered if he had encouraged, or discouraged, his son from following the same path. Having survived the setbacks of a broken home, education at Gordonstoun and being christened "Zowie," he had the good sense to change his name to Joe and is now studying for a doctorate in philosophy at Vanderbilt University in Nashville, Tennessee.

"Whether it was me encouraging Joe to be curious about life, or whether it was just a genetic thing, I don't know." He made a point, he says, never to brow-beat him about anything: drugs, sexuality, his choice of career. "The only times when I've lapsed into strictness"—the word *lapsed* seems significant—"is in the matter of fundamental morality, that it's wrong to harm or to steal, the requirement for honesty. I do think I'm basically an honest person and I know that he is a very honest person."

Bowie took custody of Joe after the break-up of his marriage in 1976, when Joe was five. "He's seen when I was really in absolute, abject agony over my emotional state; the heights of my drinking or drug-taking. He's seen the lot. So he's had the full dose of me—more than he'll ever need again."

Predictably, perhaps, the son could not be more different than the father. Joe doesn't smoke or drink; he has been in a stable relationship with his girlfriend for the past five years; he is a keen rugby and American football player. "I look at him sometimes and I'm amazed we're related. But we have just the most wonderful relationship."

The journey from the playing fields of immoderate excess to the tempering pastures of sober middle-age—via the public confessional to recant on the sins of the past—might amount to a textbook lesson on Bowie's generation, and for many of his contemporaries. "I guess that's probably known as maturity," says Bowie with a laugh. "I just matured late."

His marriage to Iman, he says, came at a point when he realised for the first time that "I was actually beginning to find my life really pleasurable, and I just wanted to share it with someone else. And one person was all I wanted."

For a while he was in a relationship with a dancer named Melissa Hurley, more than 20 years his junior, but the age difference, he says, was too great. "I recognised that it could only bring trouble in the future. So I let go of that. Then when I met Iman it was just so instantaneous. It was really one of those overnight things. In fact, it was *so* overnight we knew we should wait a couple of years before we got married, to make sure we weren't kidding ourselves. And fortunately we weren't. It's just been such a joy."

They married in Florence in 1992 in the modern style, attended by just a few close friends and a team from *Hello!* magazine. "You couldn't tell what was sincere and what was theatre," Brian Eno remembers. "It was very touching." Eno credits marriage with having transformed Bowie. "Since he's got married he's been very up. And a real pleasure to be with from that point of view."

Eno first started working with Bowie in his recuperative period in Berlin in 1976, producing a trilogy of albums in that period—*Low*, *Heroes* and *Lodger*—and last year's album *Outside*.

"The condition David was in in the late Seventies, you'd probably describe as slightly manic-depressive," he says. "I mean, I don't think he had a recognisable condition or anything, but he was unpredictable moodwise and he could become very depressed. He was pretty up and down. Now, most of the time, he's pretty up." It is as if, says Eno, Bowie has "sorted out the bottom half of the curve."

Bowie wants to play me some of the tracks from his forthcoming album, *Earthling*—a title that plays none too subtly to Bowie's new persona as an ordinary, affable, if somewhat arty, bloke. In the studio an engineer cranks out the songs at full volume. It is always a potentially awkward moment, listening to a performer's work when he is sitting beside you—how do you compose your face into a rictus of approval if the songs are awful? In fact, they sound like the strongest he has recorded in years: densely textured—"industrial rock," says Bowie—yet rich with the sort of commercial hooks that have been absent from his more recent work. Bowie was always clever at appropriating musical styles and stamping them with his own signature—the "white boy" soul music of *Young Americans*; the ambient electronic atmospheres of *Low*. Earlier in the year he played some festival dates with the new generation of techno groups such as the Prodigy and the Chemical Brothers—the paterfamilias among the young pretenders—and he has artfully incorporated the new trend of drum 'n' bass into some of his new songs.

Bowie's biggest-selling album, *Let's Dance*, was recorded 13 years ago, and, as is so often the case, success brought problems. The conventional wisdom about Bowie's recording career is that up until then he had always been one step ahead of the mass market. *Let's Dance*, which sold six million copies around the world, was where the mass market finally caught up. And ever since then, Bowie has been one step behind.

Bowie acknowledges that the mid-Eighties was the lowest point in his career. With the success of *Let's Dance*, he says, he suddenly found himself performing to what he describes as "a Phil Collins kind of audience" and, for the first time in his career, he started to tailor his work to what he imagined his audience wanted to hear, rather than what he wanted to play. "Basically, I got myself into a terrible mess." What saved him, he says, was meeting the American guitarist Reeves Gabrels.

"Reeves could see that I was compromising to try to get mass acceptance, and it just wasn't working. And he said to me, why are you doing what you're doing when it so obviously makes you unhappy. Do what makes you happy."

With Gabrels, Bowie formed the group Tin Machine, deliberately submerging his identity in an attempt to be just "one of the boys." It was, he now admits, "a disaster touched with glory. A glorious disaster." Critics were hostile, audiences bemused. Record sales negligible. "But for better or worse it helped me to pin down what I did and didn't enjoy about being an artist. It helped me, I feel, to recover as an artist. And I do feel that for the past few years I've been absolutely in charge of my artistic path again. I'm working to my own criteria. I'm not doing anything I would feel ashamed of in the future, or that I would look back on and say my heart wasn't in that."

It is not commercial success that now concerns him, he says, so much as "feeling that I'm still somewhere in the dialogue"—not only in the field of pop music, but wherever his interests happen to take him.

"I do feel that there is a much more inclusive feeling among the arts communities in general—music, literature, the visual arts. And I'm determined that if I want to paint, do installations or design costumes, I'll do it. If I want to write about something, I'll write about it." He has recently discovered the pleasures of collaboration—"action" paintings with Damien Hirst, installations with Oursler and a continuing series of *Outside* albums planned with Brian Eno. This will lead to a stage production for the Salzburg Festival in the year 2000, to be produced by Robert Wilson.

He was always a work obsessive, he says—"I don't like wasting time." But nowadays he is careful to make sure it doesn't affect his relationships. "I have dinner with friends; I *remember* to phone them up!" His tone of voice suggests a novel pleasure in the commonplace rituals of friendship.

"I think the internal and exterior values in my life have kind of leapfrogged over each other into a more positive area," says Bowie—which, I think, is his characteristically roundabout way of saying that he feels particularly good about life.

"Being as much of a chameleon as David has been is, at the least, unconventional," says his friend Brian Eno. "The worst thing for anybody is to not have a clear sense of yourself and be terribly worried about it. But I think he's come around to the idea that you can either think you have a very clear sense of yourself, or not worry about the fact that you don't. Now he thinks, who cares?"

"It's true," says Bowie. "I really do feel an overwhelming thankfulness that I can get out of bed every day; that I still have all my faculties, and that nowadays my appetites seem to be sane ones. That's enough." He falls back on to the sofa with a laugh. "Sometimes I'm so happy I depress people."

CHANGESFIFTYBOWIE

David Cavanagh | February 1997, *Q* (UK)

With him now being, as Cavanagh poetically puts it, a demicenturion, Bowie seemed to be in an even more thoughtful and reflective mood than usual in this feature from *Q*. Particularly noteworthy is the revelation of how deep his self-disillusion ran during his mid-eighties artistic slump.

Cavanagh recalls, "Parts of this interview took place on Bowie's tour bus, traveling between Boston (where he'd played a gig at the Avalon) and New York, where he was working by day on the *Earthling* album. When the bus arrived in New York, everyone got off except for Bowie and Reeves Gabrels, who stayed on, cranked up a Prodigy CD, pulled the curtains, and locked the doors." —Ed.

Planet Earth is blue and on January 8 David Bowie will have been living on it for 50 years. Tributes and accolades arrived early. In the first two months of 1996, Bowie was inducted by David Byrne into the Rock And Roll Hall Of Fame in New York. Then, he received the Outstanding Contribution To British Music award at the Brits in London. By November, he had completed work on his 21st studio album, Earthling. This year, David Bowie will become the first rock star to sell himself off on the Stock Market in a Bowie Bond issue scheme to be worth £30–50 million.

The day after his birthday, Bowie will give a charity concert at Madison Square Garden, where his four-piece band will be augmented by special guests including Lou Reed, Foo Fighters, Sonic Youth and Robert Smith of The Cure. In the coming weeks Bowie also plans to read two recently published biographies of himself, Loving The Alien by Christopher Sandford and Living On The Brink by George Tremlett.

A particularly galvanised demicenturion, Bowie has put a great jolt of energy into the Earthling album, which comes out in February. Combining jungle and rock in often startling ways, Earthling has a non-concessionary stance that takes several listens to become acclimatised to. And Bowie's online fans are already deep in discussion on the official Web site.

"Dear Mr. Bowie," wrote a woman called Crystal on December 2. "I wish to thank you for the imaginative ride through your music and thoughts. It has been both thought-provoking and a pleasure. PS. At one time I fancied changing my name to Crystal Japan."

An immediate response followed from someone claiming to be David Bowie: "Hallo darling. I think Crystal Clit would be a better choice, you icy bitch. Now bend over and prepare to be cornholed by a thin white duke with a thick white dong."

"Oh, *he's* back is he?" the real Bowie groans later that day. "No, I usually post anonymously to get a better dialogue going."

A better dialogue than *that?* Is there any? Anyway, however Bowie spends his 50th birthday (he spent his 40th skiing and can't remember further back than that), he does not intend to monitor Earthling's sales figures from the comfort of his Swiss home. Instead he is going to tour the hell out of it, hopping aboard the European festival circuit this summer, just like he did last summer. Bowie's delight with the album—and with the musicians in his band—is so infectious that even his 25-year-old son Joe has remarked on it.

"He says, 'God, you really like what you do, don't you?' " Bowie reports with the laugh of a lifelong smoker. "But it does really give me a buzz. I love being excited by what I do. I'm still playing Earthling every day. I've not stopped enjoying it."

It is early September, 1996—a New York afternoon, and David Bowie is at Looking Glass Studios on the ninth floor of a building on Broadway, where he and his new/old band are two-thirds of the way into the recording of this surprising Earthling thing.

There are four musicians in the band: drummer Zachary Alford, who's previously worked with Bruce Springsteen and The B-52's (he's in the Love Shack video); bassist Gail Ann Dorsey; guitarist Reeves Gabrels, who has played with Bowie since 1988; and keyboard genius Mike Garson, who looks a bit like Robert Morley and who recorded and toured with Bowie between 1972 and 1975.

They are taking a break and Garson is showing his bandmates some old photos of the mid-'70s Bowie line-up. There's one of Garson with an afro. There's one of Bowie at Radio City, New York, in November 1974, looking gaunt and seasick. There's one of the whole band together.

"Look at Luther!" Bowie laughs, spotting his former BVs bloke Vandross. "Carlos Alomar. And who is this guy? I don't remember him."

Garson names him as Emir Ksasan, the bass player who preceded George Murray. As Dorsey and Gabrels crane to see, Bowie recognises guitarist Earl Slick (whom he calls Frank), David Sanborn and Warren Peace. Then his eyes darken as he notices the imprint of his old management company at the bottom of the photo. "MainMan," he sighs. "Fucking MainMan."

He brings out a slide which he is considering using for artwork on the new album. It was taken in 1974 at UCLA with a Kirlian camera, which photographs energy fields. The left half of the slide shows the circumference of Bowie's forefinger immediately before taking cocaine.

The other half of the photo was taken 30 minutes later. (In fact, he has written helpfully on the back: "Just before doing coke" and "30 mins later"). In the "before" photo, Bowie's finger is a neat circle with a little outer rim of darkness. In the "after" photo, however, his finger has an angry, frazzled halo, as thick as a washer. This was clearly no average line of cocaine.

"Not in 1974 it wouldn't have been, no," Bowie admits. "Highly dangerous camera it was, too. It would regularly explode. Nic Roeg wanted to use some examples of it in The Man Who Fell To Earth, but it wouldn't film well enough."

So saying, Bowie snaps out of the mid-'70s, leaps to his feet and takes Q into the next-door studio to hear some rough mixes of new tracks. While the songs play, he's constantly out of his seat, explaining how certain of the effects were generated ("no samplers"), or where a solo will go. He points at the speakers whenever there's a good bit coming. Seven Years In Tibet is his current favourite: it has piledriving drums, an itchy saxophone sound, and it has just been added to the live set.

It was while enjoying himself on the festival roundabout last summer that Bowie decided to keep the momentum going. As soon as the tour ended, he and the band immediately hit the studio. This week they're back on the road, playing a four-date tour of small clubs which sold out instantly. Meanwhile, Bowie is back to an album a year, and proud of it.

"It's funny, you know, when I was a kid, we would do two albums a year," he recalls. "Two albums a year! And I loved it."

Bowie now believes that he is the only 50-year-old in British rock whose music really challenges the listener. While his superstar profile might seem to align him with cosy old Rod Stewart and the grand old Rolling Stones, he describes his current attitude as that of "a not terribly retrospective person, who is really enthusiastic about life and really keen to be different from everybody."

Musically, his tastes are in jungle, in nerve-shredding guitar, in computer cut-up lyrics and, of course, in the avant-garde. In this sense, at least, he is the same David Bowie who made Lodger and Scary Monsters And Super Creeps. Those songs from his illustrious past which he sees fit to play live—which include "Heroes," The Man Who Sold The World, Scary Monsters (And Super Creeps) and All The Young Dudes—are often rearranged so violently they defy recognition until he starts the vocal.

"It's unfortunate when musicians qualify their work with, Now that I'm married, now that I've got kids, I've got to be more creatively pedestrian," he muses. "Whereas there's people like myself, Neil Young and Scott Walker who move with the way life flows."

For Bowie, this has resulted in the following developments: a warm embracing of jungle and drum'n'bass; forming a touring band of very dissimilar musicians and personalities, whose common thread is that they each "excite" their leader; taking a more active role on the youngsters' gig circuit (for example, playing the Phoenix Festival as opposed to Wembley Stadium); and not really bothering about how many old-style fans he might lose on the way. Convinced that his current band out-hammers even The Prodigy, he is now talking of playing raves in Europe this year.

"I know what happens when I play the classics," he sneers, a little impatiently. "I know the outcome. So why would I want to do it again? Other than for financial remuneration, which frankly I don't need. There's a few of us now reaching our fifties and sixties, and I don't want to throw my chance to experiment away. You see, once you've gone so far, you can't turn back. And I've come that far. I'm there. I'm in my land. I'm doing it."

He catches himself up with a laugh.

"In ten years' time, when I'm playing to halls with no audience whatsoever, my contemporaries can turn round and say, Well, that's the reason we didn't do what you did. But we'll see. At least I'll have the chance to see how far you can go in this life."

It's the following night, Bowie's tourbus is heading back to New York from Boston, where he and the band have just played the penultimate date of their club tour.

The show was a strange affair. Loud and punishing in places, it focused heavily on 1. Outside and new songs. The crowd, with an average age of perhaps 28, was visibly much hotter for songs like Breaking Glass and Moonage Daydream. Under Pressure, played faithfully like the record (with Dorsey doing the Freddie Mercury bits), received the loudest ovation. Meanwhile, one girl held aloft a bouquet of flowers for 20 minutes continuously, until Bowie finally acknowledged her in Scary Monsters (And Super Creeps): "What a beautiful flower garden . . . lavvly blossoms."

While still a terrific singer, on stage Bowie moves with a gaucheness that ill-fits the metallic pulse of the music. There's a bit of mime, a few hand-claps at waist level . . . ooh, dear. In the quincunx din of his all-devouring band, he somehow seems a spare part, a piggy in the middle, draped in a hugely garish Union Jack frock-coat when, for all its relevance to the music, he might as well be sporting a stove-pipe hat. It's strange: fronting his own group, singing his own songs, the legendary David Bowie is the one person on stage who looks at odds.

But, on his coach home, Bowie is very pleased with the audience's response, particularly to Seven Years In Tibet. He comes forward to the front lounge of the bus for a chat. He is wearing only a white terry bathrobe and his voice is hoarse. Corinne "Coco" Schwab, his PA-cum-manageress and close friend for 20 years, tells him that tomorrow night's show in New York will be the first anniversary of the start of the tour. They've been on the road for a year. Excited, Bowie tells her he wants to play at a techno club immediately after the gig. (Tonight, he has inexhaustible stamina. Tomorrow, common sense will prevail. There will be no techno club.)

Does he feel that the new album is as adventurous and ground-breaking as albums like Low, Heroes and Lodger?

"I don't know if it feels like that," he ponders. "But it feels really good-hearted and uplifting."

It's hardly comforting, though.

"No? Blimey. I get all happy when I hear it. How do you hear it?"

A pounding, shrieking, relentless sort of sound.

"Golly." He thinks. "It's not difficult music, it really isn't. If the audiences can just open their minds to it."

What are the songs about?

"I guess the common ground with all the songs is this abiding need in me to vacillate between atheism or a kind of gnosticism," he explains, slowly. "I keep going backwards and forwards between the two things, because they mean a lot in my life. I mean, the church doesn't enter into my writing, or my thoughts; I have no empathy with any organised religions. What I need is to find a balance, spiritually, with the way I live and my demise. And that period of time—from today until my demise—is the only thing that fascinates me."

You're already thinking about your death?

"I don't think there's been a time when I haven't," he laughs, blithely. "It was ennobled with a romantic, cavalier attitude when I was much younger, but it was still there. Now it's measured with rationality. I know that this life is finite and I have to accept that."

What's stopping you from believing in an afterlife?

"I didn't say I didn't," he says quickly. "I believe in a continuation, kind of a dream-state without the dreams. Oh, I don't know. I'll come back and tell you."

Did the years when you took a lot of drugs do any lasting damage?

"I've been a really lucky sod," he admits, shaking his head. "I'm extremely fit. But then I've never had a brain scan. I remember reading about the effects of vast amounts of amphetamines and cocaine, and the holes they leave in your brain. They specified the amounts you had to take to produce sizeable holes, amounts I far exceeded. I thought, Oh God, what the hell's going on up there?"

Listening to the albums you made in the early '70s, it seemed that you didn't think there would be a 1996 or a 1997.

"Oh didn't I? When did I stop thinking that, then?"

It was all very apocalyptic.

"Oh really?" he chuckles. "Well, I know what you mean. But a lot of the negativity when I first started was about myself. I was convinced I wasn't worth very much. I had enormous self-image problems and very low self-esteem, which I hid behind obsessive writing and performing. It's exactly what I do now, except I enjoy it now. I'm not driven like I was in my twenties. I was driven to get through life very quickly."

Did there come a realisation in middle age that you weren't the most important person on the planet?

"No, it was in fact the antithesis of that. I thought I didn't need to exist. I really felt so utterly inadequate. I thought the work was the only thing of value. Now I'm starting to quite like me. You know, we really should continue this conversation with . . . people who talk about that stuff. I don't really. . . ."

Did you know, growing up, that you shared a birthday with Elvis Presley?

"I was absolutely mesmerised by it," he grins. "I couldn't believe it. He was a major hero of mine. And I was probably stupid enough to believe that having the same birthday as him actually meant something."

You saw him play in New York in 1971.

"I did. I came over for a long weekend. I remember coming straight from the airport and walking into Madison Square Garden very late. I was wearing all my clobber from the Ziggy period and I had great seats near the front. The whole place just turned to look at me and I felt like a right cunt. I had brilliant red hair, some huge padded space suit and those red boots with big black soles. I wished I'd gone for something quiet, because I must have registered with him. He was well into his set."

Do you remember where the first British date of the Ziggy Stardust tour was?

"Ooh . . . my God. I really don't know. Aylesbury?"

It was at The Toby Jug in Tolworth, between Surbiton and Cheam.

"Ha ha haaa! Oh, that's perfect. Ziggy at The Toby. It was probably a pub. Things moved quite fast in those days, but Ziggy was a case of small beginnings. I remember when we had no more than twenty or thirty fans at the most. They'd be down the front and the rest of the audience would be indifferent. And it feels so special, because you and the audience kid yourselves that you're in on this big secret. It's that English elitism and you feel kind of cool. It all gets so dissipated when you get bigger."

Which of your old albums do you still manage to listen to?

"Not Ziggy," he laughs. "Actually, I started listening to Low again when I heard Trent Reznor was a big fan of it. I went back to it to find out why and I started to hear the breaking down of the drum sounds and obvious signposts to the way he writes. It was fairly instructive. And what a damn good album it was. I also think Station To Station is great. I've listened to it a few times."

Exactly how true is the story that you can't remember making Station To Station?

"Very true. I would say a lot of the time I spent in America in the '70s is really hard to remember, (sighs) in a way that I've not seen happen to too many other artists. I was flying out there—really in a bad way. So I listen to Station To Station as a piece of work by an entirely different person. Firstly, there's the content, which nobody's actually been terribly clear about. The Station To Station track itself is very much concerned with the stations of the cross. All the references within the piece are to do with the Kabbala (*a set of mystical instructions supposedly given to Moses on Mount Sinai and often said to have links with ritual magick*). It's the nearest album to a magick treatise that I've written. I've never read a review that really sussed it. It's an extremely dark album. Miserable time to live through, I must say."

What would have happened if one of your unsuccessful singles in the mid-'60s, such as Rubber Band or You've Got A Habit Of Leaving, had been a huge hit?

"Ha! I'd probably be in Les Miserables now. I would have been doing stage musicals. I could almost guarantee it. Oh, I'm sure I would have been a right little trouper on the West End stage. (*Laughing*) I'd have written ten Laughing Gnomes, not just one."

He pauses to tuck into a sandwich. In the rear lounge of the bus sits a group that includes Schwab, Dorsey, Alford and Garson. The latter is a phenomenal keyboard player who brings a strong visual presence to the show. He'd not seen Bowie for 18 years until he was summoned to play on the 1993 albums, Black Tie White Noise and The Buddha Of Suburbia.

"We used to call him Garson The Parson in the Spiders, poor love," Bowie grins. "When he was into Scientology. But it did cause us one or two problems. I was thinking about having him back in the band and the thing that really clinched it was hearing that he was no longer a Scientologist."

Garson is steeped in classical and jazz music (*he's made 10 solo albums*) and tends to stay out of the jungle area on Bowie's new songs. At sound-checks, he executes astonishing flourishes of concert piano without even looking at the keyboard. He is enjoying working with his old boss again.

"I felt that spiritually he had advanced," he notes of meeting Bowie again after so many years. "He was much more calm and stable to work with on a daily basis. His actions were a lot more sane and rational. But the essence of who he was as an artist was exactly the same."

Is the new music completely different to play compared to the 1974 stuff?

"Well, David's music still has the essence of rock but it's actually rather more advanced. There's a lot of layers and complexity on both 1. Outside and the new album. Reeves, you know, views guitar playing almost like a reinventor of the instrument."

Reeves Gabrels, a guitarist whose squealing style antagonises as many people as it pleases, is arguably the most important musical influence on Bowie over the last 10 years. And he's probably the most controversial musician ever to play in a Bowie band. It was Gabrels who urged him in 1987 to rethink his direction entirely.

"He knew that it had gone wrong after Let's Dance," claims Gabrels, who met Bowie through his wife, Sara, a publicist on the Glass Spider tour. Gabrels was a virtuoso guitarist from Boston whose love of Bowie's music had been curdled (as had most people's) by the poor quality of

Tonight and Never Let Me Down. Bowie, too, was bored rigid by these albums.

"I was something I never wanted to be," Bowie admits. "I was a well-accepted artist. I had started appealing to people who bought Phil Collins albums. I like Phil Collins as a bloke, believe me, but he's not on my turntable twenty-four hours a day. I suddenly didn't know my audience and, worse, I didn't care about them."

Full of doubt and loathing for his increasingly bland music, Bowie scarcely bothered turning up to the recording sessions for Never Let Me Down.

"I was letting the guys arrange it, and I'd come in and do a vocal," he recalls, "and then I'd bugger off and pick up some bird."

Privately, he saw only one escape route: retirement. This became his intention.

"More than anything else, I thought that I should make as much money as I could, and quit," he confesses. "I didn't think there was any alternative. I thought I was obviously just an empty vessel and would end up like everyone else, doing these stupid fucking shows, singing Rebel Rebel until I fall over and bleed."

No wonder he's so grateful to the dry-witted, 39-year-old Gabrels. The guitarist told Bowie that the answer lay in reinvention. Bowie, who had reinvented himself between five and seven times in the 1970s alone, installed Gabrels as his new lead guitarist and first performed publicly with him in April 1988 at a benefit gig at the ICA in London. Within a year they had formed Tin Machine, a vilified and soon-abandoned quartet which blew a lot of Bowie's cobwebs away and cheered him up considerably.

Nine years later, it is still Gabrels's guitar-playing that sorts out the men from the boys in a David Bowie audience. Some of what he plays sounds downright horrible. Or is it genius? Or is it both at once? And couldn't he just put a sock in it occasionally? As knowledgeable and enthusiastic discussing techno as he is Aerosmith, Gabrels is part-intellectual and part-madman. A few weeks ago, he went to collect Bowie at his hotel. Nothing unusual there, except that Gabrels was wearing a full-size Tigger (out of Winnie The Pooh) suit at the time. Bowie came out of the lift and laughed so much he walked into a wall. He is enchanted by Gabrels.

"I like players who don't try and prove what great guitarists they are, but try and show you who they are as people," drools Bowie. "Maybe give you a little clue to the cracks in their psyche. And Reeves is a good man, he really is. I just feel happy with him."

"You gotta make your choice," Gabrels will declare. "Commercial survival is Rod Stewart. Artistic survival is reinvention. Do you play Las Vegas or do you want to do something vital? That's what I think. But then, I'm a bad influence."

"Have you met Lulu?" asks Garson, who toured with her after her 1974 hit version of Bowie's The Man Who Sold The World. "She's a sweetheart."

The Bowiebus is two hours from New York. Garson soon falls asleep, while the rest of the party, including Bowie, watch a video of All You Need Is Cash, a TV documentary about the financial affairs of The Beatles. It's fairly critical of John Lennon, Bowie's old friend John Lennon, which doesn't impress him. He keeps tutting and shaking his head. And when biographer Philip Norman makes a glib comment about Lennon's relationship with Yoko Ono, Bowie turns indignant: *Shaaaat up! Who the fuck are you?*"

But Bowie is a happy man. He's got his band together, all in the same room on the one bus, and he loves them. There isn't a single group worldwide that he fears. While he can still talk respectfully—and does—of his classic rhythm sections of the 1970s, or the wonderful bass playing of Herbie Flowers, or the entertaining stories of Rick Wakeman (whom he now hears is a very good friend of Norman Wisdom), you can tell that these people rarely figure in his thoughts. He loves his new band too much.

"I care about people now," he concludes. "I never used to, probably because I never cared about myself. But I really think I care about people now—about whether they're in pain or whether they're alright."

At last, the bus pulls up outside the Essex House Hotel in New York, where Bowie and his band are staying.

Some disembark, but not David Bowie or Reeves Gabrels. Still glowing a faint orange in their stage make-up from the Boston gig, they insert a Prodigy cassette into the tape machine. And with the afterhours Central Park traffic drifting past their drawn curtains, they get the all-night rave underway.

BOWIE RETROSPECTIVE

Linda Laban | March 1997, *Mr. Showbiz* (US)

In 1997, the Internet still had the glow of the new. Bowie always loved advances in media. He is to be found enthusing over the net in this interview with the briefly-lived but lively Mr. Showbiz website.

He has also always loved exciting new music. A running joke in the T-Zers column of the *New Musical Express* in the eighties had Bowie gushing of hit new acts things along the lines of, "Great. Love them. Got everything they've done. Er, who is it we're talking about again?" The *NME* were being a little unfair on the man they also mocked via the nickname "Dame David." Bowie was no granddad desperately trying to get down with the kids. Despite being perceived as (even admitting to) using pop as a flag of convenience, he has always paradoxically been Into the Music. That he has always been hipper-than-hip is demonstrated both by his embrace of drum 'n' bass on *Earthling*—the album he was currently promoting—and his forthright opinions on current music scene sensations that litter this duologue.

Of said duologue, Laban remembers, "I basically kept Bowie way longer than I was allotted and asked him every question I possibly could. I'd heard about Bowie's charm but, even so, I was left completely enthralled. He listened and showed what felt like genuine interest in the questions. One thing that touched me was how tenderly he talked about Warhol." —Ed.

As David Jones, he was born into the wreckage of post-war Britain, and raised in a dreary South London suburb. As David Bowie in the early seventies, he shook awake the hippie music scene with a dazzling, post apocalyptic vision that has been influencing bands from the Cure to Nine Inch Nails ever since. Never one to stand still, Bowie has continued a process of artistic, if not personal, re-invention that can be seen as either calculated transformation, or ambitious redefinition of his art and his life.

Be it musical evolution or sound business sense, Bowie stands as one of rock's most enduringly successful, artful, and intriguing characters. He celebrated his fiftieth birthday on January 8, 1997, with a show the following night at Madison Square Garden in New York. Proceeds from the concert benefited Save the Children, and Bowie was joined by a cast of well-wishers that included Lou Reed, Smashing Pumpkin Billy Corgan, and the Cure's Robert Smith. The world was invited, too, via the show's live broadcast on the Internet, and highlights from the set are earmarked for a pay-per-view special early next month. A week after his birthday bash, Mr. Showbiz spoke to Bowie by phone from New York. With the celebration over, he turns enthusiastically to his new album Earthling, a project that crosses the British drum 'n' bass movement with white-noise rock.

"Hello," Bowie began, his voice a deep and disarmingly playful purr. The man who has personified rock artifice and other-worldliness comes across as a pretty normal, articulate earthling. Ever the experimenter, Bowie talked at length about his favorite new artists, recent musical influences, computer programs, playing Andy Warhol on-screen, and how he aspires to meld all of his interests together into a new performance hybrid.

Let's start with the new album. Who produced Earthling?
DB: I did. With Mark Plati, who is the mixer and engineer. It was co-written with Reeves Gabrels, who is my guitar player, and has actually been with me for something like ten years now. It's like I only met him yesterday!

You haven't done much production outside of your own records since the seventies.
DB: No, I haven't and it's rather pushed me into feeling quite hearty about the prospects of maybe doing more. There's a girl, Gail Ann Dorsey, who's our bass player, and who's also a wonderful singer—and she writes. I think I will be producing her album this year as well.

You produced Lou Reed's Transformer and many of Iggy Pop's late-seventies albums. Both of them experienced some considerable career rejuvenation as a result of those albums.
DB: Well, it was really out of my own respect and admiration for them as

artists. Both, in their own way, had been influential in what I'd done, and I wanted to do something for them.

I suppose we'd better get back to the present rather than rehashing the seventies.
DB: Well, part of the present, in fact, also incorporates Lou Reed, because he worked with me the other night at the Madison Square Garden show. That was a really lovely thing, we had a ball.

To get back to Earthling, as usual, you are credited with playing many instruments: guitar, sax, and keyboards . . .
DB: Yeah, I diddle about with everything really.

Well, more than "diddle."
DB: Well, if you were there!

The diddling comes out really well.
DB: It's very creative diddling. I know which diddle to twaddle!

New audiences probably aren't aware of you as a musician. They know you just as a singer.
DB: When I've had the courage, I've always gotten in there and played something on the albums. There are some things that I do quite well, maybe it's because of my lack of expertise, but they have a certain kind of brutal integrity to them that worked. Particular chords and things, guitar runs and stutterings on the sax. I know nobody else could do them quite the same way.

There are moments on Earthling that are reminiscent of older albums, say a piano part that maybe even harks back to Ziggy Stardust days.
DB: The piano would be Mike Garson. He worked with me right through '75, from late '73 with the Spiders, and played on the Aladdin Sane album. He's a longtime collaborator, even if he was away for a long spell going his own way. But we've gotten back together, this must be now the fourth album that he's done with me in the nineties.

Who else is on the album?
DB: Reeves, of course, has been there on just about everything since '88. Gail Ann Dorsey and Zac Alford are the two comparatively new ones to

me. They've been working with me now for about fourteen months, and in this present unit of just five of us, we've been together since January of '96.

Were they the touring band, is that how you came to them?
DB: Yeah, they came in as the touring band in '95, when we did the Nine Inch Nails tour. Then I reduced the band down because it was, I thought, just too large and unwieldy. It was a nine-piece so I took it down to a four-piece. They continued on with me through the rest of this last year. We're pretty solid as a unit now, they'll be coming again with me when I go out this year.

You referred to the Outside tour as the Nine Inch Nails tour.
DB: Yes.

Wasn't it the David Bowie tour?
DB: Well, I kinda presumed you knew I was on it! Nine Inch Nails as opposed to the Pat Boone tour.

Don't want you giving NIN too much credit here.
DB: Well, they're very good.

That was a pretty spectacular duet you did with Trent Reznor.
DB: The one song that I did with him, oh Lord, come on, tell me the name of it . . . "Hurt," that's it, "Hurt"—a beautiful ballad, one of the best songs he wrote. The tour was a really unusual combination of styles. We both felt that it was probably one of the most adventurous stylings of a tour in quite a few years. I'm not sure if many other people thought of doing that kind of combination. I haven't seen it happen too many times subsequently. We actually filmed it, and one day we'll do something with the footage.

So, you were with a touring band that you became very comfortable with, and obviously Reeves you've been with a long time. How did you come together and write the songs for Earthling?
DB: We had an extremely hard year last year. We worked our way through Russia, Japan, Scandinavia, and into Europe. We pretty much ended up doing the festival circuit in Europe, which meant working with sometimes

up to fourteen other bands. We just got really good. By the end of the tour we were the dogs' bollocks, as they say in England. I really thought it would be great if we could almost do a sonic photograph of what we were like at that time. So, Reeves and I started writing pretty immediately after we finished on the road. We went in about five days after we finished our last gig and wrote and recorded in a two-and-a-half-week period; frankly, the whole thing was put down quick.

So the music was the culmination of the four of you playing together?
DB: The arrangements and the structure of it was more or less between Reeves and myself. But the individual responses to it were interesting. With Zac, for instance, the drummer, unlike most drum 'n' bass things, we didn't just take parts from other peoples' records and sample them. On the snare drum stuff, the very fast, frantic things, Zac went away and did his own loops and worked out all kinds of strange timings and rhythms. Then we speeded those up to your regular 160 beats per minute.

(Drum 'n' bass) has gone up to 185 beats per minute now. Can you imagine? It's almost impossible to dance to!

Do you try?
DB: Well, I click me fingers and that's hard enough. It goes really quickly, somebody said it was going to hit 200 within the next six months. Two hundred beats per minute is almost impossible to entertain the thought of. Back in those days of a few months ago, it was still at 160. So Zac did all his own samples. That's very much how we treat the album; we kept all sampling in-house. We created our own soundscape in a way.

How come you went for a drum 'n' bass-influenced album?
DB: Who could not be influenced by it? It's the most exciting rhythm of the moment.

The hip-hop and jungle thing?
DB: Yeah, I still like hip-hop. I guess that new musics generally, plural, are what I've always listened to. It's always been the stuff that I thrive on. What I really adore about musics, is the stuff that starts on the edge. I can't really remember a time when I had any interest in the mainstream, except maybe when I was real young. As I hit my late teens, I just started

to like more obscure, or so-called avant-garde stuff. I've just always been in tune with it. In its way, it duplicates the situation in the late seventies where both Eno and I were listening to a lot of what was the German sound coming out of Dusseldorf, whereas I guess most other people were listening to punk. We kind of didn't want to be part of that mainstream thing because it was information we already knew. For me, it sounded almost like an expansion of what Iggy and the Stooges had been doing in the late sixties. And I was always stimulated by things that I didn't completely understand and the new technological approach by bands as varied as Can, Kraftwerk, Harmonia, and Kluster, and all those Dusseldorf bands that I found far more intriguing because I didn't quite know how it worked. I guess that's why Brian and I got so much into what's now called deconstructed or rather "rusty" industrial sound, because it just felt like oncoming information.

Something you could obviously work with. New ideas.
DB: It was very stimulating to work within. I did with it then what I generally do—I hybrid it with what I'm already doing. So it becomes like one of those French stews that you put on, and as you go past it every day you throw in another vegetable, and by the end of the week you've got this incredible mixture that tastes very hearty, but you're not quite sure what it's made of. That's kind of how I build up my music.

It is pretty exciting what's going on with hip-hop-infused rock.
DB: And it's really a dialogue that's happening in Europe; it's not happening in America at all. The most they have in North America—I don't know about Canada—but the majority of it are things like Moby. Which is okay, I don't mind Moby at all, I think he's very good, but it's not actually moving in a very interesting fashion. It's pretty standard, almost disco.

What about people like Beck?
DB: That's fun, it's kinda quirky, but he's got a tradition in people like Wild Man Fischer and the Legendary Stardust Cowboy. He's a very American folk pioneer, almost outside of folk, poet. It's quirky, but it's not setting the rules for a new language.

Were any of the songs on Earthling left over from Outside?

DB: "Telling Lies" was a song that I actually started writing just before we started out on tour, because I wanted to work on it more thoroughly in that medium. We changed the arrangement all the time and tried new ideas on it. By the time we'd gotten it finished, we really found that how we structured this particular kind of music worked well and integrated it with what we do, which, fundamentally, was hybriding a very aggressive rock sound with drum 'n' bass.

We had touched on that sound before with Brian on Outside. There are a couple of tracks on Outside, specifically "I'm Deranged" and "We Prick You," which are quite heavily jungle—as it was called then. But that was more of a narrative album, and we didn't want the music to be quite so high-profile. This time I felt free to do something which didn't have narrative to take into consideration.

"Telling Lies" was the song that first went out on the Internet last September?
DB: That's correct, with three of the versions that we'd gone through. The one on the album was the one that I ultimately thought was the best. It was also, of course, the latest.

You seem to be very active on the Internet, what with the birthday show broadcast last week and the "Telling Lies" premiere.
DB: Well, I get about! I'm a right little surfer!

Seriously, you're interested in that side of it?
DB: It's not a bad pastime. It's something that I could quite easily lose myself in for a couple of hours. That's the trouble, it's so bloody addictive. I have fun with it, but I'm very careful, actually, because of that. I also find that when I do get on it, there's such a lot of crap to get through before you find anything truly interesting. You're spending half your time going to different pages and wading through this rubbish.

That's an aspect of it that I'm not particularly delighted with. I must admit that I find it much easier to get involved with it when on tour. When you find yourself in Cleveland, or Akron, or something like that, and you've done the local museum and there's nothing much else to do except watch who goes in and out of the McDonald's.

It's a bit of a savior in that situation.

DB: Yeah. It's quite fun to do. I also carry a couple of art programs with me that I slot into the computer. I knock out some graphics. (In fake advertisement-ese.) That's when I have fun with my computer! I even chip in occasionally, sort of anonymously—throw false rumors in and get everybody at it. Well, why not? I love the idea of misinformation, anyway.

How did you get interested in the Internet?
DB: It wasn't the Net that I got intrigued with first, it was the computer. My son had always been into computers. We'd fooled around with a couple of programs that he was working with and he said, "Dad, you're into art and all that. Why don't you get these two things, you might like them?" One program was called Kidpix, which is an art program for, like, six-year-olds. I think it's wonderful, I still use it. There are two others, more sophisticated ones, Painter and Photoshop.

This was around 1993, so I started messing with those, and I did a whole series of lithographs based on work that I'd done on the computer. It was inevitable that somebody then got me into a modem and I started. (Adopts woeful, Cockney junkie voice.) I came home and found I was going on the Net every night. This went on for a long time, and eventually I found a group of Net Anonymous that I joined. We shared our problems with each other, and I think I'm off it now.

Where do you see it going in terms of its impact on music?
DB: Croydon!

That bad?
DB: Croydon with a K! Where's it going? For a new artist, who's got a lot of material but no audience and can't get gigs, and there's no real record company interested in what he's doing, then at least to establish a new audience and get somebody interested in what's he's doing. To be able to put pieces of what he's doing on the Net and have them download it for free, does at least give him the opportunity for a window. I think it's pretty good for people like myself, especially those of us who over-write, which I do. The trouble is I write too much—for my company! The record company only wants to deliver an album once a year—and that's fast—or one every eighteen months, and it's so frustrating when you've got a backlog

of material. I read the same thing in an interview with Prince a few weeks ago. He has exactly the same problem because he's also an over-writer. For some of the stuff that the more corporate companies wouldn't be interested in releasing—because it's either too esoteric or arty or "avant-garde-a-clue," or whatever—getting it on the Net is a good way of getting an audience for it. At least it's going somewhere, and you don't feel like it's all stored up in a cupboard where nobody will get to hear it.

Can't you, if some of the stuff is too out there for your record company, can you not go to an independent and have a little release on the side?
DB: Yeah, but it still takes a few months even with an indie, to get the album together and get the artwork for it and all that. Whereas with the Internet, you could virtually put stuff out on the Net as you write it.

It's immediate.
DB: That's the compelling thing about it, its immediacy. On tour it was great being able to do things like "Telling Lies" at a show and then get on the Net about an hour later, after the show, and you're being told if it was any good or not. That's great. The feedback is tremendous, it's so fast.

Do you think that American audiences will embrace the coming wave of British electronic artists?
DB: There's a question, isn't it? I wonder. I don't see that big a hope for it, only because of past experience. You look at something like reggae and how little it was embraced by the American public. I think it was embraced a lot more by Canada. In the rest of North America, you can hardly say it's worked its way into the fabric of music by any means. They don't embrace so-called outside musics, musics that are not indigenous to North America, very easily. That may be a real problem. I don't know, we'll just have to see. There's been a couple of warm signs: there's two jungle clubs in New York, and a couple in L.A., but that's the coasts. That is not mid-America, and I don't know if in Akron we're going to see junglists. There's more of a market for industrial, there always has been in America. But it's the techno and the drum 'n' bass aspects, I'm not sure that they will ever really achieve the grandeur that hard rock achieved over here, or grunge, or whatever. They'll always be some audience for it, and that's good enough for me.

A couple of the British bands are having a stab at it, the Prodigy did quite well.
DB: Yes they did, they certainly got some kind of reaction. There's a new interesting multicultural band called Pigeonhed, that's not exactly jungle. But what I think they have a problem with in America is the idea of multicultural music where it has more than one influence, more than one cultural influence. They've always had a problem with that, the idea of things that are hybrid or mixed in any way seems to be problematic to the American. It's a much easier thing to fall into in Europe. Although we still have our problems over in Europe, the whole landscape there is a lot more tempered than it is in the States where the abyss between races is really terrible.

I'll tell you something, the good news is when Tricky was working in New York the other week, it was the first time that I've witnessed a mixed audience in America for a long, long time. That's pretty good. Maybe one can almost think of drum 'n' bass as possibly, if it does get a head start in the States, doing something about the social level. It might be interesting to see exactly how music can again affect society as it did so much in the sixties.

Or attempt to.
DB: At least attempt to, and the attempt is not a bad thing, to at least have tried.

There is a track on Earthling, "I'm Afraid of Americans."
DB: Well, yeah, I'm not actually specific of what my fears are in the song but I mean. . .

Is it more Americana than actual persons?
DB: Yes, it is actually. That one is about Americana and it's the inevitable Johnny song. Poor dumb Johnny, he keeps cropping up. He's like a traditional figure to have a knock at. He just wants to comb his hair and get a car.

It seems that you are talking more about the homogenization of cultures and the way everything is becoming so bland and unified.
DB: Yeah, I'm always dead scared of that. We're living in an age of chaos and fragmentation, and we should grab it positively and not be scared of it and not see it as the destruction of a society, but the material from which

we rebuild a society. It is discomforting to see people sorting through the wreckage and trying to pull out absolutes again. That's really troubling. It just becomes so intolerant, and that's not what we want. That's not what we want, is it?

Okay, let's have a couple of comments on what it's like to be fifty. Here you are, David Bowie at fifty.
DB: Fab. But, you know, I don't feel fifty. I feel not a day over forty-nine. It's incredible. I'm bouncy, I feel bouncy.

Are you as productive and happy with doing the music thing as ever?
DB: Yeah, I don't think there is much in my life that I would change. I don't think there is anything, really. Over the last ten years or so it's just gotten to a place that I could honestly say that I probably enjoy myself more now than I did twenty-five years ago. I can quite definitely say that.

You still have the acting going.
DB: Yeah, but I don't take that very seriously. I have fun with it when I do get these cameo roles—they're fun to do because they aren't very long periods on the set. You don't think you're wasting your time for eight weeks, stuck out in a trailer park somewhere. I don't have the ambition to be an actor.

What about the role as Warhol in Basquiat?
DB: That was great. It was a ten-day shoot and it was in New York, so that when I wasn't needed I could run off and play. It was easy and there were good people in it. Chris Walken I've known for years. It opened and closed in less than a week—we all thought it would, but we also feel that it's really a very, very good movie.

The Warhol character had me in stitches, very funny.
DB: Oh good, I'm pleased. I'm so fed up of people portraying him as this cold, calculating man. Because he wasn't. I just thought that he was this rather insecure queen who didn't quite believe how big he was and didn't quite know why. I found it very funny, he was just very funny. Unwittingly, half the time. He was a human; he wasn't this machine at all. He's always made out to be such a menacing figure, and he wasn't. He was just this guy living a life like everyone else and struggling through it most of the time.

I think that really came through to the audience in the scene where he had died. You really felt it.

DB: Those people who knew him really were moved when he died. It was so unexpected and it shouldn't have happened.

So, what tour plans do you have for Earthling?

DB: We start rehearsals in April and we will be touring from May through Christmas. This one's really extensive, a long, long tour. I've only got a couple of minutes left actually—before they have to put the drip in!

Looking back at both the Glass Spider and Outside tours, are you now convinced that you can translate a narrative story line onstage?

DB: If I ever had an ambition, I guess the culmination of everything I do would be to produce something that could be called a theatrical musical event. I daren't say "musical," because it's not what I'm thinking of. But, it has to go to the arena somehow. The only thing that really gets lost is dialogue. I'm convinced that there is a way to explore the idea of a straight narrative piece for rock theater that can go and travel to arenas. I know I'll do that one day. I will do it. I'm getting nearer to how it could be done. I'm beginning to understand how it could be done.

I guess you're going to be spending a lot of time in arenas this year. So it'll give you a few more ideas.

DB: Yes, I'll be able to suss it out a bit more.

Where do you see yourself going after the tour—is there going to be another album?

DB: I don't think I could say that there would be specific events. The one thing that I do know is that I just don't foresee a point when I wouldn't be making music. Not quite as constantly as I am at the moment. I am really enjoying the process as never before in my life. I could never explain how satisfying it is at the moment. The other thing is that the visual arts, over the last five years, have become much more important in my life and I'm still doing a lot of work in that area. Doing a lot of shows, doing collaborations with people. I think those two things will continue to go very much hand in hand.

"NOW WHERE DID I PUT THOSE TUNES?"

David Quantick | October 1999, _Q_ (UK)

This interview feature in _Q_ magazine on the cusp of the new millennium nominally promotes Bowie's new album _"hours . . ."_ However, the famously flippant interview technique of David Quantick sees Bowie descend into a playful mood—although that doesn't actually prohibit the unveiling of some interesting autobiographical tidbits. Aside from the despicable nature of London suburb Croydon, one crucial topic addressed is how on earth Bowie ended up duetting with Bing Crosby in the latter's 1977 Christmas TV special.

Says Quantick, "I was more than excited to interview Bowie, him being my all-time musical hero and that. It was such a joyful, pleasant experience that afterwards I noticed my jaw hurt, literally from grinning for an hour without a break."

Note: for the song "7" read "Seven."—Ed.

Bleecker Bob's is a second-hand record shop in New York's Greenwich Village. David Bowie is a frequent visitor, though it's hard to see why.

"If you're a singer, Bob tends to call you an asshole," Bowie reflects, "And he'll put on some record that's guaranteed to embarrass you. In my case, it's generally The Laughing Gnome or Uncle Arthur."

When not having his back catalogue thrown in his face, Bowie is in New York to promote his new album, tediously called hours . . ., his first for a new label (Virgin). Where previous releases 1. Outside and Earthling were, respectively, mad art rock and drum'n'bass-influenced pop, both in the avant-Bowie tradition of Low and Heroes, hours . . . is almost straightforward. Despite the rock beast that is The Pretty Things Are Going To

Hell (a track whose title alone refers to material on Pin Ups, Hunky Dory and Iggy Pop's Raw Power), acoustic semi-ballads prevail, lyrics are oddly emotive, and one song, What's Really Happening, has a lyric written by Alex Grant, who won an Internet contest to write the lyric to a Bowie song. Boringly, the Internet is a big Bowie interest—he even runs his own Internet provider, Bowienet, and Web site. Visitors to www.davidbowie .com are entertained by archive family photos, shots of Bowie in his underwear (captioned "where's my trousers?" by Bowie himself) set lists from the '60s (Bowie notes that his 1966 group The Buzz used to perform The Supremes' Come See About Me. "Oooo, camp," he notes parenthetically), and answers to fans' questions. Outstanding among the latter is a reply to Adrienne Renee Tlapa from Illinois, who asks, "David, can you recall what the writing on your Japanese cloak said?" Bowie's response: "It may well have said, Get your potatoes here."

For now, Bowie is ensconced in a conference room at his record company in New York and he is in a very good mood. At 52 and a half, the former David Robert Jones appears in ripping health. He has longish ash-blond hair like a girl, and is dressed in expensive-looking smart/casual trousers and shirt. Only his wonky eye suggests that he might be from Mars. In fact, he lives in Bermuda with his lovely wife Iman and enjoys a close relationship with his son, Duncan Haywood Zowie Jones (who prefers, for some reason, to call himself Joe).

Over the course of the next hour, Bowie will do all of the following: impersonate John Peel, criticise a major British town, adopt the foetal position, try and be nice about Ricky Martin and unfavourably compare Bing Crosby to an orange. Notorious for agreeing with anything an interviewer says, in the next 60 minutes he will say "Yeah" 12 times and "No" only once.

We begin, naturally, with Croydon . . .

On your Web site, why is there a link to an estate agent in Croydon?
I've got this thing about Croydon. It was my nemesis, I hated Croydon with a real vengeance. It represented everything I didn't want in my life, everything I wanted to get away from. I think it's the most derogatory thing I can say about somebody or something: "God, it's so fucking Croydon!" It was gonna be the big second city to London, but it never came

to be. Bits of it they put up, these awful faceless office blocks, complete concrete hell. I suppose it looks beautiful now. . . . I haven't been back in a few years but I guess things take on a certain beauty if there's distance . . .

A lot of songs on this new album seem to be about wrong choices and missed opportunities. How personal a record is this?
This album was me trying to capture the idea of songs for my generation. So what I had to do was sink into a situation psychologically, that was less than happy with life, which in my case is not true. I had to create the situations. There's a lot about this guy falling in and out of love and being disappointed and all that. I actually don't have all that, but it was a good exercise in trying to capture what I see, even in my friends, the kind of half-lived lives they have, and it's really sad and you can't do anything about it, and they feel unfulfilled and disappointed and all that.

Is this anything to do with the song 7?
Seven days to live, seven ways to die . . . I'd actually reduce that further to twenty-four hours to live. I'm very happy to deal and only deal with the existing twenty-four hours I'm going through. I'm not inclined to even think too heavily about the end of the week or the week I've just come through. The present is really the place to be.

Is this why you keep inventing genres and moving on? Most people could have based whole careers on just one of your albums.
Even me! Ha ha ha! "Why didn't I stay with the Young Americans sound?!" I could still be doing that. Ooh, I wouldn't half be unhappy. I'd be so unhappy if I'd got myself into a . . . rut, as my mother used to say. My dear old mum. (*Loudly*) "You're in a bit of a rut, aren't you?" She said it about herself. "I'm in a rut." I think I probably thought then, I'm never gonna be in a rut if that's how you turn out.

7 also mentions both your parents and your brother (*Terry Jones, who spent much of his life in a mental hospital*) . . .
They're not necessarily my mother, father and brother; it was the nuclear unit thing. Obviously I am totally aware of how people read things into stuff like this. I'm quite sure that some silly cow will come along and say, (*adopts silly cow voice*) "Oh, that's about Terry; his brother, and he was

very disappointed about this girl back in 1969, whenever he got over her. . . ." That sort of thing comes with the territory, and because I have been an elliptical writer, I think people have—quite rightly—gotten used to interpreting the lyrics in their own way. I am only the person the greatest number of people believe that I am. So little of it has anything to do with me, so I just have to do the best I can with what I've got—knowing that it has a complete second life by the time it leaves me.

And then there's The Pretty Things Are Going To Hell. That's not a song, that's a CV.
Ha ha! That was really dangling a carrot, wasn't it?! That's such a fun song. It's a good song. I like it a lot. I can't wait to do it live.

What's it like being the only person ever to work with both Lou Reed and Lulu?
Now I am not sure if that's—opprobrium, or if it's my apotheosis. I like it. I believe . . . I'm not sure, but I believe that working with Bing (*Crosby, on the unnatural Little Drummer Boy*) led to Bono working with Frank (*Sinatra*). I set a precedent there. . . . I think the thing with Bing is the most ludicrous . . . it's wonderful to watch. We were so totally out of touch with each other.

Can you remember what you were thinking when you did it?
Yes. I was wondering if he was still alive. He was just . . . not there. He was not there at all. He had the words in front of him. (*Deep Bing voice*) "Hi, Dave, nice to see ya here . . ." And he looked like a little old orange sitting on a stool. 'Cos he'd been made up very heavily and his skin was a bit pitted, and there was just nobody home at all, you know? It was the most bizarre experience. I didn't know anything about him. I just knew my mother liked him. Maybe I would have known (*sings*) "When the mooooon . . ." No . . . (*hums*) "Dada da, da dada, someone waits for me. . . ." That's about the only song of his I would have actually known.

What about White Christmas?
Oh yeah, of course. I forgot about that. (*Kenneth Williams voice*) That was his big one, wasn't it?

Apart from Bing Crosby, you've always pushed your enthusiasms. What compels you to say, Go and listen to The Velvet Underground?

It's the closet teacher in me. I love introducing people to new things. One of the major things about being a dad is when you've got someone there you can (*laughs*) inflict your passions on. Poor kid. You tend to say, "Oh, another thing," or "You'll love this. . ." Like, they've seen Star Trek. . . . "Ah but you wanna see what the Russians were doing with Solaris (*unwatchably boring 1972 sci-fi flick by director Tarkovsky*)." It's just great to have people take in all this new information and then watch them go away and do something. (*Deep '50s American voice*) "My work here is done!" It's a dad thing, really. I'm not a bad dad at all. I think I'm quite a fun dad. I'm not a brother dad—you know those, "Oh, we're like brothers, me and my son." He's terrific, my son.

If the Web site photos are to be believed, he looks like you.

He's a lot bigger. He's a rugby player and a sporty guy, weightlifter and all that.

While there have been many Bowie images, we have never had a fat Bowie.

I dunno. All that muscle—if he stopped training. . . . My Uncle Jim used to say that. He weight-trained 'til the day he died. He'd say (*teeth-clenched voice*), Gotta do it, 'cos if I stop, it'll just turn to fat. Uncle Jim learned every single word in the Oxford Dictionary, that was his life's work. He was an absolutely extraordinary bloke. He worked in the steel mills in Sheffield. He loved research and academia, he had a fantastic library, but he never had the chance. My mother's family was very poor. It was a great shame he never was able to apply that mind. You could sense this frustration in him. I always thought he should have written, you know.

As the first pop singer born after the war, do you think you bridge two eras?

I'm very aware of that. I think there's a fundamental Englishness to what I do which makes me not actually very out of the ordinary at all. You can equate some of the earlier stuff, in a way, to a kind of Jarvis. . . . I recognise what he does as being something that I'm quite sympathetic to, but we weren't alone. Syd Barrett had a fundamentally English thing going. You would never get a Syd Barrett in America. They would be lunatics.

Wasn't English psychedelia all Winnie the Pooh and cups of tea?
Yeah. If you look back at John Peel and all that, reading Tolkien. . . . "And then this little gnome went off, clippetty-cloppetty." It's fucking Listen With Mother! What's psychedelic about this? "Are you sitting comfortably?" Ha ha! When you listen back to the stuff Peel used to do on Marc Bolan's albums, it was potty, really, really silly. It wasn't at all hip, although for some reason we thought it was hip at the time. It's daft, and it's really suburban.

What about the other kind of rock? The Mick Jagger school of authentic delta blues from deepest Surrey?
Absolutely. That school of music is the antithesis of how I think about music. I admire that ability to have developed a craft, but it is like a potter who succeeds with one style of pot, and just makes it and perfects it his whole life, and this pot is just something he could put up there against the Etruscans and it would stand there in dignity and all that.

What would your pot be?
More like something out of K-Mart! Wa ha ha ha! I don't know. Sort of, you pays your money, you makes your choice! I'm more of a supermarket of things, rather than a craft shop. Oh, this is becoming very silly! (*Peter Cook*) "I'm less your corner shop, more your . . ."

Woolworths?
Woolworths. It's funny, for me it's K-Mart. But they're American as well. I never knew, when I came over here, that Woolworth's was American. "Oh, look, they got a Woolies". . . Ha ha ha!

On the Web site—being Bowie—you recommend lots of books but surprisingly—despite being Bowie—the books you recommend are far from obscure.
Yeah. Again, I'll read a real eclectic mix of books. I've read everything Stephen King's written. I love Stephen King. Scares the shite out of me. But I really like Julian Barnes as well, which is another world.

The first real one for me was Jack Kerouac, On The Road, which gave you the urge to get out of Bromley, Penge, Sidcup, and all that. Croydon . . . just driving through the whole of the States and going out to California and Big Sur, down to San Francisco . . . and thinking, God, I wanna do that, I do not wanna go down to Bromley South station and take the fucking train to Victoria station and work in a bloody advertising office again.

If you hadn't done that, who do you think you would be now?
Ha ha! (*Bowie wraps his right arm round his head and puts his left thumb in his mouth*) What do you mean? An alternative life to the one I've led? I think probably two. One would have been a full-time painter, which I would have liked very much. And the other would have been . . . I'm not quite sure that "librarian" would have been quite the right word. Something where I was quite close to books and research. I love poring through books. I like the objects; as much as I like the Internet, I could never give up my library. Wife and the library, those are the two things that I probably would never give up.

Nic Roeg recently said that you were "very studious" and took a lot of books to the set of The Man Who Fell To Earth.
(*Embarrassed*) Oh God. But I had too many books. I took four hundred books down to that film shoot. I was dead scared of leaving them in New York because I was knocking around with some pretty dodgy people and I didn't want any of them nicking my books. Too many dealers, running in and out of my place . . .

What did you look like at this time?
Did you ever see the video where I was singing with Cher? Plastered hair . . . I'd got this thing in my mind that I was through with theatrical clothes and I would only wear Sears & Roebuck. Which on me looked more outlandish than anything I had made by Japanese designers. They were just like this middle America dogged provincialism. They were loud check jackets and check trousers. I looked very bad. And very ill. I looked very ill and very badly dressed.

I remember being over a dealer's one night when Sly Stone walked in. I looked like this ultra mid-America person, but with (*laughs*) blond and red hair that was all stuck to my scalp with "product," they call it these days, hairspray in those days. And he walked in and looked at me and he said, (*ironic Sly Stone* voice) "Huh! Bet *he* takes a lot of drugs." I was angry, because I *did* take a lot of drugs! "How dare you! I'm David Bowie! I do more drugs than you've fucking looked at!" It was so funny, it was hysterical. We met each other a long time after that and laughed about that. But it seemed so offensive. I thought, he's judging me by the clothes I wear! Is that funny or what? His whole thing was, who's this straight? And I was so angry. I wanted to go (*breathless Tony Hancock voice*), "Let me tell you how many drugs I take!"

How many drugs have you taken in your life?
Ooh, five . . . six! I took everything from elephant tranquilliser back down again. But that's such a pat story, the whole drug thing, I can't even begin to get into that.

It'll end up in the tabloids. "I Took Sly Stone's Drugs."
"I Sold Sly Stone's Drugs," that would be the story with me. (*Cockney reporter voice*) Not content with Bowie bonds . . . sells drugs to his contemporary rock star friends . . .

Would you say that you were a busy man?
Yeah . . . I guess my addiction probably sees its way into becoming work-obsessed. But I can't say that's any different from what I've always been like. The difference now is I do have a social life as well as a work life. The early part of my life I really only had time for what I was doing and it caused me to become very reclusive. I have to admit, to be simplistic about it, the '70s were very much like that, I started coming out of it a little bit during the late '70s. Working with Eno in Berlin started to change my life to a degree, and I think it took me nearly all of the '80s to work out what it was I wanted from life.

I guess the whole thing came to a wonderful conclusion when I met Iman, because it was like I'd been given a prize or something because I'd made those decisions. The decisions came first and then (*laughs*) it was, Well, you've been a good boy, so this is how you're going to spend the rest of your life. Gosh! Ha ha! It is *the* lesson. I've learnt nothing else, nothing. But old Bob (*Dylan, we imagine*) was right, I know far less now than I knew then. But I was so much older then, I'm younger than that now.

As our time is nearly up, we start talking about music. Bowie reveals that he was recently asked to produce both Red Hot Chili Peppers and Marilyn Manson, but he was too busy for either. He gives the impression that he was keener on the former than the latter. He mentions Asian Dub Foundation as a favourite act, but confesses that he has been a little out of touch lately. This, he claims, was a deliberate part of the process of making the album.

"I went out of my way not to listen to anything during the last eight months," he says, adding, "Unfortunately I haven't been able to get away from Ricky Martin. Talk about prodigious . . ."

He mentions you favourably in interviews.

Bowie makes a weird noise.

"Arhhhh . . . I know! That's why I'll be careful here. I don't know. I don't really know much about him or his music, I just know I keep seeing him on the telly and he's on the radio and stuff like that. Um. He's not irritating in the way some people are, I'm just aware of his presence . . . am I getting out of this?"

He throws back his head and laughs as only a man who hates Croydon can.

"Ha ha ha ha!"

BOWIE: MOST STYLISH MAN

Dylan Jones | October 2000, *GQ* (UK)

With his scrawny frame, mismatching eyes, and (for a long time) crooked teeth, David Bowie has always made for the unlikeliest of sex symbols. However, there is no denying that he is a looker.

It is obvious that Bowie enjoys being a Pretty Thing. He has been a dandy ever since he appeared on television as a seventeen-year-old mod speaking up for the rights of the long-haired male. His penchant for using his none-too-shabby body as a canvas in his career led to the much-overused but nonetheless true description "style chameleon." Even during the days of his arctic nadir (*Let's Dance*, Tin Machine), he still looked a million dollars.

It wasn't too huge a shock, therefore, that in 2000, even with Bowie gone fifty, the readers of the UK version of *GQ* voted him Most Stylish Man of the Year. In gratitude, he held court to the magazine. Strangely, there is not much talk of fa-fa-fa-fa-fashion in the published article, but instead an interesting catch-up on his career and aims.

Neither the new *Pin Ups* album or the Ziggy Stardust "extravaganza" mentioned have come to pass. –Ed.

Bowie is back, big time. Not because he's producing his best records in years, not because he's managed to flout convention and define the Zeitgeist like he used to in the old days and not because of any bond issue or Internet nonsense. No, Bowie's back because he's turned into a monstrously important live attraction. Bowie shows these days are nothing less than events. His appearance on the Pyramid Stage at Glastonbury this year was a monumental return to form, comparable with Elvis' 1968 TV comeback. Performing a minutely calibrated greatest-hits set that included "Under Pressure," "Golden Years," "The Man Who Sold The World," "All The Young

Dudes" and "Rebel, Rebel," Bowie played his first Glastonbury since 1971 with the air of a star in his prime.

"I was quite overwhelmed to see so many people singing the songs," he says. "And they were such a young crowd, younger than most of my fans. Some of my recent albums have been picked up by the Nineties generation, but then they don't know the early stuff. I think it's a surprise when they hear them all at once and think, 'Did he write that?' I know that because, in America especially, when I do 'The Man Who Sold The World' the amount of kids that come up afterwards and say, 'It's cool you're doing a Nirvana song.' And I think, 'Fuck you, you little tosser!' "

There can be only so many Bowie concerts left and he wants to make them all nights to remember. When the Rolling Stones turn into a global jukebox every few years it is a perfunctory exercise for band and audience alike. With Bowie you get the feeling you're watching the new Sinatra. Harry Connick Jnr, eat your heart out.

While Sinatra didn't make a classic record for the last 20 years of his life, his concerts were like religious conventions, loaded with memories. Elvis Presley was on his way to assuming Sinatra's mantle but he made the mistake of not only becoming embroiled in cabaret, but also he then went and died. Bowie has done neither and it's a short-odds bet that his records will be better than either Sinatra or Presley's were in their dotage.

Of course, Bowie has none of Sinatra's bar-room swagger. He is a reformed alcoholic so he won't be accompanied on stage by a tumbler of bourbon, although his cigarette consumption has earned him the nickname "Ciggie Stardust." The fags have certainly helped his vocal cords. His singing voice gets better all the time, and has become so deep and honeyed that Bowie is turning into something of a full-blown crooner. In many ways he has hidden behind his singing technique for years and now that technique—the rich baritone he used on "Wild Is The Wind," "Heroes" and "Absolute Beginners," compounded by the mockney lilt that insists on swapping vowels ("day" for "die" etc.)—has become his calling card.

"I think I've got more control over my voice these days," he says. "For years I felt that I was lucky to be able to carry a tune and it was a useful device to make those records, but I never thought of myself as a singer. But I'm actually thinking about what it is I'd like to do as a singer. I've not reached any conclusion yet. I think the album I'm going to be doing late this year is going to be a vehicle for my voice."

His influence can still be seen and heard in the most unlikely places. He was the basis of Harland Miller's recent novel *Slow Down Arthur, Stick To Thirty*, but Bowie found it particularly hard going. "I kind of quite like the idea, though I'm not sure he's a very good writer," he says.

He's still an influential clotheshorse, too, which is why *GQ* readers have voted him the Most Stylish Man Of The Year.

"The question I always ask is: would I have been given this award if I didn't do the interview and photo session?" he says quizzically. "I'm not one for awards at all. Most of the music awards are on the basis of, if you turn up, you'll get it. And I say, fine, I don't want it. If you want me to have it, give it to me and I might surprise you and turn up. Otherwise, fuck off! But if your readers have chosen me . . . then I feel privileged, it's pretty marvellous."

He actually seems more pleased about Paul Smith being knighted. "It's fantastic news. He's a one-man industry and he has brought so much money to Britain. I guess those kinds of awards should be about the industrialists of Britain. He's definitely worth the honour. Paul is one of my favourite guys and I'll go out of my way to try and wear his things because it's such a great advert for Britain. There's a certain sharpness and irony about his clothes and I've never had a Paul Smith suit fall apart on me. British clothes are so well made. It's like Brit art and British music: strange stuff but it's actually very well made."

The most significant event in his life this year has been the arrival of the new Bowie offspring. So giddy with excitement is he that he intends to move his family back to Britain. "There is no way I'm bringing up my child in America. No way. We'll be back over to London, without a doubt. 'Right, darlin', we better look around for the English House!' "

The rest of the year is frantic. First he's recording his own version of *Pin Ups*, reclaiming around a dozen of his very obscure, very old and, in some cases, really very naff songs and re-recording them. The highlights include a new version of the first single he ever released as David Bowie—"Can't Help Thinking About Me," from 1965—as well as "I Dig Everything" and "The London Boys" from the same period. "A lot of them were so cheesy," he says. "I said to Goldie we should do a drum'n'bass version of 'The Laughing Gnome' but he didn't seem up for it." After that comes *Bowie At The Beeb*, a double CD of the material he recorded for the BBC between 1967 and 1972. The album will be accompanied by a DVD featuring the showcase he gave at the BBC's Portland Place studio this summer.

After this it's time for Ziggy again, and Bowie's much-rumoured return to the glory days of the Spiders From Mars. When he refused to allow the producers of *Velvet Goldmine* to use any of his Ziggy-period songs he said he was preparing his own glam-rock extravaganza, and this is it. He won't, however, be donning the catsuits and platform boots. "I won't be in it, let's make that clear. Not me, mate! I won't even be Ziggy's dad!"

So, this won't be *Ziggy Stardust And The Last Crusade*? "Yes! Indiana Stardust! But unfortunately, no."

Nor is Bowie writing new songs for the Ziggy project. "I've pulled out a good deal of scraps that were never used at the time. Some of them are only 30 seconds long, but I'm extending those. I thought, 'OK, is this crap and is that the reason why it never appeared on the first one or is it OK and should I try and do things with it?' So I've taken those six tracks and thrashed them out and made them into songs that will support the original. One's called the 'Black Hole Kids' which is fascinating."

Bowie found all this stuff languishing in one of the many boxes of archive material he keeps at his home in Switzerland. He has over 800 cassettes of recordings, including dozens of conversations with Incredibly Famous People, hundreds of concert recordings ("I found virtually the whole of the soundboard tapes for the '74, '76, '78 tours. Every fucking one!"), superstar jams with the Stooges and the Stones and some other stuff he would prefer we didn't go into (including a visit to see Iggy Pop in hospital in L.A.). Most of it was recorded during Bowie's infamous "Warholian" period, when he would record and Polaroid everything that happened to him, including, it's alleged, the odd sex session. One of the funniest recordings involves Rolling Stone Ronnie Wood visiting Bowie in L.A. The duo are sitting in the den, idly playing "Golden Years" while, every so often, Ronnie stops to hoover up huge lines of Gianluca. "It's hysterical," says Bowie. "*Very* rock'n'roll."

Ciggie Stardust keeps quieter counsel these days, his only addiction being his beloved Marlboros. The older he gets the more dignified he becomes, even if he refuses to see it himself. "My career has benefited so much more from the mistakes than from the things I've got right," he says. "I can always learn something from the cock-ups! I see myself as something of a blunderer. I get carried along on tides of enthusiasm. My whole life has been like that. If I'm introduced to something that fascinates me, within three hours I'm the world expert."

How does he feel about the "new Sinatra" tag? Can he easily hang it on himself? "Oh, he would not be happy with that! Sinatra's daughter, Nancy, once stupidly suggested that I play him in a movie. God he hated that. 'I don't want a fag playing me!' He was absolutely terrified that I might be taken seriously. He hated long hair, hated anything limey! I do relate to Sinatra in that my tours are getting fewer and fewer. I don't tour just for the sake of touring any more. If you see me live these days you know I want to be doing it. I don't need to tour for money. And I know that people feel like that when they go and see me. They may not even like the material but they'll say, 'Fuck me. He's prancing about, isn't he?' Because I am. I love it.

"There's an awful lot of luggage that comes with them for both the audience and myself. Ten years ago I said I didn't want to sing my big hits again, but I'm 53 now and I'm different. I've never been the kind of person who's wanted to walk through anything I do, whether it's a relationship or a stage show. And if there's no real enthusiasm I tend to walk away from it. I walked away from my older songs for years because I'd been doing them for so long, there was no resonance in them for me any more. But I've changed. I went to see Wire the other week and they didn't sing one song of theirs that I like! Not one! If I'd paid money I'd have been really pissed off!

"I started feeding old songs back into the show around '97 when we were doing the festival circuit. With festivals you have to presume not everyone's there for you. You have to think, 'Fuck me, I'd better give them something they know!' Then I'd play a few songs from *Scary Monsters*, *Low* and *Heroes* and throw in things like 'Fame' and 'Under Pressure,' which is an irresistible festival song because of the association with Freddie [Mercury]. Knowing this year that I had Glastonbury, I thought, 'I'll just go for it. I've got nothing to sell, no album out there. I'll just give them what they want.' Although there are still things like 'Young Americans' and 'Space Oddity' that I won't do. When I feel I've left those songs for enough, maybe I'll sing them again."

So, David Bowie: *GQ*'s Most Stylish Man Of The Year as well as the new Sinatra. Let's just hope he doesn't start wearing that bloody trilby.

"IT MEANS MORE TO ME THAN ANY NUMBER OF HIT ALBUMS, THIS. THANKS VERY MUCH."

John Robinson | December 2, 2000, *New Musical Express* (UK)

This feature's ungainly title is the result of the fact that it was David Bowie's "acceptance interview" after having been voted by *New Musical Express* the most influential rock 'n' roll artist of all time. As such, the piece was the climax to an issue devoted to a rundown of the artists concerned.

By now, the *NME* had a different demographic to that which had bought the paper in the Ziggy Stardust days: most older music lovers had long since graduated to the monthly glossies, whose era was kick-started by the launch of *Q* in 1986. As such, the readers of the paper were too young to properly appreciate how questionable the award was. Bowie was undoubtedly a pioneer in many areas, but in the sense of setting the sonic template for rock his importance was minimal compared to Elvis Presley, the Beatles, Bob Dylan, and the Rolling Stones.

However, the areas in which he was important—extreme eclecticism, post-modernism, studied decadence, the intertwining of image and music, the blurring of sexuality—give a clue as to why he acquired so much support amongst the recording artists who, over the course of a year, responded to the question of which musicians had exerted the most influence over the current music scene: those things tend to make an artist seem more cool than simple humanity, craftsmanship, and unironic invention. There also has to be a very strong suspicion that the aforementioned artists suffered in the voting because of a steep artistic decline (in the Beatles' case, in their solo careers) that, in the main, Bowie had avoided.

Nonetheless, the award was significant and a testament to an affection generated by an artistic integrity that was impeachable only during the mid-eighties. Even his repudiation of that slump marked Bowie out as almost unique: how many of his self-deluding peers have claimed anything other than uniformly high quality for their back catalogues?

It has to be admitted that this interview will confirm the primary objection of Bowie-haters, namely that he has often seemed to be motivated not by a love of rock or pop but by his own

356

ego. Or as he puts it here, "I was always more interested in changing what I perceived as popular music. . . ." —Ed.

David Jones, of Bromley, cannot be with us today. Some elements of the young man remain—the odd coloured eyes, the result of a childhood fight, the unmistakable suburban London note to his voice—but really everything else has changed, and changed by his own design. The hair from long, to permed, to exuberantly feathered. The music, from acoustic doominess to glam rock, to funk, to European synthesizer drones, to drum'n'bass. And the name, of course. From Jones to Bowie.

He's done, y'know, quite a lot, David Bowie. Experimented with drugs and Japanese theatre (though not at the same time), and with Nietzsche and funk rock (very nearly at the same time). Been a pupil of mime. Written a song about a garden gnome that no one can seem to forget. Been at the top, then packed it in to form a band with some men in grey suits. He's been a poster boy for Luv ice cream, and appeared in a science fiction film without the blessing of conventional genitalia. He's had a "German period," which we'll talk about, and embraced the possibilities of the Internet, which we won't.

He's David Bowie, a resident of New York, and it's for some of these reasons that he's been voted as *NME*'s most influential artist of all time. Marilyn Manson has taken his make-up and otherworldly appearance. Suede have taken his riffs and his seedy glamour. Radiohead have, like him, chosen to make extremely experimental music at the height of their popularity. Not that any of these people don't bring uniqueness to what they do—but as Bowie himself has been influenced, so in their turn have they. He's happy about it. And he hopes you're happy, too.

The phone rings. You know what? It's The Thin White Duke.

There's not a lot David Bowie regrets having an influence over, it turns out. But there is one strata of society he wishes he could have helped out more.

"I really think I should have done more for gnomes," he says. "I always feel a bit guilty that I just put my feet into the water, and never sort of dived into the deep end. I really could have produced a new sensibility for the garden gnome in Britain. Gnomes should have been explored more deeply."

How so?

"The hats," Bowie continues. "I should have worn the hat more. I tried the beard in the early '90s, but because I'm blond it didn't really take off. I talked to Goldie and A Guy Called Gerald about doing a drum'n'bass version of 'The Laughing Gnome,' but it just didn't fly. When drum'n'bass becomes fashionable again, that's the time to leap onto that particular bandwagon—gnome and bass."

David Bowie chuckles, influentially. His gnome past is behind him, and he is content to additionally discuss those parts of his past that are not specifically gnome-related. What is most apparent, though, is that as well as being disarmingly flattered by being considered influential ("It's quite a thing," he says), David Bowie is a man as comfortable talking about what has influenced him, as the influence he has brought to bear on others.

This has always, essentially been his thing. In a similar way to how Damon Albarn has often been able to pinpoint the mood of a nation in a song, Bowie, for an enviably long time between 1970 and 1980 was *right there*. He was ahead of the game, and took new strategies, new techniques and new ideas and translated them all in his own songwriting. To listen to a David Bowie album from this period is to hear a pristine modernity, all the then-current technological ideas the backdrop to his music. The fact that these records still sound brilliant today tells you less about opportunism, and something about genius.

"I've always cited who my influences are," says Bowie. "I felt it was important for people to be able to see how things are put together at any given stage. I let people know what's going through my head. I've been quite vocal about that over the years. It often amuses me to see bands who lie about who they're listening to, because they don't want people to know who their real influences are. They leave a trail of red herrings. It's disingenuous, to say the least. I've always loved the process—to see how things are put together."

The way that input from other sources worked on Bowie produced truly remarkable records, and did so while still maintaining a huge popularity. He may not have been the first to do so, but Bowie in the '70s reached for goals that sounded impossibly far-fetched or pretentious, but were brilliantly realised. He's modest about their effect, and won't be drawn on who he sees as benefiting from them, but this was all very much in his plan.

"I wanted to make the context wider," he says. "More points of view and perceptions from other areas. Like the arts, theatre—expand the vocabulary. I thought it could be more of a basket of ideas rather than insular and referring only to itself all the time, like the hippy thing. I took my cue from John Lennon in terms of . . . I saw how he was able to integrate other interests of his into his music rather than just have it be about the music.

"I was always more interested in changing what I perceived as popular music when I was a kid," he continues. "I always thought that was a lot more flattering to the vanity than being a big album seller. It was something I've always wanted to have an effect on. A worker in any particular trade wants to leave some kind of legacy."

In the '70s, David Bowie was one of rock music's most glamorous workers, and he was helping, simply, to build classic music. He'd begun the decade as a folksy, slightly hippy naïf with an acoustic guitar, and ended it a man in a Pierrot costume walking along a beach, revisiting Major Tom, the character from 'Space Oddity' that he'd created 11 years earlier.

In between, Bowie was everywhere, in a number of highly-strung conditions, with a number of very strange people. A visit to New York helped plant in his mind some different ideas about how he could manipulate his music—he met Andy Warhol. Meanwhile, some of the oddball cast of The Factory got jobs with him.

Easy bloke to get on with, Andy Warhol?

"Nah, absolutely impossible," says Bowie. "He gave the impression there was nothing going on in there. I could never tell if he was a very lucky queen who liked bright colours and struck it lucky, or whether there was a philosophy going on there. I never really found out. I think it was half-and-half, really. Then I ran into that crowd, who worked for me in the '70s. The cast of (*Warhol play*) *Pork*. That was a strange period."

Maybe more importantly, while the style of British punk was beginning to ferment, fuelled in part by the brutal rock music that Bowie and glam had produced, Bowie involved himself in collaborations with two of the godfathers of American punk, Lou Reed and Iggy Pop. The relationship was mutually beneficial. Bowie could repay a debt to two heroes. They in turn, could be given a new lease of life.

"I was a super number one fan of both of them," says Bowie. "Lou was going through an incredibly bad patch around the time that I first met him, and he was being left on the side in terms of what his influence had been. And none of us knew what his influence was going to be—the direction of The Velvet Underground's reputation.

"I kind of feel like I found them again," he says. "When I was pushing them and Iggy, no one believed me, nobody knew who they were. Maybe in NYC, but certainly not in England. I had an acetate of the first VU album, and for me that was the key to a whole new way of writing, and what I tried to do with Lou was to make him well-known. It was as simple as that—so people would realise what a great writer he was, and by way of him, back to The Velvet Underground, and kids would get to know him. We, of course, used to play VU numbers with the Spiders as part of our stage thing. The contribution I made for him was to make it more accessible.

"Iggy is much more open to a number of ways of working. I wrote a lot of the music for Iggy. I would supply him with chord sequences, and in some cases the actual melody. I would say 'Jim, this particular song gives me the impression that it's about the Far East . . . ,' a particular set of circumstances, whatever. And I'd maybe give him an idea, and he'd run off in a corner, and in about five or ten minutes he'd have a lyric that would somewhat reflect something we'd talked about. It was much more collaborative in that way. As far as I can remember I didn't write anything with Lou. It was just like, 'Here's Lou's stuff, let's make it popular.' With Iggy, it was like, 'What d'you wanna do, son?' On the early LPs I tried to get him to sing more rather than just The Stooges kind of thing, which I think helped him to find more of a voice."

Fuelling this workload was, however, beginning to take its toll on Bowie. Resorting frequently to the traditional and hearty "musician's breakfast," Bowie may have been creating extraordinary music, but he was essentially driving himself to the brink. In terms of "nonmusical influences," drugs played a significant part.

"I didn't really use them for hedonistic purposes," he explains. "I didn't really go out very much. I wasn't getting totally out of it and going to clubs and all that; I'd never really done that to a major extent. I was really just working. I would work days in a row without sleep. It wasn't a joyful, euphoric kind of thing. I was driving myself to a point of insanity. It probably started in a major way around 'Diamond Dogs,' and from then on it was, as Trent Reznor would have it, 'a downward spiral'. . ."

The way out of the spiral proved, in part, to be Germany, and in part, the free-thinking of former Roxy Music synth wizard Brian Eno. While Bowie was going through personality-threatening crises, a number of German musicians were working on music that would influence the sound of great LPs like "Low" and "Heroes," and represent for Bowie a new lease of life.

"I think how they influenced me was attitudinal," says Bowie. "It was the stance they took. If you listen to 'Low,' 'Heroes' or 'Lodger,' I'd say there's very little Kraftwerk influence on the albums. It's almost like: 'There's a new universe one can exist in. What would I find if I went to that universe?' "

While punk in Britain vented its frustrations, and evolved into new wave, David Bowie was, frankly, quite oblivious, wrapped up in his new German universe.

"It was a very odd period for me from about '75, when I suppose punk started to make its presence felt in Britain," he says. "It's almost as though I was way out in a backwater by that time, because I'd switched to Germany and German electronica was having a major effect on me. I probably didn't realise the weight of punk and what it was doing in Britain.

"I was so fully involved with the Conny Plank studios and all of the Dusseldorf boys, it was almost like the effects of punk in retrospect. When I moved back to America in about 1980, I saw the waves that punk had created, but it was really weird. . . . I missed it. I really missed punk. It was so odd. I was in a fragile state at that time, so my outlook was fairly insular. I didn't have peripheral vision."

The new music Bowie was making, encouraged by Eno, in his fairly loose role of "making things fun" was not only among the best of his career, but was also curing Bowie, in mind and spirit, essentially, of the '70s.

"It was extremely therapeutic for me. It was a self-help, self-therapy thing to get me out of this terrible lifestyle that I'd put myself into. It was time to pull myself together and get healthy again."

David Bowie then leaves his most influential decade, and returns to the 21st Century, where he bids us good afternoon. "It means more to me than any number of hit albums, this," he says. "Thanks very much."

Really no problem, David. Thank *you*.

AS NOMINATED BY:

BRETT ANDERSON (SUEDE)
"Suede have always had a very strong sense of where we came from. I find England strange and unique and beautiful, and I think that's why I was initially attracted to Bowie. People assume I love 'Ziggy Stardust,' but my favourite David Bowie albums are 'Heroes' and 'Low.' "

BRIAN MOLKO (PLACEBO)
"I remember being 11 and seeing the video for 'Ashes To Ashes' for the first time. I was quite fascinated by it."

ED O'BRIEN (RADIOHEAD)
"I just admire David Bowie in the '70s. He was on a mission. His albums were hit and miss sometimes, but he was brilliant because of that."

PAUL DRAPER (MANSUN)
"He's always made ground-breaking music, but better than that, he always looks brilliant."

BOWIE'S MOST INFLUENTIAL LPS

"HUNKY DORY" (EMI, 1971)
The influence of New York in full effect, features the song 'Andy Warhol,' as well as 'Queen Bitch,' a song footnoted on the sleeve: "White light returned with thanks." It sounds like a glam Velvet Underground.

"I don't really think Andy Warhol was as influential on me as people would like to imagine. What did I like about him? A few of his quotes. Everything could be reproduced. The idea of that was great. Him as a persona, that wasn't something I wanted as part of what I did. It goes back to Lou and the Velvets. It was by way of the Velvets, I got a fleeting interest in Warhol."

"THE RISE AND FALL OF ZIGGY STARDUST AND THE SPIDERS FROM MARS" (EMI, 1972)

Bowie's persona for the ultimate tragic rock'n'roll star. Mick Ronson supplies the riffs, while the band wear rock make-up and foot-high storm trooper boots. Bowiemania erupts.

"That was the first really successful cross-pollination for me. I took what I had found exciting about Eastern culture, and kind of bastardised it and made it very colourful. What was going on in Japan, in graphics, or in fashion. A certain kind of look. A lot of the costume changes were nicked from Kabuki theatre, and I thought that was an interesting hybrid of East and West. Which I don't think many people would associate with him."

"STATION TO STATION" (EMI, 1976)

Sleeve from the movie *The Man Who Fell To Earth*. Inside no less bonkers: Kraftwerkian manoeuvres in title track, the weird funk of 'Golden Years,' and 'Wild Is The Wind,' by Dimitri Tiomkin, Bowie's best cover version.

"While I was living in California around 'Station To Station,' I was experimenting with the new European sound, which is why there's such a heartfelt response to Europe on that album, because I was getting pangs of homesickness, and I really was excited with what was going on there. And I got back in touch with Brian Eno. Those two things . . . I thought, 'This is going to be a wonderful avenue to take.'"

"LOW" (EMI, 1977)

The cover's a pun—a shot of Bowie in profile, suggesting the, ho ho, "low profile" nature of the record. Half instrumental. Features excellent proto-Weller song "Be My Wife."

"It was made in France, but it was under the influence of the Dusseldorf bands—Harmonia, Kluster, Neu! and Kraftwerk. It was the Liverpool, or the Seattle of Germany. 'Be My Wife' owes a lot to Syd Barrett, actually. Not Floyd themselves, you understand. He was just as important to Bolan, too. Boly and me used to look up to him as the man in the late '60s. The fact he didn't sing with an American accent was really important. 'Like, great, you can do rock'n'roll in English.'"

"HEROES" (EMI, 1977)

Again, half instrumental. Title track arguably most enduring Bowie song.

"That really plodding tempo and rhythm, both are from 'Waiting For The Man' and the chord sequences are . . . what they are. I'd got over the majority of my emotional decline, and felt like I was coming back to who I should have been. I felt some substance in my emotional make-up, and I guess there was a certain healing going on, spiritually and emotionally. On that level it's as much about me as it is about the protagonists in the song. 'We can get out of this. I'll be OK, in my case.' "

CONTACT

Paul Du Noyer | July 2002, *Mojo* (UK)

In 2002, David Bowie's album *Heathen* aroused no little excitement amongst his fan base. Not only was it his first collaboration for nearly a quarter of a century with Tony Visconti—always considered his best producer—but it saw the artist engaging with some of the current musical fashions.

Yet just a paragraph or two of Paul Du Noyer's feature for retro-themed British glossy *Mojo* was devoted to the new product. As ever, Bowie good-naturedly allowed the interviewer to set the agenda, and what Du Noyer wanted to talk about was not so much what Bowie was doing in the New Millennium, but how he had got to this point. The result was an easy-rolling, revelation-packed exploration of Bowie's career from its beginning to the Berlin Trilogy. —Ed.

"I really wanted to write musicals more than anything else," remarks David Bowie, remembering the days before a certain carrot-headed extra-terrestrial turned him into a rock'n'roll superstar. "At the time I thought that was probably what I was going to end up doing. Some kind of new approach to the rock musical, that was at the back of my mind. The initial framework in '71, when I first started thinking about Ziggy, was as a musical-theatrical piece. And it kind of became something other than that . . ."

It sure did. Fate decreed that his 1972 LP *The Rise And Fall Of Ziggy Stardust And The Spiders From Mars* would become a turning point in musical history. So it's strange to think how close it came to being a West End war-horse, playing to tourists from Ohio and coach parties from West Bromwich.

We should be thankful that it did not, for David Bowie was made for greater things. And the *Ziggy Stardust* album ushered in a staggering run of albums: quite the strongest of any artist since Dylan or The Beatles. Though he'd done good work before (he now counts early album *The Man Who Sold The World* among his personal favourites), nothing prepared the world for *Ziggy*. Nothing, in fact, prepared David Bowie for the events that were about to sweep him up and turn him into that decade's defining figure.

He is naturally flushed with paternal pride, right now, at the delivery of this year's album, *Heathen*. Yet it's a record with several echoes of the old Bowie, and will put many long-term listeners in a retrospective frame of mind. Most notably it reunites him with producer Tony Visconti, a collaborator on some key releases of the '70s. *Heathen* is also imbued with a considered songcraft that recalls such earlier milestones as *Hunky Dory*. And one track, Gemini Spacecraft, repays a debt of honour to its writer The Legendary Stardust Cowboy, by way of a thank-you for donating a part of his name to that aforesaid carrot-headed extra-terrestrial.

"Obviously a lot of crafting did go into the new material," confirms Bowie, in his New York office, "because I was determined that Tony and I shouldn't rest on previous reputations. Such a lot of the albums we did together are held up in fairly high esteem, we didn't want to tarnish that. And I remember the thing that made what we did very successful was often doing very well-crafted songs. So I sat myself down at the beginning of last year and made myself start stockpiling pieces that I thought were quite strong beginnings. There was no way for me to go in just freewheeling. . . . The new one has a strong narrative thread to each of the songs. It's not particularly abstract. It's quite personal and it relies strongly on melody."

While the release of *Heathen* and his directorship of this year's Meltdown programme will have restored "the Dame" to British thoughts, he remains for now a New Yorker by adoption: "It is," he observes in his best Duke of Edinburgh, "just a *kick-arse* place." A family man for the second time around (his wife Iman presented him with a daughter, Alexandria, in 2000), his general contentment is only disturbed today by the interruptions of the phone and pressing deadlines for the rehearsal of his current band. But he consents to while away a morning in talk of that fabled '70s sequence which made his reputation.

And so we turn to Ziggy. He played guitar, he prowled a desolate London landscape in a quilted jumpsuit, he let the children boogie and he became a rock'n'roll suicide. Or did he? Not only was Ziggy Stardust aborted as a musical: the storyline of his adventures is probably too fragmented to qualify even as a concept album. "There was a *bit* of a narrative," Bowie contends, "a slight arc, and my intention was to fill it in more later. And I never got round to it because before I knew where I was we'd recorded the damn thing. There was no time to wait. I couldn't afford to sit around for six months and write up a proper stage piece, I was too impatient.

"I'm glad in the long run that I just left it like that. Because I never drew a template for a storyline too clearly, it left so much room for audience interpretation. A couple of years ago I was seriously near to putting something together. But every time I got close to defining him more, he seemed to become less than what he was before. And I thought, I should just bloody well let go of this, because it's not right. So I left it. Project abandoned."

The credible "rock musical" remains an elusive beast to this day, and Bowie himself has not picked up the gauntlet. "No, I'm as guilty as anyone. Possibly because of my natural impatience, I just don't discipline myself enough to see something through. *Diamond Dogs*, I suppose, got near that. It was my usual basket of apocalyptic visions, isolation, being terribly miserable. . ."

From *Ziggy*'s opener, Five Years, through to *Diamond Dogs* and beyond, the apocalyptic strain does recur in his work—or, if not quite apocalyptic, then the anti-Utopian outlook of *1984* or A Clockwork Orange that is sometimes called "dystopian."

"Dystopian, absolutely," he smirks. "I went to the doctors for it. You always think you've got an ulcer but it's just heartburn. . . . No, in retrospect, it *has* been a strong theme in the work that I've done down the years. In fact, I think if there is any consistency to what I do it, it's going to be the lyrical content. I'm saying the same thing a lot, which is about this sense of self-destruction. I think you can see the apocalyptic thing as the manifestation of an interior problem. There's a real nagging anxiety in there somewhere, and I probably develop those anxieties in a 'faction' [fact/fiction] structure."

As an example of his faction-writing, Bowie offers that singular astronaut Major Tom, who first appeared in his 1969 hit Space Oddity, and re-emerged 11 years later in Ashes To Ashes: "The second time around there were elements of my really wanting to be clean of drugs. I meta-morphed all that into the Major Tom character, so it's partially autobiographical. But not completely so: there's a fantasy element in it as well. It probably came from my wanting to be healthy again. Definitely. And the first time around it wasn't. The first time around it was merely about feeling lonely. But then the limpets of time grabbed hold of the hull of my ship; it was de-barnacling by the time I got round to Ashes To Ashes. No leave all this out, actually, the barnacles . . . Jesus Christ!"

Yes, you've gone a bit Captain Birdseye.

"I know. Davy Jones's locker!"

The Davy Jones who became David Bowie chose rock music, he now suggests, because it was a career where he could take all his interests with him. "You couldn't really do that in accounting. Because I loved art and I loved theatre and the ways we express ourselves as a culture, I really thought rock music was a great way of not having to relinquish my hold on any of those things. I could drag square pegs into round holes: butcher the pegs away until they fitted. It's kind of what I attempted to do: a bit of sci-fi, a bit of kabuki here, a little bit of German Expressionism there. It was like having my friends around me."

With the solitary exception of Space Oddity, (and by '72 it was fast receding in the public memory), Bowie's career took an age to warm up. At the time of his breakthrough with *Ziggy*, he'd been making records for eight years without a chart placing—as Davie Jones & The King Bees, Davy Jones, The Manish Boys and, from 1966, as David Bowie. "Well, it took me a long time to get it right," he states. "I didn't know how to write a song, I wasn't particularly good at it. I forced myself to be a good songwriter, and I became a good songwriter. But I had no natural talents whatsoever. I made a job of work at getting good. And the only way I could learn was see how other people did it. I wasn't one of those guys who came out of the womb like Marc." (A reference to Bolan's T. Rex song, Cosmic Dancer: "I danced myself right out the womb.")

"I wasn't dancing, I was stumbling around."

Marc Bolan was the nearest thing to a real-life role model for Bowie as he sketched out *Ziggy Stardust*: in the year the album was conceived, 1971, T. Rex were at the height of their powers. Bowie's old friend had become Britain's first sensation of the new era: a boy who dreamed up a whole persona for himself, and who seemed to become an overnight rock'n'roll star by sheer force of willpower.

"Oh yeah! Boley struck it big, and we were all green with envy. It was terrible: we fell out for about six months. It was [sulky mutter] 'He's doing *much* better than I am.' And he got all sniffy about us who were still down in the basement. But we got over that.

"You know how we first met? It's so funny. We both had this manager in the mid-60s [Les Conn]. Marc was very much the Mod and I was sort of neo-beat-hippy, though I hated the idea of hippy because my brother had told me about beatniks and they seemed far sexier. Both Marc and I were out of work and we met when we were poured into the manager's office to whitewash the walls.

"So there's me and this mod whitewashing Les's office. And he goes, 'Where d'you get those shoes, man?' [Bowie does a perfect impression of Bolan's fey but icily determined manner.] 'Where d'you get your shirt?' We immediately started talking about clothes and sewing machines. 'Oh I'm gonna be a singer and I'm gonna be so big you're not gonna believe it, man.' Oh, right! Well I'll probably write a musical for you one day then, 'cos I'm gonna be the greatest writer ever. 'No, no, man, you've gotta hear my stuff 'cos I write great things. And I knew a wizard in Paris,' and it was all this. Just whitewashing walls in our manager's office!"

Between Bolan's amazing success, and the public indifference to his own *Hunky Dory* (released in late 1971, it did not pick up serious sales until the *Ziggy* era), was Bowie ever pessimistic at this point?

"No, I never ever felt that, because I still liked the process. I liked writing and recording. It was a lot of fun for a kid. I might have had moments of God, I don't think anything is ever going to happen for me. But I would bounce up pretty fast."

Sure enough, Bowie bounced up incredibly fast in 1972. No sooner was *Hunky Dory* in the shops than he'd shorn off the golden tresses; he toured

Britain with a brand new look and a set of songs from his next LP, already in the can. In Ziggy Stardust, the transgender space boy who becomes a rock'n'roll star, Bowie had spawned a self-fulfilling prophecy.

Yet, having turned David Jones into David Bowie, why did he need a second reinvention? The answer seems to be that Bowie required Ziggy Stardust as a kind of body armour: an imaginary rock idol to help him become the real article. With this device he could escape the diffident, quizzical Englishman of *Hunky Dory* to become more like his current obsessions: Iggy Pop, the wild child, and Lou Reed the dark priest of decadence.

"It became apparent to me that . . . I had an unbearable shyness; it was much easier for me to keep on with the Ziggy thing, off the stage as well as on the stage. It also seemed a lot of fun, a really fun deceit. Who was David Bowie and who was Ziggy Stardust? But I think it was motivated by shyness as much as anything. It was so much easier for me to be Ziggy."

Even before he hit big with *Ziggy*'s preview single Starman, Bowie began to shape the 1972 agenda through a Melody Maker interview in February of that year, wherein he declared he was gay. The cat was suddenly among the pigeons.

Why did you say it?

"I found I was able to get a lot of tension off my shoulders by almost 'outing' myself in the press in that way, in very early circumstances. So I wasn't going to get people crawling out the woodwork saying [seedy, muck-raking voice]: 'I'll tell you something about David Bowie that you don't know . . .' I wasn't going to have any of that. I knew that at some point I was going to have to say something about my life. And, again, Ziggy enabled me to make things more comfortable for myself. There was an excitement that the age of exploration was really finally here. Which is what I was going through. It perfectly mirrored my lifestyle at the time. It was exactly what was happening to me. There was nothing that I wasn't willing to try, to explore and see if it was really part of my psyche or my nature. I was terribly exploratory in every way, not just culturally but sexually and . . . God, there was nothing I would leave alone. Like a—it's a terrible pun, but—like a dog with a bone, I suppose! So I buried it!"

Yes, very often, I hear.

"The quote has taken on far more in retrospect than actually it was at the time. I'm quite proud that I did it. On the other hand I didn't want to carry a banner for any group of people, and I was as worried about that as the aftermath. Being approached by organisations. I didn't want that. I didn't feel like part of a group. I didn't like that aspect of it: this is going to start overshadowing my writing and everything else that I do. But there you go."

Before we knew it, there was a bizarre pastiche of "gayness" about, whereby the most meat-and-potato bands became what was called glam rock. Some of it was pretty poor, wasn't it?

"Oh, bloody awful. Some of the stuff that we encouraged—and I have to pull Roxy into this as well—Good Lord, we should be ashamed of ourselves. It was so dire. It lent itself to really despicable performances because you had to move into really outré areas to make it work; and if it didn't work well, my God, it came crashing down. The one I think of is this American character Jobriath. Woah! What a mistake that was. Very strange guy, he was at like every concert when I first went to the States, my number one fan."

But the cultural incongruities could sometimes be delightful. Quite aside from *Ziggy* itself, Bowie wrote the absolute anthem of 1972 in the song he gave to those doughty tractor boys Mott The Hoople, "All The Young Dudes."

"If they were doing OK at the time," says Bowie, "I don't think they would have wanted to link up with me, because they were quite macho, one of the early laddish bands. But things weren't good, and I literally wrote that within an hour or so of reading an article in one of the music rags that their break-up was imminent. I thought they were a fair little band, and I almost thought, This will be an interesting thing to do, let's see if I can write this song and keep them together. It sounds terribly immodest now but you go through that when you're young: 'How can I do everything? By Friday!' So I wrote this thing and thought, There, that should sort them out. Maybe I got my then management to phone up their people: 'David Bowie's written you this song.' And it worked! I was flabbergasted. And then I wrote them Drive-In Saturday, but by that time I think they thought 'Oh, we don't need that wimpy glam-rocker any more.' I think they would have done it great."

The beauty of All The Young Dudes, in a way, was that it crystallised the emergence of a new pop audience, too young to belong to Woodstock and the '60s.

"Yeah. You have to try and kill your elders. We had to develop a completely new vocabulary, as indeed is done generation after generation. The idea was taking the recent past and re-structuring it in a way that we felt we had authorship of. My key 'in' was things like Clockwork Orange: that was *our* world, not the bloody hippy thing. It all made sense to me. The idea of taking a present situation and doing a futuristic forecast, and dressing it to suit: it was a uniform for an army that didn't exist. And I thought, If I took the same kind of thing, and subverted it by using pretty materials. . . . That Clockwork Orange look became the first uniform for Ziggy, but with the violence taken out of it."

As the mention of Drive-In Saturday suggests, Bowie's own ideas were already on the next project, *Aladdin Sane*. "There was a point in '73," he says, "where I knew it was all over. I didn't want to be trapped in this Ziggy character all my life. And I guess what I was doing on *Aladdin Sane*, I was trying to move into the next area—but using a rather pale imitation of Ziggy as a secondary device. In my mind it was Ziggy Goes To Washington: Ziggy under the influence of America."

But it looked like Ziggy under the influence of lots of things, didn't it, what with the lightning bolt through his head. Were things already slipping out of control? Bowie says not.

"No, not really. That came later. I just knew it was over. I kind of thought, How am I gonna wrap this up? Also, I was incredibly drained. The touring schedules that MainMan were putting us on were insane. D'you know, the extraordinary thing is that we never played Europe. We never left England except for America, and we went to Japan, and that's it. And I was beginning to miss Europe.

"*Then* I started getting into a very bad period. I mean, it really developed. My drug addiction really started, I suppose you could pin it down to the very last months of the Ziggy Stardust period. Not in a particularly heavy way, but enough to have probably worried some of the people around me. And after that, when we got into *Diamond Dogs*, that's when it was out of control. From that period onwards I was a real casualty.

I've not met many people that . . . I was in a very serious state. You just have to look at some of the photographs of me, I cannot believe I actually survived it. You can see me at the Grammies, for instance, with Lennon, it terrifies me. It's a skull. There's not an ounce on me. I'm just a skeleton.

"I have an addictive personality. I'm quite clear on that now. And it was easily obtainable and it kept me working, 'cos I didn't use it for . . . I wasn't really a recreational guy, I wasn't really an out-on-the-town guy. I was much more 'OK, let's write 10 different projects this week and make four or five sculptures.' And I'd just stay up 24 hours a day until most of that was completed. I just liked doing stuff. I loved being involved in that creative moment. And I'd found a soulmate in this drug, which helped perpetuate that creative moment."

You mean cocaine?

"Yes, cocaine. Well, speed as well, actually. The combination. And apparently a lot of elephant tranquilliser went in there too!"

In the chemically-fuelled euphoria of Bowie's first taste of super-stardom, he revisited the notion of a rock musical. The first plan was to interpret 1984, until the idea was nixed by Orwell's widow. "So I changed track real fast and converted it into *Diamond Dogs*, which was more of an effort than *Ziggy*. Thinking back, we didn't do anything on stage with Ziggy: all I had was a few costume changes. It was just the songs and the trousers. That's what sold Ziggy. I think the audience filled in everything else. But *Diamond Dogs* I intended to do something for. We had a bit more money by then—though not enough, apparently: it actually put me into bankruptcy. But that kind of started a lot, the *Diamond Dogs* show, in terms of you could do something more interesting on stage than just wear blue jeans. It was quite fun, but I got bored half way through and threw the set away, so I've only got myself to blame."

Still, if the ginger mullet were not long for this world, Bowie had not yet finished his assault upon America. Suddenly came the breathless but sophisticated "plastic soul" of *Young Americans*, accompanied by the stat-utory image overhaul. "I guess the dawning of it was some take on the Puerto Rican street look with a zoot suit, which kind of got it back into more conventional looking clothing. Even though it's pretty bizarre when you see it now, the *Young Americans* thing was an attempt to turn the visual around as well as the music.

"With people like Carlos Alomar and a few of my girlfriends at the time, I was really seeing a lot of American nightlife, including the Latin clubs, and it was terribly exciting to me. It rekindled the affection for soul and R&B which I had in the '60s. In fact the reason I left my very first band, The Kon-rads, was that they wouldn't do Marvin Gaye's Can I Get A Witness? It had been a major thing for me in my youthful days. And it all came back with a vengeance, seeing it for real in the States. It was unlike anything I'd seen or witnessed before."

But it was one thing playing blue-eyed R&B covers in the Marquee Club (of the sort he revived on his 1973 covers LP *Pin Ups*). It was quite another to record in America itself, and with black musicians too. Did he not think, 'This is a bit much,' coming over from England and doing this?

"It honestly never occurred to me," Bowie protests. "I was so hermetically sealed from everything. I was so in my own universe, that so much didn't occur to me about how other people thought. I had no idea I was even famous. I really had no idea. I just had this real creative thing going on and I went for it all the way. No, it didn't occur to me at all. I just knew it was a fantastic band. Obviously we ran into race problems down in the South. But it was years before I realised I was one of the only white artists in rock working with a multi-race band.

"And I think what we were doing at that particular time was important. In its own way it opened doors just as *Ziggy* had opened doors. The *Young Americans* period developed an alternative approach to what you could do with rock and pop music. For me it was another successful hybrid: of European melody against an R&B rhythm section."

In Bowie's subconscious the call of Europe was becoming audible. But first he underwent the parallel experiences of filming The Man Who Fell To Earth and recording *Station To Station*. At the same time he undertook to record a soundtrack for the movie. The exact chronology of this busy time is further confused by its having been the height—or depth—of his druggiest period.

"Did the film work come next? Ah, you tell me! Possibly! I know I had a lovely hat. It was *that* period. A fedora: the Borsalino."

The hat was one instance of another stylistic re-vamp, this time occasioned by the character, Thomas Jerome Newton, that he played in *The Man Who Fell To Earth*. Newton was a dapper yet inwardly-decaying space alien, maintaining a mere façade of human authenticity. It was a role the Bowie of those days seemed born to play. And as with Ziggy before him, the boundary between creator and creature grew indistinct. "They all started to overlap each other," Bowie confesses. "The frame of mind I was in, there was no real split from one to another. To me [yappy, cocaine-paranoid voice], *it all made sense, man!* Oh boy, what days they were . . ."

The soundtrack venture collapsed amid some rancour and dispute: "I got angry about it, with no real rational reason. I thought I should be contracted by the film company to do the soundtrack, not just make a presentation of ideas, a stupid, juvenile reason but I kind of walked away from it. Ola Hudson—who in fact was Guns N' Roses guitarist Slash's mum—she was my girlfriend, you see. I used to put him to bed at nights, little Slash. Who'd have guessed? Anyway, I got Ola involved as the wardrobe mistress of the film: she designed all the clothes for it, and she continued designing clothes for *Station To Station* as well."

It's the *Station To Station* ensemble that we recall as Bowie's Thin White Duke look—perhaps the most dashing of them all. "It was extraordinary," he says, "and I must give Ola full credit for the all-black, very conservative look: 'Nobody's done that on stage before, that would be so cool. Why don't you just take Newton on stage?' Then I had an idea of the French matinee idol, with the waistcoat and all that."

And always the little packet of Gitanes popping out.

"Exactly. The function of the cigarettes became a function of the stage. And I got addicted to 'em!"

They are very serious cigarettes.

"Oh yes, but with me, of course, no problem. Forty a day."

It was in this year, 1976, that Bowie disengaged himself from an L.A. life that had nearly wrecked his health and mental equilibrium. He finally toured Europe, too, and would eventually re-locate to Berlin. The same Germanic vibe that tainted some of his more outlandish interviews of the time was heard, more constructively, in his new music.

"This is where I have to give Kraftwerk their due," he says. "I had an import of *Autobahn* in the States, probably in the year it came out, 1974. I just got so hooked on this band: Who are they? Who are they connected to?

"And so I came across Tangerine Dream and Can and eventually Neu! and this whole new sound happening in Germany. I thought, Wow, I've seen the future and it sounds like this. I very much wanted to be in the swim. It's interesting that when I go back and listen to what Tony [Visconti] and I did with those albums, *Low* and all that, there really is not as much influence from the German sound as one would have expected.

"It's still a very organic, blues-driven sound. It's swathed in extraordinary atmospheres, partially from Eno, a lot from Tony Visconti himself and my choice of playing rather dotty old synthesisers, quite Beatlesque in a way. But again the actual rhythm section is not a metronome, electronic sound like the Germans were doing: it was Dennis Davis and George Murray, Carlos Alomar [some of the *Young Americans* crew, in fact]; it was another hybridisation that I thought might be fabulous. If I took what I'd found in America, brought it back to Europe and combined it with what was happening in a sonic way in Germany, I'd just see what would happen."

The return of Visconti to this tale, with *Low* in 1977, completes one circle of our conversation, since it was with that producer that Bowie had made his first fully-rounded album, *The Man Who Sold The World* in 1970. It begins a larger circle, too, in that Visconti would remain at Bowie's side for the next stupendous sequence of albums (*Heroes, Lodger, Scary Monsters*), returning for the third time on this year's *Heathen*. But that is a wider circle than we can discuss today. "My schedule," Bowie groans, "is just beyond belief."

From across Bowie's New York office a telephone rings.

"Oh shut up!" he snaps. "It's been a hell of a morning. They were Beckett's last words, you know: 'What a morning' . . ."

DAVID BOWIE: LIFE ON EARTH

Ken Scrudato | July 2003, *Soma* (US)

"I wasn't there to waste the opportunity talking about guitar sounds and producers" admits Ken Scrudato in this feature from America's *Soma*. As said magazine describes itself as "the seminal voice and vision of independent, avant-garde arts, fashion, culture, and design," it shouldn't come as too much of a surprise that Scrudato and Bowie engaged in a conversation that took in such deep subjects as nihilism, existentialism, recontextualization, and even the end of the world.

Music does get a look in, though. New album *Reality* is mentioned, and Scrudato even manages to wrest from Bowie the reason that *Outside* (whose title was actually preceded with a "1.") failed to develop into the trilogy he envisaged.

Recalls Scrudato, "He said, 'I'm going to play you some of my new music, and I'd love for you to tell me what you think.' All I could think was, 'What would I possibly say if I actually don't like it?' I sat down on a chair opposite him and he quickly slid down the couch he was on and asked me to sit right next to him. Funny, the artist who had so cagily cultivated artifice and an image of icy detachment, turned out to be one of the most gracious and unguarded people I'd ever interviewed.

"I was particularly struck by his admission that culture had reached a point at which nothing new would ever be possible again—especially as he had been responsible for so much of its modern evolution." —Ed.

"You know how I know it's the end of the world, Lenny? Because everything's been done. Every kinda music, every government, every hairstyle. How we gonna make it another thousand years, for chrissake?"

—Max Peltier in *Strange Days*

We almost manage to fool ourselves, don't we, with all of this earnest blather about cutting-edge contemporary art and culture? But if you actually asked someone the last time that art/music/film/whatever truly altered their perceptions of the world, you'd doubtless get but a few wishy-washy answers . . . on a good day. And anyone who thinks Radiohead and David Lynch have changed the world might do well to find a time machine that can blast them into a front row seat at the debut of Stravinsky's "The Rite Of Spring" or pull up a Dadaist chair next to Hugo Ball at Café Voltaire in Zurich, 1916 . . . and discover what it actually meant to subvert the status quo. Or maybe one could just throw on Ziggy Stardust and pretend that 31 years haven't passed.

Sorry. This IS supposed to be about David Bowie. And the inevitable final judgment of the man who in actuality no more fell to earth than sold the world will be a strained one. Is he a hero, because he dared take us to Mars when actual astronauts had barely set foot on the moon, and because he desecrated, decimated, and dismantled that second most sacred of all human realities: sexual identity? Or is he to be scolded for going too far too fast, and leaving everyone, including himself, with nothing left to do?

Well, there's actually little doubt that the former is true and the latter is something that he likely had no desire to obstruct. "I'm responsible for starting a whole new school of pretension," he once and brilliantly put it. No kidding, that. Bowie meant it.

Unfortunately, though, no manner of blame-gaming is going to halt the horrific postmodernist beast as he spirals us into a hopeless nostalgia for culture that once upon a time changed our perceptions of the world. Nay, the beast also mocks us with such agonies as Lilith Fair. Bastard. No wonder the drugs of choice are now Prozac, Paxil, and Zoloft. How else would that innocuous bilge actually sound okay?

What's most striking about David Bowie, twenty-first century Boy Edition, is his absolute dignity. He himself admits that he's no longer doing anything that he hasn't done before; thus, he cannot be counted amongst the blathering ones. And if it's true that, as Camus put it, "Art does not tolerate reason," Bowie is still the consummate artist, whatever the context.

As Herr Bowie is at it again, I was given the peculiar privilege of holing up with him in a room at Looking Glass Studios; there he played for me new music from his upcoming album, *Reality*, due out in September. He was courting me! How bizarre. (He also later apologized for having a bad hair day. Bad hair?!!! You must be kidding, David.) Not surprisingly, he didn't have to try all that hard to convince me of his continued relevance. I could hear it from the first song, a ferocious post-punk-space-rock steamroller that sounded like it might have been accidentally left off *Lodger*. ("So, this won't be your all ballads album, then," I cleverly remarked.) A haunting, Teutonic dirge followed, then a spooky cover of Jonathon Richman's "Pablo Picasso," and a few more clattery, futuristic rock songs. It was powerful and unpredictable stuff; and, yes, relevant.

But I wasn't there to waste the opportunity talking about guitar sounds and producers. Let the muso mags concern themselves with such things. (Okay, he did work with Tony Visconti again on this album.) What I wanted to know was this: David, in this dismaying, disappointing new postmodernist world, why, and how, are you still bloody doing this?

You're continuing to confound, musically. Are you confounding yourself as well?

"I'm very happy that it sounds like what my intention was, which was to make an album that reflected being here in New York. I mean, I've been in New York on and off for ten years now. . . . I'm a New Yorker! Iman and I have lived here for eight of them. Apart from a brief sojourn in L.A. . . ."

Oh, sorry about that.

". . . which still I can't get. I don't get it, I really don't get it. We made immediate efforts to get back here again (laughs). Because I do miss it when I'm not here. You know, I've lived here longer than I have any other city. It's really bizarre."

You came into your own at a time when there was an active exploration of artifice and pretense. And you readily explored your pretenses where others would think that was not the proper way to conduct one's self as an artist.

"Yes, absolutely, sure."

You escaped into these characters that were able to speak for you . . .

"I'll qualify that, but yeah."

Could you have stood on a stage before 20,000 people at any point in your life, and told them what you wanted to say without the . . .

"Well I've always told them what I wanted to say."

But could you have told them without something to channel it through?

"Without a character? Yeah, I really stopped writing them for myself, anyway. I went through such a traumatic period in the late '70s that it really changed my path. I just haven't written in that sort of narrative way [of late]. Well, I suppose there was something of that sort in the *Outside* album. That was Brian [Eno] and I going off on some kind of strange tangent; we wanted to kind of lay down a manifesto of what the early '90s was about. I think it was right on the money."

One of my favorite albums.

"Thank you very much. I must say that my core of fans, those that really know my albums, really liked it. It had a whole host of characters, and had I the motivation and the attention span, it would have been nice to have carried it out more fully. We did record an awful lot of stuff, and there really is every intention of going through it and putting out Part II and Part III. The second title was *Contamination,* and boy was that accurate. And it would have been nice to have somehow done it as a theatrical trilogy. I just don't have the patience. I think Brian would have the patience."

It's his job to have patience with genius.

"Well, he's one himself."

Culture as we knew it to be able to affect the world in other than a very straightforward emotional way is, essentially, finished . . .

"Well, yeah, that's the postmodernist thinking. The end of culture has arrived. I think really the intention of what they were saying is more that we'd be repeating in different ways everything that has gone before. I'm not so sure that the culture itself is finished, but it won't produce anything new."

But the Internet is not finished.

"It is as far as I'm concerned. (laughs hard) Have you tried to buy anything lately online?"

Yeah, but that's just credit card problems. If you've seen some of the stuff that's been unleashed . . . it's got an underlying quality of subversion. It has given voice to people that have never, ever had any concept of having twenty, fifty, a thousand others hear what they have to say.

"Yeah, yeah, absolutely! But in a way, you're still as hidden on the Internet. There must be a million bands on the Internet now; and how many are you gonna stumble across?"

Right.

"I don't know, I think the more worrisome part is that there's so much that one can find out through the Internet; but I don't think people take advantage of it in quite the right way."

People are afraid of certain information.

"Yeah. For instance, I'm a big pusher of a site called Truth-Out.com, which I think is a fantastic collection of essays and articles about politics and world affairs. It's really a fabulous storehouse of information of what's written in the alternative press, or the rest of the world's press, that never really sees the light of day here. I know that not that many people go to it, and it seems a great shame."

Back to your music, with the way things have evolved, clearly you do it now just for the joy of it. You must, however, have a sense of the recontextualization of what you do. Because there was the idea in '77 that music could change the world, and no one gets that privilege anymore as a rock band . . . to change the world. So, does it feel daunting now?

"Hmm. I just think that maybe there were several of us dealing in this newly found pluralistic vocabulary, this whole George Steiner-ism of life, you know? (note: Steiner is the author of a 1971 book titled *In Bluebeard's Castle: Some Notes Towards The Redefinition Of Culture*) But I think that the world caught up really quickly, and everybody is so totally aware of the kind of vocabulary that we were throwing around at that time, that one feels kind of superfluous now. I still enjoy what I do. But I don't think what I do is terribly necessary . . . at all. And I'm really not doing much that's terribly different from what I was doing back then. But it's for. . ."

For the love of it.

"Yeah, yeah. Absolutely."

Well, when you look at even contemporary conceptual art, is it hard not to feel a sense of futility?

"Yes! Of course! But I'd rather turn that futility into . . . well, I think it becomes a futility if you give credit to the idea that we are evolving, or supposed to be evolving. It looks like futility if you think that there is some system that we should be standing by. A religious system, or one of civilization's philosophies, something that we should hold by and say this will get us through and all that. But I think if you can accept—and it's a big leap—if you accept that we live in absolute chaos, it doesn't look like futility anymore. It only looks like futility if you believe in this bang up structure we've created called 'God,' and all. It's like, don't tell me that the whole system is crumbling; there's nothing there to crumble. All these structures were self-created, just to survive, that's all. We only have a moral code because, overall, it helps us survive. It wasn't handed down to us from anywhere."

Well, there is that story . . .

"I know. I've heard that story (laughs)."

Mankind has God for hope. We trade faith for hope.

"I know. It's kind of a tragedy, and it's probably a hindrance, really. I think what we're going through right now, what people are beginning to feel, is that there's a transition taking place. We're leaving all those old structures behind, whether we like it or not; they are all crumbling. And it's not a moral decay. This is the way the world is evolving, the way we are changing."

I wonder sometimes if we're just supposed to destroy the world; that we don't possess the ability not to.

"I don't think we are. I don't think we're going to destroy it at all. I'm not that pessimistic. I just believe we're going through a transition where we will become a humankind that accepts chaos as our basic premise. Accepts that it's how we exist. And I think that we're halfway between the structures and the chaos theory at the moment. You really see it evolving."

But I'm not sure the earth can hold up to it. It may actually not survive our progress.

"Oh, shucks! (laughs)"

Oh, but you and I will be long gone!

"Well, I'm not going to tell my daughter that. I'm going to tell her that she's going to have a great life, and it's a terrific world, and that she should embrace all experiences . . . carefully. You see, I HAVE to do that. It's really important for me to work hard on developing a positive attitude. Because it's not for me anymore, and I'm very keenly aware of that. I just can't get that selfish. And it's very, very easy for me to vacillate over into the more depressing, nihilistic, and dark side of life. It's always been too easy for me to do that; and I just don't need to do that now. It comes through in my writing because it's the only space I allow myself to function in that particular way."

It's where you're working it out.

"Yeah. And it's like that old adage that Brian uses: In art, you can crash your plane and just walk away from it, which you can't do in real life, of course. You present a darker picture for yourself to look at, and then reject it, all in the process of writing. There are some songs on [the new album] that I just don't agree with. The fact is, I've written them. It's come out."

It's like you're having a dialogue with yourself.

"And I think that's what's left for me with music. I thought I had something to say before; I must have had something to say. I was young! (laughs) And I knew everything then. Now I really find that I address things with myself. And that's what I DO. Where would I focus if I couldn't do what

I do? If I hadn't been able to write songs and sing them, it wouldn't have mattered what I did. I really feel that. I HAD to do this."

That's very existentialist. Which is something that I've always gotten from your work. People will tend to focus on the nihilism in your work . . .

"But it is more existential than nihilist."

I've always seen you as embracing the idea that your possibilities are your own.

"I've always felt comfortable with writers like Camus. But people would read that as being so negative. And it wasn't! It just made absolute sense, what he had to say."

They say that there's no actual human nature, that human nature is just this mountain of everything that we've ever done.

"Yeah. A style mountain! (laughs) We are about style. Style is our choosing what we wish to have represent us. And that will make us who we are. It's such a peculiar thing. I don't want the table with metal legs, I want wood legs. And it goes from the table to your philosophy of everything you do and touch. You make a choice about the style of it."

But going back to your period of exploring different levels of pretense, people would tend to see you as someone who was afraid of the world. And instead, I saw you as someone who was not afraid of going as far into yourself as possible to discover those choices.

"I thought it was very courageous, yeah. At the time, I didn't really realize how deep in it I was. But in immediate retrospect, I would think, fuck, I'm really pushing myself out on the boat. But I was just going my own way. The only people I knew were strange, anyway, Iggy and all. There weren't too many good ol' boys around me."

So, you're doing a massive tour for this record.

"Yes. And it's going to be really tough, because I haven't been on a big tour for a long, long time. And this tour coming up in September is going to be pretty huge. The luxury of my situation is that I can and will be able to take my wife and baby with me. When it's fair, when I can put them in a house in Europe and fly in and out. Which is actually quite feasible in Europe, because nothing is very far away.

So, how do you still manage all of this? How do you just keep on going?

"I'm not sure how many I've got left, you know? But making music is really still at the top of my pile. I really enjoy it so much; I love writing it, and I love creating it. And I think we all have a longing for something that can engage our systems, and that we can nurture ourselves with—a romance of life. It becomes harder and harder to plug into that particular feeling, I think. But what else would I do other than what I do?"

SUCH A PERFECT DAY

Mikel Jollett | July/August 2003, *Filter* (US)

This feature from US magazine *Filter* sees another journalist rather stunned to both find himself in Bowie's presence and discover that he is not just a musical titan but a flawed human being like anyone else. The difference is that said writer is now in a similar position himself: the interview took place a few years before Mikel Jollett underwent a Damascene conversion that saw him switch his career in journalism for the role of frontman for indie rockers The Airborne Toxic Event.

    The interview is more entertaining than revelatory—if you don't count the fact that Jollett produces from Bowie the disclosure that he hates country music. —Ed.

It was all very strange. Great, but strange. I was sitting there in David Bowie's studio in Soho, on a little leather chair in front of these two huge studio speakers taking notes on the songs from his new album [*Reality*] while he was sitting behind me on a couch flipping through a magazine, glancing up every now and then to check my expression. I had a little red notepad and an old pen and I kept thinking, "Jesus, I hope I don't run out of ink." And then out of nowhere, Bowie [and Ziggy, and the Thin White Duke, etc. . .] jumped up [he's all smiles and nervous energy, that guy] and said with a grin, "Hope you don't mind if I read your notes. . . " I stuttered. He laughed and went back to the couch. I looked down at my notepad which read:

Thought 1: This song is going to get a lot of airplay.
Thought 2: He's going to make a serious comeback.
Thought 3: I love my job.

The song was called "Loneliest Guy," a theatrical piano ballad filled with sadness and longing. It ended. He jumped up again, turned to the engineer [a youngish dude with Creed hair and a pasty tech-guy-expression], and said, "All right Mario. How about we cue up 'Pablo Picasso'?" I grinned. He grinned. He knew he had something good. I was giddy. "Pablo Picasso" started, a loosely electro-synth, British-rocky cover of the Jonathan Richman song. The speakers rumbled, Bowie's voice all gritty and chopped down, "The girls would turn the color of an avocado, as he would drive down the street in his El Dorado." There was a build up as flamenco guitars washed in and out of the mix, and then it all fell away when the voice said, "Some guys try to pick up girls and get called an asshole, this did not happen to Pablo Picasso." Which was great. Because it meant at least two things. One, that David Bowie was in a good mood in life and back to making music for the sake of making music—just fucking enjoying it. Two, that we were about to have a really nice chat because it was clear that I loved the songs and [despite the fact that he is considered by many to be among the most influential musicians of the 20th century], he was a nervous, frenetic, and utterly insecure artist first. And he wanted to be told that his songs were good. And I was the guy to tell him. That was the strange part. Well, there's more.

The songs continued to play—six in all—and he continued to stand up and smile with his hands on his hips saying things like, "Oh this one's based on this author who wrote rather bad science fiction stories," and "You hear that? That's David Torn on guitar. Doesn't sound like one, eh?" He was rather short (about 5-foot-9) and bubbling with energy. A shadow of grey stubble fell over his chin while wisps of towhead blonde hair tumbled to his eyes—a striking juxtaposition of age and agelessness. I mostly sat there in the chair and wrote things, realizing that this was a very rare moment in life—a moment in which one must try with all diligence not to fuck up.

It's easy to get caught up in such things: the New York studios, the cross-country plane rides, the major-label publicists who usher you to and fro. It's more than a little overwhelming. And very easy to be intimidated. But sitting there with David Bowie, I got the sense that he felt that way about it too. And I was surprised to notice—through his comments, his gestures, his school-chummy quips—an uncanny sincerity. And it wasn't because he was relaxed. Most rock stars are relaxed in their lair. It was because he was nervous. He was trying to win me over because he could tell I was nervous too. He was, um, cool. [As in "Is James a nice guy? Yeah, he's cool."] Which is a preternaturally bizarre way for a person to be when they've sold more albums than Britney Spears and have more money than the Queen.

"There's nothing worse than when you play your own album, and you really hate it. It's happened in my past before. I think, 'Why am I doing this? Why am I playing this? I've got to remix everything.' " He laughed as he said this presumably because he didn't feel that way this time around. The listening session was over and we were now sitting alone in the studio on the couch nine stories above the shops, street vendors, hipsters and sidewalk construction of New York City. There was a certain swishiness to him as he brushed the hair from his forehead, with his legs tucked under his torso. It was not hard to imagine him taking on the persona of an androgynous, bisexual, rock star from outer space—as he did in 1973. Not because he was weird. He wasn't. But because he seemed one of those people who would try anything. Again, cool.

"I wrote it here in New York," he said as he stood to look out the window, his hands in the pockets of his jeans. Fire escapes and brick buildings framed his figure against the glass and the light engulfed him. "There's a certain kind of energy that you get here. I really felt the sidewalk. There's a twang when the foot hits the ground. I knew what it sounded like. And that's what I wanted to get onto the vinyl."

He sat back down on the couch and looked up brightly, "I've had a sentimental attachment to this city since I was, like, 17. It's because around that time, I'd bought the second Bob Dylan album—the one where he's walking down, I believe it's Bleecker Street. And he's got the girlfriend with him. And I thought, 'this guy is so cool looking.' [Then as an aside, to me] It's always the clothes first, right? [We both laughed.] Well, I'm English. What do you want? Then I played the album. I loved the music. And it was absolute dynamite. It was like this 60 year old guy voice in this young kid. I thought, 'This is the Beats. It's everything that's great about America in this one album.' So I was already nostalgic for Bleecker Street and all that."

I tried to ask a question about playing Andy Warhol in the film Basquiat, but he interrupted the official flow of the interview [as was his habit] rather suddenly by saying, "I can't believe I'm sitting here doing an interview with no product in my hair. [He laughed hard. Bowie knew Bowie jokes, it seemed. He's insecure and looking for approval, wanting me to take part in the joy of being around him.] I feel like a dork. [I tried to console him, telling him 'No it looks good.'] Oh, I hate my hair. I've got that hair where if I don't have half a pound of lard in it, it's just horrible."

Which led quite naturally to a short discussion of Andy Warhol. Another monumentally influential artist. One with whom Bowie was often said to have an afinity. "Like anybody else," he said, "I never knew him. I mean what was there to know? It was very very hard with Andy. To this day, I don't know if there was anything going on in his mind. Apart from the superficial things that he threw out. Whether that was hiding something deeper, I really don't know. Or whether he was just one of those canny queens who got the zeitgeist, but not cerebrally. Everything he said was like, [Intoning in a dead-on Andy Warhol queeny drawl] 'Wow, did you see who's here?' And it was never never any deeper than that level. [Again the drawl] 'Gosh, she looks great. How old is she now?' Lou [Reed] knew Andy, of course, much much better. And he always says that there was an awful lot happening in his mind. But I never saw it."

The original point of the discussion had been lost, David's flair for jumping about from idea to idea being what it is. I was trying to find out what it must be like to play the role of a person he'd known who'd become a historical figure. I was about to circle wagons and re-present the question [a socially-awkward ploy for the erstwhile journalist] when it occurred to me that someone might feel the same way about playing him. He sat up, getting excited and said, "Velvet Goldmine was that. The guy in that movie was supposed to be me, apparently. I'll tell you what, [His voice dropped an octave to a tone in which one leans over to reveal something] I thought he was as charismatic as a glass of water. I thought surely I've got more zing than that. He was more Warhol than me being Warhol, that guy. He was a good-looking kid and all that and I thought, 'Whoa, thank you.' Obviously they didn't see the teeth that I had back then.

"The thing is, that film came from a distinctly American perspective. And glam never happened in America. It was so intrinsically a British thing. You had to understand the idea of these bricklayers and blokes like that who suddenly put on make-up. It was just funny." The strange thing about all this was that David Bowie generally resents questions about that era of his career. It was short. One incarnation of many. There was Ziggy Stardust, yes—in 1973—for a little over a year. But there was also the mod singles on Pye records in the late '60s, then the trippy singer/songwriter of "Space Oddity" (not to mention the professional mime who'd founded his own company) and the long-haired sweeping stylistic mélange of Hunky Dory in 1971. Then, after Ziggy, there was the plastic-soul obsession of Young Americans in 1975, followed by the introduction of the soul obsessed avant-garde persona of the Thin White Duke with Station to Station . . . the cocaine paranoia which led to a trip to Berlin and a new-found love of electronic experimentation found on the late '70s Brian Eno-produced albums Low, Heroes, and Lodger . . . the dance pop a la Let's Dance in 1983 . . . and of course the actor, the record producer (for Lou Reed and Iggy Pop, among others), the front man of Tin Machine (inspired by the Pixies and Sonic Youth) . . . and so on and so on and so on. [And that list doesn't even include the various pursuits of the '90s].

But, all of his incarnations, Ziggy Stardust seems to be the one that just won't go away. Which isn't to say that he still hadn't a certain pride of authorship for the lipstick-soaked beast he'd unleashed upon the world, "The other thing of course is that it only lasted for 18 months. From beginning to end. The entire movement. We'd all moved on—Roxy [Music] and I moved on. Of course there were the Johnny-come-latelys the Jerry Glitters and all that. They were awful anyway. We didn't like them. We were very snobby about it. There were three of us: T. Rex, Roxy and me. That was it. That was the entire glam rock school. It wasn't even a movement."

Which brings us to the core paradox at the heart of David Bowie's career. Over 40 years and 25 albums, having been through operatic grunge and electronic music (first German electro, then dub 'n' bass), gray business suits and ladies dresses, massive live productions and an intimate tour of tiny clubs in the five boroughs of New York City—he is at once the most influenced and influential musician in rock and roll. Everybody wants to be Bowie and Bowie wants to be everybody. Which may be a statement about art and transience and channeling and the lack of authorship which is the foundation of post-modern thought—or it may simply be a statement about a guy who's really fucking into music.

I presented this paradox to him there on that couch inside his studio on the ninth floor of that building in New York. He thought for a long time, sort of looking down, scratching his head, and said, "I guess I soak up everything I listen to. I'm the hugest fan of music. I still to this day . . . a band like Grandaddy still excites me to go and see. [I interjected: 'I love Grandaddy.' He animated, raising his voice, sounding exactly like a geeky fan.] I haven't gotten the new album, it just came out, Sunday [I tell him I would have brought him a copy—and this is perhaps the most surreal thought in a day of surreal thoughts: that I would be bringing David Bowie a copy of an album so he could have it—like I would for anyone. And that is his appeal. He's still excited by it. He's still in the mix.] Oh man, I've been pushing them for two or three years solidly. Because I'm so tired of them not being recognized by anybody. A discovery like that—like a Grandaddy or a Pavement—there are certain bands that you think, 'Oh, that's exactly what I want to say,' Or rather, 'That's how I want to say things.' You know, you feel a kindred spirit with these people."

He was really into it at this point, building momentum, "My pool of references was so diverse, that what I put out was tainted by very odd things. That sort of facility I've had has helped me to understand music. [And then, in a grand oratorical style, coming to a conclusion] I never cut anything out . . . [followed immediately, as an aside, under his breath with] . . . except country and western, of course. [He laughed because I laughed so hard. He looked at me with a smile, cracking up.] It's true, isn't it? Aw fuck. Don't you hate that fucking music? Dreadful. I cannot bear it. And I love America. I love everything about America. But that thing—I never got it. When Mick [Jagger] said, 'Oh, I love it.' I said, 'What do you see in that stuff?' It's like all these hick—[catching himself] oh, I should shut-up."

And that's when the clocks began to melt. We'd moved on to a discussion of the end of rock and roll. The fact that rock music was now caught in this self-referential spiral in which new artists no longer merely referenced older ones, but straight-up copied them—the exact same sort of denouement suffered by jazz and classical music, two art forms far more obsessed with their pasts than their present or their future. And just then, the publicist leaned in through the door, looked at me, pointed discreetly at her watch. The time was almost up. And it occurred to me that it was all ending too soon: the interview, rock and roll, David Bowie. And so it was at that point when we were discussing it, and at this point when we are documenting it, when it is perhaps best to get out of the way, and simply let the man speak, because he says great things and there is precious little time left . . .

"Let's put it down to post-modernism. It's almost like the cat is really set against the pigeons. When Nietzsche said, 'There is no God.' That really disturbed the 20th century. And it fucked everything up— philosophically and spiritually—when he said that. And I think when the post-modernists in the early '60s put around the idea that nothing new will ever be devised again, it kind of fucked things up too. It's a trickle down thing. That idea has definitely become part of our thinking. [He paused here, sensing a change in theme. A crossing over.] And you know, you do start to wonder: Radiohead, as much as I love them, is it basically kind of Aphex Twin with a backbeat? You know, I mean, how new is that? And is that important anymore, I wonder. Should we not be quite so keen to think that the original is the be all and the end all? Our culture is put together . . . it's style, not fashion—I'm very emphatic about that—style is how we put our culture together. It's why we choose a chair. Because it looks a certain way. I mean, why bother? Why do we have a choice of chairs? We need to have that to kind of say so much about ourselves."

He was staring down at his hands, folding a piece of paper, caught up in it, "But that's what's interesting about it. I'm older and the sense of idealism was so clear-cut in the '60s. I remember when I was 16 or 17 years old. I was such an idealist about what could happen in the future and all that. I just don't know. I can't read whether younger people—and I won't say 'young people' because I would include you as 'younger people' [he looked up at me]—actually can feel that sense of idealism in the same way that I probably felt it back in the '60s. [So here was this odd little paternal moment between me and David Bowie. And it occurred to me that it could have been with just about anyone who reads Filter. I just happened to be there. He was thinking, and he kind of looked up and said] Is it harder for you guys to feel that there definitely are certain things that we should abide by?"

I answered him. It's not important what I said. Feel free to fill in your own answer here: _____.

"Yeah the contradiction really fucks you all up doesn't it?" is his reply.

You could probably mail your answer to him. I'm sure he'd love to hear from you. Because Jesus, the guy is a sponge for the zeitgeist—chaos theory in mathematics, the search for a unification theory in physics [to no avail], the evolution of post-modernism to post-post-modernism to a return to classicism and a search for meaning. I don't know if he reads these books or talks to these people or if he's just the sort of person that senses such things when he walks down the street—but one way or another, he knows it. He gets it. He's soaked it up.

"I think now, we don't have a God. We don't have really a trust in any kind of politics. We are completely and totally at sea, philosophically. And I don't think we want new things. I think we're kind of scrounging around among the things we know to see if we can salvage some kind of civilization which will help us endure and survive into the future. We don't need new. [And then emphatically] We are fucked. We've got enough new. Enough! [He yelled into the ceiling. This is the moment, remember it.] I think we will feel a lot more content when we are able to accept that life is chaos. I think it was an awful thought 10 or 15 years ago. But I think we are beginning to become more comfortable with the idea that life is chaos and it's as simple as that: it is chaos. There is no structure. There is no plan. We are not evolving. We have to make the best of what we got. And if we can become happy about that, I think we ought to establish a lifestyle in which we are more content."

He paused for a second while the intellectual dust settled, then sort of perked up and blurted out with a laugh, "What did I just say?"

I began to review, but then the time was up. He said—

"It's lovely to have talked with you. I'm so sorry we don't have longer . . ."

DO YOU REMEMBER *YOUR* FIRST TIME?

Paul Du Noyer | November 2003, *The Word* (UK)

In this feature from UK magazine *The Word*, both writer and artist go down memory lane.

Paul Du Noyer gives us an insight into how a fan's relationship with an artist can change as he becomes a professional writer with ready access to his old idol. Bowie, meanwhile, explores in public his motivation for his bizarre (and reneged-upon) 1990 decision to stop playing his old hits in concert, and in doing so effectively admits that it was because he was worried that his new songs of the period would not bear comparison to his old material.

Also in this article may lie a clue as to why Bowie would shortly abandon talking to the press, and indeed making music. The references to his wife and child that pepper the dialogue suggest that his domestic bliss is now how he defines himself, rather than recording or providing sparkling copy to interviewers. —Ed.

In a day of hard, Biblical heat in Summer 2003, a black limousine sweeps into a sun-baked side street. From its air-conditioned interior David Bowie peers out and sees, penned in, his most devoted disciples. Behind the temporary crowd barriers they have waited patiently all day; many have travelled across New York state and some, the passenger recognises, are hard core fans from Britain. My own eye is drawn to a tall boy at the front of the scrum whose luxuriant hair is in the orange and blond style of *The Man Who Fell To Earth*. He'd be a dead ringer if he weren't Japanese.

We're in Poughkeepsie, a town sufficiently far from New York City for rock'n'roll acts to audition their new material in some privacy before going on tour. Our venue is a rock club called The Chance that still looks like the tiny picture house it used to be in the days of Charlie Chaplin and Buster Keaton. David Bowie's band have been rehearsing in there all afternoon and now their leader has arrived to join them. The fans outside, who've got their tickets through Bowie's online community, cheer and whoop with every new intro they hear. *Suffragette City, The Man Who Sold The World, Rebel Rebel* . . .

Noticing the English fans on his way in, Bowie laughs in exasperation. "I did tell them it wasn't going to be a long show." He remembers that he's decided not to play the whole new album tonight—we're still a month away from *Reality*'s release date—because he calculates there would be a live bootleg selling on eBay by tomorrow.

Within minutes Bowie is on stage with the band for the remainder of the sound-check. He's in a white T-shirt and jeans with black boots and the successfully resurrected *Station To Station* haircut. In the right light he could have just stepped right out of 1976. There's some comradely banter with the musicians, but all the technical conversation is channelled through guitarist Gerry Leonard, a young Irishman who's been made Bowie's musical director. Across the stage's tangle of cables stand the striking bald bass-player Gail Ann Dorsey and the none-more-rock'n'roll guitarist Earl Slick. Another Bowie band veteran, Mike Garson, sits massively behind his keyboard looking like Marlon Brando in *Apocalypse Now*, playing those broken toy piano sounds that dramatised *Aladdin Sane*.

It's a rather business-like procedure. "That OK for you, Pete?" Bowie enquires of his soundman, periodically. Frowning figures from the Bowie organisation are looking obscurely busy, as do various tour personnel who will soon be steering this show around the world. A New York publicist briefs the TV crew lining up for a quick interview. At the still centre of it all Bowie peers into the book of lyrics on a music stand in front of him, and occasionally crouches at the stage front to confer with Coco Schwab, his personal assistant since time immemorial. David Bowie does not possess a mobile phone, but in Schwab he has its nearest human equivalent.

Sound-checks soon lose their allure for the noninvolved and though it's fun to observe Bowie close up I opt for a breath of fresh air. In a small compound behind the club the limo driver is performing a manoeuvre called "turning the talent's car around," to smooth said talent's eventual exit.

The fans are reddening in the afternoon heat and anticipating sundown. I talk to a girl from England who proudly states she first saw Bowie at Hammersmith Odeon in 1973. Which sets me thinking of my own first time . . .

That was a little earlier, in late 1969. Though Bowie had just scored a quirky pop hit called *Space Oddity* he was still not personally famous and was touring Britain at the bottom of a bill headlined by Steve Marriott's heavy "supergroup" Humble Pie. Supporting them, for those were the dying days of the package tour, was an assortment of hairy phenomena including Dave Edmunds' Love Sculpture and bands that were probably named after the Tolkien hobbits they generally resembled. What I chiefly recall was how uncomfortable the lowly Bowie looked. Shy and unamplified, he was a curly-permed folk singer on a night of rock monsters.

The Liverpool Empire crowd was a gruff mob of dandruffed trogs in RAF surplus greatcoats and no quarter was given. He fluffed a few numbers and had to start again, then played his hit and walked off to a thin mix of faint applause, jeers and silence. I felt for him but more than that believed I had seen an otherworldly genius—the wild-eyed boy from Freecloud. Being so new to live music I thought everything that night was amazing, but only Bowie haunted me. He seemed to disappear for a few years after that, until *Hunky Dory* appeared in 1971 and I discovered him all over again.

Back in Poughkeepsie, a little later in the evening, the club has filled up with Bowie fans, though the ones who've arrived tonight look less hard core than those who kept vigil in the day. In fact there are surprisingly few signs of outright devotion—no *Aladdin Sane* lightning stripes or spangly pierrot costumes, to be sure. Perhaps the American take on Bowie is more conventionally rock than England's fond conception of him as space age panto dame.

The band begin by romping through the new album's title track, *Reality*. In the darkness to the side of the club, Bowie's wife Iman is spirited inside, surrounded by minders and unnoticed by the crowd. The capacity is just 500 and I've found a berth up front, so I'm only a couple of yards from Bowie's microphone.

It's not the nearest I've been, though. The mind drifts back to my second Bowie gig, in a grim little boxing venue called Liverpool Stadium.

It was 3 June 1972 and I stared up at the evening's challenger in thrilled bewilderment. We'd been expecting the Hollywood blonde look of *Hunky Dory*'s LP sleeve, but he was already transformed into the figure that would appear on his next album cover, *The Rise And Fall Of Ziggy Stardust And The Spiders From Mars.*

Hair cropped back into a tousled proto-punk look, he led a band who wore the same quilted jumpsuits and boots and yet—far from seeming fey—looked as brutal as any pug who'd ever fought in that boxing ring. The Spiders' style, I'd later understand, was very *Clockwork Orange*, but for now I exulted in finding an act who were doing precisely what I needed to see. That is to say, they were finally killing the 1960s.

How I loathed hippies and velveteen loon pants. For the decade of peace and love I felt the disgust that only an adolescent zealot can feel. I looked up at Bowie that night with gratitude and adoration. He sang *Hang On To Yourself* and all the Ziggy songs we'd never heard before. By the summer's end I knew every word of them and I believe I still do.

A short while after that, in my first week living in London, I bought an A-Z and looked up "K. West" in the phone book—every Bowiehead knows it as the illuminated sign on *Ziggy*'s cover. Looking for Heddon Street was my first encounter with central London and my mental map of the city has grown up around it. Just off Regent Street, I seldom walk down that way without paying a visit—it's full of smart restaurants now but in those days was just a dusty alleyway of the rag trade. Strange to recall, I was so enchanted by Heddon Street that I didn't bother looking for a building that stands almost directly behind it—the old Apple HQ in Savile Row, where The Beatles had played their last public gig a couple of years before.

Thirty-one years later and the Bowie who prances before me is shockingly unchanged, his only appreciable weight gain being some muscle around the pectorals and biceps. He wears a short denim jacket, artfully tapered to the slimness of his hips. Soon he'll be down to his T-shirt and the air pierced by feminine squeals. What's so different nowadays is Bowie's relationship to us, the crowd. Early Ziggy was rather polite on stage. He didn't say much and took care to thank us for any applause. Yet everyone felt they were in the presence of, well, strangeness. His distance was unbridgeable. The young Bowie's charisma was so unusual that the notion of a foundling child abandoned by cosmic gypsies was not so difficult to swallow.

Amid his family of fans, by contrast, the 2003 model is like a jolly gay vicar in charge of a tombola evening. "How have you been?" he asks. "Ooh, I like your new shoes!" He gives every appearance of being most relaxed person in the room. Listen, he keeps telling them, it's only a show. "Don't look so nervous!" Shouldn't that be the other way around?

"I don't know what's happened," he'll say to me later, "whether it's having a child recently. . . . It's not that the work doesn't seem a priority, but it puts it in perspective. You realise that working in a front of a crowd is not a life-threatening situation. It's just going out and singing some songs. It's nothing more than that. This has been coming home to me and I've enjoyed it a lot more. Shows have become something else for me in recent years. 'Here's me, here's the songs I write, you'll like some of them, some you won't have heard of and others you just won't like.' I'm very comfortable with it. And I'm not particularly a gregarious person, so it's something almost of a social breakthrough."

So I'm looking at the new, normal David Bowie and his new, normal fans and thinking how extraordinarily normal it all seems compared to the old days. But as the last chord dies and the house lights go on, I'm tapped on the arm by a scarily blank-eyed woman who has spotted my backstage pass. "Will you take me in to meet him?" she says, in the disconnected voice of a sleepwalker. "I have to meet him. I am his *biggest* fan." She nods solemnly. "Totally."

With a slight shudder I remember the years I worked in the *NME*'s old office in Carnaby Street. The visitations of lunatics were not uncommon, but by far the largest constituency of these were David Bowie fans. Being so bad at telling them to go away I used to spend whole hours listening to their mad claims that Bowie had arranged to meet them there, or that they were charged by higher powers to become his successor on earth, or . . . whatever.

There was often a troubling undercurrent of mental dysfunction in Bowie's music, and in the weirdness that his persona seemed to provoke. I suddenly feel a little bit nostalgic, to be honest.

Bowie got home from Poughkeepsie at about 1:30 last night, but still arose this morning at his usual time of 6:30. He likes to step out early from his downtown apartment. It's his favourite time in New York City, he says, when there's nobody else about except the workers he meets in Chinatown, delivering the day's vegetables to market. It's a long way from the Bowie of *The Jean Genie*, his wide-eyed Brit-boy song of praise to the city that never sleeps.

Does he, I wonder, still recognise the New York of those days? The days of slash-back blazers and pulling the waiters? "I guess it's a lot more homely now," he says. "That was a more romantic vision than I would have now, but then again I was living another kind of life. A late night life. I would come alive around four in the afternoon. I'd be out all night long. I'm sure that side is still out there, but it's just not my New York any more."

We're sitting in the Manhattan studio, Looking Glass, where he recorded *Reality*. He points to various corners of the room like a tour guide, telling me where the different players would stand. A baseball cap, pulled tight around the head, crushes the great mane of hair and makes him seem smaller than he did last night. He wears a crisp white T-shirt, jeans and trainers, and flops on to the sofa as tea is served. Does New York feel like home nowadays?

"Yeah, it really does. It's a bit like being on a holiday in a place I've always wanted to go to, that doesn't come to an end. So 'home' is not quite right, is it? I always feel a stranger here. I am an outsider. I really am still a Brit, there's no avoiding it. But I've got friends here. I probably know this town better than I know the new London. London has changed beyond belief since I've been coming to America. I can walk around here and find my way far better than I can in Chelsea. I've forgotten all the streets. [He mimes befuddlement.] Where did Clareville Grove used to be?"

When I arrived at JFK the other day the immigration official put me through the usual routine, squinting suspiciously at my journalist visa and asking the purpose of my trip. "David Bowie? Is he still alive?" I assured the man, politely, that he was. "Hmm. Looked half dead last time I saw him. . . ." But of course the 56-year-old Bowie looks entirely alive and enviably well. As well as the replica 1976 haircut his face, though lined with age, is structurally unchanged since Ziggy Stardust's time. There's even a significant improvement, presumably a concession to US misgivings about British teeth, in the gleaming dental work—Bowie's smile used to remind you of a Gothic graveyard.

From his handsomely refurbished pegs protrudes the tooth-pick that we suddenly see in all his publicity pictures. Like most ex-addicts—and Bowie declares himself to have an addictive personality—he loves to talk about his old tormentors and cannot keep off the topic of cigarettes. "The bane of my existence" he groans. His chosen weapon of defence, the tooth-picks are herbal (Australian Tea Tree, apparently), with what he describes as "a strange, minty taste." Inevitably he's now found himself addicted to them.

He's in tip-top physical shape, though. About three times a week he submits to a personal trainer whose speciality is making boxers out of rowdy kids from New York's tougher districts, and Bowie laughs when he wonders what the guy made of him, this frail English aesthete who couldn't punch his way out of a paper bag. "I think he took me on out of sheer bemusement. But I really am pretty disciplined. I work out a lot now. I really only started when our baby was born, because I just wanted to be around longer: 'Come on, pull it together, Bowie. You used to be fit, do it again.'"

According to Bowie the arrival of daughter Alexandria, three years ago, changed everything in his domestic routine. Though he tries to keep abreast of current music (The Dandy Warhols, Polyphonic Spree and Granddaddy receive approving murmurs) the only song he gets to hear regularly, he says, goes *The wheels on the bus go round and round* . . . "I tell you, time is the factor. A littl'un takes up a lot of your hours because they want to be looked at. Look at me, Daddy! Entertain me! So I don't go out in search of things any more. And it's such hard work because there is a *lot* of crap out there."

More and more he's found himself returning to vinyl. "I'll tell you what I was playing the other day: Daevid Allen who was in Gong and Soft Machine. I think all the strands of glam rock are in that. He preceded us by about two years. And so did Kevin Ayers. Soft Machine, especially with Robert Wyatt, were great London favourites. They were like 'our heavy band, man.' " Another path has taken him from the dub poet Linton Kwesi Johnson, back to the proto-rap of Gil Scott-Heron and The Last Poets and to the 1950s "word jazz" of Ken Nordine, looping around to the modern, socially conscious hip hop star Mos Def. Like the scholarly cove he has become, Bowie enjoys making connections between stuff, from fusions of the spoken word with music to the *griot* storytellers of Africa.

What else does he do? "We go and see a movie occasionally but all that's changing. Being a homebody really does things to you. I haven't been able to get out to the theatre, which I used to love. The last theatrical event I got to see was *The Lion King*." (His daughter, he reports was duly impressed: "best piece of theatre *she's* seen.")

He's been famously keen on the Internet, of course. He tends to his online fan community, Bowienet, like a particularly diligent shepherd. (We all know Bowie has adopted various guises down the years, but who among us ever predicted "Internet Service Provider" would be one of them? And yet it was.) He still spends a chunk of each day in cyberspace, he says, especially when he's researching his novel.

A novel? He grins, almost shyly. "It needs about a hundred years of research, and it'll never be completed in my lifetime, but I'm having a ball. I start with the first female trade unionists in the 1890s in the East End of London and I'm coming right through to Indonesia and the political problems of the South China Seas. I'm picking up these extraordinary things I never knew. And it's so easy to do research on the internet. It's something I've been writing for the last 18 months and it's hideously hard. The trouble is my through-line started splintering at some point, because I kept finding so many interesting things and I'd have to go, 'No, come back to the story, stop going off at tangents. Just show that you can write a fucking story that has a beginning, a middle and an end.'

"It's so epic that I'm not sure I'll ever finish. Maybe the notes will emerge after I'm dead. They're interesting notes! There's an awful lot of 'Did you know?' [He puts on a suburban pub-bore voice.] Ha ha! 'Did you know that in the 1700s the population of London was 20 per cent black?' They all lived in the St Giles area, there were black pubs. . ."

You should read Peter Ackroyd.

"Oh! I *love* Peter Ackroyd. I've read everything he's ever written. I was supposed to ring him and I must get round to doing it. That disquieting underbelly that he sees in London, that's how I perceive it too."

One imagines that the young Bowie's early visits to New York were—as *The Jean Genie* suggests—a punishing vortex of Andy Warhol parties, prodigious ingestion of drugs, unfettered creativity and open-all-hours sexual exploration. Lower on the agenda, perhaps, were rambles across the grey expanse of the *New York Times*.

But his conversation nowadays—hesitantly high-brow, earnestly liberal-left—suggests a Manhattan academic. The new *Reality* album is laced with local references and is stamped with the cultural aversion to George Bush that's standard in New York circles.

"New York informs it," he says of the record, "but it's not the content of the album. It's a lot more about New York than I expected it to be, but I would not want it to be considered my New York album. It's more about the times it was made in."

Although some of *Heathen*'s songs had a desolate, 9/11 air about them, they were actually written before that day. Those on *Reality* were written after. And his adopted home, New York City, was in the middle of it all.

"A hard black line was scored through the history of New York on 9/11," he says. "It really has changed everything in this culture. Even in the most subtle ways. I was amazed at the way New Yorkers came together during the black-out [the power failure of August 2003]. That was absolutely unprecedented. I think the last time was in about 1977 and I wrote a song called *Blackout* because I was there then as well. I remember burnings, looting, it got very nasty. But this time around everybody was looking out for everybody else. It was extraordinary. There was no looting. Normally it's rule number one, there's a black-out, all the alarms are off, loot. But this time was extraordinary. There is definitely a sense of community here that there wasn't before."

He brings up the conspiracy theories that 9/11 was, if not instigated by the American government, then at least exploited by them in furtherance of plans they had all along. A lot of his suspicions arise from the website of a neo-conservative think tank, The Project For The New American Century, whose members have included Bush's inner circle and which advocates US domination of the post Cold War world. "My amazement," he says, "is that nobody, apart from certain left wing writers and magazines like *Mother Jones* has tumbled on to this site or made much of it."

(When I get back to London I find he's emailed me some addresses. Go to www.newamericancentury.org for a statement of the group's manifesto and, for an opposing view, www.informationclearinghouse.info /article1937.htm.)

"So I can't make sense of the fact there seems to be a plan and nobody seems to recognise that plan. Everything is other than what you are told it is."

But this mistrust of appearances is an old habit of Bowie's—he was always pop's prime subverter of the "authenticity" yearned for by other rock artists. Now it's at the heart of his new album, and in its very title. You're left in no doubt that the word *Reality* has implied inverted commas around it, or at the very least a question mark.

"The word has got such a lot of spin attached to it these days. It's become very hard to say Reality without putting virtual in front of it, or TV after it. So it's been debased but there again, what has been debased? The actuality of reality is so much in flux now. It's different realities for different people."

Being an old-fashioned seeker after absolute truth, myself, I'm disinclined to this post-modern doctrine that there is no such thing. Bowie himself admits to a few reservations: "I know that a person in a Third World country isn't going to give a fuck whether we believe there are or there aren't any absolutes. Because there *are* absolutes for them, indelibly so, poverty and so on, absolutes of survival from day to day. So the definition of the word is the luxury of an elite few in the West."

But when I start to mention a Tom Wolfe satire of post-modernists, Bowie bridles at the name: "Oh, I admire the fluency of his writing, but he's a very egocentric writer. There's something narrow about his world view, very puritan, that makes me not warm to him." (Allow me, all the same, to recommend Wolfe's collection of essays, *Hooking Up*, which is cruelly pungent about the intellectual fashions of our times.)

From satire we turn to mysticism and somehow get on to George Harrison, whose *Try Some, Buy Some* is covered on *Reality*. "For him," Bowie muses, "there is a belief in some kind of system. But I really find that hard. Not on a day to day basis, because there are habits of life that have convinced me there is something solid to believe in. But when I become philosophical, in those 'long lonely hours,' it's the source of all my frustrations, hammering away at the same questions I've had since I was 19. Nothing has really changed for me. This daunting spiritual search.

"If you can make the spiritual connection with some kind of clarity then everything else would fall into place. A morality would seem to be offered, a plan would seem to be offered, some sense would be there. But it evades me. Yet I can't help writing about it. My cache of subject matter gets smaller and smaller and is rapidly reduced to those two or three questions. But they're *continual* questions and they seem to be the essence of what I've written over time. And I'm not going to stop."

My allegiance to Bowie never wavered in the 1970s. In the finest traditions of teenage snobbery I declined to see his big Ziggy Stardust tour because I resented all the new fans who had just discovered him. And whilst I loved *Aladdin Sane* and *Diamond Dogs* I couldn't overlook the crimson mullet, the leotards and general frightfulness of glam-rock style. With the soul-boy makeover of *Young Americans* I could at last consider Bowie sartorially acceptable and, by 1976, consented to attend his next big tour, the "Thin White Duke" dates that accompanied *Station To Station*.

His style this time around was impeccable—the black suit and white shirt, the Gitanes packet in his waistcoat, the blonde sweep of his pre-War Berlin quiff. It's a good look and one he's reprised successfully of late. Queuing up at Wembley I took malicious pleasure in spotting the silly glitterheads who'd been wrong-footed by the new regime and still dressed like clowns in Bacofoil. That same week in May his film *The Man Who Fell To Earth* went on release and there was a curious tendency, in London tube stations that carried the movie poster, to draw a tiny swastika on Bowie's cheekbone. I started seeing The Sex Pistols at the 100 Club and noticed the artier types sporting that same little swastika.

I saw him again whenever he came around, on Iggy Pop's 1977 dates, then at Earls Court and—his mass-market breakthrough—the *Serious Moonlight* tour of 1983. By now a music journalist I became used to seeing him around, and watched a whole Clash show in New York standing next to him and Joey Ramone. I ought to have been ecstatic, but somehow I wasn't, partly because I'd lost the sense of wonder you can only feel as a kid outside the industry process, and partly because the new David Bowie was not as fascinating as the old one.

In the 1980s, we saw a sunnier David on the boulevards of pop but for me it was not an improvement. While the physical excess and mental turbulence of the 1970s were at least matched by marvellous music (*Ziggy Stardust, Low* and so on) the next decade found him coasting along with mediocre records such as *Never Let Me Down*. Such was my disillusion that I remember having complimentary tickets for his Glass Spider Tour in 1987 and deciding, on the spur of the moment, to give them away to somebody in a pub.

Speaking today, Bowie recalls it as a period of creative crisis.

"My own success as a songwriter and performer, I think, really flies or not on whether I'm doing it with a personal integrity. All my biggest mistakes are when I try to second guess or please an audience. My work is always stronger when I get very selfish about it and just do what I want to do. Even if they're dismissed, and perhaps rightly, there were a couple of albums in the '80s that did exceptionally well for me—and I'm not a huge selling artist—but they're not albums I'm proud of. I'd much prefer to say that I did *Buddha Of Suburbia* [his 1993 soundtrack for the TV series]. I feel much more comfortable about that than about *Never Let Me Down* even though it was a really big seller."

The symptoms of this crisis were Bowie's 1989 "farewell" to his back catalogue (which he toured under the *Sound + Vision* title) and that awkward spell as a band-member of Tin Machine. Many were sceptical of the former and scornful of the latter. I came away from one of his press conferences frankly unconvinced that we had heard the last of *Space Oddity*. But with hindsight these twin gestures are at last looking like the beginning of Bowie's revival. The *Sound + Vision* shows were visually stunning and the Tin Machine gig I saw in Kilburn was—you'll just have to trust me—fantastic.

Shortly before Tin Machine I met Bowie in person for the first time, interviewing him in New York. I was by now too much of an old hand to feel nervous. When it was suggested I take along an old LP sleeve for him to autograph I spurned the idea as un-professional. But it was impossible, through our conversation, to stop a fan's lifetime of memories unspooling in my mind. The man himself was entirely charming, and so he has seemed in each of the four subsequent encounters I've had with him. It's as if a chap who spent his early career as an honorary extraterrestrial has subsequently applied himself—with cub scout seriousness—to the role of affable earthling. But he cannot be as ordinary as all that, because he is, of course, David Bowie.

This rather obvious fact came home to me with startling force on the day in the 1990s when I had to chaperone him around a magazine awards ceremony. Simply escorting him and Iman through a packed hotel lobby and bar, down to his allocated table, was to realise how contorted our reactions to a celebrity can be. The conversational babble, hitherto deafening, dropped to near silence when he entered. And while nobody wanted to give the impression of rubbernecking, every eye flickered across him, then back and back once more. The crowd, without prompting, re-assembled itself in the style of the Red Sea meeting Moses. Only the paparazzi (whose presence I had scarcely registered two minutes previously) scorned to play the game; everyone else made some attempt—however unsuccessful—not to gawp too obviously, whereas the snappers flew into the feeding frenzy of seagulls around a whelk-stall.

The long-term Bowiephile has to be prepared for the occasional lonely vigil. For me this occurred with the 1989 release of Tin Machine's hard-rockin', suit-wearin' first album. I've defended the record against overwhelming odds ever since. Not only is it more tuneful and exciting than it's given credit for, it served a higher purpose in rousing Bowie from the lethargy that he'd descended into. Happily, I've now found someone who agrees with me. The snag is that his name is David Bowie: –

"I *love* Tin Machine! I'm a huge fan. I really rate a lot of that work. At least 50 per cent of what we did was good. It was exciting stuff and some of it, in its way, was reasonably innovative. There wasn't much around that sounded like it at the time. There was something in the air that I just felt, *This* is what the world is like right now. It felt like that. But there were such volatile personalities in that band, you never knew from night to night how it would go. There was nothing you could depend on. Somebody would be out of their minds, not be able to play—or even turn up in some cases. But when we were 'on' it was incredible.

"And audiences *loved* that band. *Outside* is a really popular album with my lot, they love it, but I'm telling you, the audiences for Tin Machine had the greatest nights. When it was bad it sucked a big one, but that's what that band was all about. It was a terrific experience and really made me feel good, because now I felt I could make decisions about what I wanted to do over the coming years. There was nowhere to hide with that band. We had everything against us—and it was good!"

Why do you think they were so disliked?

"The consensus was that they thought it was a huge hype, because I was saying I was 'part of the band.' There was nothing I could do or say to convince people, but I *was* just part of that band. I can't say it louder. When I made the decision that we were going to carry on as a band it was really run on democratic lines. I was part of the band. And a lot of people didn't like that and I never understood why. It had always been accepted when I was playing piano with Iggy in the '70s—no big thing was made of it."

When you announced in 1990 that you were dropping all your old songs, was it because you were oppressed by your younger self? I've had the feeling your recent work has been a bid to achieve equality with your past.

"That is absolutely on the money. It was such turmoil for me at that point. I knew there had to be a real life change. I could either pull myself together or just find some other occupation that I actually enjoyed doing, become a painter or something. I didn't know if my songs were any good. I'd spread myself very thin and I didn't want to be intimidated by my own catalogue, so I thought I would really have to begin again. For myself, I would have to start anew, build a new catalogue and see where it takes me. What will I be like as a writer? Let's do it and find out.

"And as the '90s progressed I felt my writing was getting stronger and stronger. I knew it was different, it might not have the frantic energy of some of the more youthful stuff but that's the way it is when you get older. But there was a certain quality to the writing. And quite frankly, over these past three or four years, I'm really happy with the way I'm writing. I now feel very confident about touring and putting new songs against old songs. I don't feel intimidated, it's as simple as that."

"It occurs to me that we have been living under a lot of stress in the last few years. The halcyon days are well and truly over. It's just cyclic, isn't it, the anxiety? That's why I keep trying to be positive. The last time, there was the Bay of Pigs [a prelude to the Cuban Missile Crisis of 1962]. I remember how scared my Mum and Dad were, they really thought that was it, we're gonna go up in a nuclear holocaust. Every now and then you get one of those and you think, Well, we pulled back last time and I've got a three-year-old daughter now and we are *definitely* going to pull back this time because *she is going to have a great life, dammit*. When I keep coming back to that I can't afford to be negative any more. It doesn't behove me to be the nihilist any more, even for creative reasons. I have to be positive.

"Hopefully there is a sense of that on the album. It's not 'woe is me,' it's not a *Diamond Dogs*. I want the ultimate feeling after hearing it to be a good feeling. That there is something to be said for our future and it will be a good future.

"George's song, *Try Some, Buy Some*, means a lot to me now. When I first heard that song it had a very different narrative to it. Now my connection to the song is about leaving a way of life behind me and finding something new. It's overstated about most rock artists leaving drugs, it's such a bore to read about it. But when I first heard the song in '74 I was yet to go through my heavy drug period. And now it's about the consolation of having kicked all that and turning your life around."

Do you feel better for having gone through all you did?

"That's the scary part, I really don't have too many regrets. I have personal regrets about myself and my own behaviour and people I let down considerably during those years. But that's how life was for me, that's how my life has been, and I can't see it in terms of regret. If I think I wasted years of my life, then perhaps I should have gone into [a] completely different venture, outside music. So I don't regret it in that way. If I was told it was all going to happen again and I was able to retain the memories of what went down last time, I don't think I would do it that way at all. I wouldn't do it because it's too risky. I might be dead next time, that's the major thing. Or come out of it really clinically unbalanced. Knowing what I know now . . . I wouldn't do that to myself again."

Do you think you've been lucky?

"Do I feel lucky? I'm supposed to say luck had nothing to do with it . . ."

Or blessed?

"I should call one of my albums that. I'm blessed. I could thank God. Yeah. But which one?"

CREDITS

"Don't Dig Too Deep, Pleads Oddity David Bowie" by Gordon Coxhill. First published in *New Musical Express,* November 15, 1969. Copyright © IPC+ Syndication. Reprinted by permission of the publisher.

"Oh You Pretty Thing" by Michael Watts. First published in *Melody Maker,* January 22, 1972. Copyright © IPC+ Syndication. Reprinted by permission of the publisher.

"David at the Dorchester"/"Back at the Dorchester" by Charles Shaar Murray. First published in *New Musical Express,* July 22 and 29, 1972. Copyright © IPC+ Syndication. Reprinted by permission of the publisher.

"Goodbye Ziggy and a Big Hello to Aladdin Sane" by Charles Shaar Murray. First published in *New Musical Express,* January 27, 1973. Copyright © IPC+ Syndication. Reprinted by permission of the publisher.

"Bowie Finds His Voice" by Robert Hilburn. First published in *Melody Maker*, September 14, 1974. Copyright © 1974 Robert Hilburn. Reprinted by permission of the author.

"Bowie Meets Springsteen" by Mike McGrath. First published in *The Drummer*, November 26, 1974. Copyright © 1974 Mike McGrath. Reprinted by permission of the author.

"Bowie: Now I'm a Businessman" by Robert Hilburn. First published in *Melody Maker*, February 28, 1976. Copyright © 1976 Robert Hilburn. Reprinted by permission of the author.

"Goodbye to Ziggy and All That . . ." by Allan Jones. First published in *Melody Maker,* October 29, 1977. Copyright © IPC+ Syndication. Reprinted by permission of the publisher.

"12 Minutes with David Bowie" by John Tobler. First published in *ZigZag,* January 1978. Copyright © 1978 John Tobler. Reprinted by permission of the author.

The editor of this book wishes to extend his grateful thanks to Alain Valdes for provision of scans.

ABOUT THE CONTRIBUTORS

Mick Brown is the author of six books, including *American Heartbeat*, *The Spiritual Tourist, Performance* (an anatomy of the cult film classic), *The Dance of 17 Lives*, and *Tearing Down the Wall of Sound: The Rise and Fall of Phil Spector*. He writes across a wide range of cultural subjects for the *Telegraph* magazine.

David Cavanagh is an Irish-born music journalist who between 1990 and 2013 worked for *Select, Q, Mojo*, and *Uncut*. His book about Creation Records and the UK independent scene, *My Magpie Eyes are Hungry for the Prize*, was published in 2000. He is currently working on a book about music radio.

Gordon Coxhill started as a music journalist but went on to become a teacher on the Aegean island of Syros. He wrote at length about his two decades there, and his concurrent travels within Greece, in *Passing Thyme*, describing them as "more formative" than interviewing many of the biggest stars of the 1960s and 1970s.

Adrian Deevoy is a London-based journalist who has written for a variety of publications including *The Times*, the *Los Angeles Times, The Sunday Times, The Times of India, Q, GQ*, and *The Mail on Sunday*. He has conducted extensive interviews with Bob Dylan, Prince, Madonna, and George Michael.

Back in the day, **Robin Eggar** was a press officer at RCA Records, where he was allowed to answer the phones the day Elvis died. He then managed punk band the Members and record producer Steve Lillywhite before becoming the *Daily Mirror*'s rock writer. He has written for *The Sunday Times, Esquire, You Magazine, The Face, Time Out, NME, The Observer, The Word,* and *Rolling Stone,* plus ten books on everything from fitness, adventure sports, and Chinook helicopters to sixties sex gods.

Robert Hilburn was pop music critic at the *Los Angeles Times* from 1970 to 2005, when he left to write books. He has since produced two best sellers, a memoir entitled *Corn Flakes with John Lennon* and *Johnny Cash: The Life,* the definitive biography of the country music legend.

Mikel Jollett was a journalist and aspiring novelist before, at the age of thirty-one, finding his calling as a musician. He is the frontman of the Airborne Toxic Event. He has said of his time as one of the editors of *Filter* magazine, "It was just me and my friends Tom, Steve, and Greg. None of us knew what we were doing. We'd travel around and talk to bands we really liked. It was great."

Allan Jones joined the staff of *Melody Maker* in 1974 at the age of twenty-two following an application letter that was signed off with, "*Melody Maker* needs a bullet up its arse. I'm the gun—pull the trigger." He became editor of the title in 1984. He interviewed so many of the great and good in music that his anecdotes were enough to provide a regular, long-standing feature titled "Stop Me If You've Heard This One Before." The latter appeared in *Uncut,* the movies-and-music magazine he launched in 1997 and remained editor of until 2014.

Dylan Jones is the award-winning editor of *GQ* magazine. Among his many books is a collaboration with a man later to become British prime minister: *Cameron on Cameron: Conversations with Dylan Jones.* He was the chairman of the Prince's Trust *Fashion Rocks Monaco.* In June 2013 he was awarded an OBE for services to publishing and the fashion industry. He was once nearly a member of Buzzcocks.

Whether by choice or fate, **Linda Laban** has spent her life listening to music, hanging around recording studios, chasing interviews, and hustling for the best vantage point at gigs. The Boston and New York-based London native's work has been published by SXSWorld, M for Music & Musicians, Spin.com, MTV.com, *New Musical Express, Record Collector, Revolver*, the *Boston Globe*, the *Seattle Times*, the *New York Post, Kerrang!*, and *Rolling Stone*.

Angus MacKinnon is a former writer, mainly about music, and commissioning editor, mainly of nonfiction. He says, "Most of my professional past seems an utterly foreign country to me now." He is now a full-time father.

Mike McGrath is host of the nationally syndicated public radio show *You Bet Your Garden*, garden editor for WTOP News Radio in Washington, DC, and contributing editor and columnist for *GreenPrints* magazine. In the early 1970s he was a rock and roll reporter—his first interview was with Captain Beefheart; his second with Pink Floyd. He was also an editor at Marvel Comics in New York, where he produced the premier edition of the British reprint weekly *The Mighty World of Marvel*.

Charles Shaar Murray's journalistic career got off to an explosive start: the 1970 "Schoolkids Issue" of underground paper *Oz* in which he made his print debut led to an obscenity trial for its editors. He joined the *NME* in 1972 and went on to become a founder contributor of *Q* and *Mojo* magazines. His writing has also appeared in the *Evening Standard, Guitarist*, the *Guardian*, the *Independent*, the *Independent on Sunday*, the *Observer, MacUser, New Statesman, Prospect, Vogue*, and *The Word*. He is the author of the award-winning *Crosstown Traffic: Jimi Hendrix and Post-War Pop*.

HP Newquist is a writer who over the past two decades has written about topics ranging from music to medicine. He was editor-in-chief of *Guitar* magazine and is currently the executive director of the National Guitar Museum. He is also the author of numerous award-winning books, all of which are featured at www.newquist.net.

Paul Du Noyer's writing career began on the staff of *New Musical Express*. He went on to edit *Q* magazine and in 1993 launched *Mojo*. Subsequently he wrote books about John Lennon and the musical histories of his own home town Liverpool and his adopted home London. He retired from music journalism after a nine-year stint at *The Word* magazine and is currently preparing a new book.

David Quantick is a music journalist and television writer. He once caused David Bowie to sing part of "The Laughing Gnome" for possibly the first and only time in front of an audience.

Chris Roberts lives in London and has written about music, films, and pop culture for many years. He has published books on Michael Jackson, Lou Reed, the Gothic arts, Kate Moss, Scarlett Johansson, and Talk Talk, among others. The first album he ever bought was *Ziggy Stardust*. He has interviewed David Bowie four times.

John Robinson is an associate editor at *Uncut* and a contributor to the *Guardian Guide*. His features have also appeared in the *Guardian,* the *Daily Telegraph*, the UAE *National*, and *Uncut*.

Ken Scrudato has covered music, travel, hotels, nightlife, art, and the vagaries of culture for many of the top independent US style and culture publications, including *BlackBook, Filter, Billboard,* the *Hollywood Reporter, Flaunt*, and *Surface*. His editors are usually to be found begging him to include a few random facts amidst all the bombastic blather about political and cultural context. He also does travel, event, and hotel consulting.

David Sinclair began his career as a musician in groups including TV Smith's Explorers and London Zoo. He became a music journalist for the *Times* in London, *Rolling Stone, Q*, and *Billboard*, and wrote books about ZZ Top and the Spice Girls. Since 2006 he has written, recorded, and released three albums on the Critical Discs label. His album *David Sinclair 4* is released in 2015.

Steve Sutherland is editorial director at IPC Media. He became editor of *New Musical Express* in 1992, following a tenure as assistant editor at stablemate *Melody Maker*. His *NME* editorship lasted until 2000 and—much to his excitement—encompassed the Britpop era. He has described David Bowie as the artist he met who impressed him most.

David Thomas is an award-winning journalist with thirty years experience working in Fleet Street, as well as for major magazines in Britain and the US. He has edited *The Magazine, Punch*, and *Sunday Today Extra*. He has published nine novels and a dozen nonfiction books under his own name and as Tom Cain, written film scripts, and has been translated into some twenty languages.

After working in accountancy, insurance, and banking by day and writing for *ZigZag* by night, **John Tobler** joined CBS Records in 1974, where he became ABBA's first UK press officer. He would later write ABBA's official biography and the sleevenotes to their multi-million-selling compilation *ABBA Gold*. In 1976, he started freelance work at BBC Radio One, interviewing dozens of acts, including the Eagles and the Sex Pistols. He runs the small independent Road Goes On Forever record label.

Michael Watts has been a journalist, magazine, and features editor at several major British newspapers, including the *Financial Times* and the London *Evening Standard*, and was also a London correspondent for the *Los Angeles Times*. During the 1970s he wrote about rock and jazz for *Melody Maker*. Working out of London, New York, and L.A., he covered the greatest music stories of that era for what was then the oldest music paper, from the rise of punk rock and the Sex Pistols to the death of John Lennon.

Dominic Wells was editor of *Time Out* (London) for most of the nineties, winning four BSME awards for Editor of the Year. In the noughties he was editorial director of AOL (UK) and assistant editor at the *Times*. He is now a freelance journalist and screenwriter, with a film blog at www.londonhollywood.net. As a teenager he hung pictures of Bowie on his wa-wa-wa-wall, and played *Ziggy Stardust* every day for two years.

Steven Wells was a quintessentially eighties UK music journalist, seeing his work as indivisible from the mission to bring down Margaret Thatcher. His career began in the guise of the agitprop poet Seething Wells before he acquired a berth at the *NME*, for whom he wrote for a quarter-century. He also wrote for *The Guardian* and the *Philadelphia Weekly*, scripted radio comedy shows, and authored the novel *Tits-Out Teenage Terror Totty*. He died of cancer in 2009, aged forty-nine.

INDEX

ALSO AVAILABLE IN THE
MUSICIANS IN THEIR OWN WORDS SERIES
FROM CHICAGO REVIEW PRESS

-- -- -- -- -- -- -- -- -- -- -- -- -- -- -- -- -- --

COLTRANE ON COLTRANE
The John Coltrane Interviews
by Chris DeVito

"A fascinating and important compendium of the jazz icon's own words. . . . Through these gripping and revealing interviews, Coltrane comes alive. . . . Though many solid books have been written about Coltrane, this compilation of source materials provides an intimate view of the man and his music. Certainly one of the best music books of the year."
—*Library Journal*

TRADE PAPER, 416 PAGES • ISBN-13: 978-1-55652-004-4 • $18.95 (CAN $20.95)

HENDRIX ON HENDRIX
Interviews and Encounters with Jimi Hendrix
by Steven Roby

"This beautifully edited and annotated collection provides abundant insights into the heart and mind of one of the 20th century's most influential artists. Jimi's story has been told ad nauseam, but often the hype overshadows the human, and the legend subsumes the man. Here we have Hendrix in his own words, with all of his confusion, contradiction, vulnerability, beauty, and brilliance intact." —*Guitar Player*

Cloth, 384 Pages • ISBN-13: 978-1-61374-322-5 • $24.95 (CAN $27.95)

JUDY GARLAND ON JUDY GARLAND
Interviews and Encounters
by Randy L. Schmidt

"Garland is often seen, nowadays, as a sort of tragic figure, a superstar who achieved great heights and crippling lows, but here we see her perhaps as she would want to be remembered: a eager, supremely talented woman who never stopped dreaming of a brighter future for herself."
—*Booklist Online*

Cloth, 480 Pages • ISBN-13: 978-1-61374-945-6 • $28.95 (CAN $34.95)

KEITH RICHARDS ON KEITH RICHARDS
Interviews and Encounters
by Sean Egan

"All of the infamous incidents are covered—Brian Jones' drowning death, Richards' 1967 drug bust and subsequent jail time, the violence at Altamont, and Richards' public feuding with Mick Jagger, most notably after Mick's knighthood. But what also comes through is his still-burning admiration for the Chicago blues musicians who were his greatest influence and his wariness of fame. Great reading for Stones' fans." —*Booklist*

Trade Paper, 288 Pages • ISBN-13: 978-1-61374-788-9 • $18.95 (CAN $20.95)

LED ZEPPELIN ON LED ZEPPELIN
Interviews and Encounters
by Hank Bordowitz

"This telling is refreshing and does the unthinkable: it makes Led Zeppelin, beloved to the point of worship, actually likeable." —*PopMatters*

Cloth, 480 Pages • ISBN-13: 978-1-61374-754-4 • $28.95 (CAN $34.95)

LEONARD COHEN ON LEONARD COHEN
Interviews and Encounters
by Jeff Burger

"This is a must for Cohen fans." —Starred review, *Booklist*

"Burger's discerning editorial hand selects those conversations with Cohen that offer insights into his music. For longtime fans as well as newcomers to Cohen's work." —*Publishers Weekly*

Cloth, 624 Pages • ISBN-13: 978-1-61374-758-2 • $29.95 (CAN $35.95)

MILES ON MILES
Interviews and Encounters with Miles Davis
by Paul Maher, Jr.

"Here is Miles Davis's less familiar voice, his speaking voice. . . . Maher and Dorr gather together Davis's greatest hits in Q & A, and they make compelling reading."—Jack Chambers, author, *Milestones: The Music and Times of Miles Davis*

Cloth, 352 Pages • ISBN-13: 978-1-55652-706-7 • $24.95 (CAN $27.95)

TOM WAITS ON TOM WAITS
Interviews and Encounters
by Paul Maher, Jr.

"Absolutely required for Waits fans old and new, this pile of interviews is a magic mountain of weird."—*PopMatters*

Trade Paper, 480 Pages • ISBN-13: 978-1-56976-312-4 • $19.95 (CAN $21.95)

SPRINGSTEEN ON SPRINGSTEEN
Interviews, Speeches, and Encounters
by Jeff Burger

"This book is a must for any Springsteen lover as it has so much – not only a wide range of interviews in all media, here and overseas, but a collection of beautiful speeches written and delivered by the Boss over the years. Journalist-author Jeff Burger's love of the subject comes across in this vast profusion of unexpected material he's discovered, allowing the reader to view Springsteen from many angles, and over the decades."—*American Songwriter Magazine*

Trade Paper, 432 Pages • ISBN-I3: 978-I-55652-544-5 • $17.95 (CAN $21.95)

Available at your favorite bookstore
or by calling (800) 888-474I

CHICAGO REVIEW PRESS

Distributed by IPG
www.ipgbook.com

www.chicagoreviewpress.com

5/23

31901056964572

1×